KU-308-092

Edited by
Prodromos Panayiotopoulos
and Gavin Capps

World Development
An Introduction

U.W.E.L.
LEARNING RESOURCES

ACC. No.
2266734

CLASS

CONTROL
0745314074

337
WOR

DATE
27. MAR. 2002

SITE
DY

Pluto **Press**
LONDON • STERLING, VIRGINIA

First published 2001 by Pluto Press

345 Archway Road, London N6 5AA
and 22883 Quicksilver Drive,
Sterling, VA 20166–2012, USA

www.plutobooks.com

Copyright © Prodromos Panayiotopoulos and Gavin Capps 2001

The right of the individual contributors to be identified as the author
of this work has been asserted by them in accordance with
the Copyright, Designs and Patents Act 1988

British Library Cataloguing in Publication Data
A catalogue record for this book is available from
the British Library

Library of Congress Cataloging in Publication Data
Applied for.

ISBN 0 7453 1407 4 hardback
ISBN 0 7453 1402 3 paperback

10   09   08   07   06   05   04   03   02   01
10   9   8   7   6   5   4   3   2   1

Designed and produced for Pluto Press by
Chase Publishing Services, Sidmouth, EX10 9QG
Typeset from disk by Stanford DTP Services, Northampton
Printed in the European Union by Antony Rowe, Chippenham, England

UNIVERSITY OF WOLVERHAMPTON

Harrison Learning Centre
City Campus
University of Wolverhampton
St Peter's Square
Wolverhampton WV1 1RH
Telephone: 0845 408 1631
Online Renewals:
www.wlv.ac.uk/lib/myaccount

Telephone Renewals: 01902 321333 or 0845 408 1631
Please RETURN this item on or before the last date shown above.
Fines will be charged if items are returned late.
See tariff of fines displayed at the Counter. (L2)

Contents

List of Examples

List of Tables

viii

List of Figures

This volume is dedicated to all those who protested outside the WTO Conference in Seattle and to the undergraduate and post-graduate students we have taught and learnt from over the years, at the University of Wales, Swansea, the Open University, the University of Central Lancashire and the London School of Economics.

The first duty of Education is to educate the educator – Karl Marx

Preface

The study brings together a wealth of material on the Third World which points both to the inequalities within globalisation as well as its potential for improving the human condition. The study analyses 'World Development' in historical perspective and attempts to place the current concerns of the 'anti-capitalist' mood – so evident at the World Trade Organisation's Seattle Summit during November 1999, and subsequently at Melbourne and Prague – on a more informed basis. This is a development education publication which makes accessible to students and teachers both qualitative and quantitative material on the working lives of people throughout the Third World, on country experiences and on debates about development, globalisation and industrialisation. It is also the case that many readers may be or are about to become involved in small-scale development in their own or other parts of the world. This book is also addressed to them, or at least those among them who want to know about the wider picture. This broader picture, or if you like macro picture of world development, provides the structures in which human agency and small-scale development can take place. If you can make sense of the wider picture, your own small contribution may make more sense.

The book has been shaped by the interests of the authors as teachers and researchers in development studies. A number of the authors have taken an active interest in the promotion of development education as an important dimension of development itself. Prodromos Panayiotopoulos assisted the pioneering work of the Wales Joint Education Committee (WJEC) in establishing, for the first, inclusion of Development Studies in the school curriculum. The WJEC AS level in *World Development* became the model for the AS level taught at UK-wide level. Gavin Capps assisted in the production of development education teaching material for the AS level. The book has been written as an aid to students and teachers in development education. It is influenced by the proposition that 'development' is not simply something that happens 'over there', but also something which is relevant 'here' in the shaping of a multi-cultural, internationalist outlook among young people, based on respect for human diversity and in solidarity with those resisting the notion that 'nothing can be done' about the poverty facing millions of people in the Third World.

Another influence in writing the book is that at one time or other the authors were students or lecturers in the Centre for Development Studies (CDS) at the University of Wales, Swansea. CDS was responsible for pioneering studies and analyses on the role of the 'informal sector' in Third World employment. Chris Gerry carried out seminal research on artisans in Dakar, Senegal, and translated for the first time in English the work of Milton Santos. Research carried out by Ray Bromley, Chris Birbeck, Gavin Kitching, Mike Cowen, to name a few, influenced the development of a 'Swansea school'. One key concern of this school was how capitalist or market relationships reproduced themselves at the smallest level, i.e. amongst the self-employed, micro enterprises and the peasantry in the Third World. Many students, including three of the authors, were influenced by these ideas and applied them in their studies in diverse locations: in the study of refugee enterprises in the Gaza Strip, rural enterprises in South Africa and Galicia (northern Spain), 'informal enterprises' in Nairobi, immigrant enterprises in north London, in the role of particular industries, such as the construction industry, the garment industry, and so on.

An important influence in shaping the book is a concern amongst the authors about the role of Non Governmental Organisations (NGOs) in development. NGOs are diverse and range from international NGOs to local grassroots organisations, social movements, and people's organisations and it would be unwise to generalise about their role in development. However, one common tendency is for NGOs to see development as a collection of projects which frequently act in isolation from each other and from the wider society in which they operate. Another tendency is for international NGOs to show a political unwillingness to challenge the structures of poverty in the Third World, or the inequalities in international relations between their own developed countries and the Third World. In part this is the result of increased dependence on government funding. In the UK, depoliticisation is explicit in the legal status of NGOs which is overseen by government appointed Charity Commissioners. The combined effects of the 'projectisation' and depoliticisation of development underpin what can be seen as NGO 'reformism'. By this it is not meant that incremental improvements in the human condition and more importantly showing that something *can* be done about poverty in the Third World are not important. Far from it. At the same time, however, many NGO workers themselves feel an unease about their work and many are aware that what they do is unlikely to alter the pattern of poverty in the Third World without some pretty fundamental changes to the order of things. The book is also an attempt to address this discontent. This discontent was graphically illustrated at the 'Battle of Seattle' which saw some NGOs inside the WTO Conference (trying to work from 'within'), whilst others outside the Conference were being given the full treatment by Seattle's finest constabulary. The events at Seattle have radicalised and politicised many rank and file NGO workers and people involved in campaigns for labour rights, against environmental degradation, for ending the Third World debt. Many of them are raising increasingly awkward questions both about the nature of globalisation and the official positions of their organisations. The book provides them with supporting material in this project.

This book is also the result of the support shown by many people. Whilst too many to mention individually, this book would not have been possible without the toleration shown by the people we live and work with. In particular we want to thank all the workers at Pluto Press and Chase Publishing Services, Monica O'Connor and Robert Webb, without whose labour the production of this book would not have been possible. We also acknowledge the support given by Roger van Zwanenberg both for the patience shown during the preparation of the text, and the active interest taken which helped to shape both the form and content of this book. A special thanks is owed to Alison Doogan.

List of Abbreviations and Acronyms

AIP Apparel Industry Partnership, US
AMRC Asia Monitor Resource Centre
APEC Asian Pacific Economic Forum
ATOs Alternative Trade Organisations
CAP Common Agricultural Policy
CMT Cut, Make and Trim
CODELCO Corporacion del Cobre, Chile
CPC Communist Party of China
ECGS Export Credit Guarantee Scheme
ECLAC United Nations Economic Commission for Latin America and the
  Caribbean
EEC European Economic Community
EOI Export Orientated Industrialisation
EPB Economic Planning Board, South Korea
EPZs Export Processing Zones
EU European Union
FDI Foreign Direct Investment
FLA Fair Labor Association, US
GATT General Agreement on Tariffs and Trade, pre-runner of WTO
GDP Gross Domestic Product
GNP Gross National Product
GSP Generalised System of Preference
HDI Human Development Index
IBRD International Bank for Reconstruction and Development (The World
  Bank)
ICMs International Commodity Agreements
IDTUM Institute of the Democratic Trade Union Movement
IDA International Development Association
IFAT International Federation for Alternative Trade
ILO International Labour Organisation
IMES Institute for Migration and Ethnic Studies
IMF International Monetary Fund
ISI Import Substituting Industrialisation
KCTU Confederation of Korean Trade Unions

LLDCs Least Less Developed Countries
MFA Multi-Fibre Arrangement
MFN Most Favoured Nation
MVA Manufacturing Value Added
NAFTA North American Free Trade Association
NGOs Non Governmental Organisations
NICs Newly Industrialising Countries
NIEO New International Economic Order
OECD Organisation for Economic Cooperation and Development
OPEC Organisation of Petroleum Exporting Countries
PPP Purchasing Power Parity
PQLI Physical Quality of Life Index
SAPs Structural Adjustment Programmes
TNCs Trans National Corporations
UNCTAD United Nations Conference on Trade and Development
UNDP United Nations Development Programme
UNICEF United Nations International Children's Emergency Fund
USAS United Students Against Sweatshops, US
WDA Wales Development Agency
WTO World Trade Organisation

Summary of Contents

OVERVIEW OF CONTENTS

Section 1. World Development: Globalisation in Historical Perspective provides an introductory overview in which the other sections can be located. It outlines the key phases in the making of the international capitalist economy, from the sixteenth century to the present, and shows how each phase fundamentally defined and redefined the relationship between the first industrialised nations and the rest of the world. It focuses on recent shifts in the world economy, the impact of globalisation and the debt crisis. Section 1 also introduces the main themes, concepts and analytical terms that are used throughout the rest of the book.

Section 2. Globalisation: Industrialisation and Trade explores the main contending economic development policies which are currently available to the developing countries. It looks at the different theoretical positions that inform policy and assesses their validity in the light of the country and global experiences outlined in the following sections. Three policy areas are investigated: Import Substituting Industrialisation (ISI), Export Orientated Industrialisation (EOI), and Trade Policy. The section also investigates the role of immigrant labour and enterprise in the urban centres of the developed economies.

Section 3. Country Studies provides a series of country case studies with similar and contrasting experiences of economic development. It considers the industrial transformation of two Southern European Newly Industrialised Countries (NICs) – Cyprus and Spain – as well as the Asian and Central American examples of South Korea, China and Mexico. Each country case study contains profiles of real people who personify the different types of social actors involved in the globalisation and industrialisation process and represent the winners and losers of the experience of transformation.

Section 4. Commodity Studies uses the examples of different commodities, all strongly associated with developing countries, to illustrate a range of issues generated by globalisation and international trade: 'Copper' explores the historic production–manufacturing link between Chile and South Wales and considers the effects of international copper price movements on people and the industry; 'Tourism' illustrates both the environmental impact and the economic stimulus provided by the growth of the tourist industry in

Spain; 'Textiles' allow us to examine the role of 'sweatshops' in the Third World, the role of gender in shaping sectoral employment, and the impact of protectionism used by the developed countries in the form of the Multi-Fibre Arrangement.

Conclusions reflect on the extent to which globalisation and industrialisation can be seen as a necessary condition for the development of capitalism on a world scale, but not necessarily as a sufficient condition for 'development' itself.

SUMMARY OF SECTION CONTENTS

1.1 The Expansion of Europe: Mercantile Trade 1500–1750 This period witnessed major transformations in the economic life of Western Europe. From the late fifteenth century onwards, competing European nations expanded across the world to locate and monopolise new sources of wealth and luxury goods. Mercantilism linked the accumulation of gold and silver from the New World to the Treasuries of the European powers and established for the first time a systematic link between trade and state policy. European expansion and rivalry over the control of trade, drew a growing portion of the world into rival commercial networks.

1.2 Industrial Capitalism and 'Free Trade' 1750–1875 Until the mid-eighteenth century, European industry was little more than a by-product of overseas trade. Typically, this was associated with the triangular trade and the plantation economy based on slavery. The growth of industrial capitalism, unlike mercantilism, however, demanded greater supplies of raw materials and world-wide markets for manufactured goods. The 'Manchester' (manufacturing) lobby of 'Free Traders' in the UK challenged the previous protectionism and this led to a situation where for the first time in human history, commerce was subordinated to industry. 'Free trade' became the rallying cry of the strongest and during this period it was associated with Britain – the world's first industrial power.

1.3 Imperial Trade and Imperial Rivalries 1875–1945 British economic supremacy was challenged by the industrialisation of Germany and the US. This led to a new phase of international rivalry as each industrialised nation competed for a share of the world's resources and markets with increased ferocity. During this period more parts of the world were clearly delineated and colonised by the rival European powers. This period also saw the growth of powerful industrial corporations which became identified with particular states. This meant that commercial rivalry assumed the more dangerous form of national rivalry with the implied and applied threat of state force to defend the 'national' interest. This combination between industrial capitalism and colonial expansion characterised 'Imperialism' during the late nineteenth century.

1.4 Superpower Competition and the Long Boom 1945–1970 The post-war global economy continued to show a sensitive link between military and industrial priorities and this underpinned superpower rivalry between the USA and Russia. The Bretton Woods institutions established under US leadership were entrusted with the task of managing global development. The post-war boom created a more liberal world economy characterised by very high and sustained levels of growth. Among the newly independent countries, a select number made significant steps towards industrialisation during the 1960s and 1970s, but most Third World countries remained locked into a primary commodity dependency.

1.5 Debt, Crisis and the Third World 1970–1990s The end of the long post-war boom saw the collapse of the Bretton Woods system, an increased protectionism used by the industrial countries, declining primary commodity prices and increasing interest rates on loans taken. This laid the basis for the 'debt crisis' and IMF and World Bank stabilisation and adjustment programmes on a world scale. The world from the 1970s onwards became a more unstable and difficult to predict place – as the collapse of communism graphically illustrated. The world economy also became a more complex place. The polarisation of the Third World between the Newly Industrialising Countries (NICs) and the Least Less Developed Counties (LLDCs) was an important phenomenon of this period. The 'success' of the East Asian NICs was used by the IMF and World Bank as the basis for a new development paradigm.

1.6 Globalisation in the Millennium A new development orthodoxy of globalisation emerged during the 1990s driven by a near universal acceptance of free market ideology. The growth of the East Asian NICs, an unprecedented expansion in world trade and Foreign Direct Investment (FDI), the expansive activities of Trans National Corporations (TNCs), is said to be breaking down national boundaries and reducing the role of states in development. The section argues that not all the characteristics associated with the globalisation model are as straightforward or positive as the model suggests, or indeed that the phenomenon is a contemporary experience, as much of the preceding material suggests.

2.1 The Latin American NICs: Import Substituting Industrialisation (ISI) Industrialisation policy in Latin America initially appeared as a response to the global market failure experienced during the 1930s. Populism shaped ISI policy and continues to influence the contemporary discourse on Latin American development. One conundrum is the inability of large sections of Latin American manufacturing industry to compete in global markets. This has created immense balance of payments problems as heavy industrialisation was financed by external borrowing. In order to service the external debt Latin America has relied more and more on the export of primary commodities which has placed previously marginal areas under increased pressure. This suggests that industrialisation is a condition which can co-exist with a dependency on primary commodity exports, and this points to an important continuity in the relationship between Latin America and the global economy.

2.2 The East Asian NICs: Export Orientated Industrialisation (EOI) The East Asian NICs have experienced phenomenal rates of growth and have attained in terms of World Bank income ranking, 'development'. The primary purpose of this study is to consider what happens to economies which are the most globalised, or at least the most dependent on production for export. An illustration of this is offered by the 1997 Asian financial crisis which resulted in some of the largest 'rescue' packages in the history of the International Monetary Fund. None of this was predicted by the major institutions. The crisis places question marks over neo-liberal assumptions, given that it was a crisis with origins in the private sector and that it involved some of the most open, globalised and market-friendly economies in the world.

2.3 Competing Perspectives on Trade Policy Weakness in commodity trade often appears as a defining condition for the least industrialised countries. The section presents a number of policy options presented by a variety of development agencies. We examine the activities of specialised Alternative Trade Organisations (ATOs) and 'fair trade'. We also examine the standard International Monetary Fund (IMF) and World Trade Organisation policy of 'free trade' and this is contrasted with the advocacy by the United Nations Conference on Trade and Development (UNCTAD) of 'South–South' trade. A review of commodity trade and sub-Saharan Africa is used to illustrate the nature of the problem.

2.4 People Trade: Globalisation and Immigrant Enterprise Despite restrictions on the free movement of labour by the developed countries, cities like London, Los Angeles, Amsterdam, New York, Paris, have been fundamentally shaped and reshaped by immigrants. This dimension of globalisation is examined in a comparative study of immigrant participation in the garment industries of these cities, as workers and as entrepreneurs. The section suggests that the restructuring of the garment industry, and the women's fashion-wear sector in particular, may be a more critical factor in the incorporation of immigrant groups than characteristics associated with any single ethnic group. This introduces a note of caution on the assumption that a causal connection exists between enterprise, work norms, practices, and the ethnic origin of entrepreneurs and workers employed by them.

3.1 Cyprus: Industrialisation Under Conditions of Globalisation A key sectoral dimension in the rapid economic transformation of the Cypriot economy was the role of the export garment industry which accounted for the employment of one-quarter of all manufacturing workers in the 1980s. The garment industry was promoted by the government of southern Cyprus in order to provide employment opportunities for displaced refugees and to act as a source of foreign exchange. The section examines a crisis faced by the Cypriot garment industry and which brought together Cyprus, Libya (Cyprus's largest export market) and London Cypriot garment manufacturers. The section illustrates the difficult to predict nature of globalisation and considers the impact of externality.

3.2 Spain: Economic Development Under Conditions of Autarky Spain is a case of late industrialisation in Europe. This was influenced by the Franco dictatorship of 1939–76 and the actions of the economically dominant social classes in controlling investment and policies. The long period of dictatorship gave economic development in Spain particular characteristics. It was also influenced by rising incomes which were a key factor in the development of a mass car market in Spain. In order to be able to understand the reasons for both, autarky and the late industrialisation in Spain, we look at the development of engineering and car production. Another study looks at the role of the tourism industry, the largest in Europe (see Section 4.2). Spain was the fifth biggest car producer in the world in the mid-1990s, behind the USA, Japan, Germany and France and in front of Italy, Korea and the UK.

3.3 South Korea: Free Market Miracle or Mirage? Forty years ago, South Korea was a poverty stricken, agricultural country with socio-economic indicators comparable to those of present day Bangladesh and Mozambique. Today, it is a world leader in the production and export of cars, ships and hi-tech consumer goods. The case study considers the neo-liberal argument that the industrialisation of South Korea represents a 'miracle' of the free market. The section points to evidence which suggests that the profound changes in the South Korean economy over the last three decades were sensitively linked to state direction. The study concludes that South Korea has not industrialised either through the miraculous operation of the free market or the servile qualities of its citizens. The section also examines the impact of the 1997 Asian Crisis on South Korea, and considers its social and economic and political consequences.

3.4 Mexico: The Long March of Industrialisation Mexico achieved industrialised status during the 1970s but the process has longer historical roots. Economic growth accelerated during the 1930s under an Import Substituting Industrialisation (ISI) model. Mexican industrial policy has changed dramatically in the last few decades. Today industrial policy continues under a specific form of Export Orientated Industrialisation (EOI). This change of gear was virtually forced on the government by the balance of payments crisis faced in 1982 and the near default by Mexico on its foreign loans which sparked an international financial crisis. The *Maquilas* and production for export increased in significance during the 1980s and 1990s. The *Maquilas* acted as the model of free trade for the North American Free Trade Agreement (NAFTA) established in 1994 linking Mexico, the US and Canada.

3.5 China: Breaking the Iron Rice Bowl Chinese industrialisation cannot be understood without an appreciation of the humiliation inflicted on the people of China by the Imperialist Powers of Europe and Japan. Nationalist aspirations for self-determination were articulated by the Communist Party of China (CPC) which came to power in 1949 and saw industrialisation as a means of 'catching up' with the industrial economies, and so rendering China militarily capable of standing up to the imperialist powers. In this, Chinese state-directed industrialisation finds parallel experience in other large Third World countries. China, however, differs from other experiences in one novel respect: it is attempting to complete two transitions at the same time – from a command to a market economy and from a rural to urban society. This has no other historical precedent.

4.1 Copper: Chilean Miners – British Smelters in the Mid-Nineteenth Century Copper has played a central role in the Chilean economy from the early nineteenth century up until today. Chile was the largest copper producer during the late nineteenth century and again since 1990. Despite this leadership in mine copper production, Chile sees little value adding processing, that is the transformation of copper ore into refined copper and its transformation to goods such as wire, sheets, bolts, etc. The case study looks at the emergence of the copper smelting industry in Chile in the mid-nineteenth century as an early example of specialisation. One illustration of the evolving global division of labour was the development of an unequal interdependency between Chile and the Swansea Lower Valley in South Wales.

4.2 Tourism: The Spanish Tourism Industry The tourist sector has been an important component in the industrialisation of Spain and earned the hard currency needed to pay for imports used in the engineering and car industries. Rapid tourism development has radically changed the livelihoods of millions of people. The 'success' of tourism has not been without social and environmental costs. The construction of high-rise buildings, frequently concentrated in coastal areas and characterised by unacceptably high levels of population density, was made possible by a disregard for basic and transparent planning procedures. This was an important feature and legacy of the Franco dictatorship. The case study suggests that the interdependency between Western European tour operators and Spanish hoteliers is far from equal.

4.3 The Global Textile Industry: An Engendered Protectionism The textile industry is a microcosm of the world economy and offers a commodity illustration of the global manufacturing system. The case study investigates the relationship between gender and industrial work and offers insights into the inequalities of world trade exemplified by the Multi-Fibre Arrangement (MFA). The textile industry reaches out to the High Street fashion stores and daily confronts consumers in Europe and the USA with an expansive plethora of country of origin labels. Today more people are asking questions about what lies behind the country of origin and designer labels. The case study provides contextual explanation.

Introduction

Since the beginnings of time, human beings have organised themselves in various ways around providing for their material basic needs of food, housing, clothing, heating and so on. Out of the provision of these needs developed enormous sophisticated cultures all over the world. Over the last 400 years and more particularly over the last 200, all this has altered quite fundamentally. Over this last period we have seen a massive expansion in productive capability and an important dimension of this appears in the development of Science and Knowledge about how and why things work, and the application of such knowledge to trade and in the production of goods and services. This new knowledge was used to make war, to exploit nature and people, to produce more food, in particular, and to combat diseases. As a direct consequence we have over this short period increased everything around us, especially ourselves in great numbers.

These changes we have called 'development', 'progress', 'Industrialisation' or 'growth'. The names we use to characterise them have altered over time, but they all infer change of a quite distinct type, which today we all take for granted as normal. Only if you look at these changes in terms of history will you see how quite fantastic are these changes in relation to what went before. We can talk about 'transformation' in ways that could not have been recognised before this period. Just imagine trying to cross a sea by sail with the wind against you and compare that with what happens once you have an engine to drive a boat. For millennia, virtually all human beings lived from farming; today fewer and fewer people make a living from agriculture, producing ever more food. Whilst previously a community's economic activity was determined by Nature, rain, seasons, that might be considered to be relatively easy to predict, it is now in constant movement of growth and change in response to less predictable fluctuations, for example, in agricultural prices and in the cost of agricultural inputs of an industrial origin, such as fertiliser, pesticides, diesel. In the case of factory farming, we see a situation in which agriculture has effectively become a branch of industry.

Change and the speed of change is in-built into our lives in ways that could not have been conceived of before this period began. The speed of these changes has become ever quicker over these 400 years.

1

One qualitative change appears in the proposition that before the last 400 years of human development, wealth was finite and typically appeared in the form of land ownership, in how many Knights a Lord could master behind his banner, or the amount of trade and plunder gained in an expedition. The amount of wealth or lack of it was a known thing. Today there simply are no boundaries to the creation of wealth and the potential this holds for human welfare is almost unimaginable. Yet, we live in a world characterised by deep inequalities. According to the *Human Development Report* produced annually by the United Nations Development Programme (UNDP) 358 billionaires own as much wealth as half of the world's population (UNDP, 1996). Figures from the World Bank on a developing country in Africa, like Tanzania, show that the average yearly income per person is US$90 and most people will only live until they are 52. Conversely, in a developed country like the USA the average income per person is US$24,700 and the average life expectancy is 76 years (World Bank, 1995a, p. 162). There are such differences between the rich and poor countries that they can literally seem to be worlds apart. At the same time, however, the life expectancy of young black American men in the capital city of Washington is comparable to that found in some of the poorest countries in the world like Bangladesh. The US Treasury Secretary points to a situation where 'a child born in New York in the 1990s is less likely to live to the age of five than a child in Shanghai. A child born in Bangladesh has better life expectancy than a child born in Harlem' (Larry Summers, quoted from the *Independent*, 10 February 1998). This suggests important continuities within global inequality.

The inequalities between and within the developed and developing countries are reflected at global level in the share of industry and trade. The developed countries account for the vast bulk of the world's industrial production and this is reflected in the composition of exports. Manufactured exports make up 76 per cent of all developed country exports, whilst in reverse, primary commodities account for 61 per cent of all exports from the developing countries (Todaro, 1997, p. 41). In the 'poor' countries (using World Bank income definitions) 61 per cent of the labour force work in agriculture, whilst in the 'rich' countries only 4 per cent do so. At the same time, however, workers in low-income countries by sheer force of numbers make up nearly half of the world's industrial workers (World Bank, 1995a, p. 2). Within the above there is considerable differentiation between and within the regions of the world. One contrast appears between the high (94 per cent) dependency on primary commodity exports by low-income sub-Saharan African countries and the centrality of manufactured exports and employment in the middle- to high-income East Asian Newly Industrialised Countries (NICs). Figures and trends like these have informed the view that industrialisation lies at the centre of development, or at least in the raising of per capita incomes.

While inequalities in living standards and relative shares of industry and trade divide the world into 'rich' and 'poor' nations, economic activity also unites them. The developed and developing countries have been historically integrated into one world economy which connects them in many ways. A Third World country like Tanzania will probably import manufactured goods, like agricultural machinery, from the developed countries. Similarly, Tanzania exports raw materials and agricultural goods like coffee beans for consumption in the West. In historical terms, writers such as David Ricardo and in contemporary terms organisations such as the World Trade Organisation and World Bank, have emphasised the mutually beneficial aspects of trade. They argue that each economy should specialise in producing the goods to which it is best suited and can produce at the lowest price. In this view, the ability to trade in specialised goods in which a country has a 'comparative advantage', is more important than each country developing a similar industrial capacity. Other views, such as the early critique of globalisation presented by Argentinian economist Raúl Prebisch, pointed to an integration characterised by 'unequal exchange', rather than mutual gains from trade (see Section 2.1). Prebisch and many developing country governments argued that the industrial economies of the West have always gained the most from this kind of integration.

There are important debates and disputes about the distribution of the benefits of development, industrialisation and globalisation. One continuity appears in the appeal of the 'old orthodoxy' which argues that industrial production increases productivity and raises standards of living and that the developing countries will always remain poor unless they pursue policies to industrialise and achieve a more equal position in the world economy. This view is supported by the general observation that countries which have moved away from an agricultural to an industrial economy, have significantly increased per capita incomes (see Table 1.1). There are few examples of countries which have attained high standards of living and 'developed' status through agricultural specialisation. Denmark and New Zealand are rare examples.

The Newly Industrialising Countries (NICs) appear as the strongest challenge to the image of the developing countries as a homogeneous bloc of primary commodity exporters. The 'banana republic' syndrome, or the reliance on a small range of primary exports for most foreign exchange earnings, stands in marked contrast to the export-led success of manufacturing industry in the East Asian NICs. Another contrast is that NICs such as South Korea, Singapore, Taiwan, Hong Kong, show a strong performance not only in terms of per capita incomes but also important social development indicators, such as infant mortality, life expectancy and rates of literacy. This is reflected in their high ranking in internationally recognised ways of measuring development, such as the Physical Quality of Life Index (PQLI) and the Human Development Index (HDI). Indeed, according to World Bank ranking by Purchasing Power Parity (PPP) Hong Kong and Singapore ranked as sixth and ninth, respectively, richest countries in the world during the mid-1990s. At the same time, however, there is a historical association between the NICs and authoritarian political systems. South Korea is emerging from nearly three decades of military rule and repression of the labour movement remains an important continuity. Of the Latin American NICs, Brazil, Argentina and Chile have made recent transitions to democratic government but remain saddled with the debt accumulated by the military.

The experiences of the NICs appear in sharp contrast to those faced by most of the developing countries during the 1980s and 1990s. For most of the developing countries the experience consisted of declining per capita incomes and negative rates of growth. Indeed the 1980s were described by the South Commission (1990) (a think-tank of developing country leaders) the 'lost decade' from the point of development. This included in most sub-Saharan African countries declining primary and secondary school enrolment, which served as an important proxy indicator of development in the post-independence period. Much of the development crisis was accounted for by falling commodity export prices, fuelled by economic stagnation and high unemployment in the industrial economies for most of the 1980s and 1990s. The combined impact of high debt repayment due to the scissors effect of rising interest rates and low export earnings, resulted in many cases in Balance of Payments deficits and a resort to further borrowing from Western Banks and agencies such as the International Monetary Fund and the World Bank, which attach stringent conditions to such high risk lending. Until the crisis which unfolded in Asia during 1997, economic vulnerability in the Third World was typically associated with weakness in commodity trade and appeared as a particular concern for the least industrialised countries, or those most dependent on fluctuations in world export prices of primary commodities such as minerals and agricultural products. The Asian crisis suggests that industrialisation has not 'liberated' the NICs from the 'tyranny' of world markets, and this illustrates new and more complex vulnerabilities for developing countries in the world economy. Severe question marks have been placed over the future direction of the East Asian 'miracle' economies and the extent to which they represent a sustainable model of growth and poverty reduction for other developing countries.

Aim of the Book

HOW TO USE THE BOOK

The primary purpose of *World Development* is as a development education publication. It is a comprehensive introductory guide for students, teachers, volunteers, NGO workers and activists in development. The book examines the substantive issues surrounding development, industrialisation and globalisation and places them within a historic context. It outlines the historical development of the global economy and assesses the current prospects for developing countries. The book contains in-depth analyses of how particular industries operate at local and global level, drawing from case studies of textiles, tourism and copper. There are also case studies of specific countries, including Cyprus, South Korea, China, Mexico and Spain.

The book is structured into self-contained sections which can be read in isolation or in conjunction with others. This is indicated by cross-referencing in the text. There is a summary of contents at the beginning of the book and every section contains a short overview and summary for quick inspection. The book contains examples in the shape of case studies for every section. Many of them are about the lives of working people in the Third World and this offers qualitative insight into the impact of development. There are also tables, figures and summaries of key points relevant to each section. The above can act as teaching and learning visual and oral aids. The life stories are short enough to be read in class. Any one of these can act as an engaging introduction to the issues raised by the book. It is these qualitative dimensions of development, i.e. how processes are apparent in the lives of real people in actual given situations, which make this book different from other books on the subject. We have tried to avoid too much technical language. Where such terms are used we have included a glossary of terms. The book also contains an extensive bibliography and suggestions for further reading. These items are at the end of the book.

The purpose of the book is to examine the substantive issues raised by development, industrialisation and globalisation in a theoretical and practical manner. It outlines the historical development of the global economy and assesses the current prospects for the developing countries. It also compares national experiences of industrialisation and examines the industrialisation and trade strategies available to developing countries today.

The book is particularly concerned with investigating recent trends in the world economy and what these mean for the Third World. One key dimension appears in conclusions drawn from the globalisation thesis which argue that the developing countries are even more dependent on international trade and foreign investment. As a result, individual Third World states appear as even less able to pursue their own national strategies of development. Many of the Third World countries have also experienced severe economic difficulties and have fallen into debt. Loans secured from Western banks and international agencies such as the World Bank and the International Monetary Fund, have conditions attached, typically in the form of Structural Adjustment Programmes (SAPs) which favour free trade policies and openness to the global economy. Again, this is taken as evidence of the increased dependence and weakness by the Third World on the global economy. Whether such pessimistic but popular explanations present an accurate description of the condition in the Third World is subjected to critical assessment. The book in presenting diverse outcomes allows the reader to draw informed conclusions.

In theoretical terms the book points to competing interpretation presented by neo-liberal and structuralist thinking. Opposing conclusions about self-regulation by markets or state intervention and mutual gains from trade or unequal exchange, raise wider questions about the relationship between poverty, development, globalisation and industrialisation. Neo-liberal thinking points to residual (or internal) explanations for slow rates of income growth in most of the developing countries and suggests that people and countries are poor because they are excluded from global markets, typically, by inappropriate domestic policies pursued by their own governments. Structuralist thinking points to relational explanations for the continuity of poverty (such as in the impact of colonialism) and suggests that most developing countries are poor not because of exclusion from world markets, but rather because of the selective nature of their integration into world markets, typically as primary exporters.

The book deals with questions raised by the practical experiences of the Newly Industrialised Countries. Export Orientated Industrialisation (EOI) and production for export can be seen as a practical application of neo-liberal thinking with the East Asian NICs as a complementary example. Import Substituting Industrialisation (ISI) and production for the home market can be seen as the practical application of structuralist thinking and one involving considerable intervention by the state. Typically, ISI and variations such as 'self-reliance' played an important role amongst the largest of the developing countries with relatively bigger domestic markets such as Brazil, China, India. It is also the case that EOI played a more significant role in smaller economies undergoing industrialisation, such as Hong Kong, Singapore, South Korea, Taiwan, whose smaller domestic markets left them with little option but to produce for export in order to gain from economies of scale.

The book emphasises that the process of development, industrialisation and globalisation carries costs as well as benefits for different sections of people in any society. There are important implications for gender and environment. The transition from agricultural to industrial production can undermine rural communities and lead to urban centres which are overcrowded and lacking in basic amenities. One dimension of industrialisation appears in the urbanisation of poverty itself. At the same time, the urban centres of the developing world are also centres of great wealth and of optimism. One dimension of this appears in the role played by urban workers and organised labour in the struggle for democratic rights in Latin America, South Africa and South Korea. A key concern of the book is to examine the processes of change and their impact in the shaping and re-shaping of social divisions in society and in their effect on people and their livelihoods.

The primary theoretical concerns of the book are an examination of the 'old orthodoxy', namely that industrialisation creates not only a more interdependent global economy but also one in which the conditions necessary for development on a world scale are made possible. At the same time, much of the experience teaches us that industrialisation is not a sufficient condition for development. It is for this reason that the book begins by looking at the conditions in Europe and in particular Britain which made possible the world's first 'industrial revolution'. It was this combination between industry and military power which allowed the USA to dominate development in the second half of the twentieth century. Another concern of the book is about the meaning of 'development'. We all use the word as though we know what it means, yet even a small amount of knowledge shows that development processes are not only extraordinary in the changes they introduce, but are also very complex. One conventional view is that Development represents an improvement in the human condition. Another view is that Development represents the uneven development of capitalism on a world scale. The two do not necessarily mean the same thing. The book offers material which allows the reader to draw informed conclusions both about the meaning and impact of development. The book purposefully presents extensive material on the Newly Industrialising Countries which offers the best supporting evidence for the neo-liberal proposition that free markets, rather than development intervention represent the best way forward for improving the human condition. We have resisted the temptation to dwell at length on the economic horror facing most people in the poorest countries of the Third World, precisely in order to test neo-liberal assumptions on their strongest ground. This is an important concern of the book and one which underpins both the descriptive and analytical narrative. Some of the questions which are raised by the book are listed below.

INTRODUCTORY QUESTIONS

- What is the impact of industrialisation and what are the specific mechanisms of globalisation? How does this appear in different historical periods, amongst different sectors, regions, people and communities in the Third World?

- What is the relationship between industrialisation, globalisation and development? Is industrialisation and the development of capitalism on a world scale a necessary and sufficient condition for development?
- What is 'free trade'? Does it simply represent the interests of Trans National Corporations, or is it a policy which might be in the interest of the Third World countries?
- What is the role of international organisations and agencies such as the World Trade Organisation, the World Bank and the International Monetary Fund, in shaping the pattern of development in the Third World?
- Do the structures of the world economy invariably work against the interests of the Third World? If so, why is it that some developing countries have industrialised, while others have not? Do the NICs represent a sustainable model of growth for other developing countries?
- Does globalisation mean that governments in the world, and even more so in the Third World, are rendered incapable of influencing the direction of domestic policy? Who are the 'winners' and who are the 'losers' in world development? What shapes this outcome?

Section 1

World Development: Globalisation in Historical Perspective

Introduction

Gavin Capps

The development of capitalism on a world scale began in Europe. This was characterised by the development of the urban crafts in the Italian and German medieval city states which (for the first time) in human history represented the irreversible victory of town over country. The break-up of the feudal manorial estates and the expansion of commodity production (that is, production and exchange for sale) appeared initially in the form of specialisation in production and exchange between these city states. The expansion of the world economy appeared initially in the form of 'windfall' profits made from trade in scarce commodities, such as precious minerals and spices by European merchants. This is referred to as the period of 'mercantile trade'. The subsequent development of 'machinofacture', that is the increased application of machinery to production and the development of the factory system, laid the basis for a development which was different in scale and kind to that of mercantilism.

British capitalism appeared as a particularly powerful force because before any of the other European nations and city states, it had made the transition to nationhood and the potent connection between imperial expansion and industrialisation. Whilst in this section it is argued that industrialisation began in Europe, by this it is not meant that industrialisation is the property of Europe. Colonial expansion and imitative industrialisation policies by the ex-colonies, means that industrialisation has spread (albeit unevenly) to all parts of the globe acquiring as in the case of Japan, North America and the Asian and Latin American NICs, specific national characteristics. This is examined in Sections 2 and 3. In this section, we analyse the historical development of the global economy, the transition from mercantilism to industrial capitalism and the manner in which the expansion of Europe evolved from imperial acquisition and protectionism and towards 'free trade'. This evolution formed much of the context from the late fifteenth to the late nineteenth centuries. The expansion of industrial capitalism and the rise of the USA from a peripheral colony of the British Empire to the world's dominant economy by the late nineteenth century provided a sobering challenge for Europe. This was graphically illustrated in superpower rivalry between Russia and the USA for most of the latter part of the twentieth century. This bi-polarity had important consequences for their respective clients in the Third World. The section concludes by examining the historical roots of contemporary problems facing the Third World, such as the debt crisis which unfolded in the developing countries during the late 1970s and questions raised by the globalisation thesis. The section introduces basic concepts used to explain world development, globalisation and industrialisation.

One key sub-text in the intricate relationship fashioned between the expansion of Europe and what came to be the Third World was in the impact of the Enlightenment. The Enlightenment was in part driven by the phase of early mercantile exploration and attempts to offer explanations for the biblically unaccounted for peoples of the world. This curiosity when combined with innovations in Science and Technology, contributed to the questioning of the natural order of things and also questioned the rights of divine kings. In both England and France this culminated in popular revolutions which led to the beheading of both Louis XVI and Charles I. The rolling heads of kings of state symbolised the development of the 'Enlightenment model' which lies at the heart of ideas about 'modernisation' in the Third World. The model drew from the experience of the French Revolution during which the bourgeoisie achieved three major objectives in its struggle with the dying feudal order: first, the abolition of the monarchy and the introduction of democracy in the form of a constituent assembly; second, the break-up of the large landed estates held by the nobility; and third, national unification and the development of the nation state. The model was used in the newly independent countries and in their subsequent evolution, to point to the poverty of the ruling elites and their inability to meet even basic criteria necessary for development and modernisation.

1.1

Gavin Capps

The Expansion of Europe: Mercantile Trade 1500–1750

OVERVIEW

The period covering 1500 to 1750 can be seen as the era of merchant or mercantile trade. It witnessed major transformations in the economic life of Western Europe, as its feudal societies disintegrated and inter-state rivalry grew. From the fifteenth century onwards, competing European nations sent sailors, soldiers and merchants across the world to locate and monopolise new sources of wealth. Desirable luxury goods and precious metals, such as spices and silver, were extracted from the Americas, Africa and Asia through plunder, extortion and trade. European expansion drew a growing portion of the world into its orbit, through the development of rival commercial networks on a global scale.

EMPIRES AND TRADE: THE WORLD BEFORE EUROPE

To understand the changes that were to occur between 1500 and 1750, it is useful to sketch out the kind of world that Europe would soon encounter.

Two features stood out in the world of the 1400s. The first was the immense diversity in the types of economic activity found across the globe. For example, some people, like the Amazonian Mundurucu 'Indians', lived on what they could hunt or gather. By contrast, the nomadic Mongols of central Asia moved herds of animals across great areas, trading with and raiding the settlements and towns that they encountered. In Han China or Hausa Nigeria, small peasant farmers cultivated the land. They were controlled by ruling Chiefs or Lords, who claimed a portion of the peasants' produce in the form of tribute. Great city states were also known, like Malacca in South East Asia, which supported a population of 50,000 merchants and craftworkers through regional trade.

Alongside these differences, there were profound similarities and linkages emerging between the world's peoples. In the populous regions of Central America, China, India and parts of Africa, great empires rose up and expanded. Dynastic rulers, like the Mwene Mutapa of Zimbabwe, controlled trade, mining and production over vast areas. They incorporated surrounding societies into their empires through military expansion. The new subjects were then forced to pay tribute (a tax, in the form of produce or labour) and to adopt similar cultural norms. The example of the Incas illustrates this process (see Example 1).

The incidence of long-distance trade was also growing. New commercial networks expanded out of long-established routes. In the 1400s, ocean-going junks (trading-vessels) from China regularly reached the southern end of the Red Sea. Arab merchants were spreading their commercial nets into central Asia, Southern Africa and the Indian subcontinent. Because transport costs were high, traders dealt in luxury goods like silk or ivory. These commodities were destined for the wealthy rulers of empires, acting as symbols of their political power and prestige. Exploration and the growth of trade provided new challenges and opportunities for merchants and spread languages, religions and customs – like Islam – across whole continents. One major challenge appeared in question marks raised for the Biblical interpretations of humanity applied universally by the Christian world. In the face of an expansive system of trade which brought Europeans in contact with diverse peoples of the world, no satisfactory explanation could be provided by the Christian world-view. This provided a source for intellectual curiousity in Europe which reinforced non-conformist thinking, previously associated with christian heretical sects and humanist thinkers, and this contributed to the development of the kernel of ideas which during the late eighteenth century constituted the Enlightenment. One key precept challenged by an expansive world system was that humans were weaved around god and his representatives on Earth, typically in the form of princes of church and state.

During the fifteenth century the world was characterised by immense diversity, but it was also changing and becoming more interconnected. Empire building and trade established interdependent economic zones, binding together different populations under powerful political or religious principles. There were few societies genuinely untouched by the influence of others. As each empire sought new sources of wealth, the conditions were established for sustained commercial competition on a global scale.

EUROPEAN EXPANSION AND MERCANTILIST POLICY

For many centuries Europe was relatively marginal 'in the affairs of the wider world' (Wolf, 1990, p. 7). At the same time the Southern Mediterranean region had long-standing connections with Africa and Asia. The Italian city states of Genoa and Venice acted as a gateway for raw materials from the tropical countries (precious metals, spices) and finished products from the craft industries of the East (silk and cotton textiles). The fruits of this commerce were then sold throughout Europe by merchants.

In the mid-1400s, the expansion of the Ottoman Empire cut the lucrative Mediterranean trade in two. The fall of Constantinople in 1453 was a potent symbol of this expansion. Faced with commercial loss due to the closure of markets to the east, European merchants began to search for new routes to Asia. There was considerable success in this venture. In 1497, the Portuguese merchant adventurer, Vasco de Gama, rounded the Cape of Good Hope and reached India. Five years earlier (1492), Columbus had accidentally 'discovered' America, which he mistook for Japan. These journeys laid the basis for a wave of European ocean-borne expansion which would change the world for ever. The forces behind this expansion were greater than the pursuit of individual profits. The survival of every European state rested on new wealth too and during the fifteenth century this was marked by inter-state rivalry and war over territory and resources. Continuous military conflict drained the coffers of the rival war lords and monarchs whose sources of domestic revenue were limited by restrictions imposed by the feudal economy, which was itself in periodic crisis.

The feudal mode of production which dominated medieval Europe was based on agriculture which provided the mainstay of the economy. Most people were peasants, belonging to manorial estates. This gave them the right to individual landholding and 'common' grazing land. In return, the Lord (of the manor) was owed tribute in the form of agricultural produce and labour service. The peasants were also forced to pay taxes to the Crown. As taxes were the main source of domestic revenue, warring states could only raise money by taxing the peasants harder. When new 'poll taxes' were imposed in England during the 1500s, they were met with virtual insurrection. This source of state income was clearly limited.

The growing activities of merchants suggested an alternative source of revenue. Urban manufacturing was confined to guilds, in which a hierarchy of handicrafts workers of the same trade monopolised production, but were restricted in how much they could sell. In time, whole towns became specialized in the manufacture of particular items (e.g. textiles, metals or armaments), requiring wider markets. Merchants began to take advantage, buying up all the guilds could supply and selling it in new areas of demand. This growing commerce quickly spread across Europe and entwined with the Mediterranean trade. It also became subject to increased taxation and state control.

As European merchant adventurers located new sources of wealth, their home rulers began to actively support them. The Crowns needed the merchants as allies in their struggle with the feudal Lords, principally as a source of revenue to finance administration and war. In exchange, the merchants required a powerful state to protect their international trade, conquer colonies and defeat restrictive feudal practices at home. The alliance between the Crown and merchants is the meaning of the term 'mercantilism'. Economists like Mun wrote in the first quarter of the seventeenth century and advised the state to develop commerce and its allied industries, by using high tariffs (import taxes) to provide protection from competitive foreign imports (Rubin, 1989). Protectionist ideas extended to the international arena. Favoured merchants were granted monopoly rights to control trading zones in the name of the Crown. This gave rise to trading companies which combined acquisition with force and economic, military and territorial rivalries conducted on a world scale.

CONQUEST, COMPETITION AND MONOPOLY IN THE WORLD MARKET

The first wave of European expansion was led by the Portuguese. It tells us much about what was to follow. In 1415, a small force invaded the North African port of Ceuta, in an attempt to control the Mediterranean trade in gold. By 1500, Portuguese vessels had crossed the Atlantic and were shipping Brazil wood from an area which they named Brazil – the first African slaves would be imported to its new plantations 30 years later. In 1505, a Portuguese fleet reached India, plundering the East African great port of Kilwa on the way. This encouraged Portuguese merchants to invade the lucrative East African–Asian trade, ousting the Arab merchants who had controlled it previously.

New competitors arrived in the form of the Dutch East India Company which was formed in 1602 in order to break the Portuguese monopoly over the spice trade. The Portuguese were effectively driven out of the East. The Dutch West India Company formed in 1621 set out to do the same in the Caribbean. Similarly, by 1550 British trading companies had made inroads into the Dutch and Spanish Americas. They founded new colonies in North America and the Caribbean, where France also maintained a foothold. Finally, after years of battles with the Dutch and French navies, the British established monopolies throughout North America and South Asia. During this period simultaneous wars (in effect, World Wars) were fought for the first time in all of the world's continents.

The forms of European conquest varied from continent to continent. South America was divided between Portugal and Spain through the arbitration of the Pope during 1494 and the extensive direct occupation which followed contrasted with conquest in Asia where the Europeans rarely moved inland from the coastal trading stations. Countries like China and India were defended by large and powerful states, even when compared to the Inca Empire. However, superior naval power and commercial organisation allowed the trading companies to control their sea-lanes and redirect Asia's trade and wealth to vital ports owned by the trading companies. This was a key feature in European control of exchange.

The African continent was initially viewed as a transit point on the way to Asia and as a source of gold and ivory, via coastal trade. By the seventeenth century, however, Africa, America and Europe were being drawn into a more direct and special relationship. All hitherto European expansion was characterised by erratic windfall profits made from trade and plunder in luxury goods. British colonialism in North America and the Caribbean initiated a qualitatively new kind of international trade which was based on the production of mass goods which linked the large-scale production of raw materials for manufacturing in Europe, the development of markets for European goods in the colonies, and the procurement from Africa of slave labour for plantation production, in a 'triangular trade' (Bernstein et al., 1992).

At the heart of this development were the sugar, cotton and tobacco plantations which sprang up across the Americas. All adopted similar systems of settled, labour-intensive production, to supply the European economies with raw materials and foodstuffs. In exchange, European powers provided military and economic protection for the plantation economy. Labour which had proven so scarce in the initial period of exploration that it forced Columbus (at his peril) to compel feudal nobles to undertake manual labour, was not in short supply. Between 1701 and 1810, England exported over 2 million slaves from West Africa alone (Wolf, 1990). A slave traffic poured along indigenously organised routes, which stretched the breadth of Africa. Slaves were traded for European manufactures, like British arms or cloth – a direct stimulus to these protected industries. As the demand for plantation commodities increased, British merchants and shippers were able to reap huge profits at each point of sale in the triangular trade.

The era of mercantile trade saw the initiation of new and global processes of economic integration in which different parts of the world were linked together by private trading companies and the force of European state powers. Existing trade networks were smashed or modified by European needs. The highly diverse world of the 1400s was by now unified by a shared encounter with Europe, and also divided by the rival trading blocs which characterised the mercantile world market. During the next historical period this situation was to radically change. As the world's wealth flowed into Europe, feudalism gradually gave way to a process of capitalist industrialisation. A new type of world economy and trading system would now be constructed, the heart of which was no longer the old protectionism of mercantilism, but on the contrary the 'free trade' rallying cry of the emergent manufacturing classes.

CONCLUSIONS

The dissolution of European feudalism created the conditions for increased competition. Initially this appeared in the form of mercantilism which linked the accumulation of gold and silver from the New World to the Treasuries of the European powers. In itself this was little removed from guild-like regulations, albeit on a global scale, as rival Chartered Companies imposed restriction on the freedom of others to trade in areas under their control. Mercantilism established an important link between trade and state policy, given that the strength of a state was measured in the amount of gold and silver it had in its Treasury. Rivalry between the European states over the control of this trade drove this stage of world development. During this period a tenacious relationship was established between state and trade policy which constituted an important continuity in the evolution of the global economy.

EXAMPLE 1

For God and Profit: Conquistadors in the Americas

The Spanish occupation of the Americas incorporated an entire region into the emerging world economy. Within a generation of Columbus' first voyage (1492), gold-hungry Conquistadors (conquerors) like Hernan Cortes (1519) and Francisco Pizarro (1530) were leading military expeditions into Central and South America. The tragic end of the Inca Empire illustrates the effects of the encounter between an expanding Europe and the 'New World'.

It is a popular myth that the conquest of the Americas was a triumph of modern European society over traditional 'primitives'. In fact the opposing forces of Incas and Spaniards were remarkably similar – both were author- itarian societies in full expansion. The Incas were also conquerors. In less than one hundred years their empire had spread from the Central Andes to span the 5,000 kilometres between the Manta (Ecuador) and the Maule River (Chile). This imperial growth was forged by a professional army, con- solidating its gains with the construction of highways and control points. The Inca economy was no less sophisticated. A strict dynastic hierarchy organised the extraction of labour and goods from its subjects through a centralised state, military might and the legitimising force of religion. Great irrigation schemes were built to ensure a regular surplus of potatoes and maize. The subjugated Amerindian clans maintained communal plots of land and engaged in a trade which circulated goods between the different ecological zones of the Andes.

This way of life meant little to the Conquistadors. Their mission was to find and repatriate wealth, mainly in the form of precious minerals and metals to the Spanish Crown. They were also looking for new souls to convert to Catholicism, although this was by no means clear at the beginning. Indeed it took a theological debate prompted by the Franciscans for the Spanish to accept that Indians had souls in the first place which could theoretically be saved by conversion. Promises of riches and glory, far more than new souls, drove Pizarro into direct warfare with the Incas in 1532. He kidnapped and eventually murdered the Inca Emperor Atahuailpala and defeated his demoralised army soon after. The manner in which the last Emperor of the Incas met his death continues to shock to this day. The Spaniards threatened to hang Atahuailpala unless he complied with their demands for gold and his personal conversion to Christianity. As this form of death was culturally unacceptable to the Incas, he agreed to the conversion in exchange for promises that he would not be hanged. Following his conversion the Spaniards strangled (garotted) Atahuailpala and broke their promises to him.

The first two decades of Spanish rule decimated the Inca polity. In less than one hundred years, 75 to 90 per cent of the native American population had died from disease, overwork and the destruction of their way of life in what was referred to by the indigenous peoples as the 'Great Dying'. In 1545 vast silver deposits were discovered at San Luis Potosi (Peru) which remained for one hundred years the single largest source of silver in the world. Under these conditions direct plunder gave way to a systematic attempt to extract and transport this wealth.

Silver became the chief export to Spain and this required the development of a system of local administration and trans-Atlantic convoys escorted by warships and heavy fortification of principal ports and strategic points. The Spanish King granted his merchants and administrators (*encomerderos*) monopoly rights over mining, agricultural activities, cloth production and trade in the Americas. In turn, the Spanish colonialists forced the surviving Amerindians to work in their mines and *haciendas* (farms) at starvation wages, through a system of drafting labour, known as *mita*. Peasant families had to pay taxes to the state and produce food both for themselves and related men performing *mita* services known as *mitayos*. Women were forced to spin and weave cloth for export to Europe. Peasant agriculture became commercialised, accentuating divisions within Amerindian society. By the eighteenth century, some members of pre-conquest elites, like Chiefs, participated freely in the European colonial economy. However, the majority were so poor and exploited that the Catholic Church urged reform; but the colonial conscience rarely stretched that far.

The effect of the great outflow of American wealth was profoundly paradoxical. Spanish rulers such as Charles V and Philip II had little will to develop their backward agricultural economy. Instead, they used their bullion to build spectacular cathedrals or purchase arms and manufactures from countries like Britain. Between 1503 and 1660, Spanish gold and silver flooded out of Spain, expanding Northern European supplies by a fifth and a sixth respectively. One consequence of this was that the price of silver declined and this contributed towards the decline of Spain itself, which fell into debt and stagnation, while other parts of Western Europe were undergoing a transition towards industrial capitalism.

Gavin Capps

Industrial Capitalism and 'Free Trade' 1750–1875

OVERVIEW

Until the mid-eighteenth century, European industry was little more than a by-product of overseas trade. Typically, this was associated with the triangular trade and the expansion of ship-building. Laws, such as the Corn Laws and the Navigation Laws in Britain and its colonies respectively, existed in order to protect the interests of big landlords, plantation owners and merchant shipping. The Navigation Laws, for example, stated that trade to and from the British colonies had to be carried in British ships. This situation was radically transformed by the 'Industrial Revolution'. Beginning in Britain, a series of innovations and inventions spurred by capital investment, established the dominance of machinery in production. By 1850, Britain was regarded as the 'Workshop of the World' and its manufactures could undersell any competitor. The rapid growth of industrial capitalism demanded greater supplies of raw materials, food stuffs and world-wide markets for manufactured goods. Under these expansive conditions the old protectionism was inappropriate to the needs of the new industrialists who in the form of the 'Manchester' (manufacturing) lobby called for a policy of 'free trade'; that is, the removal of state protection and monopolies in the world market. For the first time in European history, commerce was to become the servant of industry.

THE CONDITIONS FOR THE DEVELOPMENT OF INDUSTRIAL CAPITALISM IN BRITAIN

The development of industry in Britain tells us much about the process of capitalist industrialisation. Usually, industrialisation involves technical changes, such as new inventions and new ways of organising work itself. Typically this involved the division of work into smaller components which began to resemble assembly-line factory production. It also requires social changes or more specifically, changes in the social relations of production. In feudal society, production was organised by the relationship between classes of peasant and handicrafts producers and the feudal Lords. Capitalist production is structured by a different social relationship involving new classes of capitalists and wage-workers.

For a labour market and wage relationships to exist, a necessary presupposition is the existence of a condition of competition and generalised commodity production. Marx argued that competition rested on the acquisition of commodities and that upon the acquisition of labour power itself, rested the acquisition of all other commodities. The significance of labour power as a branch of the general market of commodities was noted by Marx (1970, p. 170) not only as a historical condition comprising a 'world history', but also as one which 'can spring into life, only when the owner of the means of production and subsistence meets in the market with the free labourer selling his [her] labour-power'. The assertion that labour power as a commodity can only exist in a context of a market for free-labour was seen by Marx as conditional on two factors: that the exchange of commodities, i.e. money (wages) for labour power 'implies no other relations of dependence' and that the labourer is in no position to sell commodities other than 'that very labour-power, which exists only in his [her] living self' (Marx, 1970, pp. 167–9).

The previous era of mercantile trade stimulated the formation of capitalist relations of exchange and production in Britain through the development of the world market and the growth of the money economy. As we have seen, the growth of trade enriched merchants through new activities like slaving. This accelerated the accumulation and investment of savings and the transformation of many of them into a class of commercial capitalists, who mobilised guild handicraft producers to supply them with trade goods, such as guns to exchange for slaves. In time, many of these new commercial merchant capitalists began to reinvest their trading profits in the more direct organisation of industrial activity. The rise of 'cottage industry', or the 'putting out system', was a result of this process. Here, producers – former independent handicraft workers or poor peasants – were given the raw materials by the merchants, to be worked up in their own homes. The merchants then collected the finished goods and traded them on. In time, some merchants began to supply the home-workers with credit and tools. It was but a short step for the workers to become wholly dependent on the merchants for their income, which now took the form of a wage. Once this income-dependency was established, it was possible with technical innovations in machinery to organise workers in such a way as to specialise in different stages of production (i.e. a 'technical' division of labour). A precondition for this kind of work was the concentration of workers under one roof in a rudimentary urban-based factory system which allowed far closer supervision of work, when compared to the many dispersed rural households brought together by the previous putting out system (Dobb, 1971).

Expanding markets also transformed agriculture more directly. Some of the feudal landlords responded to the expanding demand of the growing urban centres by raising their productivity and incomes in an Agrarian Revolution which pre-dated and paralleled the revolution in industry. This process was in part facilitated by the strong organic links to state power enjoyed by the landlord class. First, the peasantry were progressively legally 'freed' from their feudal obligations and their right to land. This allowed the Landlords to rent it to them instead. In time, these 'tenant peasants' divided into a minority of commercial farmers, who began to improve their holdings and employ others (the so-called 'Yeomen Farmers'); and a mass of small-holders, cottagers and handicraft producers (such as handloom weavers) who found it difficult and eventually impossible to compete with factory production. A series of Parliamentary Acts (the 'Enclosure Acts') transferred ownership of much of the common-land to the new landlord class of agrarian capitalists, thereby depriving the rural poor use of traditional forms of subsistence such as the collection of fodder, fuel-wood and game (Hill, 1969; the Hammonds, 1948, Volumes I and II).

Taken together, these social and economic changes constituted along with the triangular trade a process of 'primitive' or early accumulation of capital. Productive wealth (capital) was concentrated in the hands of new classes of landlords, commercial tenant farmers and merchant capitalists. At the same time, small peasants and artisans found it difficult to retain ownership over productive assets such as land and tools and were increasingly divorced from means of production through Enclosure, competition and the intervention of merchants. With no other way to make a living, the growing mass of rural and urban poor were transformed into a class of wage-workers. The technical and scientific innovations of the Industrial Revolution built on and accelerated these emerging capitalist relations of production.

COTTON AND LOCOMOTION: THE DRIVING SECTORS OF THE
INDUSTRIAL REVOLUTION

The main features of the Industrial Revolution were the mechanisation of production and the development of the factory system. This signified that from this point on, manufacturing was to be wrested from the control of small-scale producers and organised by individual capitalists, employing larger numbers of wage-workers. In the UK this process began in the cotton textile industry and spread to railway building, with its twin satellites of steel production and coal mining. A study of the cotton industry is, therefore, illus-trative of the growth of manufacturing industry.

The impetus for the transformation of the cotton industry came from foreign competition. Britain entered the eighteenth century as a world leader in the production of woollen textiles. Merchants reduced costs by organising production through the rural cottage industry, where labour was cheap. Yet, British textiles were soon being undercut by cheaper Indian calico (cotton) imports. The British government at the instigation of UK textile manufac-turers responded by banning the sole supplier of Indian textiles, the East India

Company, from further importing or printing calicoes. The textile industry then substituted for these imports, by producing copies and improving the process of production.

A spate of technical innovations enabled this process. The idea of mechanising production was not new, but the restrictive practices of the feudal guilds had prohibited any major changes. As the cotton industry was in its earliest stages, these regulations did not apply. In 1769, Arkwright patented a new, water-driven spinning machine. A year later, Hargreaves patented the Spinning Jenny. Finally, in 1779, Crompton combined these two inventions in the 'Mule'. When James Watt's universal steam engine (1781) was applied to the Mule in 1790, output soared and the 'Age of Steam' had begun. This had revolutionary implications for merchant shipping, freed for the first time from the limitations of wind-power.

The vast increase in textile productivity reduced labour costs and undercut all competition. Where an Indian hand spinner took more than 50,000 hours to process 100 pounds of cotton, Crompton's steam-powered Mule cut the time to less than 300 hours (Wolf, 1990, p. 273). Cotton illustrates, therefore, not only the leading role of the sector in the development of industrial capitalism, but equally its role in the expansion of new patterns of international trade. According to the historian Eric Hobsbawm (1996a, p. 38),

> something like one half of the value of all British imports consisted of cotton products, and at their peak (in the middle of the 1830s) raw cotton made up twenty percent of total net imports. In a real sense the British balance of payments depended on the fortunes of this single industry, and so did shipping and much of Britain's overseas trade in general.

The conditions of the new working class where textile factories sprang up were appalling, yet, huge swathes of landless labourers migrated towards them. The result was a rapid process of urbanisation. In 1773, Manchester had a population of 24,000; by 1851 it had risen to more than 250,000 people. Of these, 130,000 came from the surrounding counties and 40,000 from Ireland (Wolf, 1990, p. 276). The quality of life and employment was appalling. The factories were hot, noisy and dangerous. Women and children competed with men for work, which could average 14 hours a day. The 'Dark Satanic Mills' of William Blake's New Jerusalem referred to the textile industry. The new relationship between productive capacity, grinding poverty and environmental pollution was also noted by Alex de Toqueville, French diarist and economist, when he visited Manchester in 1835:

> From this foul drain the greatest stream of humanity flows out to fertilize the whole world. From this filthy sewer pure gold flows. Here humanity attains its most complete development and its most brutish, here civilization works its miracles and civilized man (sic) is turned almost into a savage. (Cited in Hobsbawm, 1996a, p. 27)

By the 1830s, the cotton boom had turned to slump and this led many industrialists and financiers to seek new sources of profitable investment. The development of railways, with their massive demand for iron, steel and coal provided an alternative. The first modern railway, transporting coal from Stockton to Darlington, opened in 1825. Between 1827 and 1850, a burst of speculative frenzy saw the construction of railways in the USA, France, Germany and Belgium. Some 23,500 miles of track now sped goods from deep inland to the termini of ocean-borne trade. Steel boilers revolutionised shipping too. By 1865, a steamship could carry 3,000 tons of cargo from China to London in 77 days whereas sailing vessels took 130 days at a third of the tonnage. The magnitude of the 'transport boom' is illustrated by the following: in 1831 total tonnage of steamships came to 32,000 tons; by 1881 it was 18,325 million tons (Hobsbawm, 1996a, pp. 310, 350).

It was British capital, iron, machines and technical know-how which drove the 'age of steam'. Coal and iron output trebled between 1830 and 1850, while British engineers constructed embankments, cuttings and bridges the world over. It was the effects of this second wave of industrial revolution which were to establish Britain as the 'Workshop of the World'. The rapid development of mechanised factory production spread from cotton, through transportation to new branches of the economy. By 1851, over half of the British population were living in industrial cities, many under the new discipline of the factory wage system.

'FREE TRADE'

The expansion of the world market was essential for the development of Industrial Capitalism. The industries which led the 'Industrial Revolution' required a growing volume of primary commodities (raw materials and foodstuffs) to feed their factories and working classes. As the domestic market could only consume a limited proportion of manufacturing output, so new export markets had to be found. A good example of this was the phenomenal growth in British cotton textile export markets and new areas of raw cotton supply (see Example 2). The rallying cry of the new British industrialists was 'free trade'. Barratt-Brown explains that this meant 'the freedom to trade – to obtain food and raw materials wherever they were most cheaply produced and to open up the world markets for their wares' (Barratt-Brown, 1974, p. 177).

The call for 'free trade', however, challenged the old protectionist mercantile policies and the interests that they represented. English Landlords benefited from restrictions on corn imports (the Corn Laws), which allowed them to monopolise the domestic bread market. High bread prices forced up the wages of urban workers, which ate into industrial profits. The campaign for 'free trade' was led by the Manchester textile barons, more for this reason than any ideological commitment to 'free trade'. In 1846, the repeal of the Corn Laws symbolised the victory of the new, competitive capitalism over state monopolies and constraints to trade. The era of competitive capitalism (1850–75) saw the growth of specialisation in the world market with British manufacturing industry enjoying a unique position for most of this period. It was very much with the English bourgeoisie in mind that contemporaries such as Karl Marx and Frederic Engels wrote that

> The bourgeoisie has through its exploitation of the world market given a cosmopolitan character to production and consumption in every country. All old established national industries have been destroyed or are being destroyed. They are dislodged by new industries, that no longer work up indigenous raw materials, but raw materials drawn from the remotest zones, industries whose products are consumed not at home, but in every quarter in the globe. In place of old local and national seclusion we have intercourse in every direction, universal interdependence of nations. (Karl Marx and Frederic Engels, *Communist Manifesto*, 1848)

The era of competitive capitalism also ushered in a new relationship between British export industries and the state. Government investment was redirected towards creating a world-wide infrastructure in transport and communications and the maintenance of naval bases, to protect strategic trade routes. British military power was also mobilised to break down foreign barriers to its goods. The means of enforcing 'free trade' were exemplified by the 'Opium Wars' (1839–42) during which the British Navy bombarded China into 'accepting' an agreement allowing for unlimited imports of Indian opium into China in exchange for tea, and in the process established Hong Kong as a trading post.

The growth of industrial capitalism and the world market also stimulated a wave of global migration. Millions of people, who had been displaced from peasant or cottage production, moved to areas of heightened industrial or agricultural activity. Between 1820 and 1860, nearly 4 million landless labourers migrated to the USA from Ireland, Germany, Italy and Britain. Australia and Canada received a further 1.5 million Britons between 1851 and 1890. Labourers from India and China migrated to all corners of the world. The California gold rushes (1849–80), for example, attracted 111,000 Chinese migrants, while 'indentured' (contracted) labourers from China and the Indian subcontinent were dispersed to every corner of the expanding world economy: this ranged from the sugar cane fields of Fiji and Guyana to the payroll of the East African Railway Company and South African mining companies to build the railways and dig mines of the British Empire (Hirst and Thompson, 1996, pp. 22–6).

The industrialised nations entered the last quarter of the nineteenth century with immense optimism. The world economy was booming. Between 1860 and 1870, the volume of world trade increased by a phenomenal 260 per cent and British foreign investment increased by 75 per cent. The revolution in transport and communications increased global economic interdependence as capital, goods and labour flowed from zones of supply to areas of demand. By 1875 some 88 million tons of seaborne merchandise was exchanged annually between the major nations, while the value of British exports to Asia alone increased from 7 million tons in 1848 to 41 million tons in 1875 (Hobsbawm, 1996b, p. 50).

CONCLUSIONS

'Free trade' has always been the rallying cry of the strongest. In the mid-nineteenth century this became most closely associated with the English manufacturing classes and articulated in the views of the 'Manchester' free-trade lobby, within which textile and cotton industrialists were a significant force. The benefits of free trade for the English cotton industry is illustrated in its relationship with the Indian cotton industry (see Example 2). The dismantling of the barriers to trade and the protectionist policies which supported the landlord class in England and the plantation economy in North America and the Caribbean resulted in both an increased volume of British trade as well as important changes in its direction. One important change was the loss of significance to the British Empire of North America and the growth in significance of the Indian subcontinent. 'Free trade' and the ability to undercut any competitor in the world in a range of products, was the material and historically unique position faced by British manufacturing industry in the mid-nineteenth century, and one which informed advocacy for 'free trade'.

EXAMPLE 2

The Fall and Rise of Indian Cotton, 1700–1920

The changing fortunes of the Indian cotton industry illustrate how the development of a capitalist world market affected areas of foreign competition and production, often setting in motion new processes of economic change.

When European traders first expanded into India, they discovered a vibrant and highly developed textile crafts sector. Hand spinners and weavers produced cottons or calicoes – named after the city of Calicut on the Malibar coast – which were cheaper and better in quality than European textiles. Both the Dutch and British East India Companies began to commission Indian artisans to produce calicoes for European tastes. They also began to import Indian cottons for hand printing in Europe. The popularity of Indian imports was such that they began to undermine British textile producers whose inferior and expensive cloth could not compete with Indian imports. In the mid-1700s, British manufacturers lobbied the government to ban calicoes. In order to protect its domestic industry, the mercantile state ruled the English East India Company could no longer import Indian cottons. This action dealt the Indian artisans a heavy blow.

The subsequent expansion of the British cotton industry during the Industrial Revolution allowed huge volumes of cotton textiles to be produced at low cost. The demand by textile industrialists for free trade led to India being flooded by cheap British cotton exports which had the effect of destroying local handicraft production. The uneven price war between British factory and Indian handicraft production saw loss of livelihoods and immense deprivation amongst rural handloom weavers. Systematic de-industrialisation turned India into a key import market for Lancashire cottons: in 1820, the subcontinent took only 11 million yards; but by 1840 it already took 145 million yards (Hobsbawm, 1996b, p. 35).

The fortunes of India's cotton industry rose again, with British trading interests in China. British merchants sought China's tea and the Chinese demanded Indian raw cotton in return. The British merchants began to expand India's cotton acreage, by advancing money to Indian landlords. In 1850, 8 million acres were under cultivation. The expansion led to a network of British, Indian and Chinese merchants, agency houses and transporters around Bombay (the centre of 'cotton country'). With the expansion of the Indian railroad network, cotton production came to cover 17 million acres by the end of the nineteenth century.

Indian merchants amassed great fortunes through the cotton and opium trades with China. Some of this wealth was reinvested in the development of a new, indigenous, textile industry. The first mill, using British technology and Indian finance, went into production in Bombay during 1856. By 1900 there were 86 Indian-owned mills employing some 80,000 workers. Indian foremen, or 'jobbers', were charged with labour recruitment. Word of the new employment attracted poor peasant migrants from as far as Uttar Pradesh, 750 miles to the north. The growth of a machine-based Indian textile industry, with its centre in Bombay, gave rise to an urbanised Indian working class and trade union organisation. Despite the handicap of English import duties, excise taxes and capital exports from India, textiles became one area of the Indian economy in which local capitalists predominated and as such provides us with an early case of capitalist industrialisation in the periphery.

1.3

Gavin Capps

Imperial Trade and Imperial Rivalries 1875–1945

OVERVIEW

By the 1870s British economic supremacy was being challenged by the industrialisation of Germany and the USA. The arrival of other industrialised countries led to a new phase of international rivalry as each industrialised nation competed for a share of the world's resources and markets with greater vigour. The onset of a global slump during a protracted period which lasted from 1873 to 1896 intensified this competition and gave rise to a new era of 'monopoly capitalism'. During this period small companies either combined into powerful industrial corporations or grew to monopolise whole areas of economic activity. Production was increasingly organised on a national scale through the intervention of the competing states. This was a strong feature of US enterprise development which saw the most systematic application of anti-monopoly laws seen in the global economy (the 'anti-trust' laws), ostensibly in order to restrain monopoly and to ensure free competition between rival industrialists. One result of competition between rival companies which were strongly identified with particular states was that competition between them began to assume the more dangerous form of national rivalry and the implied threat of force to defend the 'national' interest. This period was characterised by a wave of territorial expansion, such as the 'Scramble for Africa', as more parts of the world were clearly delineated and colonised by the rival European powers. This combination between monopoly capitalism and colonial expansion characterised 'Imperialism' during the late nineteenth century. The relationship between state and capital introduced tremendous volatility in international relations and the two World Wars are a sobering reflection that nineteenth-century Imperialism far from producing the order expected in territorial division was characterised by immense carnage.

THE LATE INDUSTRIALISERS

The later industrialisation of other European countries, the USA and Japan presented a novel problem for the mid-nineteenth-century orthodoxies of free trade and comparative advantage developed by British political economists such as Adam Smith and David Ricardo. Comparative advantage questioned whether it was wise for them to industrialise at all. One conventional view in England was that Prussia (and Poland) should remain as dedicated agricultural producers. Thus, it was not difficult for Germany or the USA to suspect 'that many of the supposed universal postulates of classical economic theory were simply convenient rationalizations to justify and maintain British dominance' (Kitching, 1989, p. 142). In 1841, the German economist, Friedrich List, developed a theoretical defence of industrial protectionism. List argued that identities, culture, politics and economics should be seen as mutually supporting elements in a process of national development. This thinking encouraged the German government to control imports and to nationalise the banks, railways, mines and heavy industries.

State-direction in Germany pioneered the fusion of banking with industry ('finance capital') and concentrated small enterprises into powerful conglomerates. By producing in larger units, German industries reaped the advantages of economies of scale. That is, by producing in even greater amounts they could lower production costs and undercut their competitors. The USA was able to industrialise by virtue of its vast domestic resources and markets protected by tariff barriers. The relative self-sufficiency of the US economy created the material basis for both protectionist trade policies and political isolationism. Both the German and US economies also benefited from technological advances. Where the UK still relied on steam power, its rivals expanded their industries on the new foundations of oil or electricity. Between 1880 and 1890, the massive US economy overtook Britain in steel production. Within a decade, Germany was able to do the same. Britain, the previous champion of free trade, was barely able to keep up and did so by virtue of its protected markets in the Empire.

Under these conditions, there were pressing reasons for the industrialised countries to expand and compete for the world's resources and markets. Their highly specialised economies could not survive without guaranteed raw materials, foodstuffs and markets for sale. Growing economic rivalry initiated a new wave of European expansion and conquest, culminating in the 'Scramble for Africa'. In 1876, only 10 per cent of Africa was ruled by European powers. By 1900, 90 per cent was under European colonial rule (Coquery-Vidrovich, 1988). As each power brought new territories under its influence, it integrated them into its own economic sphere.

DIRECT COLONIAL RULE

Clearly defined territorial procession by the European powers increased from 2.7 million square miles and 148 million inhabitants in 1860, to 29 million square miles and 568 million inhabitants in 1914. Colonial conquest was accompanied by a huge increase in European foreign investment, from £2bn in 1862 to £44bn in 1913 (Callinicos, 1994, p. 23). In reality, the expansion of foreign investment was highly uneven. For example, Britain, still the greatest exporter of capital, predominantly invested in its traditional empire of India and the White Settler colonies, such as Canada and Australia (see Table 1.2).

The significance of the new imperial possessions for the economic and strategic interests of the colonising powers was influenced by a number of factors. Whether a territory was considered rich in primary commodities, like palm oil in West Africa, held good prospects for European settlement (like Kenya), or was of geopolitical significance, like Egypt for control of the Suez Canal, were some of the factors which led to direct European control and the development of colonial states. Direct colonial rule built on three centuries of expansion by merchants and trading posts and consolidated the international division of labour in the world economy. Now, whole global regions specialised in the production of foodstuffs or industrial raw materials. This was typified by the phenomenal rate of expansion in the production of tropical primary commodities in the colonies. Others – usually the industrial economies – processed the raw materials, consumed the food, and sent back manufactured goods in exchange (see Table 1.3). The commodity examples of bananas, palm oil and the mining industry illustrate this further (see Example 3).

The colonial states had varying levels of interest in long-term economic development and this was influenced in Africa by whether a colony was a 'settler' or 'non-settler' colony (Brett, 1973; Zwanenberg and King, 1975; Kitching, 1982). The priority of all colonies was to facilitate the production and transport of primary commodities for their home industries. This required a framework of 'law and order' and a basic infrastructure of railways or ports. The colonial states compelled peasants to produce specified primary commodities or to work on the new plantations and mines either for specified periods or more frequently in order to earn money to pay taxes, such as the Hut and Poll Tax. The general principle applied in the administration of the British colonies was that they had to be self-financing, so as not to be a 'burden' on the British Exchequer. This principle drove taxation policy and was critically linked to the demand for labour in the 'settler' colonies of Africa in which the interests of large-scale European agriculture were paramount in policy making. If the colony required more labour, then taxes would be adjusted (raised) so as to force even more Africans into European plantation or mining employment. Another general principle was each colony was kept dependent on the imported manufactures of the occupying power and there was little trade between rival territories. As a consequence, any attempts at indigenous industrialisation or agricultural development which could compete with either metropolitan capitalism or the settler plantation economy, were highly constrained by colonialism. The basic division established by direct colonial rule, between a centre of developed industrial nations and a periphery of primary commodity producers, lies at the heart of the modern world economy (see Table 1.4). At the same time, however, the world market did not prove to be entirely monolithic. We have already seen how the Indian textile industry was able to take advantage of its strategic proximity to China.

IMPERIALISM AND WAR

As Germany, a relatively late arrival to colonial acquisition, increasingly challenged Britain's industrial and naval supremacy, both countries plunged into an arms race driven by further technological innovation such as the revolution in sea and land transport, the chemical compositions of high explosives and the mass production of new weapons. The drive to industrialise also came from the necessities of modern warfare (see Table 1.5). The period from 1875 to 1914 saw phenomenal rates of growth in world output and trade. During 1850–1900, the volume of world trade grew by 900 per cent (Hirst and Thompson, 1996, p. 20). Under these conditions of globalisation, Russian economist Nikolai Bukharin pointed to what was seen as a growing contradiction between 'the increasing internationalisation of capitalist production and the persisting political organisation of capitalist societies through national states' (Bernstein et al., 1992, p. 178). The First World War and subsequent 'Great Depression' (1929–33) can be seen as practical manifestations of the necessary contradiction between capitalist production and the nation state. The Depression led to the emergence of a world economy which was very different to that before the First World War. The USA had substantially bank-rolled Britain's war-time effort and was now the holder of the largest capital reserves in the world. As such, the US economy was far more significant to the world economy when compared to the pre-war period and this had important implications. During the inter-war period each industrial nation attempted to isolate itself from the world market through strategies of economic autarky – or self-sufficiency. New tariff barriers were erected and the world market was divided into mutually hostile protectionist trade blocs. The high level of economic integration which was attained before 1914 declined and an important contributory factor was that Britain no longer had the authority or the will to impose the 'free-trade' system on other countries. One reflection of protectionism was that trade was now carried out within different 'currency zones'. For example, British colonial 'possessions' like India traded almost exclusively with Britain using pounds sterling – the so-called Imperial Preference System established in 1932. Conversely, French colonies used the franc as their trading currency. This increased the control of each power over its colonies and kept imperial rivals out. These manoeuvres in the colonies did little to substantially alter the development of the inter-war Depression. Neither did the actions of the USA which precipitated the growth of protectionism in Europe by withdrawing short-term lending to Germany. This triggered

Germany's inability to repay the war-time reparations imposed by the Allied victors at the Treaty of Versailles and contributed towards the collapse of the banking system and the growth of hyper-inflation which fed the social and political crisis in Germany.

At the same time, a different set of opportunities emerged for peripheral and colonised countries with the contraction of world trade both during the Great Depression and the two World Wars. As war and recession disrupted the existing pattern of world trade and the demand and income from primary commodities such as copper and coffee fell, so some of the largest countries in the periphery, such as Brazil, Mexico and India were forced to attempt to produce locally the manufactured goods previously imported. By default, this gave a significant push to industrialisation in new areas of the globe. This was reflected in an increasing share of manufacturing production by the Third World, from a mere 3 per cent in 1926–29 to a significant 15 per cent of global production by 1948 (see Table 1.6).

CONCLUSIONS

The restructuring of the world economy during the latter part of the nineteenth century was characterised by very high levels of integration between giant private sector quasi-monopolies and their respective states. This factor underpinned the emergence of Germany and the USA as industrial powers which challenged Britain's supremacy. As competition between different units of capital appeared in national form so the world became an increasingly unstable place. The two World Wars and subsequent Great Depression were memorials to this instability. A critical dimension of global restructuring was the displacement of the UK as the 'centre' of the world economy by the USA. This had important implications for the Third World. It is argued that during the nineteenth century when the UK acted as the centre of the world economy this created far greater demand for tropical and other primary products from the colonies and peripheral economies of the world, when compared to the USA when it began to act in the twentieth century as the new centre of the global economy. As such, growth in the USA can be said to have a 'low import co-efficient' for the developing countries (see Section 2.1). This tendency followed from the size, diversity and self-sufficiency of the US economy, as well as the strength of isolationism. This was reinforced by the high productivity gains of US manufacturing industry due to higher levels of automation and the application of fordist mass production techniques, which lowered the price cost to American consumers to such a degree that it could not be matched by rivals. At the same time, however, we noted that during this period, the disruption of existing patterns of trade had a perversely positive effect in many parts of the Third World as this encouraged domestic manufacturing industry in a forced attempt to produce locally what was previously imported.

EXAMPLE 3

'Local Episodes' in the International Division of Labour

The making of colonial economies, geared to the production and export of specialist raw materials, integrated new regions into the world market. Primary commodity production was either organised around plantations and mines, which required a supply of labour; or through the commercialisation of small-scale peasant production. The following 'local' examples illustrate some of the ways in which giant Western companies and colonial states interacted to develop new areas of primary commodity production, thereby extending the international division of labour.

Banana plantations in Colombia
In the 1870s, Colombian entrepreneurs 'opened up' a northern area of the country through the construction of a railroad, a drainage canal and irrigation channels. They initiated banana production for the North American market, but soon this operation fell under the control of the United Fruit Company. This US corporation drew on vast sources of finance to monopolise the production, transport and marketing of Latin American bananas. United Fruit's plantations have been described as 'factories in the fields'. Each employed a wage-labour force supplied by labour contractors. The contractors organised the workers into 'gangs', which carried out the hard and repetitive tasks of clearing ground for planting, weeding and harvesting. Substantial 'economies of scale' allowed the plantations to reduce labour costs and develop their own processing and storage centres. Within 35 years (1875–1910), the United Fruit Company produced 2 billion bunches of bananas from plantations throughout Colombia, Costa Rica, Panama, Honduras and Ecuador.

Mining in South Africa
The South African mining industry took off with the discovery of diamonds in 1867 and gold in 1886. Until this time, South Africa was divided between a Dutch (or *Boer*) colony, a British colony and large African settlements. The British fought the *Boers* for control of the mining territories (1899–1902) and then set about supplying vast mining corporations like DeBeers and Anglo-American with labour. Most Africans preferred to make a living through peasant farming and refused to work in the mines. This forced the colonial state to import indentured (contracted) workers from India, but it was only a temporary measure. As the demand for labour grew, so did the perception of an African labour shortage 'problem'. In 1894, laws were passed to tax every male African, unless he had been employed away from home during the year. Then, in 1913, the Land Act crowded Africans into 'Native Reserves', which guaranteed that there was not enough land to make a living from peasant farming alone. These measures forced African men to periodically migrate to the mines on short-term contracts. They then

returned to their rural homes, where the remnants of agriculture supported (or 'subsidised') their meagre wages. This system of 'labour migration' spread to neighbouring territories, through the action of other colonial states and labour recruiting companies like the Wiswatersrand Native Labour Association. Between 1904 and 1976, an estimated 90,000 men migrated from Mozambique to the South African mines alone.

Palm oil 'cash cropping' in West Africa

Palm oil was exported from West Africa to make soap and lubricate the machines of the industrialised nations. Instead of relying on plantations, giant commercial monopolies like the United Africa Company (now Unilever) bought palm oil directly from African peasant producers. These peasants had switched from subsistence agriculture to 'cash crop' production, with the growth of the market and money economy and through the action of colonial regimes. The effects of the commercialisation of small-scale agriculture were varied. Most peasant households were forced to produce palm oil, so that they could pay taxes imposed by the colonial authorities. Others took advantage of the palm oil market and grew rich through farming and trade. Between 1860 and 1900, West African farmers were supplying 50,000 tons of palm oil to the United Africa Company a year.

1.4

Gavin Capps

Superpower Competition and the Long Boom 1945–70

OVERVIEW

The Second World War provided sobering reflection on the relationship between industry, technology and war. For the first time in human history we saw the use of nuclear weapons and the application of the factory system to the killing of large numbers of people. The post-war global economy continued to show a sensitive link between military and industrial priorities. In part, it was military expenditure which drove the unprecedented rates of growth experienced in the post-war global economy. The USA and Russia emerged as the dominant superpowers from the chaos of war and effectively partitioned Europe between them, in spheres of political influence cemented by military alliances. The North Atlantic Treaty Organisation (NATO) established under US leadership was the most significant and durable of the alliances. The Bretton Woods institutions, most notably the International Monetary Fund (IMF) and the World Bank, were entrusted with the task of managing global development, trade and finance, and were similarly structured under US leadership. Both economic and military trends provided affirmation for the proposition that the twentieth century would indeed be the 'American Century'. One unresolved problem of the post-war bi-polarity appeared in the decolonisation of the European empires which gave rise to newly independent countries pursuing strategies of national development and self-reliance. The post-war period was characterised by 25 years of sustained growth in the world economy – the long boom – which created immense demand for raw materials and tropical products and provided opportunities for Third World industrialisation and development. At the same time, however, the specialisation of the colonies as primary producers during the previous international division of labour created barriers to the diversification of their economies. The Third World in the post-war period had to negotiate new difficulties. One was the extension of US and Russian superpower conflict into the newly independent countries which had the effect of undermining Third World solidarity. An additional problematic was the role of the Bretton Woods institutions: the World Bank, for example, had a specific development remit, yet it was characterised by little representation from other than the industrial countries. Relations with the Bretton Woods institutions and the rival powers shaped the concerns of the newly independent countries.

THE POST-WAR ECONOMY AND BRETTON WOODS

Europe and Asia saw the destruction of sectors of industry and infrastructure during the Second World War. Blockades and naval warfare disrupted world trade and caused primary commodity prices to fall as war-time rationing made the most ingenious use of product substitution. Yet, within this chaos, the foundations of a new global order were also being laid. In 1945 the US economy accounted for over half of the industrial output of the industrialised nations and its output was seven times that of the UK, its nearest competitor. It was under these circumstances that the USA eschewed its previous position of isolationism, departed from its historic commitment to protectionism and became the strongest advocate for 'free trade' (Jenkins, 1992). Communist Russia under Stalin had also grown in stature and influence and offered an alternative 'centrally planned economy' model to that of Western capitalism. This model became influential in a number of the emergent newly independent countries, most notably in China following the Communist victory in 1949 (see Section 3.5). These two military and industrial giants confronted one another in a bi-polarity which appeared in the form of the Cold War in Europe and actual military conflict by proxies in the Third World (see Example 4).

The two superpower blocs were highly uneven. The Western alliance brought the world's most advanced economies together, under US leadership. This created a vast international arena in which a new liberalised world economy could be constructed. This was illustrated in 1944 when the 44 nations met under US leadership to map out a future global agenda at Bretton Woods, an insignificant village in New Hampshire, USA. The driving force behind the Bretton Woods negotiations was a determination not to repeat the past cycle of slumps, protectionism and war which characterised the inter-war period. The outcome was a series of agreements which provided a framework for stimulating free trade and regulating international finance. However, there were other agendas at work at Bretton Woods. The conference was primarily a meeting of the rich, industrialised nations, and negotiations reflected a struggle between the USA and Britain for economic leadership of the capitalist world. The US aim was to open up the world market, such as the Sterling Trading Zone which still accounted for one-third of world trade in the post-war period, to US manufactures and to consolidate its domination of the Western bloc. The developing countries, meanwhile, were still colonies at this time and few were considered to have interests of their own.

In order to achieve this new economic system four main institutions emerged from Bretton Woods. The International Monetary Fund (IMF) was founded as a source of short-term finance for member states with balance of payments (trade) difficulties. It was hoped that this institution would promote international cooperation and national development. However, the USA stipulated that nations which borrowed from the IMF should meet strict loan conditionalities. These included the wholesale removal of barriers to trade and loan repayment at commercial rates of interest. The USA pushed and saw established the fixed exchange rate mechanism. This set the value of all other currencies against the US dollar which effectively superseded sterling as the international trade currency. The value of the dollar itself was fixed to the price of gold. The expectation was that this would significantly stabilise exchange rates, the volatility of which was widely seen a contributory factor to inter-war instability, the growth of protectionism and war. It also tightened America's grip on the world market, as the rest of the world was now forced to accumulate US dollars in order to pay for transactions in trade.

A second major Bretton Woods institution was the International Bank for Reconstruction and Development, or World Bank. Its charter was to provide long-term finance for productive investment. The World Bank has since assumed the major role in the channelling of Western aid to the developing countries (see Griesgraber and Gunter, 1996). Typically finance is lent on commercial rates of interest with attached conditions similar to those associated with IMF loans. The International Development Association (IDA) is the development arm of the World Bank and lends at concessionary rates of interest to the poorest countries. This accounts for less than 10 per cent of Bank lending. A third body, the General Agreement on Tariffs and Trade (GATT), subsequently the World Trade Organisation (WTO), was created with the primary objective of making substantial reductions of tariffs and other barriers to trade. This proved controversial and led to extensive discussion. In fact it was not until 1948 that GATT was finally established, as the US push for economic liberalisation met resistance from an independent India which demanded the right to protect its 'infant industries'. This and the failure to reach an agreement with the developing countries over the regulation of primary commodity prices, were some of the factors which led to the view that GATT acts to defend the trading interests of the industrialised nations (see Griesgraber and Gunter, 1997). Finally, areas of international conflict were to be resolved through the United Nations. The UN, however, was dominated by a permanent 'Security Council' of the world's five most powerful nations and drew the bulk of its funds from the USA.

Despite the problems generated by the Bretton Woods system, the system also coincided with a period of sustained growth in international trade and the world economy. Whether this can be attributed to the institutions themselves is debatable. What is clearer is that the four Bretton Woods institutions played a leading role in the restructuring of international relations in the post-war period and this had and continues to have important implications for the Third World.

POLITICAL INDEPENDENCE AND NATIONAL DEVELOPMENT

The 1950s and 1960s saw the rapid dismantling of the great European colonial empires. Within 25 years, the vast majority of colonies had achieved political independence and many introduced policies aimed at national economic development. In this, an important identification was made with industrialisation. There were a number of external and internal factors which led to decolonisation. The first factor was the rise of the USA as the leading capitalist power and architect of the Bretton Woods system. This greatly weakened the ability of the European industrial nations to hold on to their empires in the old ways, as markets reserved for their own national economies. The second factor was the decreasing importance of the colonies to the industrial countries. The drive to economic autarky, between 1914 and 1945, had involved a sustained effort by the advanced nations to reduce their dependence on imported raw materials. Technological advancements had allowed them to develop synthetic substitutes for tropical commodities, like rubber and cotton, and to use essential raw materials more efficiently. Agricultural output in the industrial countries had also increased. During the war, marginal land was turned over to farming and agricultural mechanisation proceeded apace. This further undermined the need to maintain costly occupation.

Finally, there were fundamental changes within the colonies themselves. Effective political movements for national liberation were forged out of the long conflict between the colonisers and the colonised. Despite the changes in the wider international climate, each colonial power was loathe to give up its territories without a fight, particularly where the white settlers constituted a significant force. This led to bloody and contracted struggles in settler colonies like Algeria, Rhodesia, Kenya and Mozambique. In the 'non-settler' colonies, the colonisers found it relatively easier to concede political independence once they came to accept as inevitable the proposition that the 'winds of change blowing across Africa' could not be resisted with conviction in the colonies generally. The 1960s saw a scramble to 'get out' of Africa. This was a particularly strong feature of British overseas policy following the débâcle of Suez in 1956 and the subsequent loss of confidence. On gaining political independence the new states set out policies to promote national development and self-reliance policies. This was, however, restrained by the terms of independence. Whilst the end of the British and other empires took a variety of forms, the realisation that decolonisation could not be resisted resulted in attempts by the colonisers to 'manage' the process of political independence. One common characteristic in the emergence of the post-colonial states was the imposition of conditions, most notably clauses in the 'Lancaster House' type of independence agreements, conceding the sanctity of British strategic and business interests. Another was an attempt to propel to prominence local elites, frequently educated in Britain or France, as the future leaders of the newly independent countries. These agreements often provoked tensions between the constituent parts of the nationalist anti-colonial movements. In many cases the development from liberation movement to authoritarian government was characterised by state repression of the very same forces which made liberation possible – such as the intelligentsia, independent trade unions, the peasantry and the ex-combatants – frequently in order to enforce the terms of the various 'agreements' (Shivji, 1976; Saul, 1983; Odinga, 1985).

Whilst there were diverse outcomes in the post-liberation environment one general conclusion drawn was that primary commodity specialisation was associated with colonialism and backwardness whilst industrialisation was associated with progress, increased productivity, better standards of living and economic independence. Despite tremendous cultural diversity it was this shared experience of colonialism as much as the experience of decolonisation which forged the new common identity between the newly independent countries of a 'Third World'. The identification of industrialisation as necessary for development was conventional wisdom in the post-independence period. US economist W.W. Rostow (1960) advocated a development model for the Third World derived essentially from the history of Europe, North America and Japan. In this schema 'modernity' would be achieved through a rapid and sustained phase of industrial economic growth requiring large-scale capital and technological aid from the West to the newly independent states. This strategy which drew from the experience of the Marshall Aid Plan for European post-war reconstruction, provided the rationale for the World Bank to provide aid for infrastructure and industrial projects in the Third World (Toye, 1989).

The Rostowian schema implied a continued reliance on the West and ignored the wider role played by the world market and the international division of labour. These were issues developed by Argentinean economist Raúl Prebisch who worked for the United Nations Economic Commission for Latin America (ECLA). Prebisch argued that the international division of labour worked against the interests of the developing countries in a system of 'unequal exchange'. This was defined as the tendency for the prices of developing country primary commodity exports to decline, relative to the price of manufactured imports from the developed countries. One consequence of this movement in prices was declining terms of trade, which meant that Third World countries had to export ever greater volumes of raw materials in order to import the same quantity of manufactured goods and machinery. ECLA began to campaign for trade reforms and a fairer deal for primary commodity producers. ECLA also began to promote a new and influential industrialisation strategy: Import Substituting Industrialisation (ISI). This drew on the experiences of countries like Brazil and Mexico during the 1930s (Sections 2 and 3 consider these ideas in more detail). Many newly independent countries adopted state-led industrialisation strategies throughout the 1950s and 1960s and made use of central planning. They were particularly attractive to nationalist leaders, such as Mao in China, Nasser in Egypt and Nehru in India, who were politically committed to either severing their ties with the Western dominated world market, or placing relations on a more equitable basis.

THE LONG BOOM AND THIRD WORLD INDUSTRIALISATION

The partition of the world between the superpowers introduced a perverse stability. The estimation made by senior policy makers was that the unprecedented nuclear arms race between the USA and Russia could guarantee mutual destruction. Therefore, rather than risk direct confrontation between themselves and with it the possibility of nuclear war, conflict was superseded by extensive 'wars by proxy' fought by competing states in the periphery of their empires. The arms race and the extension of international trade within which the conventional arms trade was of growing significance, were critical factors in laying the foundations for the longest boom in the history of the industrial economies (Kidron, 1968, 1974). The 'long boom' years of 1950 to 1970 witnessed the unprecedented growth of commerce and production on a global scale. Between 1948 and 1966 world trade grew annually by 6.6 per cent and industrial production by 9 per cent respectively. In the following seven years world trade grew by a further 9.2 per cent and industrial production by 6.7 per cent (Gordon, 1988). These rates of growth in the global economy far outstripped those of the nineteenth century, and it is little wonder that these were termed the 'golden years'.

Growth, low inflation and full employment became the norm in the West. The rapid expansion of manufacturing exhausted domestic supplies of labour. This stimulated a wave of immigration. Workers from Southern Europe and the old empires were encouraged to provide cheap labour for the industries and services of the centre. In Germany, Turkish 'guest workers' were only allowed to stay on a temporary basis. Despite racism and discrimination in employment and housing, many immigrants from the Commonwealth countries (i.e. British ex-colonies, like Jamaica and India) settled permanently in Britain. By 1973, some 6.4 million immigrants accounted for 7.5 per cent of the total labour force in Western Europe (Van der Wee, 1987).

Many developing countries benefited from the long boom, but there were also underlying problems. On the positive side, the rapid growth in Western manufacturing raised the demand for raw materials in absolute terms. This meant that the primary commodity exporters were able to increase their export earnings and make investments and governments were able to increase the taxable sector of the economy. One result was that public services such as education and health showed a tendency to improve in most Third World countries. Increased primary school enrolment and increased life expectancy were important dimensions of the post-war period of growth.

There was a significant shift from agricultural to industrial production in many developing countries, including India and China. Between 1965 and 1973, the average growth rates for sub-Saharan Africa, East Asia and Latin America were 3 per cent, 5.4 per cent and 4.1 per cent respectively. This compared to a figure of 3.5 per cent for the OECD member countries during the same period (World Bank, 1990).

Despite attempts at industrialisation most developing countries continued to rely on primary commodity exports as their main source of income and investment. The small domestic markets of many developing countries constrained the ability to industrialise through production for their own (limited) markets. Furthermore, whilst the volume of trade did increase, the actual prices for primary commodities were falling. Between 1951 and 1965, the terms of trade of the developing countries decreased by some 25 per cent. This, notes Jenkins (1992), was at a time when 70–90 per cent of exports from developing countries were primary commodities and 50–60 per cent of imports were manufactures. Crisis was only held off by the high levels of aggregate (total) demand during the long boom.

The pattern of Third World industrialisation was also problematic. Much of the industrial activity was centred around Trans National Corporations (TNCs) and their investments accounted for some 70 per cent of capital inflows into the developing countries during the 1960s. They were a key source of investment, expertise and technology. However, many TNCs located their operations in areas such as ports or mines, which were relatively isolated from the rest of the economy. Much was located in 'enclaves' which did little to stimulate industrialisation elsewhere.

The issues of 'balanced' growth and 'employment creation' were stated objectives in development and industrialisation strategies pursued by Third World countries. In practice, there was a tendency to move from relatively labour-intensive industries, such as textiles, to more strategic, capital and technology intensive heavy industries (such as steel production), which generated fewer jobs relative to capital invested. Heavy industry, however, depended on imported technology, know-how and energy which could only be bought as long as foreign exchange earnings stayed high; also, since industry had to be initiated from very low starting levels in most developing countries, costs were very high. This situation increased dependence on primary commodity exports in order to pay for imported technology. At the same time, however, heavy taxation of the agricultural sector to raise investment funds undermined rural life with prices paid to peasant farmers kept artificially low, partly in order to drive down urban wages. The 'scissors effect' of diminishing returns to agriculture (prompting mass rural–urban migration) and the failure of industrialisation to generate the expected levels of employment, overwhelmed industrial policy making in the Third World. Where new industries were established, they could only exist as state-run industries with few local competitors which meant that plant and machinery was frequently insufficiently and inefficiently used. One contributory factor was the low level of after-sales support provided by imported technology.

CONCLUSIONS

The post-war boom created a more liberal world economy characterised by high and sustained levels of growth. The USA emerged as the new 'centre' of the world economy and the Bretton Woods institutions provided the framework for resolving problems in international trade and finance which ensured the stability of the system as a whole. Superpower rivalry created a political space which was exploited by some of the largest Third World countries, such as India which became a favourite of both US and Russian development assistance. Whilst this period of growth also impacted favourably on the Third World, it did not resolve major development concerns. The 'employment question' became even more acute during this period. Industrialisation failed to generate the expected level of employment and accelerated urbanisation created novel development problems. Africa which in continental terms was characterised by the lowest levels of urbanisation, saw the population of its ten largest cities increase from 32 million in 1950 to over 80 million inhabitants by 1970 (World Bank, 1989, pp. 25–7). An important dimension of urbanisation in both Africa and other developing continents was the expansion of precarious urban 'informal sector' employment in which labour is unprotected and hence less costly than that covered by contractual arrangements (Portes et al., 1989). The urbanisation of poverty became an important dimension of global poverty and challenged, even during the period of the 'long boom' – the most sustained and generalised period of growth ever experienced by the world economy – assumptions by conventional development theories about 'modern' jobs and 'modern' cities. While there were diverse outcomes in the Third World which are considered in Sections 2 and 3, most Third World industrialisation was limited and characterised by highly uneven distribution, both in geographical spread and choice of sectors. Whilst a select number of NICs did take significant steps towards industrialisation in the 1960s and 1970s, most Third World countries were unable to break out from primary commodity dependence. As the world economy entered a new period of crises during the early 1970s these differences became amplified.

EXAMPLE 4

The Origins of the 'Third World'

The idea of the 'Third World' emerged during the 1950s. The term referred to the common experience of colonialism and articulated the mutual interests and objectives of the newly independent countries of Africa and Asia, and later broadened to include Latin America, in their relations with the industrial economies. From the onset, the idea of the 'Third World' encapsulated a political, an historical and an economic dimension.

The political meaning of 'Third World' developed in the context of the Cold War. The Third World countries were defined as those new states which were neither a part of the 'First World' capitalist bloc nor the 'Second World' communist bloc. Furthermore, many Third World countries did not wish to jeopardise their new-found independence by aligning themselves with either of the superpowers and becoming entangled in the East–West conflict. This generated the principle of 'non-alignment'. It was developed and expressed by the formation of the Non-Aligned Movement (NAM), following the Afro-Asia Solidarity Conference, at Bandung, Indonesia (1955). The NAM attempted to foster a collective identity between the newly independent states and encouraged solidarity against superpower domination and interference.

The new African and Asian countries were also acutely aware of their shared colonial past. This was the historical dimension of the Third World idea. The NAM adopted the principle of giving support to movements for national independence in the world's remaining colonies. In 1960, the UN General Assembly passed the 'Declaration on the Granting of Independence to Colonial Countries and Peoples', which legitimated the right to national self-rule for all colonial peoples.

The economic meaning of the 'Third World' flowed from the perception that all developing countries were enmeshed in an unequal world economy which worked against their developmental interests. For some African leaders, formal political independence was compromised by a new form of Western economic domination termed 'neo-colonialism', despite nominal political independence. This term referred to the continued economic dependence on the old colonial powers, the Western Trans National Corporations and progressively the World Bank and the IMF, as well as their influence in the shaping of policy through investments, loans and aid.

The Third World countries attempted to restructure the institutions, relationships and mechanisms which governed the world economy by forming the Group of 77 (G77). The G77 was a voting bloc of all the Third World countries (it now has 120 members) in the United Nations. In 1964, the G77 succeeded in establishing the United Nations Conference on Trade and Development (UNCTAD) to provide a forum for negotiating global economic reform with the Western powers. However, despite granting some concessions on tariff duties in 1970, the Western powers maintained the upper hand through controls of the Bretton Woods institutions. During the 1950s and 1960s radical Third World leaders such as Nkrumah in Ghana, Nasser in Egypt and Castro in Cuba, argued that the developing countries should break with the 'neo-colonial' world system and pursue strategies of national or regional development in conjunction with similar Third World states. This gave rise to ideologies and concepts such as Pan-Africanism, Pan-Arabism, South–South Trade, as points of solidarity for the post-colonial states.

Breaking out of the world economy and maintaining a genuine non-aligned stance was very difficult. This is illustrated in the experience of Egypt, which set out on a path of national development under the leadership of Gamal Abdel Nasser during the 1960s and 1970s. The ultimate aim by Nasser was to build a radical, united Arab nation with other Arab ex-colonies, such as Syria and Libya. The nationalisation of the Suez Canal by Egypt during 1956 was a potent symbol of Third World country intentions and earned Nasser the hatred of the Western powers, with the British press describing him as a 'New Hitler'. The British in a joint military action with France and Israel attempted to regain the Suez Canal. The USA refused to support the action which led to the humiliation of Britain and the resignation of British Prime Minister Antony Eden.

Initially, economic development by Egypt and attempts at industrialisation were financed through its foreign exchange reserves, built up from the export of cotton. However, when these savings ran out, Russia was able to gain influence by supplying Egypt with loans and new markets for cotton export. Also, it became the major supplier of arms and military spare parts for the Egyptian army. In this way the Egyptian economy and army became dependent on Russia whilst Israel developed a similar military dependency on the USA. In 1967, Nasser lost the 'Six Day War' against Israel which was backed by the USA. Weakened by its defeat, Egypt was forced to open its economy to the world market. The death of Nasser led to a change in direction and the acceptance of American finance and military equipment. Ultimately, the course of Egypt's development was strongly influenced by the wider context of superpower rivalry and its continued dependence on cotton exports to finance military expenditure.

1.5

Gavin Capps

Debt, Crisis and the Third World 1970–90s

OVERVIEW

The long post-war boom ended during the early 1970s. It was followed by the collapse of the Bretton Woods system and increased protectionism by the industrial countries. One important dimension consisted of significant oil price rises which fed inflation in the developed countries and worsened the terms of trade for the non-oil producing developing countries. The long-term collapse in primary commodity prices and more recent rise in interest rates on loans taken, laid the basis for an accelerated 'debt crisis' in Latin America and sub-Saharan Africa. At the same time, while these regions experienced recession and economic stagnation, a small group of East Asian countries continued to grow. An influential interpretation of their success by the IMF and World Bank was used as the basis for a new industrialisation strategy. The growing economic and political differentiation of the Third World, between the mass of primary commodity exporters and the fewer East Asian 'miracle' economies, accelerated during this period.

THE END OF THE LONG BOOM: OIL SHOCKS AND THE NEW PROTECTIONISM

The end of the long boom went hand in hand with the breakdown of the liberal post-war world economy. The USA was the cornerstone of both. It was American will which drove liberalisation forward and the strength of the US dollar which underwrote the Bretton Woods system. However, the post-war recovery of Western Europe and Japan challenged US dominance of the world market. In part this was the result of US superpower status which rested on high levels of arms spending. Whilst military expenditure was useful to defence industry contractors such as Boeing and Dow, this also redirected US investment away from other areas of manufacturing production which undermined America's international competitiveness. Another effect of the high US military expenditure was that government faced a rising budget deficit, to finance amongst others the Vietnam War. This further undermined projected expenditure on the regeneration of the US black ghettoes launched by President Lyndon Johnson in response to the mass uprisings which took place in the major cities of the USA during the 1960s. As the US economy faced decline, the dollar weakened and in 1971 US President Richard Nixon was forced to suspend the exchange rate mechanism and the Bretton Woods system effectively collapsed. The unilateral devaluation of the dollar (the basis for international transactions) had important implications for world trade and in particular the oil industry in which transactions are mainly carried out in dollars. Effectively, US devaluation meant a reduction in income for oil producers and exporters and this was the cause of the initial price hike by the Arab oil exporting countries.

The other industrial OECD countries were also experiencing economic problems. Unemployment and inflation were increasing and the rate of growth of the developed countries declined from an average of 5.2 per cent during 1967–74 to an average of 2.7 per cent for the rest of the 1970s decade. Overall, the world economy experienced an economic slow-down. World manufacturing output fell from an annual average growth rate of 6.1 per cent (1960–70) to 4.3 per cent (1970–80). The growth of world trade in manufactured exports also declined from 9.2 per cent to 7 per cent during the same period (Gordon, 1988).

The growing global economic crisis was intensified by a series of 'oil shocks' during the 1970s. The long boom was in part fuelled by cheap oil from the Middle East. Third World industrialisation also depended on this source of energy. Yet oil proved to be an exceptional primary commodity, with no clear substitute. Recognising this potential, the oil producing nations formed the Organisation of Petroleum Exporting Countries (OPEC), a cartel which forced up the price of oil, initially in response to US devaluation, between 1973–74 and again in 1978–79. The 'oil crises' radically changed the terms of trade for all oil importers and hastened the demise of the post-war liberal world economy.

The OECD countries attempted to stabilise their economies through the reintroduction of protectionist measures. A new protectionism developed in the form of emerging regional trade blocs, such as the European Common Market, with the aim of sheltering Western industry from competition with Japan and the East Asian Newly Industrialised Countries (NICs). A series of 'voluntary agreements' set limits on the amount of cars and electronic goods that they could export to the USA and Europe, while textile imports were subjected to strict quotas by the Multi-Fibre Arrangement (MFA). The MFA proved to be an important exception to the normally liberal GATT rules on trade, at a time when the developing countries were experiencing success in the international textile industry. The MFA's arbitrary nature heightened the perception that the GATT discriminated against producers in the Third World. This is considered in more depth in Section 4.3.

A good example of the new protectionism in agriculture was the European Community's Common Agricultural Policy (CAP). This subjects Third World agricultural imports to strict restrictions whilst maintaining relatively free trade between member states. The CAP provides European farmers with subsidies (in many cases to grow nothing) in order to maintain artificially high prices, thereby doubly injuring both consumers in Europe and producers in the Third World. Since subsidies are paid on the amount of land or livestock held this favours the large TNCs.

The developing countries responded to the collapse of primary commodity prices and the new protectionism during the early 1970s by proposing a New International Economic Order (NIEO). This advocated the reorganisation of international trade relations – particularly in the stabilisation of primary commodity prices – and greater access to the markets of the industrial economies. The calls for the NIEO also stressed the need for the expansion and diversification of Third World manufacturing export capacity. There were proposals at the UN for an increase in development assistance. Few of the recommendations were implemented in practice and the second oil shock of 1979 saw primary commodity prices deteriorate further, falling even far below the low point of the 1930s. This had a most damaging effect on the countries with the greatest primary commodity reliance, such as sub-Saharan Africa (see Section 2.4).

THE DEBT CRISIS

During the two decades between 1970 and 1989, the external debt of developing nations increased from $68.4bn to $1,283bn. This represented a phenomenal increase of 1,846 per cent. During this period, debt service payments increased by 1,400 per cent and were in excess of $160bn (Todaro, 1997, p. 413). The roots of the debt crisis can be found in the 1970s. During this period the Latin American and East Asian countries continued to industrialise, despite the contraction of world trade and the growth of protectionism. Much of Latin America's growth was based on heavy borrowing from international banks, at favourable terms of interest. As long as these sources of credit stayed cheap it was possible to service the loans. The expansion in credit was a direct result of the first oil price rises in 1973 during which the OPEC oil exporters amassed a considerable financial surplus, from $7bn in 1973 to $68bn by 1974. By 1980 this had reached $115bn (Todaro, 1997, p. 415). Most of these 'petrol-dollars' were deposited with Western banks. The slow-down in Western manufacturing, however, meant that traditional investment opportunities were restricted and as a result, American and European banks began to issue favourable loans to the developing countries. Between 1976 and 1982, over $350bn 'petrol-dollars' were recycled, typically in the form of short-term loans by financial markets which were themselves progressively liberalised and deregulated.

During 1979, the second oil shock and economic recession faced by the industrial economies radically reversed the conditions which had favoured international lending. The increase in oil prices while simultaneously primary commodity prices were falling and international interest rates rising, meant that debt service repayments tripled between 1976 and 1985. These problems were compounded by a tremendous increase in capital flight as Third World elites withdrew their deposits in favour of more profitable investments elsewhere. It is estimated that $200bn fled the heavily indebted countries between 1976 and 1985 – an equivalent of 50 per cent of their total borrowing. This problem was worst in Latin America. Sixty-two per cent of Argentina's and 71 per cent of Mexico's debt growth are believed to have resulted from capital flight alone (Todaro, 1997, p. 407).

Mexico nearly defaulted on its debt in 1982 amidst considerable panic by the US banks which were heavily exposed in Mexican lending. Most of the indebted developing countries became trapped in a vicious circle. Many tried to finance their widening deficits through increased external borrowing, which led them into deeper debt. By the mid-1980s, the debtor countries were paying back $11.3bn *more* to the commercial banks than they received in new loans. This accumulated debt meant that to service the loans (let alone pay the principal debt) many countries had to double and triple their export earnings, which proved impossible under the circumstances of global slump.

STABILISATION AND STRUCTURAL ADJUSTMENT

Growing instability in the world economy forced the OECD countries to consider ways to tackle the debt crisis. At the same time, the debtor nations began to approach the International Monetary Fund (IMF) for assistance. The IMF and the World Bank became involved in the process of debt renegotiation between the debtor countries and the commercial banks. The aim of these meetings was to agree a package which would refinance or defer existing loan repayment schedules. The IMF identified the 'problem' as a short-term balance of payments deficit. A not unfamiliar situation for many developing countries is that the value of imports is significantly higher than the value of commodity exports, resulting in the exhaustion of their foreign exchange reserves. This places strains on paying for imports and reservicing the debt, since these have to be paid for in foreign exchange.

The IMF intervention rested on the condition that the debtor countries adopted short-term 'stabilisation' programmes. These set out to reduce trade deficits and restore growth, by 'adjusting' the economy away from protectionism and state intervention such as in Import Substituting Industrialisation. The central role of governments was prescribed as no longer to regulate markets, but rather to create a market-friendly environment which facilitated self-regulation by removing barriers to trade and foreign investment. By adopting these policies, it was envisaged that the Latin American countries could follow the example of the East Asian NICs, which were more successful in servicing their foreign debt. Typically, an IMF stabilisation package consisted of the following measures:

Type of Conditions Attached to IMF Loans

- An export-led orientation and the removal of restrictions on trade such as undue tariffs protecting domestic industries.
- A reduction in state expenditure, such as the removal of subsidies on staples consumed by low income groups (maize, rice, sugar, cooking oil).
- Some mechanisms for reducing wages, particularly in the state sector.
- Possibly a devaluation of the local currency, as an aid to exporters.
- The dismantling of controls regulating the activities of private sector enterprises in order to facilitate inward investment (e.g. lowering or removal of corporation tax; waiving Health and Safety rules).
- The privatisation of state-owned enterprises and public sector utilities. The 'retrenchment' of public sector workers. The introduction of 'user-charges' and 'cost-recovery' in government-provided services such as health and education. An overall reduction in government expenditure as a percentage of GDP.
- Incentives to commercial farmers in the form of higher prices; support for small enterprises in the form of a soft credit regime.

The above policies flowed from the IMF estimation that the problem facing Third World countries was a temporary balance of payments disequilibrium. The effects of the above were intended to reduce consumption, including the consumption of imports. In addition, it was expected that the more favourable environment for private capital would lead to increased profits and investment steered towards private sector enterprises producing for export. As imports declined and exports increased, so an expected Balance in Payments would be achieved.

The IMF programmes were the antithesis of the state-led, 'inward-looking' strategies of the 1950s and 1960s. They reduced the state's control over national economic development and undermined the minimum social provision capacity of the public sector. Few of these stabilisation programmes actually met their original aims and often led to greater problems. Between 1982 and 1988 the IMF strategy was tested in 28 of the 32 nations of Latin America and the Caribbean. During that period Latin America financed $145bn in debt payments but at a cost of economic stagnation, rising unemployment and an annual decline in per capita income of 7 per cent. These countries 'stabilised' but did not grow. By 1988 only two were barely able to make their payments (Todaro, 1997, p. 421). Debt servicing carried high social as well as economic costs as wages fell dramatically and social provision deteriorated as bankrupt governments cut spending (ILO, 1993; Watkins, 1995, 1997).

The World Bank also began to make its aid and loans conditional on the adoption of Structural Adjustment Programmes (SAPs), which were not too dissimilar in design and intention to the measures applied by the IMF. One difference was the greater emphasis placed by the World Bank on longer term, structural changes to the economy. These policies had their greatest impact in sub-Saharan Africa (see World Bank, 1994). However, as with 'stabilisation' in Latin America, 'structural adjustment' also led to problems. By continuing to emphasise comparative advantage and the role of exports, the SAPs deepened primary commodity dependence and made many African countries even more vulnerable to fluctuations in the world market. By encouraging individual African country producers to increase the volume of exports, the accumulated effect was that key primary commodity markets were oversupplied which depressed prices even further (Chossudovsky, 1996). This was one reason for the 40 per cent decline in prices for sub-Saharan Africa's non-oil primary commodity exports during the 1980s. Africa's total external debt increased from $6bn in 1970 to $134bn in 1988, an amount equal to Africa's total annual economic output and 3.5 times its total export earnings (Hewitt, 1992). The interaction between debt, structural adjustment and declining terms of trade is illustrated by the example of peanut farming in Senegal (see Example 5).

THE NICs AND EXPORT ORIENTATED INDUSTRIALISATION

The onset of the debt crisis in Latin America indicated that inward looking, state-directed Import Substituting Industrialisation (ISI) had come up against definite limits. Countries which manufactured goods solely for the domestic market showed a continuing dependency for imported technology. In the case of Latin America, external borrowing financed the growing trade deficit and this contributed further to the debt crisis (Kiely, 1995). In contrast, a group of East Asian newly industrialised countries (NICs) continued to grow in the 1980s by aggressively targeting the production of manufacturing goods for the world market. This led World Bank economists to advocate for a new Export Orientated Industrialisation (EOI) model which aimed to replicate their formula for success. This influenced World Bank and IMF policy-based lending.

The first Third World countries to achieve significant export-led growth were the four East Asian 'Tigers' of Taiwan, South Korea, Singapore and Hong Kong. This began in the 1960s and paradoxically accelerated during the slump years of the 1970s. Most of the manufactures exported to the West were labour-intensive products. Initially, textiles and garments and subsequently electronics, dominated manufacturing industry. Some of the NICs went on to become internationally competitive in heavy industries such as steel and in more capital intensive areas of production such as cars and computers. The example of South Korea is considered in Section 3.3. The export success of the Asian NICs was emulated by other developing countries. In the 1970s, Brazil and Mexico also began to give incentives to export orientated manufacturers, alongside their traditional ISI strategy of protecting the domestic market.

CONCLUSIONS

The break-up of the post-war boom, the growth of the debt crisis and IMF and World Bank stabilisation and adjustment policies had a negative impact on the human condition in the Third World. The world from the 1970s onwards became, as during the inter-war period, a more unstable place. The crisis years heralded an epoch of wars and revolutions with the collapse of communism as the most graphic demonstration of this condition. The 'winds of change' in Eastern Europe that inspired the pro-democracy movements in the Third World and the collapse of the system of bi-polarity, had important and direct implications for Russian and US clients in the Third World: the Russian-backed Mengistu regime in Ethiopia (one of Africa's bloodiest) fell, as did the political will by the USA to continue its 34-year support for the Mobutu regime in Zaire. The world economy also became a more complex place. It was already evident by the mid-1970s that the original homogeneity of the Third World, typically associated with ex-colonial status and primary commodity dependence, had given way to a more complex economic differentiation. While the East Asian and oil exporting economies experienced positive economic growth, the impact of the debt crisis and the harsh terms of stabilisation led to falling industrial growth and rising unemployment in Latin America and Africa. The polarisation of the Third World between the NICs and the Least Less Developed Countries (LLDCs), i.e. developing countries characterised by extremely low levels of industrialisation, incomes, literacy and life expectancy rates, was an important social, economic and political phenomenon of this period. As Third World economies diverged, one important political implication was the further undermining of Third World solidarity based on a set of common experiences and common problems.

EXAMPLE 5

Peanuts, Structural Adjustment and Debt in Senegal

The West African country of Senegal provides a striking example of the vicious interplay between primary commodity reliance, structural adjustment and debt. The researcher, Robin Sharp, has written a powerful account of Senegal's economic predicament. What follows are selected extracts from his book, *Oxfam Country Profile – Senegal: A State of Change* (1994). Senegal is stuck with its peanut economy, which employs over one million people, occupies 40 per cent of all cultivated land, and provides nearly half the country's export income. While it brings in much needed foreign income, the modest peanut is now playing havoc with Senegalese financial and natural resources.

In common with all African countries, Senegal's terms of trade – the prices it can obtain for its exports, compared to what it has to pay for its imports –

have deteriorated seriously in the past decade, as world markets for primary commodities have slumped. Most of the country's peanut crop is sold for processing into oil; in one year (1985–86) the wholesale price of unrefined peanut oil crashed from over US$1,000 a ton to below US$550 – an extreme example of how unstable markets can affect primary producers.

In 1980, faced with the prospect of bankruptcy, the government of Senegal became the first sub-Saharan African country to call in the World Bank and the International Monetary Fund to devise a rescue package. The price of that rescue was a Structural Adjustment Programme, based on the principles of free market capitalism. Since 1984, the government has had to cut state services drastically, liquidating or selling off many government-run agencies, and making many public sector workers redundant.

Under the New Agricultural Policy (NAP) of 1984, farm subsidies were abolished and the government suddenly stopped providing the seeds, fertilisers and support services on which farmers had come to depend. The New Industrial Policy (NIP) has frozen the national minimum wage and liberalised the job market, giving employers more scope to hire and fire staff as they please. Under pressure from the World Bank, the NIP was also designed to reduce tariffs which protected Senegalese industry from foreign competition. Factories have closed, foreign investors are staying away and unemployment is running at 20 per cent or more. Many doubt whether the policy will fulfil its promise of economic growth.

Overhanging the economy, meanwhile, and severely constraining Senegal's room for movement, is a foreign debt which at the beginning of 1992 stood at US$3.5bn, according to the World Bank. By the time the government has met its debt-service obligations, which swallow 30 per cent of all tax revenues, and paid public sector salaries, which take another 58 per cent, there is precious little left to improve schools, health or other operational expenses.

Furthermore, the negative impact of the NAP is forcing farmers to switch back to traditional subsistence crops, simply for survival. As a consequence they have less and less to sell to feed the towns. This in turn means ever-increasing food imports, and therefore ever-increasing debt. For West African commodity dependent countries like Senegal, domestic and international trends seem to point to a deepening dependency on a global economy which is impervious to their needs.

Gavin Capps and Prodromos Panayiotopoulos

Globalisation in the Millennium

OVERVIEW

A new development orthodoxy has emerged during the 1990s. It argues that the world economy has undergone a rapid and recent process of globalisation driven by a near universal acceptance by policy makers of free market ideology. The growth of the East Asian NICs, technological innovations in communications and the opening up of cross-border trade in parts of the world hitherto closed such as Eastern Europe and China, are some of the factors driving this process. At the heart of the 'globalisation thesis' is the unprecedented expansion in world trade and Foreign Direct Investment (FDI) which is said to be breaking down national boundaries and reducing the role of states in development. One highly optimistic interpretation of this development argues that the separation between nation state and capital renders the world a more stable place and reduces the drive to war (Harris, 1990a). At the heart of this process are powerful Trans National Corporations (TNCs), which are investing across the world and organising production on a global scale. Third World economies are becoming favoured sites for this investment because of their comparative advantage in cheap labour. This is said to be integrating them into an increasingly interdependent world economy as specialised exporters of manufactured goods. While critics of this view agree that there are new tendencies in the world economy, they point out that not all are straightforward or positive as the globalisation model suggests, or indeed that the phenomenon is a contemporary experience, as much of the preceding material suggests.

THE GLOBALISATION MODEL

The neo-liberal globalisation model and its practical manifestation in World Bank and IMF policy-based lending, predicts high rates of export-led growth throughout the developing world. It points out that the East Asian NICs have been joined by countries like China and Indonesia as favoured sites for Foreign Direct Investment (FDI). This has the potential to unleash their vast reserves of cheap labour and natural resources, which had previously been locked away by inward looking national development strategies. As trade and FDI flow more freely, other developing countries will be embraced by this positive process of change. One estimation is that if present trends continue, China will be the largest economy in 2020, having already overtaken the United States, and that developing countries will represent over 60 per cent of world output and the rich industrial countries under 40 per cent (Hirst and Thompson, 1996). These changes or expected changes have important implications for labour conditions in both the Third World and the industrial economies (see Lee, 1996, 1997). Labour rights have been linked to current discussion on trade.

The conventional neo-liberal wisdom assumes that growth in one part of the world economy will lead to benefits elsewhere. Expanding international markets will reduce the need for protectionism in the West and provide new opportunities for productive investment abroad. By exploiting their comparative advantage in cheap labour, the developing economies will be able to attract this investment and industrialise by exporting manufactures to the West. However, if Third World governments continue to pursue state-led strategies of national development, they will miss out on these opportunities and become increasingly marginal to the world economy. Critics of the globalisation thesis, however, argue that many of these perceived changes and benefits have been over-emphasised or misunderstood (see Hoogvelt, 1997; Harman, 1996). It is useful, therefore, to look at the main points of the globalisation model and to assess the strategic implications of each, by asking four questions:

- Are the TNCs relocating to the Third World because of its comparative advantage in cheap labour?
- What is the relationship between TNCs and Third World states?
- Are patterns of direct foreign investment and trade integrating the whole world economy?
- What are the theoretical implications of globalisation for labour and livelihoods?

The Trans National Corporations and Cheap Labour

Until the 1970s, most TNCs were involved in the extraction of raw materials from the Third World for manufacture in the West. Others located inside developing countries in order to gain access to their domestic markets. The simultaneous impact of the recessions of the 1970s and 1980s in the industrial economies and industrialisation in East Asia, led many TNCs to restructure their activities in the face of increased competition. Significantly, this included the relocation of certain industrial processes and products to the NICs, with the output exported back to markets in the developed countries. It is this tendency which has led the globalisation thesis to claim that TNCs are now relocating to the Third World in search of cheap labour.

One of the key factors in TNC relocation was the separation of labour-intensive and capital-intensive operations within the production process. This was particularly true for products which were assembled from a range of components such as cars, garments and electrical equipment. In each case, it was possible to relocate the labour-intensive aspects of component production or assembly (which requires the maximum of labour) to the low-wage economies of the NICs. The capital-intensive operations, which require a higher level of investment in technology and a more highly educated workforce, were more likely to be retained in the developed countries. As a result, the export orientated production of the Third World has been concentrated in the textile and electronics industries, which make up most of their manufactured exports.

The fragmentation of production and relocation of labour-intensive manufacturing to the Third World has created the basis for claims over a 'global manufacturing system'. In this system, TNCs decentralise and coordinate production between factories around the world, with each providing a specialised aspect of design, component supply or assembly. Neo-liberals see this system as proof that developing countries can utilise their comparative advantage in cheap labour and integrate further into the global economy.

It is certainly true that one of the major factors behind TNC relocation to the Third World is because of cheap labour costs. Surveys of comparative wage levels between the industrialised countries and the NICs show that wages are consistently lower in the developing countries. The majority of the workers in the new factories were women in sectors such as electronic component and garment assembly. Since women are consistently lower paid than men, this reduced wages even further. However, Hirst and Thompson (1996) point out that labour costs typically represent no more than 20 per cent of the cost of the final product in manufacturing in the advanced countries, and the benefits of cheap labour are, therefore, unlikely to dominate the strategies of firms. This suggests a range of other factors which also influence investment decisions. Many developing countries, for example, have responded by providing subsidies and setting up Export Processing Zones (EPZs) which aim to attract foreign investment. These are examined in the example which follows (see Example 6). EPZs and other fiscal and physical incentives represent a hefty subsidy for TNCs – which may not be readily available in all countries of the Third World. Political stability, physical infrastructure and an educated labour force are also important factors.

Whilst global comparisons of average manufacturing labour costs are revealing, they ignore considerable sectoral variation. It is the case that the incidence of global production is higher in a narrow range of industries where the fragmentation of production is actually feasible. The relative contribution of labour and capital in different sectors may be a more significant factor in variation than the globalisation thesis acknowledges. For example, one study of the West Bengal textile industry drew the conclusion that the choice of technology (such as in the use of 'flexible specialisation') is influenced by the supply and demand for labour, and that as long as developing countries remain labour surplus economies there will be an incentive in 'sweating' existing labour and technology (Das and Panayiotopoulos, 1996). It is also the case that management techniques in European and the other industrial economies have shown an increasing preference for suppliers located close to hand. This is explicit in 'just-in-time' production, one purpose of which is the minimisation of capital tied up as stock. As such, much greater pressure is placed on the delivery system for precise amounts and styles. In the fashion industry (see Section 2.4) this is a critical issue.

For some of the reasons stated above, globalisation is limited. Indeed amongst US and Japanese TNCs the vast bulk of sales and assets are in their home country (see Table 1.7). Amongst European countries this is less clear as many invest in neighbouring European countries. In practice, this means that the trend is towards a regional rather than a truly global manufacturing system. Labour-intensive industries such as textile and electronics manufacture are an exception to this rule.

Trans National Corporations and Third World States

The second question raised in this section concerns the relationship between Third World states and TNCs. The globalisation orthodoxy suggests that TNCs have become so powerful and internationally mobile that they can invest where and how they choose. As a result, states are becoming increasingly marginal to the development process and no longer retain the ability to regulate and shape industrialisation, or other policy, within their own national borders. This is an important political conclusion which has both informed *Third Way* thinking in the UK and encouraged the view amongst trade union leaders in Europe and North America that the multinationals are too powerful to be hit by 'old fashioned' forms of workers' struggle. Harman (1996, p. 24) argues that this 'ideology of globalisation' has been a major factor in handing over victory to the multinationals.

Over the past 20 years or so, the combined effects of recession and competition have forced the TNCs to change, to expand and contract in size, as well as in their geographical distribution. There have been a spate of take-overs and mergers as rival TNCs attempt to concentrate greater productive assets under their control. As a result, the bulk of global economic activity is overseen by a smaller number of very large firms. The 100 largest TNCs control over one-third of all foreign investment and 40 per cent of world trade takes place within them. Furthermore, the revolution in electronic communications and the deregulation of financial markets means that money can move more freely across the globe. This leads to the impression that national boundaries and economic policies are becoming increasingly irrelevant to the TNCs (Simmons, 1995). Yet, when we examine the kinds of investments that the TNCs are making, it becomes clear that local conditions continue to play an important role in their operations and that governments continue to play an important role in development.

Despite the expansive global manufacturing system, most TNC investment in the Third World is aimed at production for sale internally rather than for re-export. This has led TNCs to establish locally based plants which are highly involved with the national economy and the state. They often form joint ventures with domestic industries and governments, borrow from local banks and sell shares to local shareholders and subcontract other firms to supply their local plants with components. All of these linkages with the local economy take time and careful planning, as well as adequate levels of infrastructure, a trained labour force, favourable taxation and so on, which involve complex negotiations with local governments. As a result, TNCs are reluctant to uproot their whole operation and write-off massive financial investments in plant, machinery and political patronage, even if cheaper labour or other conditions present themselves elsewhere. This interdependence is described by Stopford and Strange (1993) as one where only a few firms can operate in a 'borderless' world. Governments, both host and home, continue to play a crucial role and, perhaps paradoxically, an increasing role.

The relationship between states and TNCs can be very unequal. However, the dynamics and quality of that relationship are formed by a number of factors which may give local governments considerable room to manoeuvre. This is particularly true of the newly industrialised countries themselves. In countries like South Korea, all export orientated foreign investment was subject to careful state supervision. Foreign companies were discouraged from sectors where they might compete with local firms, while investment was encouraged in areas which the state wished to develop. One conclusion is that states continue to provide the framework within which TNCs operate and, as such, can influence the shape of industrial policy.

Patterns of Foreign Direct Investment (FDI) and World Trade

The third question posed in this section asks whether the volume of world trade and investment has grown in recent years and if it is evenly integrating new regions into the world economy.

In absolute terms, FDI has grown rapidly since the Second World War, particularly in recent years. It grew four times faster than world trade in the mid-1980s and has grown twice as fast ever since. By 1994, flows of FDI exceeded $220bn, four times the level for 1981–85. Most of this investment takes place between the developed economies and the rest is concentrated in the established Latin American and East Asian NICs and China. The greatest FDI flows are between the three main groupings of OECD countries – Japan, North America and the EEC, which accounted for 60 per cent of all FDI in the 1990s. The majority of TNCs prefer to do business in their home country or/and region in cross-border investment. In cases of extra-regional investment where TNCs physically transplant production in order to enter lucrative regional markets, such as Japanese companies investing in the UK, they do so in order to avoid physical import controls.

FDI to the Third World as a whole has increased in recent years but this has been extremely selective as Table 1.8 shows. The distribution of FDI during 1995 shows that developing countries received over three-quarters of all transfers, with China alone accounting for over one-third. Eight developing countries absorbed around two-thirds of total FDI flows. At the other extreme, the 48 Least Developed Countries received around $800m in 1993 – roughly the same size as flows to Brazil, and less than 1 per cent of total transfers to the developing countries. The concentration of FDI in a few favoured localities reflects the priorities of the TNCs. Unless a developing country can offer large domestic markets (like Brazil) or favourable conditions for production for re-export (like the NICs or China) it is likely to be written off the 'investment map'. Moreover, TNCs from each of the major states tend to invest in areas where that state retains influence, notably in ex-colonies. French firms, for example, are strongly represented in the old French empire of Western, Central and North Africa. This reinforces the selective and regional tendencies of FDI, which excludes most other developing countries. The uneven distribution of FDI away from the poorest countries is also reflected in the pattern of world trade. The 48 poorest countries in the world economy now account for less than 0.3 per cent of world trade – half the level of two decades ago (Watkins, 1997).

As can be deduced from the above, trade and investment, far from showing a benign and universal distribution, is highly selective and con-centrated in regional blocs. In 1990, 72.2 per cent of Western Europe's trade was conducted within the EEC. Similarly, the Asian Pacific Economic Forum (APEC) aims to liberalise trade between Pacific Rim countries like Japan, South Korea, Taiwan and the West Coast of the USA. In 1993, the North American Free Trade Agreement (NAFTA) formed a common market between the USA, Canada and Mexico. These regional blocs may provide new trading and investment opportunities for the developing countries which are integrated into them, yet they simultaneously exclude all other countries from the most dynamic areas of the global economy. One recent study of the cost of protectionism by the European Union (EU) indicates that it amounts to 6 per cent of EU Gross Domestic Product. It suggests that 'global protection', a measurement which takes into account all types of protec-tionism, including anti-dumping measures, non-tariff barriers and subsidies as well as tariffs, has amounted since 1990 to 14 per cent of EU output. This is two to three times higher than previously estimated (Messerlin, 2000).

Globalisation and Labour

The fourth question examines the theoretical assumptions of neo-liberal and comparative advantage thinking about globalisation, growth and poverty in the Third World. Substantially the assumption made is that industrialisation and globalisation will result in the equalisation of factor prices, or the cost of land, labour and capital. Nigel Harris concurs and writes (1995a, p. 113) that whilst global integration 'does not take place on terms of equality, nor are its effects on different countries the same [...] one of the few theoretical positions available deduces that "factor prices" will be equalised, an alarming proposition for many in the developed countries'.

Both the World Bank and the Stolper-Samuelson theorum propose that with increasing free trade there will be greater rewards to exporters (Samuelson, 1948). In terms of incomes this would see the equalisation of pay rates between unskilled workers in the developed countries and those of skilled workers, not only in the labour-intensive export industries, but also (and increasingly so) in the export service sectors of the developing countries. Current examples of this in the service sector include data-loading and processing, accountancy and software programming. Swiss Air, for example, has moved its accountancy offices to Bombay, India is emerging as a software programming centre for Silicon Valley, British police records are being loaded in the Philippines, Canadian medical records and US airline ticketing are being processed in the Caribbean, Japanese real estate transactions are being handled in China, and so on (UNCTAD, 1994, pp. 9–20).

It is expected that over time, converging wage rates would influence other factor prices towards equalisation. Affirmation of the Stolper-Samuelson theorum appears in the equalisation in income levels between the East Asian NICs of South Korea, Taiwan, Singapore and Hong Kong (the original 'Gang of Four') and the developed countries. Affirmation also appears in the declining and even negative rates of income growth amongst the least skilled and less educated workers of the developed countries. In the USA during the 1980s, for example, real wages for men with 12 or less years of schooling declined by 20 per cent (Harris, 1995a, p. 114). High rates of unemployment in the industrial economies during the 1980s and 1990s contributed to the decline of the human condition. It is reflective that during the early 1990s the Oxfam charity launched its first ever anti-poverty programme in a developed country (i.e. the UK).

It is not at all clear, however, that we are witnessing in global terms the equalisation of income levels between the developing and developed countries. The World Bank in its 1995 Annual Development Report entitled *Workers in an Integrating World* points towards the opposite, despite increasing levels of integration to the world economy. During 1990, 17 per cent of the labour force in the developing countries and the former Communist countries of Eastern Europe were employed in the export sectors. The Bank estimated that by the year 2000 more than 90 per cent of the world's workers will be working in countries strongly integrated with the global economy (World Bank, 1995a, p. 98). At the same time the Report points towards growing global income inequalities. In 1870 the average income per head in the richest countries was eleven times that of the poorest, with the ratio rising to 38 in 1960 and 52 in 1985 (World Bank, 1995a, p. 9). These trends are likely to continue as an increasing proportion of the world's workers will be living in the low-income economies (see Table 1.9). In occupational and gender terms the purchasing power of (primarily male) engineers in Frankfurt, Germany, was 56 times greater than the purchasing power of women textile workers in Nairobi (World Bank, 1995a, p. 11). Purchasing power is measured in what wages in dollars can buy taking into account inflation and this disguises higher levels of nominal income inequality.

There are diverse trends in the global economy and the relative equalisation of incomes between the East Asian NICs and the developed countries is such an important and optimistic example. The World Bank (and neo-liberal thinking) explain this success as due to market-friendly policies, effective engagement in international markets and a strong export orientation (see Sections 2.2 and 3.3).

A number of other explanations are offered to account for the phenomenon of income equalisation by the East Asian NICs when compared to most of the developing countries. The ILO (1993) points to labour scarcity in the East Asian NICs as critical in shaping the pattern of incomes. Most of the developing countries, however, are labour surplus economies characterised by limited productivity gains and powerful downward pressure on wages. Another explanation is that skilled workers in the NICs and the industrial economies get paid more because they add more value to production, substantially due to higher levels of investment in plant and equipment (Das and Panayiotopoulos, 1996).

Harris (1995b) points to the effects of immigration controls as an explanation for persistent global income inequalities. The neo-liberal model assumes free trade as a prerequisite to rising incomes. This has seen high levels of mobility by capital as exemplified by the activities of TNCs. At the same time, however, there are expansive immigration controls and restrictions on the movement of labour. Restrictions have paradoxically been given a major push by the growth of regional 'free trade' blocs such as the European Union (EU) which encourages the free movement of nationals of member states, but at the same time allows cruel restrictions on the movement of people and workers from outside the EU (such as the UK Immigration and Asylum Act). Import controls by the industrial countries extend from people to the movement of goods and services. Protectionism distorts real factor prices between developed and developing countries in a number of ways. The quota system applied in the Multi Fibre Arrangement (MFA) physically limits the amount of products which can be exported by the developing countries. Much development assistance is tied to buying goods and services from the developed donor countries. Protectionism was far removed from the free trade assumptions made either by the Stolper-Samuelson theorum or its application by the World Bank. The fear of the old protectionism of the MFA and the new protectionism (of the regional trade blocs) is one factor which has encouraged high levels of relocation by Japanese and to a lesser extent

East Asian NIC companies of physical production and jobs ('transplants') as a way of avoiding restrictions to free trade.

CONCLUSIONS

Overall, it can be seen that the effects of 'globalisation' are highly contradictory. Selected regions of the Third World and particular sectors of global manufacturing have become more integrated into the world economy through trade, FDI and an expansive global manufacturing system. However, as production and investment decisions become based on narrower criteria, the poorest countries are increasingly disadvantaged by their unfavourable location and internal conditions. As a result, not only has economic differentiation between and within Third World states accelerated during the 1990s, but for the least industrialised nations the future is highly problematic and uncertain. The 1997 Asian crisis has complicated predictions even further (see Section 2.2 and 3.3), as many of the optimistic assumptions about the 'Tiger economies' and associated rising living standards have been challenged by increasing unemployment and loss of confidence by foreign investment.

EXAMPLE 6

The Export Processing Zones

A major policy conclusion of the Export Orientated Industrialisation (EOI) strategy is that developing countries should use incentives to attract export orientated Trans National Corporations (TNCs). These are seen as a source of employment, foreign exchange earnings and new technology and skills. Since the late 1960s, developing countries have been trying to encourage this type of investment by establishing Export Processing Zones (EPZs). EPZs are designated areas from which unrestricted free trade is permitted with the rest of the world. They offer a range of incentives which are thought to be attractive to export orientated TNCs (see below).

Export Processing Zones: Incentives for Investors

- The provision of suitable industrial sites and buildings at low or subsidised rental.
- The provision of infrastructure such as telecommunications, docks, airports, roads of high standard and reliable power sources.
- The availability of financial incentives such as freedom from local taxation and export and import tariff duties for an agreed period, and possibly some element of direct subsidy; freedom from foreign exchange restrictions; assurances on freedom to repatriate profits to home country.

- A supply of low-cost labour, unhampered by union organisation or protective legislation relating to working conditions and health and safety; restrictions on trade union presence and sometimes physical repression.

The EPZs are usually segregated from the surrounding country and often enjoy special privileges. According to Takeo, the EPZ is

> like a country within a country. Cut off by barbed wire or concrete walls ... and guarded by 'zone police', the zone is an enclave in terms of customs-territorial control ... it has its own authority to which the central government functions are largely relegated ... Workers employed in the zone are often subject to special regulations (prohibition of labour disputes, for instance), have to show special passes to enter it and must often undergo body checks when they finish a day's toil. (In Wield and Rhodes, 1988, p. 291)

The success of the 'Asian Tigers' in attracting export orientated investment has led to a proliferation of EPZs throughout the Third World. The countries offering EPZs grew from nine in 1971 to 52 by 1985. By the mid-1980s, it was estimated that a total of 173 zones employed 1.8 million workers world-wide (Jenkins, 1992). There is now fierce competition between different countries and regions to attract firms to these zones, not least in the area of the 'labour incentive' industries. Singapore, for example, offers a guaranteed absence of labour disputes – or 'strike holidays' – to TNCs for a number of years. Similarly, Malaysia and Indonesia advertise their repressive labour legislation. There is also evidence of competition between developing countries to offer the lowest standards of health and safety and environmental pollution regulations. The effect has been for some of the dirtiest and most dangerous industries to relocate in the Third World.

Although the EPZs are a powerful symbol of globalisation, their actual significance is often over-estimated. In South Korea, EPZs accounted for only 5 per cent of exports in the 1980s and less than 5 per cent of employment. In fact, many firms inside EPZs are not foreign TNCs, but export orientated local companies, such as South Korean *Chaebol* (Kiely, 1995). The increasing number of EPZs suggests that desperate Third World countries are competing for a declining share of foreign investors. Unfortunately, the effect of this competition will be to drive the conditions of work and environment down further.

Section 2

Globalisation: Industrialisation and Trade

Introduction

Prodromos Panayiotopoulos

In this section we examine in more detail competing industrialisation and trade policies in both a practical and theoretical manner. In industrialisation policy previous mention was made of Import Substituting Industrialisation (ISI) and Export Orientated Industrialisation (EOI) (see Section 1.6). In Section 2 we compare and contrast these policies with reference to contemporary and historical regional experiences. The section points to elements of continuity as well as change between ISI and EOI and in their respective relationships to market and state. Whether an economy is directed towards production for the home market or the world market is a tension with important sectoral and political implications which are also revealed in country case studies (see Section 3). The polarity between EOI and ISI is commonly used in analysis of industrialisation. ISI is characterised by an incremental process of industrialisation, ultimately leading to the 'balanced' growth of a range of industries. EOI is characterised by specialised production for export which places the emphasis on 'leading sectors' of the economy. A representation of the key characteristics of the two approaches, and the assumptions made by respective advocates, are included in Figure 1. We draw from the experiences of the Latin American Newly Industrialising Countries, historically associated with ISI, in order to investigate this model, and the recent experiences of East Asian NICs to investigate the EOI model.

The example of Latin American industrialisation is particularly significant, given that it is the most industrialised and urbanised continent of the developing world and one which achieved political independence considerably earlier than the colonised peoples of Africa and Asia. As such, the experiences of Latin America may be pre-figurative of indicators and outcomes in other parts of the Third World. Specifically, Latin American material allows us to investigate the relationship between state, industrialisation and the 'populist', nationalist political mobilisations of the 1930s which propelled ISI to prominence. The example of East Asian industrialisation illustrates the more contemporary experience of industrialisation, globalisation and crisis. A review of the development of crisis in the 'miracle economies' during the late 1990s points to a dynamic and much more difficult to predict environment facing Third World industrialisation in the early part of the twenty-first century.

Import Substituting Industrialisation attaches a critical role to state intervention and direction. Policy was frequently framed with the political objectives of 'national economic development' and the social objectives of 'growth and equity': by this it was meant that growth had to be consistent with elements of redistribution in the benefits of development and industrial policy. Whilst the redistributory effects of ISI were variable, this approach was very much driven by a recognition of market failure – a failure graphically illustrated in Myrdal's early and influential *Asian Drama* (1968). In the case of Indian and Chinese variations of ISI, or 'self-reliance', the dispersion of industry and jobs to the poorer regions was a stated key aim of policy with the expectation that this would have a significant development impact. Export Orientated Industrialisation displaced ISI as the favoured industrial policy during the 1980s and 1990s, substantially as the result of the 'success' of the East Asian NICs. EOI represents the application of market theories of comparative advantage to industrialisation and trade policy in the developing economies. Primacy is attached to markets rather than state intervention in industrial policy with the expectation that market-based growth and redistribution would 'trickle down' to the poorest and have, similarly, a significant development impact. The World Bank during the 1970s referred to this strategy as 'redistribution with growth'.

The relationship between state, industrialisation and globalisation is a reoccurring theme in Third World development. The application by developing countries of state direction (and in some cases direct ownership) has been a characteristic feature of the Newly Industrialising Countries (NICs). Amsden (1989, p. 139) notes the high degree of intervention in South Korea as one where 'the government made most of the pivotal decisions', and suggests this was something of a general condition amongst 'late industrialisers' (also see Evans et al., 1985). Evans (1979) noted that a key component of the 'triple alliance' which characterised post-war Brazilian industrialisation was the state sector. Luedde-Neurath (1988) points to the high level of state intervention in the key role played by the Economic Planning Board (EPB) in directing South Korean industrialisation: this ranged from fixing producer prices (upon pain of fine) to directing industrial location and insisting on the use of local inputs in production.

One important dimension of both East Asian (EOI) and Latin American (ISI) industrialisation is the high levels of concentration which characterise both the private and public sectors. This is typified by giant Brazilian state-owned enterprises (such as *Petrobras*) and private sector South Korean *Chaebol*. An important relationship between market and state which derives from high levels of concentration is the frequent inter-exchangeability in personnel between the private and public sectors. This phenomenon renders too strict a separation between the two spheres of the economy as something of a sociological simplification. One study of South Korea's business elite, for example, points to a significant 36.5 per cent citing the public sector as their first 'job'. This included 12 per cent who cited the Armed Forces as their first 'job' (see Hatori, 1989, pp. 346–62).

That states intervene, and that this may even be of some positive contribution to economic development, is a proposition accepted by all except the most ideological of the free market fundamentalists. Even the World Bank nowadays accepts this proposition. *The East Asian Miracle. Economic Growth and Public Policy* is a World Bank Policy Research Report and the only publication by the Bank on the emergent NICs. It was paid for by the government of Japan. It was not only a long-delayed and unusual publication but also one which uncharacteristically for the Bank, saw Lewis Preston (President of the World Bank, at the time) drawing the conclusion that 'in Northeast Asia, some selective interventions contributed to growth' (World Bank, 1993, p. vi).

Industrialisation and trade policies are also sensitively linked to weakness in primary commodity trade. Frequently, Third World industrialisation was a response to depressed commodity prices and declining terms of trade. Protectionism by the developed countries has been a determining factor in shaping the pattern of contemporary trade. Whilst there are winners and losers in world trade this is an area characterised by deep inequalities within globalisation (see the example of the MFA, Section 4.3). Commodity weakness provides a powerful explanation for why developing countries try to industrialise. Competing perspectives on trade are investigated in this section with reference to the work of the International Monetary Fund (IMF) and 'free trade', the United Nations Conference on Trade and Development (UNCTAD) and 'South–South trade', and Non-Governmental Organisations (NGOs) and 'fair trade'. The growth of regional trade blocs, such as the European Community (EC) and the North American Free Trade Association (NAFTA) have shaped trade policy in the direction of a 'new protectionism', with restrictions on both the movement of goods and labour. Despite restrictions on the free movement of labour to the industrial economies, there are few urban centres in Europe and the USA where immigrant workers do not constitute an important section of the labour force. One significant change over time has been the growth of immigrant-owned enterprises.

2.1

Prodromos Panayiotopoulos

The Latin American NICs: Import Substituting Industrialisation (ISI)

OVERVIEW

Industrialisation in Latin America has accelerated economic differentiation between and within the Latin American economies. Central America, the Andean countries and the NICs of Brazil, Mexico, Argentina, Chile, face different problems and challenges under conditions of globalisation and it would be unwise to generalise in continental terms. This section investigates industrialisation in the Latin American NICs with special reference to Argentina and Brazil (also, see Section 3.4, Mexico). Economic development policies were strongly associated with Import Substituting Industrialisation (ISI) characterised by attempts at domestic production of previously imported industrial goods. A characteristic feature was a high level of state intervention and direction. The concept of 'people and nation' informed the nationalist and populist political mobilisations of the 1930s and these were influential factors both in the shaping of industrial policy from the 1930s to the early 1970s and in the contemporary discourse on Latin American development.

THE INTER-WAR DEPRESSION AND STATE INTERVENTION

A number of Latin American economies from the late nineteenth century onwards were used as textbook examples of the sensible application of comparative advantage. Argentina specialised in the production and export of beef and imported manufactured goods and machinery. The expansion of refrigeration made Frey Bentos 'bully beef' a household name in the UK and USA and earned Argentina large foreign exchange reserves. Brazil and the expansion of coffee production was cited as another common-sense example of the successful application of factor endowment. This perception changed radically during the inter-war depression when both Argentina and Brazil faced collapsing commodity prices on the international markets, rising stocks and over-production. Since beef and coffee regulated the national economies the implications were quite severe.

During 1929 Argentina was the first country in the world to abandon the Gold Standard (that is, the 'pegging' of national currencies to the price of gold) and faced immense debt repayment difficulties. It introduced exchange controls to stem the flight of capital and partly as a result of this, it was the only country in Latin America not to default on its international debt during the 1930s Depression. Falling export prices were reflected in declining terms of trade. An illustration of this was that in 1933 Argentina had to export 73 per cent more in volume terms than before 1929, in order to obtain the same quantity of manufactured imports. Latin America as a whole had to export 60 per cent more (Love, 1980, p. 50). These were the conditions which informed the thesis of 'unequal exchange' presented by Argentinian economist, Raul Prebisch (see Example 7).

In Brazil the expansion of coffee production in the high regions of the state of Rio de Janeiro from the mid-nineteenth century onwards, saw Brazil accounting for 80 per cent of world output by the beginning of the twentieth century. Defending the interests of King Coffee was the paramount principle of economic policy. Typically this meant that during situations of economic crisis the exchange rate was adjusted to suit coffee exporters. A frequent response consisted of devaluation which made coffee exports cheaper. This made it easier for Brazil to sell even more in volume terms, with the expectation, thereby, that this would compensate for falling prices and maintain coffee exports, jobs and incomes. This model worked reasonably well until the 1930s Depression, during which a crisis of unprecedented proportions was faced by Brazil. Between 1929 and 1933 Brazil saw a 60 per cent fall in the price of coffee and a 40 per cent devaluation. At one point during 1931 coffee traded at $0.08 cents, when compared to $2.25 in 1929 (Pereira, 1984, p. 18).

Celso Furtado, a Minister of Planning in Brazil under President Kubitschek during the early 1950s, suggests that whilst under the conditions of the inter-war Depression exchange rate adjustment was a limited tool, it did, however, have the effect of increasing volume output by about 25 per cent. Indeed Brazil continued to grow and harvest more coffee even though the cost of production was actually much greater than the selling price. Rising stocks fed further price decline and the government was finally forced to intervene by buying the coffee surplus and destroying it. Coffee beans were used at one stage as fuel to power steam trains. As Furtado writes,

At first glance it seems absurd to harvest the product in order to destroy it [...] to guarantee minimum sales prices [however] was in reality to maintain the employment level in the export economy and indirectly in the productive sectors linked to the domestic market [...] what is important to take into account, is that the value of the product destroyed was much less than the amount of income created. We were, in reality, building the famous pyramids Keynes would describe years later. (Furtado, cited in Pereira, 1984, pp. 17–18)

The reference by Furtado to Keynes is quite revealing. Keynes was also a major influence on other Latin American thinkers in the inter-war period and was an important influence on Raúl Prebisch's development of the theory of 'unequal exchange' as explanation for Latin America's weakness in the world system of trade. Keynes also legitimised arguments in favour of state intervention and this influenced the policy direction of Prebisch's thinking (see Example 7). Keynes argued that the developed economies could take demand-side counter-measures to recession and unemployment by pumping government money into public work schemes (which hypothetically could take the form of building pyramids). The expectation was that this would re-create lost incomes and initiate a wage multiplier effect (i.e. a spiral of demand). By maintaining the level of employment it was hoped this would maintain the level of aggregate demand in the economy, as the incomes of those now in work created a demand for a range of goods and services which would not otherwise be present. Keynes' thinking influenced governments world-wide.

POPULISM, NATIONALISM AND INDUSTRIALISATION

One critical and general assumption made by national policy making and planning for industrialisation is that a number of key economic variables (exports, imports, rates of savings, growth, etc.) can be regulated or at least influenced to the degree of producing a desired effect. Yet the early experience of ISI suggests that external shock, rather than domestic determinants, was the critical element in industrial change. Furtado (1976) refers to 'forced ISI' to describe the situation facing Brazil and Argentina in the inter-war Depression. It was the disruption of the world trading system which initially made it necessary to substitute for previous imports through local production. In Brazil this was a perverse effect of devaluation which had the objective of increasing volume output in coffee (in order to maintain employment) but meant that in reverse, imports mainly of manufactured goods became much more expensive and prohibitive to import. Luis Pereira (1984, p. 19) estimates that 'defending coffee' resulted in a 50 per cent increase in the prices of manufactured imports which gave a price opportunity for domestic industry to compete with imports.

Policy evolved over time from an ad hoc response to external shock to a more clearly defined industrial policy characterised by an extensive system of protectionist measures to favour domestic industry. Policy was influenced by an eclectic combination of ideas. Keynes was an influence on economic policy. Mussolini was an influence on government. More significant was the influence of nationalist and populist politics characterised by figures such as Juan Perón in Argentina and Getulio Vargas in Brazil. Wynia (1984, p. 145) points to the Vargas regime in inter-war Brazil, as substantially driven by 'strong nationalist rhetoric, promising to liberate the country from the tyranny of world markets and economic control by foreigners'. Nationalist and populist politics facilitated the emergence of a state planning apparatus during the 1930s.

The word 'populism' is a derogatory term used to describe diverse political mobilisations which appear to have very little in common. Kitching (1989) uses the term to describe the peasant parties which grew during the inter-war Depression in Eastern Europe and which made an appeal to nationalism (Pan-Slavism), the Orthodox Church and anti-Semitism. Hewitt (1992, p. 75) refers to the urban populism of Getulio Vargas as 'moralist, emotional and anti-intellectual'. For 20 years Vargas dominated Brazil and laid the basis for the 'economic miracle'. Vargas came to power in a coup during 1930 and held power until 1945. The *Estado Novo* established by Vargas was modelled on the Italian fascist state. In 1950 Vargas was elected President, but in 1954 pro-American army officers worried about Vargas' nationalist policies threatened a coup. Rather than agree with their demands, Vargas chose to commit suicide.

Getulio Vargas can be seen as part of a long tradition of *caudilismo* (rule by military strong men) which includes the parallel historical experience of Argentina under the leadership of Juan Perón, and in a more troubled application contemporary Cuba under Fidel Castro. Populist politics, however, represent more than simply another coup. Wynia (1984) describes the take-over by Vargas in 1930 as a 'revolution from above' which according to Pereira (1984, p. 15) 'drove from power the agrarian oligarchy that had dominated Brazil for four centuries'. In order to attack the landed oligarchy Vargas assembled an alliance between different and frequently opposing sections of society, such as politicians, young junior army officers, industrialists, middle-class professionals and organised labour. An appeal to 'youth', 'modernisation', 'people and nation', was used in varying measures at different periods to maintain the unity of the difficult alliance assembled by Vargas. In the balancing act between the various classes in society, to some Vargas appeared as the champion of social justice who (for the first time in Brazil) introduced social insurance and labour legislation favouring workers. To others he appeared (paradoxically) as 'the long awaited leader of the march towards constitutional order' (Wynia, 1984, p. 140). To industrialists, Vargas appeared as the champion of rapid national economic development. The construction of *Volta Redonda* in 1940, which still remains Latin America's largest steel complex, acted as a potent symbol of this intention.

Between 1929 and 1935, while Europe (with the exception of Russia) faced economic stagnation, industrial output in Brazil increased by nearly one-third (Pereira, 1984, p. 19). To middle-class professionals and the petty bourgeois intelligentsia, Vargas appeared as a youthful and dynamic figure affirming Brazil's determined drive towards 'modernisation'.

Populism: Key Characteristics

- Authoritarianism/military rule/personification of power.
- Nationalism/demands for equality of nations.
- Modernisation/industrialisation/development.
- Attack on forces of conservatism such as the landed oligarchy as a barrier to modernisation.
- A balancing act between opposing classes in society.

THE 'GOLDEN PERIOD' OF ISI IN BRAZIL: 1956–61

The post-war period was characterised by high rates of growth in the world economy. One dimension was the stabilisation and increase in commodity prices, relative to the 1930s. Under these conditions 'defending coffee' was no longer a priority. This signified the reversal of exchange rate policy. Whilst in the 1930s the currency was devalued in order to promote coffee exports, in the post-war period the currency was revalued in order to allow industrialists to import cheaper capital goods, i.e. machinery and technology.

The post-war period in Brazil also saw the expansion of a 'techno-bureaucracy' of technical experts (such as Prebisch and Furtado) which gained wide influence in policy making. This was a particularly strong feature of the Kubitschek administration (1955–60) which continued, albeit in a more subtle manner, with the corporatism of the Vargas regime. The period 1955–61 is seen by the advocates of ISI as something of a 'golden' period in which the Brazilian government began to act for the first time as a deliberate instrument of industrial policy and to make extensive use of both protectionism and planning (Pereira, 1984). During the Kubitschek administration a number of policy measures were introduced, which despite subsequent radical changes, continue to characterise Brazilian industrialisation.

It was during the Kubitschek period that the car industry took off which gave a boost to a components industry and machine tool sector. Indeed by 1958 something like 67 per cent (in values terms) of industrial equipment and machinery used in Brazil, were produced in Brazil (Pereira, 1984, p. 31). Whilst in 1949, 64.5 per cent of consumer (light industrial) goods were imported, by 1964 this was reduced to 1.6 per cent (Harris, 1990a, p. 75). Clearly, these sorts of indicators suggested that ISI was meeting important objectives in substituting for imports. By the early 1960s commentators pointed to the 'exhaustion' of the ISI model and confidently suggested that Brazil had reached 'independent' development (Pereira, 1984, p. 31). Conventional wisdom argued that the Brazilian 'economic miracle' was based on ISI. This saw industrial output grow by an average of 10 per cent per year during the ten-year period 1951–61 and laid the basis for an even bigger spurt of growth during the late 1960s. The Kubitschek administration articulated other important and more difficult to measure objectives. As Luis Pereira (who was a former Finance Minister of Brazil) writes,

[Kubitschek] perceived the opportune historical moment through which the country was passing and guided his government along two major lines: forced industrialisation at full speed and, more importantly, his confidence in the potential of Brazil and its people. His industrialism and the extraordinary support that he gave to Brazilian industrialisation, often proceeded despite the industrialists; his unlimited optimism was a direct negation of the colonial inferiority complex, particularly in relation to people of Anglo-Saxon origin, that was then widespread in Brazil. (Pereira, 1984, p. 27)

THE CRISIS OF ISI IN BRAZIL

The crisis of ISI in Brazil appeared in the 'exhaustion' of current ability to substitute. The crisis was manifested in declining rates of growth, the 'fiscal' crisis of state, hyper-inflation and 'law and order' politics culminating in a military coup during 1964. State intervention to promote and to protect industries such as *Petrobras* in petrochemicals and *Electrobras* in electricity generation, was very costly. Public Sector Expenditure accounted in 1960 for over a quarter (25.9 per cent) of total expenditure in Brazil and a massive 48.3 per cent of capital formation (i.e. acquisition of new assets). Taxation as a percentage of national income increased from 14.7 per cent in 1947 to 22.9 per cent in 1960 (in the UK it was 28.2 per cent in 1960). One necessary characteristic of ISI was that consumers were expected to pay more for manufactured goods produced locally as tariffs discouraged imports and competition, and this contributed to a scarcity of industrial goods and was a significant factor in rampant inflation. The annual rate of inflation during the 1950s was 20 per cent and in the 1960s 50 per cent. The compound rate of inflation from 1930 to 1960 was a staggering 3,195 per cent (Pereira, 1984, pp. 35–7).

Policy makers in Brazil – a poor and underdeveloped country at the time – saw industrialisation and development as closely interwoven and the choice as 'either development with inflation or price stability with stagnation' (Pereira, 1984, p. 37). The toleration of high levels of inflation, the deliberate distortion of prices through tariffs, and subsidies to state enterprises were policy measures which appeared as necessary features of ISI. As such they became characteristic features of ISI in crisis.

The military coup of 1964 which ousted President Joao Goulart of the leftist *Partido Social Democratico*, had the support of the landed oligarchy and sections of the private sector (such as the *Grupo Multibilionarios*) who formed a key part of the 'Triple Alliance' of state, local private and foreign capital (Evans, 1979). Most of these large Brazilian private sector firms were founded before the First World War (see Table 2.1) and were the major beneficiaries of ISI and state protection. A number of them saw the advantages of production for export, mainly for the Latin American market, and came to see ISI as a barrier to future development. The purpose of the coup was ostensibly to suppress inflationary tendencies in the economy, not a task usually associated with the Armed Forces. The military identified rising wages as the primary cause of inflation and most of the repression was directed against organised labour. Military rule lasted for 20 years (1964–84) (see Humphries, 1988).

The 1964 coup in Brazil signified a radical change in direction for the ISI model. Whilst the mechanisms of ISI remained relatively intact, the military removed restrictions on profit repatriation for multinationals and pushed for the 'opening-up' of the economy. This saw a growing presence by US TNC subsidiaries and a much increased emphasis on an export orientation for the Brazilian economy.

EXPLANATIONS FOR THE CRISIS OF ISI

Various explanations were offered for the crisis of the ISI model. Structural-ists such as Celso Furtado and Osvaldo Sunkel pointed to the gross disparities in income distribution as a major constraint to demand-side economic growth. Sunkel pointed to the tendency for continuing dependence (rather than independence) for Brazilian and Argentinian industrialisation, char-acterised by a growing external debt, and the necessity to import the latest technology, until such time as it was substituted – by which time another (and more costly) generation of new technology appears (see Panayiotopou-los, 1995, pp. 13–19).

Neo-liberal explanations for the crisis of the ISI model form part of a wider critique of state planning. Whilst planners in Brazil and Argentina may have been more astute than their contemporaries in China during the 'Great Leap Forward' (see Section 3.5, China), neo-liberals point to a general tendency for the techno-bureaucracy to use its privileged/monopoly position to extract profits from the state, in the manner that the slum landlord extracts rent from a tenant. Neo-liberals refer to 'rent-seeking' to describe this activity, and 'rent-seeking states' to describe the political structures of ISI (Jenkins, 1992, pp. 159–60). Lal (1983) and the World Bank (1996) point to privileged ISI industries as secure behind protective tariffs and shielded from competitive pressure, and therefore, inefficient and costly to operate. Heavy government subsidies to import capital goods and an overvalued currency to make imports cheaper (and exports in reverse more expensive) both overvalued the local currency and discriminated against exporters.

Todaro (1997, p. 468) suggests that Trans National Corporations (TNCs) have been major beneficiaries of ISI, provided they could relocate themselves behind the protected tariff walls. Frequently the costly import of capital goods consisted of subsidiaries purchasing from parent or sister plants. The growth of American subsidiaries was a particularly strong feature of the post-Second

World War period and 68 per cent of US industrial subsidiaries were in fact founded during this period (see Table 2.1).

CONCLUSIONS

Latin American industrialisation appeared initially as a response to global market failure typified by the collapse of commodity prices. The Latin American NICs have been characterised by a long transition from ISI to EOI and from dictatorship to democracy. It is reflective of the long transition, however, that Brazil and Argentina still export considerably less than Hong Kong or Singapore which are tiny in comparative population terms. During the 1990s Brazil still accounted for only 6.4 per cent of total manufacturing exports from the NICs, Argentina 1.0 per cent and Mexico 3.2 per cent. Hong Kong accounted for 16.7 per cent and Singapore 13.0 per cent (Todaro, 1997, p. 425). Despite industrialisation in Latin America, the continuing inability of large sections of manufacturing industry to compete in global markets has produced immense balance of payments problems. Much of the energy demanding heavy industrialisation was financed by external borrowing. Brazil and Mexico are the most heavily indebted developing countries in the world. One response by Brazil, Argentina and Chile has consisted of attempts to create a Latin American free-trade zone (Mercosur) in the expectation that this would result in greater continental gains in trade.

One paradox of the current situation is that in order to service its external debt, Brazil has relied more and more on the production of primary commodities. It is not only the world's largest exporter of coffee and tobacco, but also of iron ore. It is the second largest exporter of soya beans and third in the export of beef (Todaro, 1997, p. 426). The expansion of primary commodities as a source of foreign exchange earnings has created conditions for the geographical extension of production to previously marginal areas and this has placed the people and environment of areas such as Amazonia under intense pressure. One representative example in Brazil has been the *Grande Carajas Programme*. This linked the interior of Brazil to 'export corridors' in the largest development project seen in Latin America.[1] The industrialisation of the Latin American NICs shows that this is a condition which can coexist with a dependency on primary commodity exports and this suggests important elements of continuity in the relationship between Latin America and the global economy.

EXAMPLE 7

Argentina: Raúl Prebisch and 'Unequal Exchange'

Raul Prebisch was born in 1901 in Tucuman, Argentina and educated at the University of Buenos Aires. He acted as Under-Secretary of Finance for

Argentina during 1930–32 and was Executive Secretary to the UN Commission for Latin America, 1948–62. During 1962–64 he became Director-General of the Latin American Institute for Economic and Social Planning. Prebisch came to international prominence as Secretary-General to the UN Conference on Trade and Development, 1964–69 (see UNCTAD, Section 2.3). At the age of 81 he came out of retirement to act as adviser to the civilian government of President Alfonsin in Argentina. Prebisch died in 1986.

One key factor in the adoption of ISI was the emergence of the structuralist analysis of dependency influenced by the ideas of 'unequal exchange' presented by Raúl Prebisch. Initially structuralism appeared as an attempt to understand and explain the economic impact of the inter-war Depression on Latin America and in particular its impact on Argentina. Prebisch who faced the impact of the inter-war Depression and collapsing commodity prices as Under-Secretary of Finance for the Government of Argentina, wrote:

> In my younger years, I was a neo-classicist [neo-liberal]. I strongly believed in the Walras-Pareto theory of general equilibrium [An econometric similar to the Stolper-Samuelson theorum; see Section 1.6] and was fascinated by its mathematical elegance. Under the free play of economic forces, according to that theory, resources would be allocated in the best possible way [...] I recommended orthodox anti-inflationary measures to eliminate the fiscal deficit and suppress inflationary tendencies. [Prebisch also writes, however, that] the world depression had a tremendous intellectual impact on me. I had to abandon the belief in free trade [...] I departed from orthodoxy when I had to face a serious balance of payments deficit and advocated a resolute industrialisation policy. (Prebisch, 1984a, p. 175; 1984b, p. 1)

The economic problems of Argentina were analysed by Prebisch as sensitively linked to the changing trading relationships with its new major trading partner (the USA) when compared to its previous major trading partner (the UK). Prebisch argued that when in the nineteenth century the UK acted as the world's major growth centre, trade with Argentina developed quite rapidly. This was due to the high import coefficient of the UK economy, or the tendency by the UK to generate more demand for imports as its economy grew, when compared to the USA in the twentieth century. The US economy was far more self-sufficient and required less imports. It had an abundance of natural resources (e.g. beef, oil, cotton), a large domestic market and for these reasons was until the post-Second World War period strongly protectionist.

The trade deficit with the USA appeared, therefore, as a structural characteristic of Latin American trade, rather than a momentary disequilibrium. From this observation Prebisch (1959, pp. 251–74) went on to generalise about the nature of world trade and to challenge the assumptions by theorists of comparative advantage about mutual gains from trade as the engine of economic growth. Prebisch abandoned free-trade ideas and the belief, widely held at the time, that market mechanisms alone would provide optimum conditions for economic growth, and went on to argue in favour of state intervention. In 1944 Prebisch used for the first time the terms 'centre', 'periphery' and 'unequal exchange' to describe the relationship between the USA (as 'cyclical centre') and Latin America (as 'periphery') in inter-American trade.

A 'System' of Unequal Exchange

- 'Unequal exchange' is a trade relationship between the 'periphery' (primary exporters) and the 'centre' (industrial exporters).
- This relationship is characterised by inequality, one in which the centre uses its monopoly of technical progress to impose disadvantageous prices upon the periphery. Its expression (therefore) becomes declining terms of trade for developing countries.
- Technical progress in the centre results in higher wages. In the periphery, the opposite was true, as surplus labour (such as rural to urban migrants) act as a downward pressure on wages and trade union power.
- Protectionism by the periphery can be used in two ways to alter the above trading relationship: (i) through the imposition of import tariffs. This would have the effect of making imported industrial goods more expensive, and therefore give a boost to domestic industrial production in the periphery; (ii) through the subsidisation of industrial exports from the periphery. This would have the effect of lowering the price of industrial exports and dependency on primary exports.
- Prebisch's analysis influenced developing country policy makers in the adoption of Import Substitution Industrialisation (ISI) and advocacy for South–South trade.

2.2

Prodromos Panayiotopoulos

The East Asian NICs:
Export Orientated Industrialisation (EOI)

OVERVIEW

The Asian NICs of South Korea, Taiwan, Singapore and Hong Kong have all experienced phenomenal rates of growth. The rapid industrialisation of South Korea is perhaps the most dramatic (see Section 3.3). The 'Gang of Four' have all attained in terms of World Bank income ranking, 'development'. It is important in this sense, therefore, to make a distinction between the above and the 'second generation' NICs of Thailand, Malaysia, Indonesia and the Philippines where per capita incomes are lower and in the last two cases, significantly so. The primary purpose of this study is to consider what happens to economies which are the most globalised, or at least the most dependent on production for export. An illustration of this is offered by the 1997 global market crash which appeared as a 'domino effect' of collapsing Asian currencies and market prices, resulting in some of the largest 'rescue' packages announced in the history of the International Monetary Fund (IMF). The Asian financial crisis also impacted on Brazil, South Africa and Russia. None of this was predicted by the major institutions. The Western banks continued to lend. The IMF gave the 'miracle' economies sound ratings.[1] Major South Korean companies relocating to the UK were seen as critical 'partners' in regional employment policy. Tony Blair commented favourably on the high levels of social cohesion in the Asian countries. The view during the 1980s that the Asian emergent economies were driving global rates of growth in the face of European stagnation led to the publication of articles with titles such as 'Can the West Survive?'.[2] The Asian crisis severely dented such assumptions, at least those held about the role of the market and state in development. This was more acutely felt amongst the 'first generation' NICs in which prudential direction by the state was a frequently cited reason for 'success'.

THE 'DEVELOPMENTAL STATE' IN EAST ASIA

The concept of the 'developmental state' has been widely used to describe the functional relationship between the interventionist 'strong' state and the private sector in East Asia. It has been widely argued that it was the quality of this relationship which provided the necessary precondition for rapid industrialisation in South Korea and Taiwan (see White and Wade, 1988; Wade, 1990, 1996; Johnson, 1982; Leftwich, 1994). Robert Wade pointed to three levels of causation in growth which are critically influenced by state direction. First, very high levels of productive investment and even higher levels of investment in key (leading) industries with a high degree of exposure to international competition. This involved the selection of particular industries and companies for export promotion often through the medium of export subsidies: in the case of South Korea a graduation from labour to capital-intensive production has seen textiles, ship-building, car production and electronics actively encouraged by the state. This has brought South Korean companies in conflict with European trading partners, who point to examples of 'dumping' at prices below the cost of production as 'unfair trading' (Harris, 1990a). This sectoral intervention by the state is frequently ignored by neo-liberal analyses. As Wade (1990, p. 12) notes, the conventional neo-liberal position argues that market failure (if at all recognised) can rarely be improved by a sectoral industrial policy. Wade argues that this omission matters 'because it is in the histories of specific industries that one can most clearly see the government in action' (Wade, 1990, pp. 28–9) (also see Sections 3.1 and 4.3).

A second critical factor was the nature of specific government economic policies which underpinned investment policies. These included incentives, controls, mechanisms for spreading risk and the transfer of technology. Third, and perhaps more significantly, the developmental state thesis points to the specific institutional arrangements of support for industrialisation policies: in this, one representative proposition put forward is that the East Asian NICs represent a 'more effective way of putting the institutions of capitalism together' (Wade, 1990, pp. 4, 27). The conclusions which follow from this analysis are: that it is the corporatist and authoritarian arrangements in East Asia which have provided the basis for the market guidance which has enhanced capital accumulation. The argument that the 'strong' (but market-functional) state has durable capacities to assemble the specific institutions of support for industrialisation does not explain, however, the experience of South Korea, where bitter industrial disputes over the last three decades have punctuated industrialisation. Neither can compliance theories explain the acceleration of popular movements for democratisation, such as the student movement in Indonesia. One generalised impact of the financial crisis was that it also became a deepening social crisis, and this challenged the political legitimacy of the ruling classes throughout the region (Sparks, 1998, pp. 3–54; German, 1998). This led to the overthrow of the Suharto regime.

THE CRISIS AND THE RESCUE

The 1997 crisis appeared initially as a financial crisis typified by collapsing exchange rates and market prices. The worst affected was Indonesia where between 1 July 1997 and 18 February 1998 the value of shares declined by a massive 81.2 per cent and the exchange rate by 73.5 per cent against the US dollar. In South Korea the figures were 32.3 per cent and 48.1 per cent respectively.[3] The financial crisis began in July when (after futile attempts) Thailand allowed its currency (the *baht*) to free-fall, which sparked a burst of selling in the currency markets that spread quickly to Indonesia, the Philippines and Malaysia (see Example 8A, Chronology of Crisis).

The 'domino effect' caused immense concern in the financial markets and during August, Thailand with support from Japan and other Asian countries agreed to a $17bn rescue package with the International Monetary Fund. The role of powerful currency dealers such as George Soros in fuelling the crisis, led the Prime Minister of Malaysia (Mahathir Mohamad) to launch a fierce attack against Western 'speculators' and the IMF, which he accused of trying to 'subvert' the Asian economies. Rather than submit to the IMF, Malaysia was to impose its own IMF-style reforms including cuts in public expenditure with the aim of reducing its current account balance of payments deficit to 3 per cent of GDP by 1998. By October, Indonesia had to accept a $23bn IMF package (subsequently increased to $33bn) and agree to cut spending, reduce its current account deficit and to close several banks. During November, South Korea after struggling to meet repayments on short-term debt of around $110bn, was forced to turn to the IMF for help. One reflection of the breadth of the crisis was that during the same month the Japanese authorities closed down Yamaichi Securities – the country's fourth largest brokerage house.

During December, South Korea agreed terms on a $57bn IMF rescue package. This was the single largest intervention in the IMF's history. During a relatively compact period (of less than four months) rescue packages by the IMF and World Bank to the value of US$100bn were put in place. Concerns about the speed of intervention were raised by amongst others, Jeffrey Sachs, ex-consultant for the IMF in Bolivia and Russia, who noted that policies intended to dictate economic conditions to 350 million people in Indonesia, South Korea, the Philippines and Thailand, were undertaken 'without any public debate, comment, or scrutiny'.[4] The pattern of disbursement in packages was shaped by the realisation that the large foreign debt was becoming difficult to service. Much of this debt was of short duration and was owed to Western banks. Even more was owed to Japanese banks which during 1997 accounted for over half of foreign investment in Thailand, 40 per cent in Indonesia and a quarter in South Korea. Over 60 per cent of the total East Asian debt was set to mature (i.e. had to be repaid) within two years or less (see Table 2.2). Much of this was scheduled to mature during 1997. The rescue packages launched by the IMF were, above all, attempts to rescue banks with a large debt exposure to the crisis-hit economies. This was reflected in money allocated. A breakdown of the Indonesian rescue package shows that of the $19.8bn actually disbursed by the World Bank-led donors to Indonesia between July 1997 and April 1999, minimal sums went into social expenditure and most went into servicing loan repayments to the international donors. Social development projects amounted to something in the region of $780m, or 3.9 per cent of the total (see Example 8B, Indonesia: Anatomy of a 'Rescue' Package). Curiously, given the contribution by short-term capital lending to the crisis, the answer to the problem from the World Bank was for even shorter-term lending. It proposed the establishment of 'Emergency Structural Adjustment Loans' (ESALs), with shorter repayment periods and higher charges than the Bank's normal loans.[5]

IMPACT OF THE CRISIS

Commodities, companies and regions with high exposure to the Asian NICs were the most severely affected by the crisis. Copper and nickel prices fell as demand in the Asian NICs – which consume between 25 and 40 per cent of world production – declined. The crisis had specific implications for the economy of California, which is not only the world's ninth largest economy but also dependent on the East Asian NICs for over 50 per cent of its exports. Australia's wool and coal exports collapsed. Vietnam saw its exports to South Korea slump by 60 per cent during the first two months of 1998. As a result of contraction in South Korean and Japanese ship-building, China faced the possibility of further steel plant closures. The crisis forced the IMF in its 1998 World Economic Outlook to halve its forecasts of world growth from 4.5 per cent to 2.0 per cent (IMF, 1998).

One impact of the crisis was the contraction of expansion plans by large East Asian firms such as the South Korean *Chaebol*, which during the previous period responded to US and European protectionism by adopting 'transplant' strategies: that is, the physical relocation of production capacity inside the protected area. This was particularly felt in the semiconductor industry which accounted during the late 1990s for 13 per cent of South Korean total exports. This included a Hyundai investment of $1.3bn in Oregon, USA, which it claimed would be the world's largest semiconductor plant. Hyundai Semiconductors also announced its biggest ever investment programme in Europe (at Dunfermline, Scotland), at a cost of £3bn with the expectation that it would create 2,000 jobs to produce the next generation 64 megabyte D-ram memory chips. Samsung opened a large electronics complex in Cleveland, UK. Chung Hwa Picture Tube, a Taiwanese electronics company, announced plans to build a manufacturing capacity in Scotland, creating 3,300 jobs. South Korean multinational Lucky Gold Star (LGS) announced a major investment in Bridgend, South Wales and the creation of 3,000 jobs. The Welsh Development Agency (WDA) gave LGS a subsidy of £30,000 per job 'created' in this manner. One impact of the crisis was that these expansion plans failed to materialise. The proposed Samsung plant on Teeside and 1,600 jobs were shelved. The Hyundai Semiconductor plant in Dunfermline (Gordon Brown's constituency) was put on hold. LGS abandoned the recently completed Bridgend plant, built with funds from the WDA, and was itself threatened by liquidation. The Asian crisis also exposed the weakness of regional employment policy in the UK which saw 'high-tech' Japanese and more recently, South Korean inward investment and jobs, as the driving force of 'economic regeneration' in areas such as Teeside and South Wales.[6]

Whilst the crisis began as a financial crisis which impacted in various ways on the global economy, it also became a deep social crisis which challenged the political legitimacy of the ruling classes throughout the region. One immediate problem of devaluation was that the cost of imported raw materials and technology became very high. The same was true of imported foodstuff. Some of the first people to join the demonstrations by students in Jakarta against the Suharto regime, were women demonstrating against price rises. Unemployment reached record levels in the Asian economies, real wages declined drastically, prices for basic commodities increased and social services were cut back. People tried to cope by rationing food, pulling children out of school and by disposing of personal assets. The most severely affected by the crisis were workers, the urban poor, day labourers, or those most dependent on paid wage work. Factory closures and job losses increased. South Korea saw over half a million jobs lost between October 1997 and January 1998, most of them in ship-building and related industries. The increase in unemployment and weak social protection schemes in Asia prompted fears about 'social unrest'. Those in employment faced declining real wages. According to the International Labour Organisation (ILO), in Indonesia the rice equivalent of the daily minimum wage fell from 6.28kg to 4.76kg during 1997.[7]

The overall impact of the crisis revealed new tensions for development in the region. Whilst it is the case that poverty remains entrenched, particularly in the low-income economies of Indonesia and the Philippines, for many in East Asia the prospects were not that they would remain in poverty, but rather that millions of households would be pushed back into poverty. One result of two decades of rapid economic growth and rising per capita incomes was that the incidence of poverty in East Asia declined substantially, from about 60 per cent to 20 per cent of the population. The crisis threatened to undo this in a matter of years. According to estimations from the World Bank, if economic activity declines by 10 per cent in Indonesia, Thailand, Malaysia and the Philippines, then the number of people in poverty in these countries would double to 90 million. At this rate, most of the poverty reduction effects of economic development during the previous two decades would be lost.[8]

The most vulnerable in the crisis were the estimated 7 million immigrant workers sucked into the previous booming economies of Thailand, Malaysia, South Korea, from even poorer neighbouring countries such as Bangladesh, Burma, Philippines. Malaysia is a country in which immigrant workers have been an integral part of the economy from the mid-nineteenth century onwards. During the late 1990s 1 million workers (10 per cent of the labour force) came from neighbouring countries. In the construction industry an estimated 80 per cent of the workers were immigrants. It is not an exaggeration to say that Malaysia was built by immigrant labour. This was more or less acknowledged in immigration policies and public attitudes which were not unsympathetic to labour migration during the period of growth. During 1997, however, immigrant workers in Malaysia began to be scapegoated. The media, normally heavily influenced by government, began to carry news items blaming immigrants for spreading 'diseases' and 'viruses'. It was under such conditions of the build-up of prejudice that the Malaysian government carried out mass expulsions of immigrant workers. At least one documented mass killing of deportees took place in Malaysia which was carried out mainly against Indonesian and Bangladeshi detainees. By April 1998 one camp had processed 17,000 undocumented Indonesian immigrants. This is the description of the detention camp, following a macabre incident:

> The authorities took the extraordinary step of introducing poison, perhaps an overdose of a sedative, into water given to detainees. The goal was to subdue them before repatriation. At 9pm they were given a handful of rice, dried fish and a bowl of water. Shortly after this many detainees began to vomit blood. When the detainees realised that those who did not drink the water did not vomit, they knew something was wrong. The cry went up 'they are poisoning us'. This triggered riots which were brutally suppressed: 'ringleaders' were shot dead, and others tortured, beaten and robbed before being deported.[9]

The casualties of the crisis were not only found amongst the immigrant workers and the urban poor, but also from the ranks of Asia's billionaires. According to the list of richest people published by the Forbes magazine, during 1997 the number of billionaires (in US$) in the region declined to 44, down from 56 the previous year and 119 in 1996. The richest man remained the Sultan of Brunei, down $US2bn from the last year. The biggest losers were billionaires involved in property and financial services. The single biggest decline was registered by former Indonesian President Suharto (at $US4bn).[10]

EXPLANATION FOR THE CRISIS

In trying to offer an explanation for the crisis of the EOI model, one needs to be reminded of the standard neo-liberal explanations for its previous success. Commentators and policy makers (such as the World Bank) have argued that amongst the East Asian NICs, Export Orientated Industrialisation represented the wise application of conventional economic theories which see global trade as the 'engine' of growth and development. They suggest that the East Asian NICs succeeded because the market mechanism rather than state direction was at the heart of transformation. For the neo-liberals, South Korea (in particular) was nothing less than a 'free market miracle'. One crude but accurate description of IMF and World Bank conclusions is, that if other developing countries and the ex-communist countries opened-up *their* national economies to global markets, then they too would experience their own economic 'miracles' (see World Bank, 1993, 1995a, 1996).

The 1997 crisis, however, questioned neo-liberal assumptions in two novel ways. First, it was a crisis of some of the world's most open and globalised economies which until recently were held up as examples of sound macroeconomic management by the World Bank and IMF. Second, and unlike previous financial crises in the Third World, it was a crisis which had its origins in the private sector (see Hellenier, 1998; Jomo, 1998). The neo-liberals have responded (as the IMF now does) by pointing to the need for greater attention to the deficiencies of capital markets, or at least of short-term lending. The IMF now argues for greater controls on inward investment. One conclusion drawn from the East Asian crisis was that the opening of economies 'prematurely' to free capital flows, when they are char-acterised by a combination of weak banking systems and open capital accounts, 'was an accident waiting to happen'.[11]

An important contextual and complementary explanation for the crisis has focused on the role of 'deficient' political institutions. 'Crony capitalism' was a term first used in the Philippines to describe the government of Ferdinand and Ismelda Marcos in which a few select private sector companies closely linked to the regime were the main beneficiaries of government contracts, foreign exchange, credit and the distribution of overseas aid. The term is used to describe diverse networks of self-interest linking government and the private sector. The term has been applied in an ever-increasing propensity to states which include military dictatorships (as was Indonesia) and formal democracies (like Thailand). One significant network of self-interest existed around the person of President Suharto of Indonesia. A daily manifestation and irritating reminder of this to the citizens of Jakarta was the person of 'Tutu' Siti Hardiyianti Rukmana (wealthy busi-nesswoman and Suharto's eldest daughter). 'Tutu' had the contract to manage the capital city's toll gates, where the invariable grinding traffic jams accompanied by a cacophony of tooting horns earned 'Tutu' her popular nickname. Ten people around President Suharto controlled 975 companies with total assets of Rp62.5bn. Most of these were owned by sons, daughters and in one case a brother-in-law of the President's daughter. One stepbrother was also a key patron of the militia in East Timor which gained notoriety, as demands for independence grew. The most significant was Liem Liong a personal 'friend' (and golf partner) of the President who controlled large chunks of the export sector and single-handedly owned 600 companies with combined assets of Rp42.1bn. One key mechanism of 'cronyism' was the Bank of Bali into which contributions were paid by aspiring Suharto business partners to the many charitable foundations controlled by the President (see Example 8C, Indonesia: President Suharto Network).

The above network accounted for a significant proportion of GDP. President Suharto's personal wealth was estimated at £33bn, or the same amount as the rescue package launched by the IMF. The political power of those most closely embedded within the 'crony state' allowed the non-bank private sector to accumulate unhedged (uninsured) short-term foreign loans that far exceeded official foreign exchange reserves, by an estimated 70 per cent during mid-1997.[12] Further, the political power of the Suharto network allowed conditions in which the banking sector operated with a high level of non-performing loans. A more significant contribution to this may have been the willingness of foreign banks to lend to the private sector enterprises controlled by the Suharto network, in the full confidence of political support at the highest level. These issues raise profoundly political questions about the financial markets themselves.

Perhaps a more substantial explanation for the crisis has been the prolonged impact of recession on the Japanese economy. During the first quarter of 1997 Japan's GDP fell by a phenomenal and annualised rate of 11.2 per cent. By April 1998 the government of Japan announced its seventh fiscal package to revive the economy. The latest envisaged £70bn in temporary tax cuts, public work schemes and low cost loans.[13] These measures failed to bring the economy into growth. The over-exposure by Japanese banking institutions in the form of short-term loans to the East Asian economies made them even more vulnerable to default and at a time when many of them faced the pressure of liquidity. Japanese capital, and US markets, drove much of the extension of industrialisation in East Asia. One cumulatory effect of the expansion in the number of NICs is that the US market has a larger pool of suppliers and contractors and this made it more difficult for any NIC to enjoy the unique advantages of the 'first generation' NICs typified by South Korea (see Section 3.3). The scissors effect of Japanese capital and US markets moved against the Asian NICs. This suggests more complex processes than those described by Robert Wade and Frank Venereso, who come close to saying (on quite flimsy evidence) that the 1997 crisis was somehow engineered by the US Treasury to destroy a rival model of capitalist development (Wade and Venereso, 1998, p. 20).

CONCLUSIONS

The 1997 Asian financial crisis revealed a number of theoretical and practical tensions in 'globalisation'. The crisis challenged neo-liberal assumptions on the relationship between economic liberalisation, free markets and growth, given that it involved some of the world's most open, globalised and market-friendly economies, and that the crisis had its origins in the private finance sector. The crisis also challenged the ability of the 'developmental state' to guide economic development and placed even bigger question marks on its ability to reproduce conditions of compliance in development. The crisis which generalised from the finance sector to the economy of the region as a whole, became a social crisis which undermined the living conditions of millions of households in the South East Asian NICs and drove many of them back into poverty. The price paid by workers, and in particular immigrant workers, whose labour made possible the 'economic miracle' in the NICs, graphically reveals 'who gets hurt' in globalisation.

EXAMPLE 8A

Asia: Chronology of Crisis, 1997

2 July Thailand allows the *baht* to fall, sparking a burst of selling in the currency market that spreads rapidly to Indonesia, the Philippines and Malaysia.

11 August Thailand, with support from Japan and other Asian countries agrees on a $17bn rescue package with the International Monetary Fund.

31 August Malaysia's Prime Minister, Mahathir Mohamad, launches an attack against Western 'speculators' and the IMF, which he accuses of trying to 'subvert' Asia's economies.

31 October Indonesia accepts $23bn IMF package (subsequently increased to $33bn). It agrees to cut spending, reduce its current account deficit and close several banks.

21 November After struggling to meet repayments on short-term debt of around $110bn, South Korea turns to the IMF for help.

22 November Japan's authorities close Yamaichi Securities, the country's fourth largest brokerage house prompting renewed panic about the health of its financial system.

25 November Thailand and the IMF agree on new, lower growth projections for 1997 and 1998 of 0.6 per cent and 0.1 per cent respectively.

3 December South Korea agrees terms on $57bn IMF rescue package – the largest in the IMF's history.

5 December Malaysia imposes IMF-style reforms including cuts in public expenditure with the aim of reducing its current account balance of payments deficit to 3 per cent of Gross Domestic Product in 1998.

17 December Japan announces latest in a series of reflationary measures including unexpected income tax cuts. After an initial rally, the stock market again returns to pessimism.

18 December IMF releases a second tranche of Korean loan as voters elect opposition leader Kim Dae-jung as the country's new President.

21 December New IMF World Economic Outlook sharply cuts forecasts of world growth by half as a result of the Asian crisis.

EXAMPLE 8B

Indonesia: Anatomy of a 'Rescue' Package. World Bank Financial Support to Indonesia (July 1997–April 1999)

October 1997 $4.5bn over three years as part of the $33bn international rescue plan.

November 1997 $34.5m for Information Infrastructure Development Project (Information Technology development).

December 1997 $20m Banking Reform Assistance Project.

March 1998 $360.7m for rural development, education, environment and transport projects.

June 1998 $225m Kecamatan Development Project for rural development.

July 1998 $1bn Policy Reform (budgetary) Support Loan; $45m Fifth District (rural) health project; $21.5m Early Child Development project; $3.7bn (later reduced to $2.7bn) as part of IMF-led Consultative Group (donors) Meeting for Indonesian package.

March 1999 Interim Country Assistance Strategy; $31.5m Corporate Restructuring Technical Assistance Loan.

April 1999 $128.9m Sulawesi and Eastern Islands Basic Education Project.

Summary: Cumulative bank lending to Indonesia as of March 1999 approaching $25bn, of which $19.8bn disbursed, $8.2bn repaid; projects: 75 active, 207 closed.[14]

EXAMPLE 8C

Indonesia: President Suharto Network

Bambang Trihatmodjo (son) 50 companies/assets Rp4,041bn.

Siti Hardiyianti Rukmana (daughter) 55 companies/assets Rp4,666bn.

Hutomo Mandala Putra (son) 40 companies/assets Rp2,093bn.

Bob Hasan (friend and golf partner) 90 companies/assets Rp6,706bn.

Sigit Haryoyudanto (son) 39 companies/assets Rp650m.

Siti Prabowo (daughter) 23 companies/assets Rp378m.

Probosutejdo (stepbrother) 38 companies/assets Rp378bn.

Sudwikatmono (cousin) various partnerships.

Hashim Djodjohadikusumo (brother-in-law to President's daughter) 40 companies/assets Rp1,550bn.

Liem Sioe Liong (friend) 600 companies/assets Rp43,100bn.[15]

Prodromos Panayiotopoulos

Competing Perspectives on Trade Policy

OVERVIEW

Commodity trade and policy alternatives for the developing countries are presented by a variety of development agencies. This section offers illustrative material on the activities of governmental, non-governmental organisations (NGOs) such as Alternative Trade Organisations (ATOs), and the International Monetary Fund (IMF). The IMF's standard advocacy for global free trade is contrasted with the United Nations Conference on Trade and Development (UNCTAD), which actively works with developing country governments in the promotion of 'South–South' trade. Both are contrasted with the more localised work of NGOs. Policy is closely linked to external constraint and structures which influence the actions of the various agencies. Section 1 examined some of the historical factors (including the role of colonialism) in the development of commodity trade. Section 4 examines in greater detail particular commodities. The key issues raised in this section are how trade policy impacts upon different sections in society. A review of Commodity Trade and sub-Saharan Africa is used to illustrate the nature of the problem.

AFRICA'S COMMODITY DEPENDENCE

A major impact of colonial rule was the restructuring of the economies of colonies in ways which involved the expansion of cash crop and mining production for export. These were to become the major source of income for the newly independent countries. Cash crops, minerals, metals and fuel are referred to as primary commodities (or simply 'commodities'). To be a primary commodity exporter – by its very nature – implies considerable disadvantage in the world system of trade. In the case of primary products the 'income elasticity of demand' is relatively low: that is, any increase in national income leads to a smaller demand in the quantity of primary commodities, when compared to manufactured goods. Michael Todaro, an American development economist, points out that

it has been estimated that a 1 per cent increase in developed country incomes will normally raise their import of foodstuffs by 0.6 per cent, agricultural raw materials such as rubber and vegetable oils by 0.5 per cent and manufactures by about 1.9 per cent. Consequently, when incomes rise in rich countries their demand for food, food products, and raw materials from the Third World nations goes up relatively slowly whereas their demand for manufactures, the production of which is dominated by the developed countries, goes up very rapidly. (Todaro, 1997, p. 427)

The continuing dependence by most African countries on a small range of export commodities is the most pronounced of any region in the developing world. Copper accounts for 98 per cent of all export earnings by Zambia; petroleum for 95.8 per cent of Angola's earnings and coffee for 95 per cent of Uganda's. In Ghana cocoa made up 59 per cent of earnings and in the case of Mali, 58.6 per cent of earnings came from the export of live animals (see Table 2.3). Much of the development crisis during the 1980s and 1990s has been strongly associated with declining commodity export earnings and the deterioration of terms of trade. During the period 1973–90 commodity prices fell by almost 40 per cent and this accelerated during the 1980s. The sharpest decline was in tropical beverages: coffee, cocoa and tea.[1] As we noted in Section 1, during the 1980s declining commodity prices led to a growing inability to service the debt. As the most commodity dependent continent in the developing world, Africa was hit with particular ferocity (see South Commission, 1990).

Africa's share of world and developing country exports has shown a steady decline from the mid-1960s to the 1980s. Even in commodities in which Africa enjoyed some historical comparative advantage, there has been a decline: by the late 1980s Africa's world market shares for spices, palm oil, cocoa, coffee and copper had fallen between 20 and 40 per cent. One pessimistic projection (by UNCTAD) was that by the year 2000, Africa would contribute a mere 1 per cent to global Gross Domestic Product (GDP).[2] The above sorts of trends inform attempts to offer solutions for the commodity crisis facing Africa and other commodity dependent countries.

SOLUTION 1: THE IMF

One manifestation of Africa's commodity crisis is expressed in low foreign exchange earnings (required to pay for imports). This results in a balance of payments (trade) deficit and a resort to borrowing. Borrowing from agencies such as the International Monetary Fund and the World Bank become conditional on the implementation of a short and standard programme of 'market-friendly' policies to resolve the deficit (see Sections 1.5 and 3.3). The IMF sees free trade as an instrument for addressing the deficit both in trade and in government expenditure. It is envisaged that the 'problem' can be resolved during a short one- to three-year duration. Critical to understanding the impact of IMF policy has to be an appreciation of the diversities to be found in how people make or earn a living, and how IMF specific policies can affect different income groups in different ways.

One fairly representative policy measure consists of the reduction of public sector expenditure. The sacking ('retrenchment') of civil servants and public sector workers – including in areas such as health and education – has been a characteristic feature of countries under IMF conditionality and World Bank structural adjustment. According to the International Labour Office Report for 1993 (ILO, 1993), the number of teaching jobs in Gambia declined by 20 per cent; in Mali the teachers' union reported a fall in membership (to which cut-backs contributed) from 20,000 in 1980 to 8,000 in 1991. In Ghana, by the end of 1991, 50,000 public sector workers were retrenched, over one-third of them teachers. Frequently, women workers in the public sector fare worse: in Benin, for example, whilst women constituted a mere 6 per cent of all public sector workers, they made up 21 per cent of workers retrenched. The positive and negative multiplier effect of public sector employment and incomes is frequently ignored in the designing of structural adjustment trade-based policies, in Africa and elsewhere (see Raghavan, 1997, pp. 1–31).

The above policy environment, which originates from attempts to balance the deficit, has influenced the way the state operates in every aspect of life. Frequently, cut-backs take the form of increased 'user-charges' and this has been identified as one of the major reasons for low levels of participation by youth on training programmes. One evaluation of DANIDA's (Danish bilateral agency) support for Kenya's youth vocational training organisations, found very low enrolment and declining community support. This was attributed to factors such as uncertainty over employment opportunities and certification, poor facilities and training and the high fees charged. For example, whilst tuition fees at the Institutes of Technology (IT) and Technical Training Institutes (TTI) came to KSh3,200, by the time other costs to participants are included (such as boarding, caution fees paid as insurance for damages, tool kits, exam fees, etc.) the overall costs triple to three times the value of tuition fees at KSh9,600. The evaluation concluded that the 'main reason for the low enrolment at the ITs and the TTIs are the very high fees which are charged' (Panayiotopoulos and Gerry, 1997, p. 213).

Another representative policy is the liberalisation of external and internal prices and the removal of price restrictions and distortions. These include the removal of subsidies and price control on staples (maize, sugar, oil). This policy may have a differing impact on sellers and buyers of food. A poor rural household may, if it has the capacity to produce and transport goods to market, command a higher price for its products in this context. In reverse, wage and salaried workers, particularly in the city-based public sector facing cut or frozen salaries, find it more difficult to maintain their standard of living in a context of price rises. Amongst the urban unemployed, the casually employed, the retired, and the urban 'informal sector' dependent on local markets (and local incomes), the situation may reach critical proportions. It is emblematic of the consequences of IMF-type policies, that World Bank analysts (Moser et al., 1993) nowadays write of redundant urban civil servants as representing a strata of the 'new poor' (see Example 9, 'The Government Official').

The experience of the African countryside undergoing IMF conditionality or structural adjustment policies does not, however, mean that incentives to commercial farmers necessarily result in better prices for all farmers. Ghana, which has been applying these (ostensibly) short-term policies for 14 years, has seen cocoa prices paid to commercial farmers rise. At the same time, however, farmers have seen the prices for (often imported) industrial inputs such as pesticides, fertiliser, building material and so on, rise even more. This experience suggests that declining terms of trade, which are a structural feature of global trade between agriculture and industry, have not been addressed by short-term policies designed to be targeted at country level. The World Bank itself, in reviewing 14 years of structural adjustment policies in sub-Saharan Africa which originate from attempts to balance the deficit, concludes that under current projections, it will take another 40 years before the region returns to the per capita income levels of the mid-1970s. In the case of Ghana (seen as one of the most successful 'adjusted' countries in Africa) the Bank estimates that it will take 50 years for the average Ghanaian to cross the poverty line (see World Bank, 1994; also see Doogan et al., 1996; Watkins, 1995, pp. 71–108).

SOLUTION 2: THE UNCTAD APPROACH

The United Nations Conference on Trade and Development (UNCTAD) is an agency which came out of demands by developing countries for a fairer deal in the global economy: an end to protectionism, debt-forgiveness and a commitment by the developed countries to make available the equivalent of 0.7 per cent of their GNP for development assistance, were some of the demands raised. The first General Secretary of UNCTAD was Raúl Prebisch, who argued theoretically and empirically that the system of North–South trade was characterised by 'unequal exchange' (see Section 2.1).

UNCTAD advocates for a fairer trade regime for Africa and other developing countries. It argues for developed countries to open up their markets to trade from the South, and for developing countries to expand regional trade, or 'South-to-South' trade. UNCTAD in a report on African trade prospects has argued that industrialised countries should provide more open markets for African exports of primary and manufactured products. The report also recommended that at international level there is the need to step up efforts to re-establish International Commodity Agreements (ICMs). These are agreements between producers and consumers which have the ability to limit production, and thereby, by reducing available 'buffer stocks' push up commodity prices. Most ICMs collapsed in the 1980s (UNCTAD, 1990). It was in response to UNCTAD pressure, that GATT (the forerunner to the World Trade Organisation) and the European Community introduced the Generalised System of Preferences (GSP) which provides special tariff preferences for developing country manufactured exports (Coote and LeQuesne, 1996; Tussie, 1987).

The problem facing UNCTAD is that it is not a heavyweight organisation and has few funds at its disposal. Recently its body which monitored the activities of Trans National Corporations has been closed down by the United Nations – UNCTAD's funding body – after pressure from the USA and the UK. A key constraint to its policy recommendations for South–South trade becomes the nature of developing country exports. Whilst the Newly Industrialised Countries of Asia and their dependence on manufactured exports are examples of the growing differentiation amongst the economies of the South, sub-Saharan Africa remains heavily dependent on primary commodity exports. The experience of this growing global differentiation suggests that there is some basis for continental South–South trade. During the oil boom of the 1970s a number of African oil exporters did increase their trade with the Asian NICs. This was reduced as oil prices fell in the 1980s.

A major problem involving sub-Saharan African South–South trade is the tendency for economies to export generally similar primary commodities. This suggests severe limits to increasing trade between African countries. An additional constraint appears in the continuing need to import capital goods (machinery) from the North. The UNCTAD prospects for South–South trade have subjectively improved with the election of the African National Congress (ANC) government in South Africa. The industrial and mining capacity of South Africa (i.e. the most industrialised economy in Africa) and Nigerian oil producing capacity create the possibility of a more serious basis for South–South trade, and one which may be of benefit to the region as a whole. Given, however, that Trans National Corporations control most of Africa's trade in industry and mining, and that the ANC and other African governments have shown an unwillingness to challenge the power of the TNCs, they would more than likely be the major beneficiaries of an 'African Renaissance' based on regional cooperation and variations of South–South trade.

SOLUTION 3: FAIR TRADE AND NON-GOVERNMENTAL ORGANISATIONS

Interventions in trade policy by Northern NGOs have proliferated in recent years. Oxfam shops now compete (tax-free) on most High Streets, alongside commercial retailers. Fair Trade begins from considerations to do with livelihoods and is increasingly seen as an instrument for meeting medium-term development objectives in rural poverty alleviation and in the empowerment of communities, at the expense of intermediaries between production and consumption. Christian Aid, for example, estimates that a jar of coffee retailed by a major store to the British consumer for £1.50, earns a worker on a Costa Rican coffee plantation less than 10 pence.[3] There are also many examples of high price mark-up by commercial retailers of 'ethnic' goods, with relatively little return to the producer. NGOs hope to overcome the weak position of peasant handicraft producers and to increase value-adding activities.

Many NGOs from developed countries have collaborated to promote specialised Fair Trade organisations. These organisations see themselves as alternative trading organisations (ATOs). Forty of these organisations have come together to form the International Federation for Alternative Trade (IFAT). The products sold by ATOs range from crafts and foodstuffs to clothes and household textiles. According to Graham Young who works for Traidcraft, the second biggest ATO in the UK, the basic principles of IFAT Fair Trade are: to cooperate with the poor and oppressed of the Third World and to improve their position mainly by promoting products made by the poor in the Third World; to increase awareness of unfair international trade structures; to promote good working practices; and to campaign for fairer global trade policies (*New Internationalist*, February 1990, p. 21). Some of the ATOs are listed. The material is taken from various websites written by ATOs themselves (see Examples of Alternative Trade Organisations).

The potential for Fair Trade is best illustrated in the work of the *Caffedirect*. This ATO is a collaboration between Oxfam Trading, Equal Exchange, Traidcraft and Twin Trading, which buys high quality ground Arabica coffee directly from farmers in Tanzania, Mexico, Nicaragua and other Third World countries, and distributes it through its own *Caffedirect* brand. During 1992, *Caffedirect* was selling about 11,000 quarter pound packets per month. By April 1994, it had sold its one millionth pack and was working in partnership with the Co-op – an important UK retailer. A significant influence on *Caffedirect* was the work of the Max Havelaar Foundation in Holland. The Foundation, whilst not distributing its own brand, attaches a 'Fair Trade' mark on coffee imported on ethical Fair Trade terms. The Foundation has captured a significant 2 per cent of the national market. Fair Trade coffees are available in 90 per cent of the country's supermarkets.[4]

One severe limit to Fair Trade as an instrument of trade policy is found in the scale of operations: since they are small they cannot apply economies of scale in production, processing and transportation. This tends to push up the retail price. Max Havelaar coffee, for example, costs up to double the price of normal ground coffee. These sorts of limits are apparent to ATOs themselves, who see Fair Trade more in campaigning terms (i.e. in 'raising awareness') than as an attempt to overcome the weakness of small farmers in commodity trade. For *this* to happen NGOs/ATOs (such as Christian Aid) argue that there is the need to reform the world trading system, along the kind of agenda mapped by UNCTAD.

Examples of Alternative Trade Organisations

Twin Trading – UK: Twin Trading helps Third World organisations to engage successfully in international trade, often for the first time. It enables producers to improve the quality and standards of their products, to do more of the processing and refining, to be responsible for packaging, transportation and export, to do their own repairs, to develop their own technical infrastructure and manufacturing capacity. This kind of aid generates independence and encourages local initiative and control. It is much more than aid, a way forward to real development.

Oxfam Trading – UK: Oxfam Trading is the largest alternative trade organisation in the UK with sales of £11m per year, largely through Oxfam shops and mail order. Fifty-five per cent of their sales are of products from small enterprises throughout the Third World which are committed to economic and social justice. Oxfam Trading staff and consultants also provide design, marketing and other forms of practical assistance.

Trading Partners – Australia: Trading Partners has links with 26 Third World countries. It deals directly with local producer groups, paying the price they determine and *never* bartering. There are no middle managers. They offer Third World producers advice on export procedures, quality standards, design and selling, and ensure that all items are produced with integrity to local traditions. Australian sale prices are based on the original purchase price plus costs. All goods are sold through volunteer networks. Trading Partners always talks about craft in the broader context of culture, not just that of trade.

Friends of the Third World – USA: This group does wholesale distribution of crafts from the Third World and poor groups in the USA. It has 11 outlets and is eager to assist others in setting up stores. Friends has a bookstore and stresses education on Third World issues.

Pueblo to People – USA: This group sells crafts and food products from Latin American producers at fair prices mainly through a mail order catalogue. Pueblo also handles development education products and materials.

CONCLUSIONS

The prospects for UNCTAD-type structural solutions for the commodity crisis affecting Africa and other developing countries was dealt a blow by the most recently negotiated GATT trade agreement. The expectations of the agreement are that it will result in a 30 per cent cut in effective protection (approximately $200bn) and that the lower tariffs will result in savings to the consumer. The bulk of the gain comes from 'freeing' agriculture from protectionism. Since the most protected agriculture is to be found in the economies of the industrial economies (EC, North America and Japan), so the main gains will be made in those countries. A breakdown of 'winners and losers' shows that Africa lost up to $2.6bn in the removal of tariffs (see Table 2.4). Clearly there are no simple solutions to commodity weakness. This problem does provide an insight, however, into the policy conclusion drawn by many developing countries, that they need to industrialise and diversify their economies. This option is not available at will. As the experience of the Newly Industrialising Countries (NICs) suggests, neither does this make developing countries any less prone to the fluctuations of the world economy.

EXAMPLE 9

The Government Official

'I was born in N'Djamena, the capital of Chad. My father worked in the offices of the French colonial administration as a senior clerk. Compared to most people's circumstances today, I suppose my childhood was fairly stable, secure and comfortable. Even though my father and uncle were active in nationalist politics in the late 1950s, when I look back, I sometimes think that very little of the dream of independence has become a reality.

'I finished secondary school, as did all my brothers and even some of my sisters. By this time, France had given us our independence and there were good prospects for educated boys to enter the government service. Perhaps because our farmers, artisans and traders are all small-scale, I have always been fascinated by the workings of big organisations such as plantations, factories and the government, perhaps because I had read so much about them at school. So, I was delighted when I was offered an administrative post with the State Cotton Corporation (SCC).

'Before long, I married, we started a family and moved into subsidised accommodation provided by the SCC. Eventually, I was promoted to assistant head of the cotton-seed oil department; my success was mainly due to my clean record, and the short course on industrial processing that I took in France. Also, the fact that I am from the same minority tribe as the enterprise's new Director-General may have made a difference: we were excluded from any top posts until he was appointed. By this time I was full of confidence: through my own efforts, I had built on my father's hard work and shared in the benefits of independence; in the future my children would inherit even greater opportunities to prosper.

'However, from the late seventies onwards, so many calamities befell my country – drought, civil war, the Libyan invasion, the collapse of export-earnings and, most recently, the big changes in government policy that we call "structural adjustment". All my hopes for the future, and all the things I had thought were certain and secure began to crumble around me. At first, though, these problems seemed only to affect other people; but eventually, the government stopped paying our salaries on time, and sometimes we would go for six months without being paid. We would have to borrow, and run up bills wherever we could. Then the rent was increased, and the housing subsidy removed, and finally, the costs of petrol, basic foods, and even schooling began to soar. My wife began driving over the border to the Cameroons to buy cloth, which she'd then sell to her friends, some of whom had opened a boutique as a side-line. We even started farming at weekends to keep costs down.

'There was worse to come. The new policies adopted by the government required massive cuts in government spending. At the SCC, we were told that we no longer had a monopoly in cotton buying and processing, and that we would have to compete with other, new organisations in an open market. For us to become a more efficient organisation, many would have to lose their jobs. At first, I thought they would just reduce the number of cleaners, truck-loaders, nightwatchmen and so on. But I was one of the first to lose my job: they had decided to close down the whole cotton-seed oil operation, because it was cheaper to import oil than have us continue to produce it.

'They didn't call it redundancy, but "retrenchment", "downsizing", or something like that. I was in despair, and for several days I pretended to go to the office, because I was ashamed and afraid to tell my family what had happened, and that we would have to move to a smaller house, sell the car, and put the children in a different school. My mood lifted when I got the SCC's letter about my severance pay (which wasn't very much), and what they called my "re-insertion package". I had to attend a course, some counselling sessions and an interview to help me "re-insert" myself into employment. Then I would be told how big an interest-free loan I would receive to start a new career as a self-employed businessman. Some of my ex-colleagues had as much as US$2,000 from this scheme; I got much less, but US$1,250 was enough for me to open a small private commercial school where we teach typing, book-keeping and basic office practice. It's really hard to find enough students to make ends meet, because money is short, so many are out of work, and competition is intense. A former neighbour of mine lost his job, too; he bought two second-hand computers from his Ministry and has established what he calls a "business school". I couldn't spend all of my loan on the school because my brother also lost his job; he was only a driver with the Water Ministry, and had no contacts, so I helped him and his family, too. I'm scared to say anything in case I've broken the rules and have to pay it all back.

'I yearn for the days when there were clear rules, where the important decisions were taken by someone else, and I felt proud to be a public servant. It's only now that I'm starting to understand that for those I used to call "ordinary people", life on a tight-rope is normal, and hardship is more common than comfort. It seems to me that most youngsters have nothing to feel confident about; they're forced to hang around on street corners, maybe queue unsuccessfully for a day's poorly-paid work, get involved in crime, or slip over the border to find work in Nigeria or the Cameroons. But life's almost as difficult there as here. It amazes me how optimistic my young students are about their future; they have the highest ambitions; they see the market as a source of endless opportunity, while it scares me to death!' (Source: Chris Gerry, from Doogan et al., 1996, pp. 46–8).

Prodromos Panayiotopoulos

People Trade: Globalisation and Immigrant Enterprise

OVERVIEW

The growth of regional trade blocs such as the European Economic Community (EEC) and the North American Free Trade Association (NAFTA) has produced the paradoxical situation of free trade and increased protectionism. Restrictions by Europe on the movement of labour and of asylum seekers are frequently cited examples of 'Fortress Europe'. This points towards an emergent tension within globalisation over the extent to which the regions of the industrial economies are effectively assuming some of the political functions typically associated with the nation state, such as the waging of war and the imposition of immigration controls. The primary functions of immigration controls serve to underpin the exercise of selection and regimentation in the construct of nation state and national identity, and this has important implications for all people in Europe and the USA. Despite restrictions on the free movement of people, cities like London, Los Angeles, Amsterdam, New York and Paris have been fundamentally shaped and reshaped by immigration. This dimension of globalisation is examined in a comparative study of immigrant participation in the garment industries of diverse urban centres.

LONDON

London is the most cosmopolitan capital city in Europe and North America and as such is used as an extensive example which amplifies issues to do with immigration, ethnicity, minority status and employment. In part this is the legacy of an expansive British colonialism, reflected in New Commonwealth immigration. London is both a great centre of global wealth and an urban centre characterised by the persistence of poverty calculated in terms of material and social deprivation. In terms of material deprivation, using indicators such as the level of unemployment, number of lone parents, single pensioners, unemployed youth and those suffering from limiting illness, London is the most deprived city in England, with 13 Inner and two Outer

London boroughs being amongst the 20 most deprived areas in the country. Whilst the relationship between wealth and poverty and the causation of social and spatial polarisation within the capital city are debatable (see Sassen, 1991; Hamnett, 1996) indicators show that the rate of unemployment is eight times greater in poor wards when compared to richer wards in London. In the poorest wards of London 96 per cent of households do not own their own home and 74 per cent do not own a car when compared to only 3 per cent and 5 per cent in the least deprived wards (Goodwin, 1996, pp. 1396–7).

London's ethnic interspersion is reflected in the fact that it contains at least 50 different language groups with 10,000 or more speakers (Storkey, 1994). The 1991 UK Census shows that London contains 12.2 per cent of the total population but nearly half (44.6 per cent) of Great Britain's ethnic minority population on the basis of country of birth data (Storkey and Lewis, 1997, p. 201). The inclusion, for the first time, of the ethnic group question in the 1991 Census, allowed us to assess the relative size of the UK-born population of ethnic minority origin. This shows that 43 per cent of London's minority population were in fact born in the UK and in the case of Cypriots this rises to over half (Storkey, 1993, p. 205). Of those born outside the UK and living in London, the largest groups were from the New Commonwealth countries with India first, followed by Jamaica, Kenya, Bangladesh and Cyprus (Storkey and Lewis, 1997, p. 207). London became the major area for Cypriot settlement accounting for 80.5 per cent of all Cyprus-born persons in the UK in 1961 and 65 per cent in 1991. Over half live in four Boroughs (Haringey, Enfield, Barnet and Hackney) situated in a relatively compact north-east London area (UK Office of Population, 1961, 1991). It is estimated that by the year 2001 more than one in three of London's population will be from minority origins.

Whilst information on the position of immigrants and their children is of variable quality, self-employment and employment in small enterprises in the restaurant, retail and garment sectors, are important areas of representation by minorities, both as workers and as entrepreneurs. The average rate of participation in self-employment whilst (marginally) higher than amongst the white group, disguises sharp differences between members of minority groups enumerated as 'South Asian' and 'Black', with self-employment rates of 20.8 per cent and 6.7 per cent respectively (Owen, 1997, p. 53). Explanations for the widely observed disparity in UK enterprise formation extension between persons of Asian and African-Caribbean origin, point to that much harsher process of racial exclusion and the inability to access bank finance as critical factors in black under-representation (Ram and Jones, 1998). There are also important generational differences between first and second generation expectations and reluctance by second generation youth to enter the 'niche' retail, restaurant or garment sectors, in the face of other alternatives (Metcalf et al., 1996; Panayiotopoulos, 1990).

Data on income disparities and ethnic minorities in London are scarce, but unemployment is consistently higher amongst ethnic groups and this is also reflected in open registered unemployment. According to ILO estimates over one-fifth of black men and Pakistani/Bangladeshi women were registered as unemployed in June 1998, when compared to an average white unemployment rate of 6 per cent (UK National Statistics, 1998, Table 2). At the same time, however, there are considerable inter-ethnic variations with estimates that three in four of Bangladeshi households are in the lower income group and Indian households nearer the income distribution associated with white households (Anderson and Flatley, 1997). Whilst variation based on class, gender, occupation and locality are critical, the tendency for members of minority groups to be over-represented in the Inner London Boroughs and wards which suffer most from deprivation, means that they are more likely to live in places where the representation of households with lower incomes is greater, even by UK-wide standards. When coupled with the tendency to work in sectors which are most systematically associated with low pay, these combined factors offer substantial explanation for the position of ethnic minorities in London and elsewhere.

IMMIGRANTS AND THE GARMENT INDUSTRY

Immigrant workers in London and New York have a long historical association with the garment industry and this is graphically illustrated by accounts of Victorian London, which show that it was not unusual for Jewish immigrant and local workers in the industry, who constituted a significant proportion of London's working poor, to hawk their own clothes in summer – when work was 'slack', in order to buy them back in winter when work was more abundant (Steadman Jones, 1976, pp. 19, 152). The expansion of the piece-rate system and homeworking were new and growing features of the trade in the late nineteenth century. Much of the work was of a seasonal nature and casual employment characterised the industry. Many Jews fleeing pogroms in Eastern Europe during the 1880s and 1890s, found employment as pressers and machinists in the clothing workshops of the East-end of London and for many this was an important stepping stone to Ellis Island or in opening their own workshops. Concerns about the social conditions of the London poor as well as a moral panic directed against the even poorer Jewish immigrant, informed the 'anti-sweating' campaign by Liberal reformers which led to the introduction in 1905 of the Aliens Act, the first-ever anti-immigrant legislation in the UK.

The post-war boom and labour demand of the European economies and action by European governments to facilitate the migration of labour provided the conditions for the most significant expansion of immigration experienced by Western Europe. Whilst this was subject to considerable local variation, in the context of the post-war European experience the concept of a formalised 'European Labour Market' emerged as a description of system-atised labour transfer (Kindleberger, 1967; Bohning, 1972; Castles and Kosack, 1973; Penninx et al., 1993; Harris, 1995b). One consequence of this labour transfer was that African-Caribbean and Indian workers in the UK have higher rates of trade union membership than white workers (Jones, 1993, p. 76). The migration of workers to the United Kingdom and Western Europe accelerated during the 1950s and 1960s and by 1970 seven per cent of the UK labour force were immigrant workers with the single largest concentration in the textile and garment industry, where immigrants made up more than one in ten of all workers. In the London garment industry during 1971 nearly one-third of all registered workers were born outside the UK (UK Department of Employment, 1976, p. 141). During 1962 the introduction of the Commonwealth Immigration Act severely curtailed New Commonwealth immigration to the UK.

The garment industry in the USA and Europe is characterised by a high representation of minorities, women workers, small firms, low barriers to entry, hyper-competition, informality and seasonal troughs. The industry makes use of relatively simple technology and, importantly for immigrants, relies on demonstrable ways of learning skills. The organisation of production is structured in a series of subcontractual relationships. In a vertical direction these include the relations between the buyers (who place the orders), the manufacturers (who provide the cloth and design) and the contractors (who provide the labour) and are referred to in the trade as Cut, Make and Trim (CMT) units. Labour consists to a large extent of homeworkers and their family helpers. Those moving in a horizontal direction include relations between contractors who frequently subcontract part of their production to other factories or to drivers who work on their own account.

The women's wear 'fashion' sub-sector amplifies further the (above) structural characteristics. The tendency in women's wear for greater fashion change and even more frequent changes in style requiring even smaller 'dockets' (quantities of output) which are frequently delivered pre-cut, militates even more against large-scale assembly-line production and further reduces the cost of entry. This factor reinforces the role of small firms and hyper-competitive behaviour between ethnic contractors through the under-cutting of the making price.

Most immigrant workers work for ethnic contractors in cities such as Los Angeles, New York and London. Bonacich (1993, 1994) points to the most common configuration in the metropolitan Los Angeles garment industry as one of Asian contractors employing Latino workers. In London, whilst half of the workers in Cypriot-owned factories are Cypriots, workers also come from a variety of ethnic backgrounds (Panayiotopoulos, 1996a). One example is illustrated in the labour force composition of a Cypriot-owned garment factory in Tottenham, North London (see Table 2.5). Whilst there are diversities in terms of the nature and extent of ethnic interspersion, CMT production is fairly standard. The basic fragments of production in CMT work require different skills and trades which are paid in different ways (see Figure 2). Cutters, their assistants and sample machinists (who make first copies to show other machinists) are on pre-agreed wages. The making side which employs most of the labour, consists of sewing machinists who are paid through the piece-rate system. Trimming requires pressers and passers (cotton cleaners and workers who do the bagging, labelling, ticketing) who are also on pre-agreed set wages. Production also requires drivers who link homeworkers to the factory and who may be on a set wage or commission. Workplace relations are structured by the need to exercise control over women machinists who form the bulk of the labour force (see Example 10A). Typically this appears in the form of the piece-rate system which links pay to effort. The rate paid for each garment is subject to individual negotiation and bargaining which involves variables such as experience, the time of the year, past rates and the availability of homeworkers.

The incorporation of diverse immigrant groups into informal labour markets characterised by casual work and precarious forms of income generation is a strong characteristic of the garment industry. This echoes the work of Sassen (1988, 1991, 1996) who directs our attention to the spatial impact of globalisation and restructuring in the urban centres of the industrial economies (London, New York, Tokyo) and suggests that one mechanism of globalisation appears in the incorporation of diverse immigrant groups into informal labour markets. Sassen (1996) suggests that it is not immigration which is causing informalisation, but rather a more complex interaction between localities and the global economy. The institutions of informality routinely applied by many of the entrepreneurs are typified by 'voluntary liquidations' and the effects of this on the casualisation of employment (see Example 10B, 'Doing a liquidation').

Many studies of immigrant workers and entrepreneurs point in a pessimistic way to the re-emergence of 'sweatshops' and the discovery of the 'informal sector' in the recession-hit economies of Europe and urban America (see Fernandez-Kelly and Garcia, 1989; van Geuns, 1992; Pétras, 1992; Sassen 1989, 1995; Bonacich, 1993; IMES, 1998). Mitter (1986, p. 59) refers to the emergence of Bangladeshi enterprise in the London garment industry as representing little more than 'a sideways shift from lumpen-proletariat to lumpen-bourgeoisie'. In this approach, immigrant participation in the garment industry is presented as a precarious response to discrimination in the (segmented) labour market, and as a collective survival mechanism in the face of ethnic and racial disadvantage. Naila Kabeer (1994, p. 329), in a study of women homeworkers in the Bangladeshi-dominated East London garment industry, suggests that labour market preference for homeworking may owe more to 'defensive social relations' adopted in response to a more contemporary British racism, rather than being due to any cultural propensities of the Bangladeshi community. In this approach the 'split labour market' is a useful term in offering explanations for the positioning of immigrant workers on the lower rungs of labour markets (Bonacich, 1972, 1973).

In contradistinction, Waldinger (1996a, 1996b) has applied the concept of the ethnic 'labour queue' to explain how minorities face, negotiate and generally overcome the structural constraints they face in cities such as New York and Los Angeles. Waldinger provides a model of 'ethnic ordering' in New York which makes use of ecological succession and 'niche' theory to explain employment changes amongst minorities. One suggestion is that some groups may be 'predisposed towards certain types of work' (Waldinger, 1996a, p. 21). The concept of the 'queue' draws from a long tradition of succession theories applied in the USA to explain the relationship between immigration and enterprise, which share common assumptions in the familiar theme about the assimilationist prowess of American society. These purported to show a gradual progression by an immigrant group on to the lower rungs of the small enterprise spectrum from which they were displaced, typically in an upward direction, by the next immigrant group. Portes and Jensen (1989) and Portes and Zhou (1996) have drawn similar conclusions on Cubans in Miami and the Chinese community in New York City.

IMMIGRANT LABOUR AND REPRESSION: LONDON, AMSTERDAM, LOS ANGELES

The relationship of immigrant labour and entrepreneurs with the regulatory agencies is complex and can be influenced by factors such as the nature of the local economy and local politics. A common relation involves conflict between minority workers and entrepreneurs with various branches of central and local government over the avoidance of taxation, social insurance, health and safety at work, and homeworking legislation. Many workers are employed illegally and paid off-the-books. The scale of the conflict is illustrated in one raid by Customs and Excise officers on premises in the Dalston and Stoke Newington areas of east London, which resulted in 44 people being charged with Value Added Tax evasion offences in the region of £2–3m. All the people charged were Turkish Cypriot entrepreneurs in the garment industry. 'Operation Anchorage' involved the use of 300 officers who raided a total of 49 premises. Among those charged were a number of accountants. Charges related to the fraudulent preparation of VAT invoices. These invoices are used by enterprises to reclaim VAT on purchases, matching payments made on the basis of sales.[1] It is worthy of note that some private sector interests and even more public agencies have felt the need for specific regulation of the London garment industry. The London-based UK Fashion Design Protection Association (FDPA) was established by leading clothing companies, many of which are owned by minority entrepreneurs, and has campaigned successfully for the creation of special legislation to cover copyright infringement (i.e. 'design pinching'). There are now new statutory guidelines on company directors to bar 'repeat' liquidations which were informed by trends in the industry. The Customs and Excise Department has created special surveillance units targeting the north and east London garment industry, in addition to periodic joint raids by the Customs and Excise Department and the Home Office ('fishing' for aliens) (Panayiotopoulos, 1996b).

In diverse locations, conflict between minority workers, entrepreneurs and the regulatory framework provides insight on the institutional framework in which they operate and the labour conditions associated with economic activity. Foo (1994) and Bonacich (1993) point to the targeting of minority contractors in the Californian garment industry for labour code violations which revealed systematic under-payment and non-receipt of benefits by employees, non-payment of taxes, non-conformity with health and safety regulations and the employment of child labour. The term 'sweatshop labour' is used by Foo (1994, p. 2181) to describe 'multiple' or serial labour law violators. Van Geuns (1992) pointed to labour conditions in Turkish-owned enterprises in the Amsterdam garment industry which included the avoidance of legislation regarding taxation, national insurance, minimum wages, holiday entitlements, health and safety at work. In some cases, workers were housed beneath or above the workshops in which they worked. In many cases passports were held by the owner (Van Geuns, 1992, p. 133). Petras (1992) suggests that the 'proliferation' of garment sweatshops in the USA has seen a growth in workers employed illegally, paid off-the-books, receiving no minimum wages, unemployment insurance, or health benefits. There were situations in which employers pay passage abroad for co-ethnic young women and documented cases where the shop owner required women to take room and board on the shop premises. Petras (1992, p. 101) concludes that under such conditions young women are 'not likely to refuse to cooperate or make demands on their protectors'.

The 1990s saw the return of an aggressive American nativism demanding tough controls against 'waves' of immigrants and the 'proliferation' of sweatshops in the USA. The proposition has been advanced by, amongst others, Ong and Valenzuela (1997, p. 167) that immigrants from Mexico and Central America to Los Angeles 'are taking jobs away from African Americans' (also see Waldinger, 1997, p. 453). This provided support for anti-immigrant views and Proposition 187 in the State of California.[2] The purpose of Proposition 187 was to drive a wedge between legal and illegal immigrants and to exclude illegal immigrants, as well as their dependents from basic services such as health and education. It was envisaged, for example, that teachers would inform the immigration services about the children of illegal migrants, for eventual deportation. In a similar way the UK Asylum Act excluded for the first time people in need from the state benefit system. In what amounted to a one-sided pogrom directed mainly at the Chicano and Mexican communities, Proposition 187 was approved by 59 per cent of the registered voters in the State of California. Most of the leaders of the black community, including some who came out of the Civil Rights movement, campaigned in support of the Proposition. Despite this, a higher than average proportion of black Americans (50 per cent) voted against, as did 77 per cent of Latino voters (Ong and Valenzuela, 1997, p. 179). Mexican Americans 'rediscovered' their ethnicity during the referendum. In a massive demonstration of solidarity in Los Angeles, up to 100,000 people marched carrying Mexican flags. This infuriated White America. On the demonstration a small but vocal group of white and black Americans took part, shouting 'We are All Mexicans'. Proposition 187 has not yet been ratified.

Ivan Light et al. (1999, p. 9) challenge the idea that immigrants are 'taking over' American jobs and suggest that existing network theory 'exaggerates the extent to which hyper-efficient immigrant networks deprive native workers of jobs, thus exaggerating the conflict of economic interest between native and immigrant workers'. The observation made and confirmed in other research is that analysis of labour transfer cannot sufficiently take into account the labour demand created by the development of minority enterprises. In this respect immigrant entrepreneurs, far from 'taking jobs' away from native workers, create employment typically linked to the employment of other immigrants and which is a significant factor in the continuity of the garment sector in urban centres such as Los Angeles, New York, London and Amsterdam (Panayiotopoulos, 1996a).

Immigrants in the European Community have faced similar hostility and in this there are important continuities in issues of informality, and in cases of the criminalisation of minority workers and entrepreneurs. Amsterdam saw a dramatic growth in Turkish-owned garment enterprises between 1987 and 1992 (see Rath, 2000). The vast bulk were small contractors in the women's wear sub-sector. The number of registered contractors increased from 275 in 1987, to 1,000 by 1992. After 1993 the sector went into sharp decline and was reduced to an estimated 300 firms by 1995. An investigation of the premises revealed that most were vacated (IMES, 1998, pp. 21, 31–2). One factor in the crisis was that sourcing policy began to look to Eastern Europe as a low-cost production centre of cheap ready-to-wear women's garments. Another was the severity of repression shown by the Dutch state which launched a comprehensive offensive against the informal practices in the industry leading to numerous raids against workshops. As IMES (1998, p. 62) noted, 'When undocumented workers were found, or when the payment of taxes and social benefits were evaded, entrepreneurs were heavily fined, leading to bankruptcy of a lot of firms, and undocumented workers were expelled.'

Amsterdam is a concentrated example of a wider phenomenon in the European Community. The drive to reduce the public sector deficit requirement to 3 per cent of GDP as a precondition of reaching monetary and political union amongst member states, has led to tight fiscal policies, cuts in social expenditure and the need to expand the tax-base. Immigrant enterprises are part of more general concerns about unregistered and untaxed economic activity. Estimates from the European Commission on the 'black economy' range from a third to a quarter of GDP in Greece and Italy to less than 10 per cent in the Scandinavian countries. In a report adopted by the Commission it is assumed that undeclared work in the European Union (EU) amounts to between 7 per cent and 16 per cent of GDP and 7 per cent to 19 per cent of declared employment (or approximately 28 million jobs). Policy has been directed at the reduction of the informal economy through greater enforcement of existing rules on taxation. The German (and Dutch) slogan 'illegal is unsocial', when coupled with the view that the black economy goes hand in hand with illegal immigration, has specific implications for immigrants and sectors in which they are concentrated, such as garments, construction and seasonal agricultural employment.[3]

TRANS NATIONAL CORPORATION STRATEGY AND IMMIGRANT LABOUR

Whilst there are continuities in the European and US garment industries, typically in the form of concerns about unemployment in the face of global competition, there are also important structural differences in the activities of TNCs, which have created both opportunities and constraints for immigrant participation in the garment industry. In the 'German' model, production tended to move offshore to minimise labour costs while a highly capital-intensive domestic textile industry supplied them with high quality fabric. The model was substantially driven by the needs of German TNC textile producers to remain competitive with Far East mass producers (see Frobel et al., 1980). In the 'British' model relatively more of the production remained onshore and labour costs were minimised by equipping factories with the best available technology, by making use of local contractors (including ethnic contractors) and by purchasing fabrics from the lowest cost source. The 'British' model had the objectives of strengthening quality and minimising delivery times and was substantially driven by a highly concentrated UK clothing retail sector. Marks & Spencer (M&S) and its historic commitment to a 'made in the UK' policy was the most characteristic example of this model. M&S placed textile and garment orders to the value of £5.7 billion in 1997, of which about 70 per cent was produced in the UK. In the 1980s this was significantly higher at 90 per cent of sales (see Anson, 1997).

The ability of the retail sector to structure (and restructure) the UK garment industry is a reflection of its highly concentrated nature and considerable corporate power. In the women's wear sub-sector (which accounts for 40 per cent of the market) M&S was the market leader at 18 per cent, with Burtons its nearest rival at 8 per cent. Women's wear made up 60.5 per cent of M&S clothing sales. During the 1990s the power of M&S was challenged by the growth of specialised UK clothing retailers such as Arcadia (an offshoot of Burtons), Next and mail-order firms (such as GUS), which between them control over one-fifth of market share. Many of them source production overseas and this has put pressure on M&S to do the same (Barnes, 1994). During May 1998, M&S asked openly for the first time its suppliers to source more of their production abroad. This has put considerable pressure on M&S domestic suppliers such as SR Gent (its major ready-to-wear manufacturer), Courtalds Textiles and Coats Viyella (its major textile suppliers) and Dewhirst (major women's wear manufacturer). Suppliers have contracted capacity in their own larger factories in areas such as South Wales and Northern Ireland. Union sources estimate that up 20,000 jobs will be lost in the UK industry as the result of this one change in M&S sourcing policy.[4] Suppliers have put pressure on their manufacturers and they in turn on their contractors to remain price competitive in the face of global competition and this has impacted on immigrant entrepreneurs and workers.

An acute crisis faced many immigrant workers and entrepreneurs in the London garment industry during the late 1990s, which was substantially driven by reinvigorated outward processing and recent developments in the market for clothing. Whilst the long-term implication of changes to the market for clothing are not certain, what is clear is that many contractors in the London women's wear sector – who as contractors are the least capable of adapting to the changes in the market for clothing – have come under intense pressure. Many factories closed down and even more were working below capacity. All faced lower making prices from the manufacturers which in turn leads to lower piece-rate payments for machinists. Many of the contractors in the quantity market where price competition and labour costs are critical factors in production, pointed to a situation where with comparable technology a machinist in London is paid £800 per month when similar work in Bulgaria and Romania can be undertaken for only £150 per month.[5] Ethnic manufacturers have responded to changes in the market for clothing in quite different ways: many are pursuing an even more active policy of outward processing. Amongst Cypriots this was typically associated with subcontracting to Cyprus for most of the 1980s. Labour costs, however, have progressively risen in Cyprus and entrepreneurs began to look for alternative locations, such as North Africa and Eastern Europe (see Section 3.1). Other manufacturers who have progressively added greater design and fashion input to production and established 'own' brand labels, responded to uncertainties in the mass market in clothes by pursuing with increased vigour a policy of moving away from quantity and towards quality production. For the contractors, these sorts of options are not readily available.

SOCIAL DIFFERENTIATION AND IMMIGRANTS

Much of the material reviewed provides insights into our understanding of how immigrant workers and entrepreneurs are incorporated in the labour markets of the industrial economies. At the same time, however, these approaches have a more limited use in revealing tensions inside ethnic communities about the distribution of the benefits of immigrant enterprise.

Both optimistic and pessimistic analyses, in drawing from the sociology of immigration and ethnic relations, necessarily apply a methodology which consists of the counter-positioning of immigrants to the host society, or of one ethnic or immigrant group to another. This methodology, whilst useful in allowing us to analyse the economic and political position of a particular immigrant or ethnic group, does not allow us the ability to investigate fully (if at all) processes of social and economic differentiation within ethnic minorities themselves. At one level there are differences between ethnic entrepreneurs and workers. At another level there are differences between immigrant entrepreneurs. Some enterprises are small, family firms or firms critically dependent on family labour input, whilst others were very large employers who recruited labour from a wide range of ethnic groups. The differentiation of minority enterprise has been a strong feature of Cypriot participation in the London garment industry where some firms have broken out of the ranks of small contractors, are significant employers in local areas, have become manufacturers and operate as micro multinational companies in international outward processing (Panayiotopoulos, 1992a, 1996b, 2000).

Lee (1992), Panayiotopoulos (1996a) and Kwong (1997) argue that structural changes can transform social relations within immigrant communities. Social stratification and the 'commodification' of immigrant communities pose problems for culturally driven claims to common ethnic identity, and in doing so invite questions about 'who benefits' from immigrant enterprise. The major criticism made by Sanders and Nee (1987a, 1987b, 1992) on the work of Waldinger, Portes et al. concerns issues to do with the social stratification of ethnic groups and their workplace relations. They suggest the need to be 'sensitive to important differences between immigrant-workers and immigrant bosses' (1987a, p. 745). They question the methodology applied by Portes et al., for failing to make a distinction between self-employment and the employment of others, and for ignoring previous findings which reported significant income differences between workers and bosses in the Cuban enclave (1987a, pp. 747–8).[6]

CONCLUSIONS

In fashion wear, historically associated with women's wear, the search for shorter supply lines looked for sourcing in-country which was relatively cheaper. Contracting and subcontracting is often used for this purpose. Petras (1992), in a study of the Philadelphia garment industry, argues that the major factor in the expansion of Chinese-owned 'sweatshops' and homework in New York, New Jersey and Philadelphia, has been the decision of American manufacturers to shift their production orders back to the USA as a cost-cutting measure. The experiences described by Petras, Bonacich and Van Geuns, are reflected in other local studies of diverse ethnic groups. Greek and Turkish Cypriots and Bengalis in London, Indians in the West

Midlands of the UK, Hispanics in New York and Miami, Asians and Latinos in Los Angeles and Arabs in Paris are all associated with high participation in this sector. In Amsterdam it was the Turkish community which provided the raw material for the development of a ready-to-wear garment industry, during the 1970s and 1980s making 'almost exclusively women's clothing' (Van Geuns, 1992, p. 128). The suggestion in these sectoral studies of ethnicity is that the restructuring of the garment industry, and the fashion-wear sector in particular, may be a more critical factor in the incorporation of immigrants, than characteristics associated with any single ethnic group (Panayiotopoulos, 1996a). This introduces a note of caution on the assumption that an optimistic or pessimistic causal connection exists between enterprise,[7] work norms, practices, and the ethnic origin of entrepreneurs and workers employed by them.

EXAMPLE 10A

A Cypriot-owned Garment Factory in Tottenham, North London

In one workplace, in the Tottenham area of north London, the following observations were made. The enterprise was owned by a Greek Cypriot family and various members of the family acted as workers and as managers. The factory produced women's wear (blouses, skirts, dresses) on a CMT basis. Some of the dockets were for less than 500 garments and up to five different styles produced per week was not unusual. The workplace was a medium-sized factory situated on an industrial estate employing 40 people, of whom half were employed as homeworkers. Work began at 8.30am (later for those with young schoolchildren) and finished at 5.30pm, Monday to Friday and 8.30am to 1.00pm on Saturdays. In the factory and amongst homeworkers directly employed by the firm, whilst the labour force was considerably ethnically interspersed (see Table 2.5), Greek Cypriot workers and African-Caribbean women machinists were seen more as 'regular', and if laid off during a 'slack period', they had 'first offer' for future work. The employment of young African-Caribbean men was unusual. Many Greek Cypriot factories discriminate (effectively) against second generation West Indian youth. Tottenham, however, is a major West Indian settlement and this is a factor which influences the local labour market. The elder brother also prided himself on being a 'progressive man' (and was in fact a leading member of the London Branch of the Cypriot Communist Party).

Inside the factory, face-to-face workplace relations were structured by wage relations and patron–client relations. A high degree of patronage was shown by management. For example, the elder brother part-owned a fish and chip shop which contained live-in accommodation and the top flat was rented to the two African-Caribbean pressers. Lifts were given to some women workers. The aunt and two other workers who lived near one of the brothers were regularly given lifts. If people worked overtime to meet a 'rush' order getting a lift home was an expected favour. Loans were often advanced to workers and sometimes gifts were given. Garments, frequently end of line or slightly damaged, were sometimes given away or bought by workers for small sums. These patron–client relations based on a high degree of informality between labour and management also had important formal enterprise functions. In this way management estimated that workers would be more likely to show flexibility over their time of work when asked to, particularly in meeting 'delivery dates'. Given the small dockets produced, there were many delivery dates and requests to 'work on' and this was a source of friction. The giving of lifts was an attempt to regulate in an effective manner the hours worked. The renting of housing to pressers was also an important way of binding workers who have a reputation for disloyalty (moving on) amongst employers in the trade. It would be less likely that workers would move on if this meant the loss of housing (source: Panayiotopoulos, 1993, pp. 125–8).

EXAMPLE 10B

'Doing a Liquidation' in the London Garment Industry

Commonly, carrying out a 'voluntary liquidation' is a means of avoiding paying creditors and in particular the payment of Value Added Tax (VAT). This is quite a widespread practice amongst UK small enterprises and it is a strong feature of the London garment industry. VAT is tax which is added to the retail price. Currently it stands at 17.5 per cent of the retail price. This tax is recoupable by the entrepreneur, but it has to be paid in the first place. This calls for fine tuning of business finance and the maintenance of two sets of accounts, one for the entrepreneur and another for the VAT money. However, as the question of liquidity (often posed in the shape of late payments to small firms) assumes a disproportionate weight in this sector, so the two sets of accounts often show a tendency to become submerged into one. By the end of the accounting period the VAT money has evaporated, frequently amongst contractors in order to make up for low making prices and to retain machinists during slack periods. The motions of 'doing a liquidation' consist of placing the company in the hands of the liquidator (typically a co-ethnic accountant) who then sells the assets (few as they are amongst contractors) to the original owner through a 'front' person. The liquidation might involve a physical relocation by the enterprise. It is of note that the Customs and Excise in the UK do not pursue routinely for the relatively small amounts owed by small contractor firms given that the cost of pursuit (of mobile enterprises) can be discouraging relative to the expected return. In a study of companies undergoing liquidations and insolvencies in the London garment industry, it was found that the majority of companies undergoing liquidation in the women's wear sub-sector were Cypriot-owned. The implications of such statistics are that

Cypriot companies in the garment sector in five or six Greater London postal code districts (out of 115), all within a relatively compact area of north and east London, can influence trends and statistics on the general state of company liquidations in the UK garment sector as a whole. One reason for this is that women's wear production has become more significant in the UK economy, and many of these companies are located in London. Company insolvencies in the garment industry contribute consistently between 5 per cent and 10 per cent to all insolvencies in UK industry. These sorts of trends have not been missed by the UK Customs and Excise Department which launches periodic raids against the entrepreneurs. This is also a source of irritation to the more established ethnic contractors in the garment industry who have accumulated assets and property (and therefore would find it more difficult to 'do a liquidation'). Many point to the non-payment of VAT by (often) co-ethnic 'rogues', as 'unfair' competition (source: Panayiotopoulos, 1996a, p. 452).

Section 3

Country Studies

Introduction

Prodromos Panayiotopoulos

This section investigates the impact of globalisation and industrialisation at country level. The selection of countries is an eclectic one. For example, China with a population of 1.25 billion people and Cyprus with a population of less than one million, may not appear as readily comparable. The addition of material from the southern European periphery may not conform to a limited spatial interpretation of the Third World. The section provides a series of country case studies with similar and contrasting experiences of economic development. It considers the industrial transformation of two Southern European Newly Industrialised Countries (NICs) – Cyprus and Spain – as well as the Asian and Central American examples of South Korea, China and Mexico. Each country case study contains profiles of real people who personify the different types of social actors involved in the globalisation and industrialisation process and represent the winners and losers of the experience of transformation. Whilst the case studies are diverse what they have in common are societies which have been subjected to incredible changes.

The transformation of the Cypriot economy, for example, can be illustrated in the following historical summary. At Year One of political Independence a mission from the United Nations Development Programme (UNDP, 1961) visited Cyprus with a brief (at the government of Cyprus' behest) of drafting a development strategy for the newly independent state. Cyprus became a member of the UN on 20 September 1960. The UNDP found a Cyprus rocked by severe economic crisis, with mass migration as its leading expression (see Panayiotopoulos, 1990). At the time per capita income stood at $600 but in the rural areas where 60 per cent of the population lived this was at $300, half the national average; only 15 per cent of households had access to piped water, reasonable sanitation or electricity. Items such as telephones, refrigerators and cars were rare commodities. Television sets, at the time a new phenomenon, were rare, and for most, a sight to be seen in a small number of *kafenes* (coffee houses). At Year 14 of independence half the population became refugees (see Section 3.1).

During 1993, the Human Development Index (HDI) compiled annually by the UNDP in the Human Development Report, ranked the Republic of Cyprus twenty-seventh (out of a total of 173 countries). This ranking takes into account purchasing power, life expectancy and infant mortality. Other material supplied by the UNDP shows that Cyprus has resolved rural–urban imbalances in the delivery of services, such as health, water, sanitation and may be seen as an example (along with other NICs) of the narrowing of the North–South gap (see UNDP, 1993, Tables 6, 10). Indeed during 1991 an event took place which was emblematic of the changes to the Cypriot economy and society: with a per capita income of $9,000, an annual rate of GDP growth of 6.4 per cent during the previous five years (1986–91), a level of unemployment of around 2–3 per cent and solid credit ratings, Cyprus said 'goodbye' to the World Bank. As one of the world's 25 'richest' nations (by World Bank per capita income ranking) Cyprus could no longer qualify as a developing country in need of development assistance. Thus Cyprus has been crossed off the international lending institutions' books.

The rapid economic transformation of the Cypriot economy based initially on the export of garments and the import of tourists, finds parallel experiences with those of a number of other smaller NICs such as Hong Kong and Singapore. Not only is there in these three cases a common, British, colonial thread and post-colonial authoritarian experiences of varying dimensions, but also similarities in spatial terms articulated in issues to do with the small size of the domestic market, the physical land-mass itself, and limited resource endowment. These are factors which are frequently used to explain under-development in the West Indies. The country studies of industrialisation in this section offer powerful evidence that capitalism on a global scale is expanding the boundaries of human contact, in ways which were unimaginable even within the time scale of a single decade. The lives of workers offer graphic detail and insight into the processes of industrialisation and globalisation.

3.1

Prodromos Panayiotopoulos

Cyprus: Industrialisation Under Conditions of Globalisation

OVERVIEW

The rapid economic transformation of the Cypriot economy from the mid-1970s onwards may be seen as part of the more general process of industrialisation. The growth of the East Asian NICs and their Latin American counterparts was also mirrored in the increased pace of industrialisation and urbanisation of a number of the Southern European countries during the 1960s (Spain, Portugal, ex-Yugoslavia, Greece, Turkey). In Cyprus, during the late 1970s manufacturing employment overtook, for the first time, employment in agriculture, signalling a fundamental realignment in sectoral employment. A key dimension of this was the role of the export garment industry which during the 1980s accounted for the employment of one-quarter of all manufacturing workers and one-fifth of all workplaces. The industry was aggressively promoted by the Cypriot government, which attached significant welfare objectives to industrial policy. At the same time, however, the globalisation of production by weakening the power of national economies subjects nation states and enterprises to an even more competitive and difficult to predict market environment. An example of this was a crisis faced by the Cypriot garment industry due to the collapse of the Libyan market, at the time the biggest importer of Cypriot garments. This experience placed an initial question mark over the 'economic miracle' in Cyprus. The strategies adopted by the entrepreneurs to survive the crisis consisted of a turn towards the European market and away from the Arab market. A critical dimension of the 'turn to Europe' was the role played by London Cypriot manufacturers, who are a significant force in the UK women's wear sector.

DEVELOPMENT OF THE CYPRIOT GARMENT INDUSTRY

The development of the Cypriot clothing industry points to a high level of intervention by the state. Support measures included a wide range of subsidies – low interest credit, export credit guarantees, duty-free importation of machinery and raw materials destined for export, low-cost sites (industrial estates) as well as connections to public utilities and supporting services (transportation, telecommunication) and other infrastructure. The Cyprus Industrial Training Authority targeted for training – both for vocational and management purposes – priority sectors such as clothing: over half of the manufacturing establishments assisted by the Authority between 1978 and 1982, as well as a massive 82 per cent of all workers trained, were involved in the textile and clothing industry. The vast bulk of supported enterprises produced for export and had a capacity of 200,000-plus garments per year (mainly in the women's wear sector). The push for exports during the Third Emergency Plan (1982–86) saw the implementation of the Export Credit Guarantee Scheme (ECGS). Export guarantees (in effect a delayed subsidy) ranged from 50 per cent in most cases (such as the Libyan market) to a massive 80 per cent in others, such as Iraq (Panayiotopoulos, 1992b, pp. 79–82).

A critical factor in the economic development of Cyprus was, paradoxically, the fracture of the Cypriot state itself. Cyprus gained Independence in 1960, following an armed struggle against British colonialism. The break-up of the Republic of Cyprus began in the form of informal partition during the inter-communal violence of 1963–64 between Turkish and Greek Cypriots, and arrived at a formal partition enforced by mainland Turkish troops in 1974.[1] The events of 1974 resulted in massive economic dislocation. In 1974 the unemployment rate stood at 39.0 per cent and GDP declined by one-third when compared to 1973. In total, something like 200,000 Greek and 65,000 Turkish Cypriots (approximately 45 per cent of the entire population) who were disproportionately drawn from the countryside, were displaced. Industrial policy towards the clothing sector characterised the developmental concerns of the Greek Cypriot state. As a labour-absorbing industry it was key to the post-1974 war period of reconstruction and development. The Emergency Economic Action Plan (1975–76) saw the promotion of small-scale and labour-intensive enterprises as the cornerstone of industrial policy and initially as one addressing the question of mass unemployment amongst displaced refugees. The Second Emergency Economic Action Plan (1977–78) shifted emphasis to more capital-intensive production. The Third Emergency Plan (1979–81) pushed for export promotion of manufactured goods (Republic of Cyprus, 1980, 1981; Mavros, 1989, pp. 11–66). At each period of planning the clothing industry was given due consideration.

The World Bank, in a country study of southern Cyprus which analysed the pattern of growth during the period of the 'economic miracle' (1976–84), pointed to clothing exports as the single highest source of commodity earnings at 11.9 per cent of total earnings during the period (World Bank, 1987). The increased employment of women in manufacturing was a characteristic and sustained feature of the period of rapid economic growth and by 1992 nearly half (46.5 per cent) of all manufacturing workers were women. Women represented over one-third of all trade union members in Cyprus during the period 1979 to 1986. Women members of the left-wing union federation PEO's Clothing Workers Section represented over one-tenth (11.5 per cent) of PEO's entire membership during the period (UNDP, 1993, pp. 168–9; Panayiotopoulos, 1992b, p. 89).

GLOBALISATION, CRISIS AND THE 'TURN TO EUROPE'

Whilst planning policy initially saw the clothing sector in employment terms, the most significant new-found role for the clothing industry subsequently appeared in the earning of foreign exchange. It was, as noted, at a compound rate of 11.9 per cent during 1976–84 the single most significant commodity and the second most important area (after tourism) in foreign exchange earning growth. Indeed, it was the collapse of clothing exports during 1984–86 which was to place the first initial question marks over the direction of the 'economic miracle' in Cyprus and graphically illustrated the effects of economic globalisation. This decline was solely accounted for by the collapse of clothing exports to Libya (Panayiotopoulos, 1996b, pp. 5–28).

The Arab countries and in particular the Libyan market were a regulatory influence on Cyprus trade during the years of rapid growth and this was a characteristic feature of trade policy. The two key elements of policy were first, that orders to the Arab markets were (relative to a small economy) large, and second, that this contained elements of sovereign trade (i.e. state to state) and theoretically greater security. In the case of Libya orders were placed by two state procurement companies. The element of export-security was reinforced by the government of Cyprus in the shape of the Export Credit Guarantee Scheme (ECGS). The centrality of the Libyan market for Cypriot clothing exports, and in turn for the overall performance of the (small) Cypriot economy is illustrated in the following: clothing exports to Libya as a percentage of all clothing exports stood at 40.0 per cent in 1981 and collapsed to 4.5 per cent in 1982. In 1984 they stood at an even bigger proportion at 54.0 per cent, and in 1986 collapsed again to 7.0 per cent. The impact of Libyan clothing exports, in turn, fed a volatility into economic activity as a whole (see Table 3.1). The major reason for the collapse of exports to Libya during 1986 was due to delayed payments for goods delivered. Libya's problems derived from the economic and military destabilisation initiated by the United States which included the bombing of Tripoli, followed by an economic boycott and the freezing of Libyan assets in European and US banks. This resulted (among other things) in a foreign exchange shortage by Libya of, in particular, dollars which act as the major currency in the industry and it was this factor which led to delayed payments for Cypriot clothing firms. This eventually led to the largest lay-offs faced by Cypriot workers since Independence (Panayiotopoulos, 1995, pp. 13–53).

ENTREPRENEURIAL SURVIVAL STRATEGIES

For many of the entrepreneurs the collapse of the Libyan market was a critical issue. In a study of 46 entrepreneurs, it was found that 20 had shed labour and three were forced to temporarily close down as a result of the crisis.[2] The entrepreneurs faced with the export market instability associated with the 'Libya crisis' made desperate efforts to turn towards the European market. Effectively this meant the displacement of Libya by the UK as the major destination of Cypriot clothing exports. This redirection of production and marketing strengthened the role of London Cypriot manufacturers who are an emergent force in the London women's wear sector (Panayiotopoulos, 1992a, 1996a, 2000). Manufacturers act as intermediaries between the buyers who place the orders and the contractors who carry out the work. The capacity of London Cypriots to deliver contracts in a context of work scarcity placed them in a strong position and this was an important variable in the restructuring of production and enterprise functions. A significant factor appeared in distinctions between social categories which were used both by entrepreneurs themselves and the public at large, in terms of whether entrepreneurs were returnees (mainly from London), refugees (from northern Cyprus), or locals. This factor influenced the nature of the entrepreneurs' social integration and was translated in one respect as problems faced by returnee entrepreneurs in the recruitment of labour. The significance of returnee entrepreneurs, however, was that they had access to work or information about work and many of them had spent ten to 20 years in the London garment industry as contractors. Most were working as contractors for London Cypriot manufacturers in Cyprus (Panayiotopoulos, 1996b, p. 12).

Most of the entrepreneurs in the study sample were contractors or subcontractors producing on a Cut, Make and Trim (CMT) basis. The vast bulk of employment (80.5 per cent) was in the women's wear sub-sector, within which the sewing of pre-cut blouses was a significant commodity dimension. Most of the workplaces were situated in residential areas, such as working-class neighbourhoods and refugee estates, with only one-fifth sited on the specially designed industrial estates and zones. The turn to Europe linked these entrepreneurs to networks of subcontracting, typically associated in the global garment industry with outward processing (see Section 4.3). At the same time, these networks made use of complementary social relations which informed the organisation of production. These often appeared in claims to a common identity involving kinship and pseudo-kinship, village and political affiliation, which were used by the entrepreneurs in daily transactions. Three London-based manufacturers, for example, relied on kin to manage operations in Cyprus. In one other case a 'communist' entrepreneurship network was revealed, linking leading AKEL (Communist Party of

Cyprus) cadres in London who were manufacturers with collaborators in Cyprus who were CMT contractors.

The role for returnee entrepreneurs was that they acted as intermediaries in the expansive relations of outward processing between London-based Cypriot manufacturers and CMT contractors in Cyprus. In the study sample, out of 46 entrepreneurs over one-third (16 cases) were contractors for one of six London Cypriot manufacturers. Another two had previously worked for them and in another 12 cases intermediaries offered information about other contractors working for them. A total of 30 establishments were found to be working for these six London Cypriot manufacturers. These networks of subcontracting were a general feature of the women's wear sector and appeared as a particularly strong feature of the production and re-export of pre-cut blouses. It was estimated that the 28 respondents who produced blouses in some capacity or other accounted for 53.7 per cent of all-Cyprus blouse production. Most of this was absorbed by the UK market (Panayiotopoulos, 1993, p. 464). An important mechanism in the relationship between international outward processing and complementary social relations was in the role of commission earned by well-placed contractors, or those with the strongest organic links to the manufacturer. This appeared as a major institution of the process of intermediation.[3] One such network of intermediation is presented in Example 11.

FUTURE PROSPECTS

One consequence of the Libyan crisis and the turn to the European market has been to place more pressure on Cypriot clothing exporters to cut production costs and to remain competitive. The 1990s have seen many casualties and a large number of exporters to the UK have closed down operations. The significance of the UK market is that during the 1990s it supplanted Libya as the major market destination of Cypriot clothing exports. This has made Cyprus exporters price sensitive to UK trends, often in unexpected ways. The *Financial Times* of London, for example, found in a survey of the clothing industry in the West Midlands area, thousands of workers suffering pay and conditions associated with the developing countries: squalid factories, workers earning less than £2 an hour for a 50-hour week and 'knocking-up' prices for contractors of £1.50 per blouse. This is making it difficult for Cypriot firms to remain price competitive. In one case it was reported that a Cypriot embroidery firm has found it cheaper to export the processing to the UK.[4]

Other dimensions of the turn to Europe have included the impact of Cyprus's entry into the European Customs Union and the progressive removal of tariff barriers. This has contributed to the halving of sectoral employment.[5] Another parallel dimension of globalisation is illustrated by the activities of some of the largest Cypriot exporters who have relocated production to lower-wage economies. The strategy of 'capital to labour' was adopted by the two largest clothing exporters in Cyprus (JET and Synek), who have relocated significant production capacity, in both cases to Jordan. Another strategy has consisted of 'labour to capital', with immigrant labour accounting for 6 per cent of all registered employment and a higher proportion (14 per cent) of sectoral employment (Republic of Cyprus, 1994, pp. 14–16.) These trends place question marks over the viability of the garment sector as a major source of employment for working women over the next decade.

CONCLUSIONS

Industrialisation and 'de-industrialisation' in Cyprus was closely bound up with the clothing industry. This experience suggests that while the expansion of the industry may be substantially attributable to promotion by domestic industrial policy, equally, this expansion appears as externally driven: the impact of globalisation articulated in a dependence on the Libyan market, its subsequent crisis and after-effects, point towards a range of variables not under the control of the government of Cyprus, but which did emanate from the consequences of its industrial policy. Whether the USA decides to bomb Libya and impose an economic boycott resulting in delayed payments to Cypriot clothing exporters and contraction on the production side, is clearly not subject to the control of domestic public or market forces. It does, however, point to the difficult to predict impact of externality. An analysis of the evolution of sectoral industrial policy needs to be informed by two crucial questions: first, what happens *after* promotion by the state has been superseded by globalisation; and second, what are the precise mechanisms of that globalisation? The case study suggests that below the visible signs of state direction lies the more spontaneous 'real world' of entrepreneurs. The mechanisms adopted by them to deal with export-market instability made use of a range of organic networks. These unofficial networks existed in parallel to the official networks found in ministry and industry circles (such as the Clothing Exporters Council or the Ministry of Trade and Industry) and reflected far more on the experiences of Cypriot migration to London, the involvement of the community in the clothing industry and the evolution of a class of London Cypriot manufacturers, than any formal channels or official policy. Outward processing by London Cypriot manufacturers made use of complimentary social networks of intermediation and this was a critical influence in both the strategies adopted by many entrepreneurs, and the nature of industrial policy in Cyprus.

EXAMPLE 11

Complex Fashions: a Network of Subcontracting

Complex Fs is situated in the village of Farmakiti and adjoins the Kokkino-horia region, an area of intensive agricultural production. The major urban settlement (Paralimni) has been recently recognised as a municipal authority. Increasingly agriculture has to compete with tourism for labour, particularly with the nearby Ayia Napa and Protaras resorts. Farmakiti stands on the Green Line, indeed the line goes through the village. Local residents often articulate the view that 'we have been left behind' (...) 'all the tourists are in Paralimni and Ayia Napa' (...) 'Farmakiti is a *ftohohori*' (poor village). A source of major pride is that a number of co-villagers were doing visibly well in the London clothing industry. Villagers offered information that one of them was building a house in the village (reputed to be worth C£150–£180,000), that 'the Pantelides and Savvas's boys have done very well because they are *prokommenoi* (upright)' and that 'they started with their fathers as *pramateftides* (travelling merchants) selling from the back of the van'. The site for Complex Fs was a sparkling white *Hacienda*-style building with verandas all around the residential top floor. The factory was situated on the ground floor. A basement acted as storage for cloth and machinery.

Mr Savvas (the proprietor) spent eight years in London, the last five years working as production manager for his brother who has a 'top factory' (i.e. gets 'first offer' for work) from Cleopatra Fashions (UK). Cleopatra Fs is itself owned by a first cousin. Mr Savvas returned to Cyprus to oversee the Cyprus end of operations, but also because he didn't like living in London. Complex Fs employed a total of 62 workers, 42 indoors and 20 as homeworkers ('when we have a lot of work'). The establishment was unionised and this acted as major source of labour recruitment. Previously, Complex Fs had another attached section employing 18 workers, but it had shut down. Instead, it subcontracts work out, with itself producing only 2,000 blouses per week and putting out 'a lot more'. It received C£1.10 per blouse, compared to 75 cents three years ago. The establishment faced lay-offs and working at below full capacity: indeed it had nearly closed down during June and July. As Mr Savvas put it, 'we were affected by Libya ... but there were other problems in England'. Although this was not elaborated on, the locals I talked to previously said that they lost a big order in England to 'Indians' who had undercut them by 'ten shillings'.

> Over the last three months, however, Mr Savvas was getting more work than could be handled and this had put him under pressure. He was generally 'fed-up' (...) 'You need *flanga* [liver, associated with patience] for this. It's frustrating! The hangers haven't arrived, buttons are held up, they wouldn't let the cloth out of the docks last night, and you got to meet delivery dates!' (Mr Savvas, Complex Fs)

Complex Fs acted as an intermediary and subcontracted to at least eight factories that I was aware of, earning 15 cents commission per garment as payment. Some subcontractors did likewise. This commission-earning by well-placed contractors was a major institution of intermediation in outward processing in a context where many entrepreneurs were resorting to CMT work as a survival strategy in the face of the 'Libya crisis'. Complex Fs had a special relationship with a number of subcontractors. Pantelides Fs and Fanos are 'top factory'. Complex Fashions and its subcontractors were exclusively making blouses which were delivered pre-cut. In a number of establishments cutting tables were not visibly present. The conversion (in many cases) of previously independent entrepreneurs to subcontractors who assembled pre-cut blouses was one important feature of the relationship between Complex Fs and its subcontractors. The impact of the 'Libya crisis' was also felt in different ways. Subcontractors took the major brunt. Whilst Complex Fs and Pantelides Fs faced uncertainty and both laid off workers, they did not close down. Two subcontractors (SKAN Dresses and Vaso) closed down for nearly a two-month period (see Figure 3). The subcontractors saw Complex Fs and London Cypriot Manufacturers in ambiguous terms:

> they are good for the Cypriot economy, but bad for us; yet if they have work all year round, we need them. (...) They give us low prices and also the middle man makes his profit for simply putting out the work. For example, if Savvas makes fifteen cents a blouse that means C£300 for every 2,000 blouses he gives out! He could *make more than me for doing nothing*! The problem is they have the contacts. (Mr Christophi, Rising Sun Fs, emphasis in original)

In the case of another subcontractor where Complex Fs provided the trimmings (except thread) and where the firm had no cutting table, suggesting a position of high dependence on Complex Fs, the relationship was described thus:

> They deliver work, at low prices on a Monday, and they wanted it on Wednesday! it's pressure all the time. My wife's not well, I got high pressure and we are in here at all times to meet delivery dates ... and then there's no work! What else can I do? I can't take up painting again [previous occupation]. I am not a young man any more. (Mr P. A.)

For Mr Savvas a critical question in relations with subcontractors was 'costings'. Costings were a 'headache' with up to 65–70 per cent of costs taken up in the form of wages and other deductions (for indoor workers). The Cost of Living Allowance (indexing of wage rises to price rises) came in for vehement denunciation:

> of course we want it ended. We get English prices yet here we pay Cypriot labour costs. If wages go up faster than the price for each garment, we get caught in the middle, on top of the English pound going down and the Cyprus pound going up. In the last two months sterling went down two and a half pence! (Mr Savvas, Complex Fs.)

(Source: Panayiotopoulos, 1996a, pp. 16–21)

3.2

Jose D. Garcia Perez

Spain: Economic Development Under Conditions of Autarky

OVERVIEW

Spain is a case of late industrialisation in Europe. The industrialisation strategies adopted in Spain can be broadly divided into those of import substitution, and export promotion after the 1980s. The particular social and economic circumstances can be divided into externally determined, such as the two increases in oil prices in the early 1970s and 1980s, and membership of the EU, and internally determined such as the Spanish Civil War, Franco's dictatorship of 1939–76, and the actions of the economically dominant social classes in controlling investment and policies. The long period of dictatorship gave economic development in Spain particular characteristics. In order to be able to understand the reasons for both autarky and the late industrialisation of Spain we propose to look at its development in historical perspective. To be able to illustrate how development strategies have been affected we chose the two most representative areas of industrial activity, engineering and tourism (the second is explored in Section 4.2). Spain is the fifth biggest car producer in the world, behind the USA, Japan, Germany and France and in front of Italy, Korea and the UK, and has the largest tourist industry in Europe. Engineering and tourism both have important backward and forward production links. The study of engineering allows us to explore the backward links of mining (iron ore and coal), the forward links of car manufacturing, and the importance of technology and investment.

SPAIN DURING THE PERIOD OF THE EUROPEAN INDUSTRIAL REVOLUTION

The most prevalent explanation for the late industrialisation of Spain is based on the consequences of agrarian reform during the nineteenth century. The agrarian reform involved a policy of selling land owned by or leased (from the state) to the Church and military. One of the main objectives of this policy, initiated in 1836, was for the state to raise capital to compensate for the grave deficit in the national balance of payments. The result was a process of partial proletarianisation and entrenched peasant production. Some small subsistence land users managed to raise the necessary capital to buy the land they had traditionally leased from the Church or their own village councils. The majority, those who could not afford to buy land, became landless peasants in the larger estates of the south (Andalucia and Extremadura) or colonised areas of more marginal land in the rest of Spain. Others joined the ranks of the economic immigrants to the New World. Investment in land by the elite which could otherwise have been used in the emerging industrial processes and, according to Tamames and Rueda (1997), lack of entrepreneurship on the part of the landed classes, as well as an immiserated population with limited demand appear as significant explanations for late Spanish industrialisation.

THE SLOW PROCESS OF SPANISH INDUSTRIALISATION

Until the first quarter of the nineteenth century artisanal industries in Spain were uniformly distributed throughout the country. With the advent of mechanisation and the division of labour in the production process the situation was modified towards regional specialisation based on the available natural resources of the areas. It is at this stage that the backward linkages of metallurgy with the mining industry developed. The northern areas of Biscay produced iron ore and Asturias coal, the south-east lead mining and copper, and Cataluña in the north-east specialised in cotton and woollen textiles.

Many industries such as iron smelting were antiquated and lacked capital investment. The first coke-fired blast furnace was installed in Asturias in 1848, more than one hundred years after the first was used in Britain. Another example of the relative technological backwardness of Spanish industry was the use of steam in the cotton industry in Cataluña in 1832 for the first time (when in Britain steam had been used since 1790) (Tamames and Rueda, 1997). At the end of the century the industry was technologically lagging well behind the main European producers and only survived because of protective policies.

ENGINEERING UNDER CONDITIONS OF AUTARKY

At the turn of the twentieth century it was expected that the protected engineering industry would expand and catch up with others in more advanced countries. Instead, the establishment of high prices to the level of the less competitive firms, and the centralisation of sales and quotas of production agreed among producers, restricted competition. The outcome was an uncompetitive monopoly and very small growth.

The Spanish economy was badly affected by world economic depression in the early 1930s, when many workers in the steel industry were made redundant, and by the Spanish Civil War (1936–39). Industrial production was disrupted during this war but was not destroyed as in the case of other northern European countries. As a result of the undemocratic character of the Franco regime, after 1939, Spain was excluded from the UN, did not receive any Marshall Aid, and continued to operate the antiquated industrial plant left almost intact during the war. The Franco state enforced a development strategy of autarky until the mid-1950s, and used the police to exact retribution on its Republican opponents and to enforce a corporatist system of pay-bargaining which ensured a compliant labour force, until the late 1960s. In terms of economic policy, tariff barriers were erected in order to protect or promote national industries. A good example was the use of import controls and tariffs in order to support the private sector Spanish steel-making industry. This resulted in shortages and in order to compensate the state intervened nationally by producing its own steel. The National Institute of Industry (INI) created Ensidesa Steel Corporation with public capital in 1950 to produce steel. Organised private sector producers saw the creation of Ensidesa as a potentially strong competitor. To meet the enormous public investment needed for the construction of Ensidesa, INI requested the participation of private capital to a maximum of 35 per cent initially, with possibilities for increase. Neither public nor private sectors invested at the projected level. When Ensidesa managed to increase the supply of steel, prices remained high because of tariff controls. The sector remained uncompetitive, highly subsidised, and protected from foreign competition (see Gutiérrez, 1990; Vázquez Barquero, 1988).

The 26 years (1936–62) of strong interventionism and protection receded with the new policy of liberalisation. Although high import taxes continued to be levied, the Spanish industry could not compete in price terms, and their stocks increased. Amongst policy makers the conclusions were drawn that the obsolescence of metallurgical industry and disorganised nature of the market needed to be 'modernised'. In 1964 the government devised the First National Plan for Metallurgy (IPSN) which remained in operation until 1972. Steel producers, including Ensidesa, organised themselves into UNESID (a coordinating commercial body) and continued to influence the policy-making process. The demands of UNESID resulted in the continuation of protection against foreign imports and UNESID producers also benefited from state subsides until 1986, when Spain entered the European Community. Because of the high cost to the state, and at a later stage in preparation for entry to the EC, subsidies decreased and a programme of rationalisation was effected. In the period between 1985 and 1995 the number of people working in the steel sector was reduced from 70,000 to 24,000 (unemployment rose considerably in Asturias, Biscay and Valencia) while new technology and working practices increased productivity 57 per cent (Tamames and Rueda, 1997, pp. 23–4). By 1995 Spanish producers were able to meet national demand and became the fifth largest producers in the EU.

THE CAR INDUSTRY

Lack of special steel and other alloys, technical know-how, capital investment in plant, and research and development (R&D) for the production of new car models, represent the main obstacles to the entry of new producers into the sector. Spain was constrained by these conditions until the late 1950s. These plus the low purchasing power of the Spanish population at the time, meant that all the early national car production attempts failed.

The expenses involved in the design, construction and marketing of a new car are too high for most developing countries, therefore production often starts under the licence of an established firm. These firms, however, charge royalties for their licences and place strong restrictions on exports especially to areas where the parent company is already selling. This was the case with the first main Spanish automobile firm SEAT starting production under licence from the Italian firm FIAT in 1950. SEAT was formed with 52 per cent of capital from INI, 6 per cent from FIAT and the rest from private investors. By 1967 FIAT increased its shares to 36 per cent and INI was no longer the main shareholder. FIAT the main shareholder restricted exports and frustrated the possibility of developing the first Spanish-designed car by SEAT. The car industry, as with engineering, was highly protected and production was mainly for the internal market.

The main constraint for the growth of the national car industry was low market demand. This spoke loudly about the nature of economic development in general. To say that the Spanish population did not have the purchasing power of other people in the industrialised countries of northern Europe for much of the post-war period would be an understatement. During the 1950s Spain saw very high levels of unemployment, rural poverty, illiteracy, and under-five mortality rates. Many people did not have access to basic services like electricity. These are indicators which today are usually associated with the Third World, rather than a European country. The economic stagnation of Spain during the 1950s was one factor which forced the government to change from a strategy of autarky to economic liberalisation. The Labour Laws of the 1959 Stabilisation Plan encouraged rural–urban migration and the transfer of capital from the areas of low productivity agriculture to high productivity manufacturing industry. The active labour force employed in the agricultural sector declined from 50 per cent in the early 1960s to 23 per cent in the mid-1970s (Vázquez Barquero, 1988; Gallego, 1979). Many of these migrants from the less productive rural areas of Galicia and Andalucia, however, were not absorbed by the incipient Spanish industrial enclaves of Cataluña, Biscay and Madrid. Many joined, for a variety of reasons, the ranks of the first group of immigrant workers recruited to work in Germany, France and other north European countries facing labour shortages during the 1950s and 1960s post-war boom (see Example 12).

The government objective of encouraging migration in the early 1960s was for a variety of reasons. First, immigration was an important safety valve for the Franco regime and a way of reducing the level of rural unemployment and underemployment, and second, that the remittances of workers abroad would reduce the balance of payments deficit for Spain, provide investment funds and raise incomes. Migrants' remittances from abroad in 1975 were worth more than $700m (Harrison, 1978). The supply of cheap labour and migrants' capital (circulated through the internal banking mechanism in Spain) for investment in the already more prosperous areas of Cataluña, the Basque Country and Madrid, contributed to their further prosperity, and to widen the regional gap. This greater prosperity, also fuelled by the enormous growth of the tourist industry since the early 1960s, increased the purchasing power of Spanish people and allowed the possibility of a mass car market.

Greater purchasing power and the reduction in the costs of production resulted in rapid economic growth from the early 1960s. From 1963 to 1972 SEAT increased production for the national market at an average rate of 7.7 per cent per year. This was mainly due to the application of economies of scale in production of the popular model FIAT 600 which specifically targeted the Spanish market. As more people could afford to buy cars and they could be produced in greater volume, so more saving could be made and this was reflected in the retail price. A FIAT 600 could be bought in real terms in 1972, that is taking inflation into account, for half the price of what it was in 1961. The price of this and the model FIAT 850 were even lower than models produced in Italy in the early 1970s, but export restrictions by FIAT (Italy) frustrated the possibility of selling abroad. Other car producers, taking advantage of the growing market and cheap labour, were also investing in Spain. Renault, a strong competitor of SEAT, started to produce its model R5 in 1955. Citroën opened a new factory in the Free Export Zone in Vigo in 1957 producing the model 2CV, and at a later stage more expensive models, for the national market as well as for export. In the 1960s the British group Morris and later on British Leyland started production of the Mini in Spain. In 1974 British Leyland abandoned production in Spain and sold its plants to SEAT. Simca, Chrysler, Peugeot, Ford and General Motors also started production in the 1970s (see Lagendijk, 1995a, 1995b).

In the 1980s greater competition, especially from Japanese producers, forced the European car industry to increase productivity. This meant the rationalisation and modernisation (greater automation) of the production process. A complex web of rationalisation measures and take-overs followed in Spain in the early 1980s. FIAT pulled out of SEAT selling all its shares to the INI who entered negotiations with Nissan, Toyota and Volkswagen. After a long bargaining period Volkswagen bought FIAT's part and eventually the entirety of SEAT in 1986. The greater automation of production (especially in Renault) and the reduction in demand (because of the economic slump deriving from the oil crisis) resulted in a large amount of redundancies. The rationalisation of production to reduce the large number of models on the market (to increase production runs and reduce costs) resulted in agreements between Citroën–Peugeot, Volkswagen–Nissan, General Motors–Toyota, etc.

By the early 1980s the Spanish car industry had changed from autarky to foreign and national investment, but it still was highly protected. Further liberalisation of trade and production (the abandonment of protection) was necessary in preparation for the entry of Spain into the EU. In 1990 import quotas of foreign quality cars into Spain were gradually removed. As a result imports of quality European cars increased dramatically, costing 2 per cent of the 1990 GNP. All import restrictions on cars and parts were finally removed in December 1992 sending indigenous suppliers and car manufacturers into economic slump. Component procurement in the international market, especially in the countries of the parent company, are increasingly becoming more important than the fate of local suppliers (Lagendijk, 1994).

The success or failure of the car industry in Spain now depends on internal and foreign markets as well as on international trade agreements. Although protection is no longer a policy instrument of government, some room for intervention is left and used to ensure the success of the industry. The Spanish government had to intervene to help the car industry from the effects of low demand in 1994. In 1994 the Spanish government offered an $825 discount to those who traded in their 10-year-old car for a new one. This kind of 'subsidy', although reviving demand, was expensive and had to be abandoned after one year. The government has also been involved in a rescue plan for SEAT. In 1995 the European Commission approved a $377m government aid package to restructure the company, involving the reduction of capacity by 29 per cent and job cuts.[1] The search for a satisfactory trade agreement between the EU and Japan will lead to a condition of further freedom in the car market at the end of the century. This involves dismantling the still existing protective barriers in the UK, France, Italy and Spain (Tamames and Rueda, 1997).

However, the most vulnerable point for the Spanish industry still is its sluggish national demand and, paradoxically, its ability (and need) to export. Spanish exports represented 74 per cent of its total output, compared with 62 per cent by France and 56 per cent and 42 per cent by Germany and Japan. Production is now extremely dependent on foreign markets and other forces beyond the control of car producers.[2] Since Spain only has 340 cars per 1,000 people compared with the 500 European average and 600 in Germany there may still be room to increase national demand. The ability (and perhaps will) to purchase more cars, however, depends on the purchasing power and habits of Spanish people and the success of the whole national economy.

CONCLUSIONS

The Spanish experience of industrialisation has been greatly affected by policies of protectionism, autarky and liberalism, pursued during different historical periods. The post-war experience of 'late' industrialisation illustrates high levels of intervention by the 'strong state'. The development of the car industry, however, suggests that the level of incomes may be a more important factor in the development of a national car market, than policies of economic autarky and social compliance. One continuity in economic policy is that the two most important ingredients in the economy, capital and labour, were under-utilised. Decision makers, themselves frequently acting under great pressure from the dominant elites, embarked on a path of underinvestment and protection. Capital which could have been released for investment was used by the dominant classes to buy land for speculation. An impoverished majority, with little influence in the decision-making process, could only purchase little of the small industrial production. The post-war boom, however, did introduce significant changes to the Spanish economy. Increased immigration to northern Europe saw a growing role for remittances in shaping the pattern of rural incomes. Rising incomes in the northern European countries led to the expansion of mass tourism and this created employment opportunities in some of the most marginalised coastal regions of Spain. In historical terms, the experience from the 1950s and 1960s onwards can be seen as representing a departure for economic development in Spain. In effect, during the boom years Spain saw an increase in per capita incomes which resulted (amongst other things) in the increase of purchasing power by the majority of the population which created immense investment opportunities for the expansion of domestic industry. It was this factor more than any other which laid the basis for a mass car market. This wealth distribution was hardly the result of policy, given the anti-distributionary basis of the Franco regime, but reflected far more on the impact of the post-war boom on the global economy, translated into rising incomes in Europe and most acutely felt in the more underdeveloped countries of southern Europe. One consequence of this was that when the long boom gave way to slump during the early 1970s, much of this employment-based redistribution went into reverse. Andalucia[3] suffers from one of the highest rates of unemployment in the European Community.

EXAMPLE 12

The Draft-dodger

Carlos was an 18 year old, who like many compatriots avoided conscription into the Spanish Army during the 1960s. 'When the papers arrived I knew I had to go. Being the son of a communist, was bad enough, but being gay as well, meant double misery. There are stories in the newspapers about the treatment of gays in the Spanish Army – being beaten, often by fascist officers. Many of my friends made the same decision. I know for my father it is a disappointment, not because I run away from the draft, but because of my sexuality. Probably he is more disappointed because I let him down with the apprenticeship. He works at SEAT and is a representative for the Workers' Commission. He is an electrician and earns good money, so he thought I should be an electrician too! He went to a lot of trouble to get me the apprenticeship and I did it for two years. He was very surprised when I got my call-up papers, since they try not to disrupt training – unless you are a 'communist'.

'I went to Paris on a "holiday". There are a lot of Spanish people working on construction sites. Some of the younger workers live on the site and others in hostels. Sometimes the police came and asked questions, usually about whether people had the right papers, but the *patron* paid them off. He was a big noise on the municipal authority. The communist union (the CGT) gave us far more trouble. They went as far as setting up a picket of the site we worked on, although it was more of a protest – otherwise I would not have crossed it. Since the other guys knew I was a "communist" they delegated me to go and talk to them. In fact many wanted to join the union. They told me to "fuck-off back to Africa!" Can you believe that!?

'I went to Brussels after that and stayed with my uncle who worked as a chef in a hospital. I stayed with him for six months, although I hardly saw him, since he worked all the overtime he could get to send money home. He got me a job as a kitchen-porter in another hospital, but then I found a better paid job in a restaurant owned by a Basque. My mother was happier. She knew where I was and that I was working. In the restaurant I worked 16 hours a day and took home less than an engineer makes at SEAT, and the cost of living in Brussels is, of course, much higher! I asked for a pay rise, but the boss – who reads *Mundo Obrero*, the Spanish Communist Party newspaper – said to me that "inflation is an in-built characteristic of the capitalist economy, and that's one reason why we have to get rid of capitalism". I got fed up and left. I saved some money while I was working, though.

'I think there is going to be a Revolution in Spain. I have sent some money to my mother but I still have quite a bit left, so I am going to India for six months. I hope it doesn't start before I come back.'

(Source: Carlos Fernandez, Personal Communication, P. Panayiotopoulos, Vondel Park, Amsterdam, 5 May 1969.)

3.3

Gavin Capps and Prodromos Panayiotopoulos

South Korea: Free Market Miracle or Mirage?

OVERVIEW

Forty years ago South Korea was a poverty-stricken agricultural country with socio-economic indicators comparable to those of present-day Bangladesh and Mozambique. Today, it is a world leader in the production and export of cars, ships and hi-tech consumer goods. South Korean companies, like Daewoo, Hyundai and Lucky Goldstar, have become powerful Trans National Corporations (TNCs) with factories across Europe and the Pacific Rim. The industrialisation of South Korea has been accompanied by an increase in per capita incomes to levels which the World Bank classifies as 'developed' country status. This is no mean achievement for a developing country. The aim of this case study is to consider whether the industrialisation of South Korea really has been a 'miracle' of the free market, or a 'mirage' of state intervention. It examines the implications of the financial and economic crises which faced South Korea and other East Asian NICs in the late 1990s and considers the social and economic consequences.

THE MILITARY

The people of the Korean Peninsula constitute a national group with common histories and shared cultural and linguistic characteristics. Prior to the nineteenth century the landed aristocracy paid tribute to the Chinese Emperor. In the early twentieth century Japan was the ascending power in the region and it physically annexed Korea in 1910 and incorporated it into its Imperial Trading Zone as a specialist producer of high quality rice and minerals for the Japanese market. Japan established a protected Yen Trading Zone in the same way that the British did in their colonies with the Sterling Trading Zone. This period can be seen as one of 'forced' export orientation. At the end of the Second World War, Korea was partitioned in a bloody civil war by the superpowers, into a communist north and a capitalist south. The price for this political arrangement which came out of the Korean War (1945–53) was 4 million deaths and the economic destruction of both North and South Korea. During the 1950s agriculture was in stagnation as farmers retreated into the subsistence economy and stopped producing a marketable surplus. A predominantly rural country ended up having to import its staple foodstuff, rice. This was one factor in the significant land reform programme introduced in South Korea during the 1950s.

The Korean War is a crucial factor in explaining the role of the military in South Korea. For most of the 1950s South Korea was an economy heavily dependent on US military aid. In 1957 a massive 87 per cent of South Korea's import bill was financed by US aid. Between 1945 and 1978, South Korea received almost US$6bn in aid from the USA. This was equivalent to the amount given to the entire African continent during the same period (Bello and Rosenfeld, 1990, p. 4). The military were the major beneficiaries of US aid and training and between 1953 and 1960 they doubled in size to 500,000 persons, becoming the major centre of power in South Korea. During the 1950s the term 'Guided Democracy' was used by the US State Department to describe South Korean military rule, presumably in order to differentiate them from their totalitarian brothers in the North. The political impetus for industrialisation came from a military driven by anti-communism and who saw in this a way of strengthening their position in the conflict with North Korea. A qualitative change in direction came in 1961 when General Park Jung Hee swept to power through a military coup. It was under this government that the pace of industrialisation accelerated and the economy was redirected towards production for export. The military formed the government during much of the period of rapid economic growth. Limited democracy was restored in 1987 following a popular uprising initiated by students and supported by industrial workers.

THE MIRACLE

One distinguishing characteristic of industrialisation in South Korea is the remarkable speed of economic transformation – even when compared to the other Newly Industrialising Countries. Between 1960 and 1986 industrial output grew by an average of 18 per cent, which was significantly higher than Brazil at 11 per cent. During the 1970s manufacturing output grew by 5.5 times whilst in Taiwan it grew by 2.5 times. During the two decades which followed the 1961 coup, South Korea experienced years during which manufacturing output grew by more than 20 per cent per year (Harris, 1990a, p. 65; Jenkins, 1992). Such rates of industrial growth were even higher than those associated with the British Industrial Revolution, and as a result South Korea managed to industrialise in a relatively compact period of 30 years, whilst British industrialisation itself was a much more protracted (150-year) experience. It is for reasons such as these that the South Korean economy appears as the 'miracle of miracles'. Production for export was the characteristic feature of South Korean industrialisation. In 1960 exports amounted to a mere 3.3 per cent of GNP. By 1975 they had increased to 28.4 per cent. The sevenfold increase in exports during the 15-year period translated to foreign exchange earnings which amounted to $107m in 1960 and $6.0bn in 1975. By 1978 manufactured goods accounted for 64 per cent of exports and by 1986 one-third of exports consisted of machinery and transport equipment.[1]

The initial period of industrialisation saw a high reliance on labour-intensive sectors and during the 1970s about 40 per cent of all exports came from the textile and garment sector. During the 1990s the sector declined in significance but in 1993 it still accounted for 19 per cent of all manufactured exports (World Bank, 1995a, p. 112). The textile and garment industry is, however, one of the most restricted areas of trade and it was partly in response to MFA quotas and restrictions (see Section 4.3) that during the 1980s the South Korean economy began to diversify and broaden its manufacturing base away from sectors such as garments. This was despite the conventional economic wisdom about 'comparative advantage' which suggested that South Korea could continue as a dedicated specialised producer. Indices of manufacturing production from 1980 to 1987 show that sectors which grew at below average rate were labour-intensive industries such as food, beverages, textiles and wood products, whilst in reverse the sectors which grew above average (and in some cases spectacularly so) were iron, steel and basic metals. The export of fabricated metal products (cars, ships, fridges), machinery and transport equipment, increased fourfold during the 1980s (see Table 3.2).

THE STATE AND THE *CHAEBOL*

The conventional neo-liberal interpretation of industrialisation in South Korea points to the progressive reduction of import duties and export-led orientation as evidence of the 'openness' of the economy. It argues that these measures subjected the South Korean economy to the 'stimulus' of international competition in the global market which acted as a powerful countervailing power to remaining distortions and protectionist policies pursued by government. This view of globalisation is challenged by a wide body of literature which points to the tenacity of state intervention in modern economies generally and South Korea specifically (see Harris, 1990a; Wade, 1990, 1996; Bello and Rosenfeld, 1990; Amsden, 1989; Akyaz et al., 1998). A practical manifestation of state intervention appeared in the framing of industrial policy and in the structuring of relationships with the *Chaebol* (large, family-owned business groups) which dominate the private sector in South Korea. The *Chaebol* employ, either directly or indirectly, most of South Korea's industrial workers and account for virtually all exports. A review of state policy suggests that extensive state intervention was a critical factor in the initiation of South Korea's export-led growth. The three areas of industrial and financial policy as well as policy towards labour are highlighted to support this view.

The Park regime set out to build a strong authoritarian state capable of subordinating the interests of capital and labour to the grand ideal of 'industrialisation'. Industrial policy was influenced by this in a number of ways. Dissenting opposition parties and independent trade unions were banned and elections were suspended. A powerful Economic Planning Board (EPB) was established which framed industrial policy and set production and export targets for key industries through five-year planning, something not usually associated with the free market. The EPB applied the 'localisation' rule, specifying the use of local inputs as a condition for inward investment. It 'selected' particular *Chaebol* for the expansion of new industrial sectors. Through the producers' associations the EPB fixed consumer prices (see Luedde-Neurath, 1988). The state also supported industry over agriculture by driving down the prices paid for rice, which had the effect of lowering the wage bill for exporters.

The government controlled financial policy as an important instrument of industrial policy. It nationalised the banking system and developed mechanisms to direct both internal and external resources in the form of Foreign Direct Investment to strategic areas of the economy. State planners guided (or 'disciplined') the *Chaebol* through the careful manipulation of finance and trade policy. Companies which met government export targets were rewarded with subsidies, cheap loans and 'bail outs' in times of difficulty. However, poor performers were penalised by high taxes, the loss of export licences and were often taken over by favoured firms (Amsden, 1989, p. 15). By 1990, some 1,000 laws regulated the activities of individual industries and companies (see *The Economist*, 1991). The key outcome of these 'carrot and stick' policies was the development of a powerful, export orientated and nationally owned industrial sector. An ever-smaller number of *Chaebol* monopolised production. By the 1970s, four 'super-Chaebol' – Hyundai, Samsung, Daewoo and Lucky Goldstar – dominated the economy. During 1984 the 30 largest accounted for 76 per cent of sales in South Korea, and Hyundai sales alone accounted for 10 per cent of GNP. During the 1990s, Samsung overtook Hyundai as the largest group (see opposite page, 'South Korea's Top Five *Chaebol*').

The third area of considerable state intervention was in its control of the workforce. During the period of rapid growth low wage costs and high labour productivity gave the *Chaebol* a significant competitive edge in sectors such as textile and garments. Throughout the 1960s and 1970s, a labour surplus in the form of rural to urban migration drove wages down. Women were particularly favoured in the labour-intensive industries, as they were considered by management as more obedient and 'docile' than men workers. In the factories, both women and men workers were subject to military-style discipline, backed up by harsh labour laws. South Korea earned the reputation of having one of the world's worst industrial health and safety records (Pilger, 1995).

South Korea's Top Five *Chaebol*

Core business sectors and related companies
Sales, Exports, Research and Development, Assets, Debt (in $bn)
Number of Employees (in 000s)
Samsung: Electronics (Samsung Electronics), machinery (Samsung
Heavy Industries, Samsung Aerospace), chemicals (Samsung General
Chemicals, Samsung Chemicals). *1991* – Sales (43.4), Exports (13.7),
R&D (1.09). *1996* – Sales (71.0), Assets (75.2), Debt (62.1), Number
of employees (164).
Hyundai: Motor vehicles (Hyundai Motor Services), electronics
(Hyundai Electronics), energy (Hyundai Oil Refinery, Seil Oil). *1991* –
Sales (39.6), Exports (5.9), R&D (0.51). *1996* – Sales (69.7), Assets
(58.1), Debt (47.6), Number of employees (187).
Lucky Goldstar: Electronics (Goldstar, Goldstar Electron), chemicals
(Lucky, Lucky Petrochemical), (Honam Oil Refinery, Saebang Oil).
1991 – Sales (25.0), Exports (7.6), R&D (0.65). *1996* – Sales (48.5),
Assets (44.2), Debt (34.9), Number of employees (116).
Daewoo: Motor vehicles (Daewoo Motor), machinery (Daewoo Heavy
Industries, Daewoo Shipbuilding and Heavy Machinery), distribution
(Daewoo Corp.). *1991* – Sales (16.0), Exports (4.8), R&D (0.42). *1996*
– Sales (38.6), Assets (37.4), Debt (28.4), Number of employees (120).
Sunkyong: Energy (Yukong, Hungkuk, Sangsa, SKI), chemicals (SKC),
distribution (Sunkyong, Yukong Shipping). *1991* – Sales (10.7),
Exports (2.6), R&D (0.06). *1996* – Sales (26.7), Assets (23.9), Debt
(18.9), Number of Employees (29).

Note: sales, exports and R&D for 1991; sales, assets, debt, number of employees for
1996.
(Sources: *Far Eastern Economic Review*, 'Asia's Leading Companies', 25 December
1998, pp. 39–97; *Financial Times*, 'Time to cut giants down to size', 10 April 1991;
Financial Times, 'South Korean groups target core businesses', 19 January 1994;
Financial Times, 'Seoul fires warning shot over chaebol', 22 January 1998.)

Two examples illustrate the role of the state in the industrialisation. The
first concerns the strategic development of 'dynamic' comparative advantage
in areas such as the ship-building industry through the application of
technology transfer. This is quite different to conventional comparative
advantage theory relying on the use of natural endowment, such as an
abundance of labour, or particular tropical commodities. During the 1990s
South Korea became the world's second largest producer of merchant
shipping. Without the ability to produce steel it is highly questionable that
South Korea would have become a major ship or car producer. Yet, when
the government made plans to establish the Pohang Steel Mill in 1970, they

were actively discouraged from doing so by World Bank advisers who argued that this was not an area of comparative advantage for South Korea, unlike labour-intensive industries such as textile and garments. This was ignored by the government and the mill went on single-handedly between 1970 and 1981 to increase steel output by 194 per cent (Harris, 1990a).

The second example concerns the complexities of globalisation and the difficulties of 'opening up' culturally sensitive sectors of the South Korean economy, such as the film industry. According to one report in the *Financial Times*, 'Teargas and fire have made an unwelcome reappearance in South Korea, not during a demonstration, but in a cinema.' Apparently, patrons left one cinema sneezing and crying after teargas was placed under the seats. At another, the screen and several seats were destroyed in a fire which police believe was started deliberately. Both cinemas were showing films, including *Indiana Jones and the Last Crusade*, imported directly by the US distributors, Universal International Pictures (UIP). Film imports have been the subject of a trade dispute with the USA for some time and during 1989 Seoul capitulated to American demands to allow direct distribution. Apparently, 'at a showing of *Fatal Attraction*, the first film allowed in under the agreement, a bag of snakes was set free in the cinema to frighten patrons'.[2] A further demand made by the USA, following considerable lobbying by Hollywood, was that the South Korean government abolish the 'screen quota system' which mandates cinemas to show Korean films for 146 days a year. This was made a condition of further US investment in Korea, and led to understandable protests by Korean actors.[3]

CRISES

The tiumphalism associated with the South Korean 'miracle' has been considerably subdued by a number of crises which faced the economy and society. Three separate but interconnected crises faced the South Korean economy. First, crisis associated with fluctuations in the world economy; second, the political crisis of 1987 which led to the partial restoration of democracy; and third, the financial and economic crisis of 1997 associated with the effects of the wider South East Asian crisis and which resulted in the adoption of an IMF 'rescue' package.

Crisis and the Global Economy

South Korean manufacturing exports grew in relation to the world economy, and as such, were affected by changes to the global economy. The South Korean economy became particularly sensitive to changes in the 'special relationship' linking South Korea with Japan and the USA. This relationship was set in motion by the *Chaebol* which moved into capital-intensive industries during the 1970s and 1980s, and in doing so became more dependent on technology transfer. Japan provided technology licences and transfers, and the USA provided 'privileged access' to its markets (Bello and Rosenfeld, 1990, p. 6). Whilst South Korea benefited from this relationship, the arrangement itself was subject to fluctuations in the global economy. The onset of world recession in the mid-1970s, for example, kept in check ambitious expansion plans by South Korea in areas such as steel and petrochemicals. During the slow-down of the late 1980s the economy shrank into single digit figures of growth and 'leading sectors' like the car industry were badly hit: exports to the US fell by 38 per cent in 1989 and 28 per cent in 1990. During 1991 the 'miracle' economy suffered a record trade deficit of $8.83bn. Virtually all of this ($8.4bn) was accounted for by the deficit with Japan, and for the first time (since 1981) South Korea also registered a small deficit with the USA.[4]

The South Korean economy has attempted to negotiate global market instability through two major compensatory mechanisms. The first is the action of government itself, and this consisted of the bailing-out of the private sector through a 'soft' lending regime. The image of generals in government lending to generals sitting on the Boards of the major *Chaebol*, whilst crude, may be seen as an accurate working description of the activities of the banking sector, which was itself for much of the period of rapid growth (until 1984) under state ownership. Financial support by government was a characteristic response to private sector crisis.

The second compensatory mechanism was a reflection of the key role played by the US market for South Korean manufactured exports. The US market, because it is very large relative to other industrial economies, is capable of much greater autonomy in the world economy and this is reflected in periodic divergences from trends common to the other industrial economies. The USA, for example, came out of the 1970s recession earlier than the European economies did. The more serious world recession in the early 1980s saw the USA enjoying a mini-boom during 1983–85, substantially driven by increased military expenditure by the Reagan administration and the perverse multiplier effect of defence industry employment. The South Korean economy because it became closely linked to the US economy benefited from this trend.

Despite the above compensatory mechanisms – which worked with reasonable predictability for most of the period of rapid growth – the extent and selectivity of the world crisis which faced South Korea in the late 1990s was quite unprecedented in scale. During 1996 the South Korean economy recorded its worst ever deficit: at $24bn it was the second largest trade deficit in the world after the USA, and significantly, it was driven by a fall in prices for exports in the new industries characterised by high *Chaebol* investment. Export prices for semiconductors fell by 61 per cent, chemicals 15 per cent and steel by 8 per cent, during 1996 when compared to the previous year. These items accounted for over 40 per cent of total exports.[5]

The Political Crisis 1987

A critical dimension of industrialisation in South Korea consisted of rapid occupational changes. The most significant realignment of employment during a 27-year period (1960–87) was the reduction of agricultural employment from 66.2 per cent to 22.2 per cent of overall employment and a corresponding increase in industrial employment from 13.3 per cent to 33.1 per cent. The number of industrial workers in South Korea increased from 600,000 in 1963 to 4.4 million by 1987.[6] The progressive maturation of industrialisation also made increasing demands on the technical capability of the labour force, and this was reflected in the large numbers of young people in higher education and training: by the early 1990s something like 2 million students were enrolled in South Korean universities.

South Korean workers have been involved in previous bitter wage disputes, and in 1980 the army massacred hundreds of striking shipyard workers in the southern city of Kwangju (Gyoung-hee, 1998, p. 52; also see Ogle, 1990). The example of the Pangrim textile workers shows that women have been at the forefront of union organisation (see Example 13). During 1987 South Korea was rocked by an unprecedented wave of labour disputes and student protests. Powerful, independent trade unions in the form of the Korea Confederation of Trade Unions (KCTU) grew in strength, and during the 'Great Labour Offensive' of 1987–90, strikes and unionisation spread from textiles to heavy industry. Hyundai Heavy Industry was a classic example of a militarised company (with regulation Hyundai hair cuts and uniform) and the industrial city of Ulsan was a Hyundai company town. Hyundai Shipyard employed one-third of the labour force. The company promoted a company union and employed 'goons' to enforce discipline.[7] The demands of the workforce were for the recognition of their own union, the release of their leaders from custody and a substantial pay rise. During December 1989 a 109-day battle began with workers occupying the plants and up to 14,000 riot police were used to storm the shipyard (Bello and Rosenfeld, 1990, pp. 40–2).

Whilst the shipyard workers were defeated at high political cost to the military, the number of strikes increased phenomenally and most were in fact successful. The number of strikes increased from 276 in 1986 to 3,749 in 1987 (see Table 3.3) and involved millions of workers who won wage rises averaging 20 per cent (Bello and Rosenfeld, 1990, p. 43). In the textile industry the hourly cost of labour increased by 25 per cent – in US dollar terms to $2.87 cents between the spring of 1988 and 1989.[8] Successful struggles by workers for economic rights gave them more confidence and this lifted the lid on the economic and social repression which was at the heart of industrialisation. Workers and students became inextricably linked with the movement for democratisation and the development of this atmosphere of resistance demonstrated the vulnerability of the repressive apparatus of the state, and in actuality pointed to powerful criticism which can be made of the 'strong state' thesis. The worker and student movement forced the government to ease restrictions on political activity and marked a shift towards limited parliamentary democracy. However, the democracy issue is far from resolved, as the letter from the Hyundai striker suggests (see Example 13). The Korea Confederation of Trade Unions – which is strong in heavy industries such as ship-building and car production – continues a semi-legal existence in some plants. Over 150 members of the International Socialists of South Korea (ISSK), associated with the UK Socialist Workers' Party, have been charged with a variety of political offences, including the publishing of their newspaper and books. A number of their members have faced, in some cases, four-year prison sentences.[9]

One important dimension of the limited return to democracy in South Korea, was to subject the relationship between the state and *Chaebol* conglomerates to much greater scrutiny. Illegal contributions to the ruling party made by the *Chaebol* surfaced during the 1987 uprising and this exposed them to financial scrutiny. The government in an effort to rationalise their activities, instructed the *Chaebol* to concentrate on 'core' businesses and made this a condition of eligibility for unrestricted access to borrowing and government subsidies for the purposes of research and development.[10] Another significant impact of demands for increased transparency was the demise of the major symbol of state intervention, great 'fixer' and friend of the *Chaebol* – the Economic Planning Board, itself. During December 1994 it was merged into the new and more supportive of liberalisation policies – the Finance and Economic Board (FEB)

Financial and Economic Crisis 1997

The crisis which impacted on South Korea and the other South East Asian economies during 1997 appeared initially in the form of a financial crisis. The 'domino effect' of collapsing share prices and currencies left no country in South East Asia unaffected. The IMF and the World Bank launched the largest 'rescue package' in their history, in order to 'save' not the poorest of the developing countries, but middle and high income economies. The financial crisis also became a social and economic crisis which was translated to rising unemployment and factory closures. In the case of South Korea and elsewhere (Indonesia, Malaysia) the financial crisis became part of a wider political crisis which questioned the legitimacy of rulers throughout the region (see Section 2.1).

The IMF in its 1997 Annual Report (based on 1996 data) wrote that 'Directors welcomed Korea's continued impressive macroeconomic performance [and] praised the authorities for their enviable fiscal record.'[11] Between July 1997 and February 1998, South Korea saw the collapse of share prices traded on the Seoul stock exchange by −32.3 per cent and the value of its currency (the *won*) against the US dollar falling by even more at

−48.1 per cent. At one stage the South Korean long-term debt rating was reduced by Moodys Investor Services, one of the two big international credit rating agencies, to junk bond status. This created the paradox whereby South Korea, a member of the industrial nations 'club' (the Organisation for Economic Co-operation and Development), had a lower credit rating on government-issued bonds than Tunisia, El Salvador and Slovakia.[12]

The South Korean crisis was in part driven by huge trade deficits financed by an increasing foreign debt. The Western banks were more than willing to lend to the 'miracle' economy. The organisation which monitors international transactions – the Bank for International Settlements (BIS) – reported that during the 18 months prior to June 1997, lending to South Korea had increased by a third (to $103.4bn). At the same time, however, the banks, aware of the economic problems facing South Korea, attached conditions to lending. Of the loans, 68 per cent ($70bn) were of short-term duration and set to mature in less than one year. This was the second highest exposure to short-term lending in Asia, after Taiwan.[13]

The critical issue facing the *Chaebol* was that they could not service loans taken out by them or their associate banking groups and both the *Chaebol* and their banks were threatened with bankruptcy. The government nationalised two banks and KIA Motors – Korea's third largest car manufacturer – rather than allow them to go bankrupt. To observers this looked like the familiar response of the government using compliant banks to support industry.[14] The severity of the crisis, however, was quite unprecedented and overwhelmed the government, as attempts to 'rally' the *won* and the value of shares the Seoul Exchange proved expensive failures.

During December 1997 the IMF launched in South Korea its largest ever 'rescue' of a national economy. The $57bn loan brokered by the IMF involved the collaboration of the IMF (itself the major donor at $21bn), the World Bank (at $10bn), Japan ($10bn), the USA ($5bn) and the other industrial economies,[15] including (symbolically) the People's Republic of China. The IMF package was given on condition that the government implemented standard 'deflationary' and export orientated policies. Typically these include fiscal tightening, high interest rates and cut-backs in public sector expenditure. Reaching an agreement was complicated by the presidential election running concurrently with the crisis.[16] The specific conditions attached to the IMF package included:

IMF Rescue Package: South Korea

- Reduction of the expected GDP growth target to 2.5 per cent.
- Reduction of current account deficit to below 1 per cent of GDP.
- Reduction of the rate of inflation to 5 per cent or less.
- Reduction of public sector expenditure and a balanced budget within one year.
- The government is 'banned' from rescuing troubled *Chaebol*.

- Reform of the 'rigid' labour laws to allow the easier sacking of workers.
- Legislation to give independence to the central bank.
- An increase in foreign shareholding limit in listed companies, from 26 per cent to 50 per cent.
- Permission for foreign banks to establish subsidiaries.
- Elimination of trade barriers; end to import licensing and certification process.[17]

The package of measures agreed to in December 1997 by the South Korean government were described by the Korean media as a 'national shame' and as representing the 'loss of national sovereignty' which would place Korea under the 'trusteeship' of foreign powers. Trade unions pointed to the likelihood of massive lay-offs, as indebted companies and insolvent banks shut down.[18] A wave of national humiliation was felt amongst the Korean people, who (with media prompting) launched a massive 'savings' campaign to pay the debt: recently married couples donated their gold wedding rings, executives waived pay rises, luxury imports were at one stage banned and the politics of 'sacrifice' was the order of the day. Under these conditions, widely reported indiscretions by the rulers of South Korea (such as reportage of imported fur coats) further fuelled popular anger.

The KCTU trade union federation (with 550,000 members) had launched a series of strikes before the IMF package was announced in order to defend jobs in companies facing bankruptcy. During January 1997 widespread strikes took place in auto, steel, ship-building and the financial and banking sector. This action was, however, limited to 'only on Wednesdays'. The KCTU also refused to make common ground with the smaller right-wing trade union confederation (FKTU) whose members in a number of companies were on indefinite strike against closures, or to defend the Korean Confederation of Student Councils (KCSC) whose members were arrested *en masse* during September 1996 and November 1997. This created a sense of demoralisation in the worker and student movement. Under these conditions, the politics of 'sacrifice' made headway. President Kim Dae-Jung, the first non-military person to occupy the post for nearly four decades, and the KCTU reached an understanding. The 'Social Agreement' saw the KCTU accepting job losses and legislation making it easier to sack workers, in exchange for promises to reform the (octopus-like) *Chaebol*. Whether this agreement lasts is a matter of debate in the Korean labour movement (see Gyoung-hee, 1998, pp. 39–55; IDTUM, 1998). What is clear, however, is that the IMF package has severely limited the room for manoeuvre available to the government of South Korea.

MIRACLE OR MIRAGE?

At the beginning of this case study, it was asked whether South Korea's industrial transformation has really been a 'miracle' of the free market, or a 'mirage' of outside help and state intervention. Much of the previous review would substantiate the view of economist Alice Amsden who answers the question thus:

> South Korea is a country that grew very fast, yet violated the canons of conventional economic wisdom [...] instead of the market mechanism allocating resources and guiding private entrepreneurship, the government made most of the pivotal investment decisions. Instead of firms operating in a competitive market structure, they operated with an extraordinary degree of market control, protected from foreign competition. (Amsden, 1989, p. 139)

Luedde-Neurath, similarly, makes the observation that,

> The South 'Korean miracle' is not a triumph of laissez faire, but of a pragmatic non-ideological mixture of market and non-market forces. Where the market works, fine: where it doesn't, the government shows no hesitation in intervening by means that range from a friendly phone call to public ownership. (Luedde-Neurath, 1988, p. 74)

It was also asked whether South Korea's export success could be repeated elsewhere. In part this is answered by the extension of industrialisation to other South East Asian economies and China, which enjoys a 'Most Favoured Nation' trade status with the USA. This is similar to the privileged access to US markets enjoyed by South Korea in its own development. Clearly, we are seeing the dispersal of industrialisation and South Korea has new competitors abroad. Other low wage countries also have embarked on export drives, while South Korea's labour costs have increased. The experience of massive trade deficits reveals important tensions in the maturation of South Korean industrialisation. First, the South Korean economy finds it difficult to compete in labour-intensive industries with the 'second generation' NICs (Malaysia, Thailand) as well as China, on the basis of cost price, since they are considerably lower wage economies; at the same time, South Korea finds it difficult to compete with the industrial economies on the basis of product quality and product differentiation. The above is complicated by selective restrictions to world trade imposed by the industrial economies.

The *Chaebol* are losing their privileged political role in South Korea and access to the American market: the USA has reacted to its own economic problems by imposing import quotas on South Korea and forcing it to accept American imports. This is one reason why South Korea's trade deficit has grown. Some *Chaebol*, like Lucky Goldstar, responded to the end of the 'special relationship' by relocating to Britain as an expected base for operations in the European market. These plans have been much scaled down by the recent crisis. Others have relocated their labour-intensive operations to low wage countries such as Thailand, China and Bangladesh, in an attempt to regain international competitiveness. This has given a push to the 'second generation' NICs.

CONCLUSIONS

The profound changes in the South Korean economy over the last three decades were sensitively linked to state direction. Since the return of limited democracy in 1987, however, the links between the state and the private sector have become more difficult to predict, both due to public protests against the political influence of the *Chaebol* and the impact of crises. One illustration of this was the willingness of the South Korean government during August 1999 – under heavy pressure from foreign banks – not to bail out Daewoo which had run up debts of $50bn. This was a condition of the IMF 'rescue' package. Rather, it was proposed that Daewoo be dismantled or effectively asset-stripped of its most profitable sectors by domestic creditors.[18] Whilst the future of Daewoo is far from certain, the willingness by government to accept this development illustrates a new direction in economic policy. The example of Daewoo also illustrates an important contradiction between finance and industry in the Asian crisis. On one hand, at the most current and much higher than assumed estimate of debts to the level of $73bn, Daewoo became the single largest private sector defaulter in the history of capitalism.[19] At the same time, according to a study by the Economist Intelligence Unit, Daewoo's Changwon facility in South Korea is the world's most productive car plant in terms of cars produced per employee.[20] The complex crisis faced by Daewoo and the hundreds of thousands of workers employed by it world-wide illustrates the fragility of the hope that South Korea represented a more sustainable market-based model which raised incomes and safeguarded livelihoods. In this sense the miracle is a 'mirage'.

The crisis faced by South Korea does not mean that industrialisation will be reversed, or that the South Korean economy will not continue to maintain a significant presence in manufacturing production for export. Indeed the economy rebounded with remarkable vigour[21] and by 1999 the World Bank raised its short-term projections for South Korea and the region as a whole (World Bank, 1999). The crisis illustrates, however, that a system based on production for the world economy, cannot but become incorporated into the 'storm and stress' of that world economy, over which only the foolhardy can predict with certainty likely outcomes. Growth and recession, however, appear as necessary parts of the same process of capitalist economic development and this suggests something less than a condition of 'sustainability'. It is also the case that the world economy is a considerably different place in the year 2000 than when South Korea began its own export drive. In the 1960s international trade was booming and protectionist measures were relatively low. Today, the world market is highly unstable, fiercely competitive and increasingly protectionist (see Jenkins, 1992). Under these conditions, the real miracle will be if the world's poorest countries can grow at all. In conclusion, it can be seen that South Korea has not industrialised either through the miraculous operation of the free market or the servile qualities of its citizens. Rather, an authoritarian and interventionist state has formed an alliance with a small number of powerful companies to break into the world economy. The success of that alliance partially rested on a combination of socially repressive policies at home and unprecedented support from the world's most powerful economies abroad.

EXAMPLE 13

Workers' Accounts of the South Korean 'Miracle'

Women Textile Workers at Pangrim, Seoul
If any one industry was associated with the South Korean 'miracle' during the 1970s, it was textiles. One of the largest textile firms is Pangrim. For a long time it seemed as if Pangrim's 6,000-strong female workforce fitted the stereotypes of 'docility' and unquestioning loyalty. In 1978, the women formed a trade union and issued a public statement which showed that there is another side to this story.

'In the dark shadows of this pride and glory, we, women workers, have for too long worked too hard and experienced too much pain. Our one reason for working is to help our poor parents. We want to wear a student's uniform, but instead we have left our home town in the country and have come to the strange surroundings of Seoul to work in a factory. We came to earn money, but it has been more difficult than we thought. In our factory we are forced to work three eight hour shifts. If we live in the company dormitory we sometimes work until 1am or 2am. We do not receive weekly holidays. We work harder than animals!

'Night shift is too tiring and so our bodies are exhausted. Therefore, we take "Timing", a medicine to keep awake. Some of us have eaten too many and are now addicted to these pills. If we fall asleep, we are reprimanded, beaten and shaken. There are many examples of this. Last night a worker was beaten by the supervisor. In our eyes, this means that the company is in fact the one doing the beating. What work do we do? We make many different types of yarn and cloth. Because the machines run continuously we are so busy that we cannot have a meal break. If the machine needs fixing, we must do it immediately or suffer the consequences of a reprimand. We are ashamed to say that sometimes we cannot go to the toilet and so must use the factory floor. The machines never stop!' (Source: George Ogle, 1990, p. 82, Program Associate for [the United Methodist] Church and Society.)

Striking Car Workers and the 'Traitor' President Kim Young-sam
In January 1997, a militant strike wave erupted in South Korea. It involved some 500,000 workers in key export industries like ship-building,

electronics, car manufacture and engineering. The workers were protesting against a new 'Labour Law', which President Kim Young-sam's government passed at a secret meeting on Boxing Day. Many workers referred to him as a 'traitor' who betrayed the democracy movement. Accusations of 'corruption' levied against the President, and his son's imprisonment for such offences, inflamed popular indignation. The Labour Law freed South Korean companies to sack workers and delay the introduction of full trade union rights. Despite bloody clashes with riot police and several imprisonments, the strikers forced the government to compromise. Kim Young-sam's image as a crusader for democracy was shattered. Printed below is a letter from a South Korean car worker to British unions at the height of the strike. It gives an indication of the 'labour relations' which characterise the 'miracle'.

'I am a worker in a Hyundai car factory in South Korea. You will know about our fight against the corrupt labour law. We are calling for solidarity towards our struggle from workers in Britain. We face a very hard fight. The government tries to repress us. Police have been used against striking workers since we started action three weeks ago. Yesterday the police attacked again with tear gas. Police fired tear gas in the subway. And there was fighting in the city of Pusan.

'As I write, the police and army have surrounded one labour cultural centre and they may attack at any time to arrest the leaders of our strikes. The Handra industry committee union leader is already arrested. The government of traitor Kim Young-sam says the strikes are illegal. We are only standing up for the basic trade union rights of workers and for justice. The police and government try to witch hunt the strikers. But workers still try to fight back. Today over 80,000 people demonstrated in ten cities! We must fight together. If they seize one labour centre, a second will follow. If we can unite the workers, we will win victory.' (Source: *Socialist Worker*, letter from Hyundai worker, 18 January 1997.)

3.4

Luis Valenzuela

Mexico: The Long March of Industrialisation

OVERVIEW

Mexico is one of the few Latin American countries that can be considered industrialised.[1] Mexico achieved this status during the 1970s, but the process of industrialisation has longer historical roots which can be traced to the early nineteenth century. Economic growth accelerated during the 1930s in Mexico under an Import Substituting Industrialisation (ISI) model which shaped policy until the early 1980s. Today industrial policy continues under a specific form of Export Orientated Industrialisation. This latter model has been favoured by new economic policies (neo-liberalism) and specific trade arrangements with the USA and Canada (the North American Free Trade Agreement or NAFTA) in operation since 1994.

HISTORICAL DEVELOPMENT OF MEXICAN INDUSTRIALISATION

Industry has played an important role in the Mexican economy for decades or even centuries. As early as 1817, before its independence from Spain, industry was estimated to contribute 19 per cent of Gross Domestic Product in Mexico (Quirós, 1973, pp. 262–4). However, at the time most of this production was small-scale artisanal rather than industrial production.[2] The latter only started in the 1890s during the rule of dictator Porfirio Diaz (1876–1910). Diaz assumed the presidency after an army rebellion and ruled with an iron hand, eliminating regional factionalism, social banditry and the most blatant forms of contraband trade and state corruption. Diaz encouraged foreign investment in Mexico and export promotion and created preconditions for a process of industrialisation. Thus an impressive railroad network was created increasing mileage from 400 in 1876 to 15,000 in 1911. This plus the elimination of the interregional tariffs in 1896 created a relatively integrated national market. The success of the export economy – exports grew by a factor of eight between 1876 and 1910 – permitted the capital accumulation necessary for investment in industry. Finally this export success and the ideology of modernisation (i.e. uncritically emulating the achievements of the development of industry in the USA and Europe) among entrepreneurs, created in them the belief that the same modernisation could be applied to Mexico.

Unfortunately industrialists had little choice but to adopt capital-intensive European and American technologies instead of developing more suitable national technologies. The former were expensive and required a large scale of production for economies of scale to apply and to be profitable. Although the Mexican population was relatively large (15 million in 1910), it was mostly rural and poor, therefore the potential market for manufactures was small. As a result industries created under Diaz rule used well under 50 per cent of their installed capacity for several decades. Furthermore these industries generated few jobs and in fact a large number of skilled workers had to be 'imported' from Europe and the USA to fill the most highly skilled and technically demanding positions in most industries (Meyer and Sherman, 1991, p. 431 ff.; Haber, 1989).

The Mexican Revolution (1910–20), although it disrupted the economy and led to a decrease in industrial output and profitability (among other factors because of forced payments to different factions), did not seriously damage industrial installations, and output and profits rapidly recovered even before 1920. A more serious threat to industrialisation was posed by the Depression of the late 1920s which hit Mexico earlier but less seriously than other Latin American countries. Mexican exports went down from US$334m in 1926 to US$97m in 1932 and imports declined in roughly the same proportion. Industrial production, on the other hand, decreased less dramatically and recovered rapidly after 1932 (FitzGerald, 1984, pp. 274–5). This recovery was the outcome of two factors. On the one hand exports (mainly silver and petroleum) started to pick up after 1932. More importantly treasury minister Alberto Pani in 1932 abandoned the policy of supporting the value of the Mexican *peso* and this depreciated in real terms by 35 per cent in less than two years. In what was a common enough experience in Latin America, this increased the protection to the Mexican industry by making imports dearer and gave a push to domestic production. Furthermore, Pani began an expansionary monetary policy, that is, he increased the amount of money available in the economy by printing notes and coining silver. This fuelled consumption and lowered lending rates; both factors, of course, increased the profitability of industry.

The above policies were continued and deepened by President Lazaro Cárdenas (1934–40). He increased real (i.e. measured in constant currency) public expenditure during his period of office by 46 per cent as compared with the previous six years. The privileged sector in this programme of investment was the economy (irrigation, public works, roads) which received an increase of over 100 per cent, transforming the state into a major actor in economic activities. This was also reflected in social policy where government expenditure on welfare (health, education) increased to 21 per cent of the total (when compared to 10 per cent during the period 1923–28) (Wilkie, 1970, pp. 98–9, 128–9, 158–9). In the political arena Cárdenas cemented a nationalist/populist multi-class alliance between peasants, workers, other popular sectors and the military under the umbrella of the state party, the *Partido Revolucionario Mexicano*. The party clung to office for 60 years under the implausible name of the *Partido Revolucionario Institucional* (PRI). Although capitalists resented an extensive agrarian reform process and a threefold increase in the minimum wage, they did welcome the 'social peace' achieved under Cárdenas, as unions were under the firm control of the government. Under these conditions industrial profits increased significantly and industrial production almost doubled between 1932 and 1940 (Haber, 1989; Cárdenas, 1984). Populism and nationalism proved a potent force for industrialisation during the 1930s and 1940s and were instrumental ideologies which underpinned political institutional support for ISI policies, in Mexico and in other Latin American countries (see Section 2.1).

INDUSTRY 1940–85: THE VISIBLE HAND OF THE STATE

The Cárdenas government can be legitimately considered as one which applied Import Substituting Industrialisation (ISI). However, under Cárdenas ISI policies were more the result of a 'trial and error' learning process than conscious decisions taken by an extensive state planning apparatus. During the 1940s and the following decades, however, a policy of ISI and decided state intervention in the economy was consciously pursued, and new state agencies were created to carry out these policies. Among these Nafinsa (Nacional Financiera, the state development bank) played a key role. Although created in 1934, it was restructured in 1940 and endowed with vast financial resources in the early 1940s. Its aims were to promote industrialisation, especially the production of intermediate and capital goods, investment in infrastructure and to promote the development of a national industrial bourgeoisie. These aims were carried out by long-term loans to the private sector and by the creation of a number of parastatal firms including steel and oil. One indication of Nafinsa's impact on industry is that it owned or financed firms which 'accounted for fully 30 per cent of the entire manufacturing capital in this period [1940–50]' (Cypher, 1990, p. 53).

Significantly, a new breed of industrialists came to the fore in the early 1940s. Small and medium sized entrepreneurs not linked to foreign interests formed the National Chamber of Manufacturers (or Canacintra). Canacintra proclaimed industrial growth as the key to further Mexican development and acted as a pressure group vis-a-vis the government to promote their cause. As a result of this pressure and the inner convictions of Mexican state personnel, tariffs jumped in 1941 and, in 1944, import licensing was introduced. Both acted as an effective barrier to prevent foreign goods from competing with a wide range of Mexican manufactures.

This protectionist policy continued, in fact increased, right up to the 1980s. However, the ISI model started to show its weaknesses in the first fiscal crisis of the period in the mid-1950s. By then the stage of easy industrialisation (the replacement of imported consumer goods by Mexican manufactures) had been accomplished. At the time, and still today, Mexico remained reliant on the import of consumer durables and capital goods. This trade deficit in manufactures had to be compensated for by surpluses of non-industrial goods. This was not problematic in the 1950s and 1960s when Mexico was a net exporter of agricultural products and again in the late 1970s and when petroleum exports soared. However, serious fiscal crises occurred in 1976–77 and 1982–83. Another problem was that the production of consumer durables and capital goods required increased investment in the sector and that meant fresh capital. The solution imposed on the government was twofold. On the one hand, Foreign Direct Investment (FDI) was given red carpet treatment since the mid-1950s and it started to grow, especially in the manufacturing sector (see Table 3.4). On the other hand, the government started to borrow heavily, initially from national sources but later on from foreign banks (see Wilkie, 1970, p. 301, and Table 3.5). These two solutions were a mixed blessing for the Mexican economy. Trans National Corporation capital flows to Mexico amounted to US$179m in the 1960s, but in the period of President Luis Echeverria (1970–76), a mild reformer, they amounted to minus US$349m. 'Investor confidence' and positive flows of capital returned after an International Monetary Fund package, which among other things reduced real wages. Also in the late 1970s tax incentives were provided to those companies operating in Mexico which exported more than they imported (Gereffi and Evans, 1981, pp. 51–2; Lustig and Ros, 1987, p. 66).

The borrowing of foreign resources created even bigger problems for the Mexican economy and laid the basis for the dismantling of the ISI strategy during the 1980s. During the period of President Lopez Portillo (1976–82) the government, overconfident of the recently discovered Mexican petroleum resources, engaged in a vigorous programme of investments. Although Petroleos Mexicanos (or Pemex, a parastatal firm) produced handsome surpluses – an average of US$5bn p.a. between 1979 and 1982 – the fiscal deficit (including that generated in other parastatal firms) grew enormously averaging US$11.2bn p.a. in the same period. On top of these deficits the Mexican bourgeoisie (and senior party/state personnel) started sending large deposits to foreign banks. Estimates of this capital flight during 1981–83 vary between US$12.5bn and US$27.5bn (Buffie, 1988, p. 152). These deficits were financed by foreign loans. As lending rates jumped in late 1980 while petroleum prices slumped, the government was caught in a vicious circle, obtaining short-term loans to pay the interest on the loans borrowed previously.

THE MEXICAN ISI STRATEGY UNDONE

The vicious circle facing the Mexican economy came to a critical point when President Lopez Portillo declared in August 1982 that the government was unable to meet interest payments due in the following days. The possibility of default – given that Mexico was the world's most indebted Third World country at the time – threatened to provoke a global financial crisis, or at least of the US banks which were overexposed to Mexican lending. This news shocked the financial world into action. In the space of a weekend the IMF assembled a US$10bn 'rescue' package. For Mexico, the 1982 crisis also signalled a radical departure from the ISI model.

By the beginning of 1983 the worst of the crisis had been at least postponed. The government had signed the IMF agreement and a new government was in office. The government of President De la Madrid (1982–88) was made up of a new type of politician. Mostly economists with postgraduate studies in US universities they were more concerned with the 'health' of the macro-economy and privatisation than the well-being of the masses. This created tensions within the delicate populist balance of forces which had held the government together since Cárdenas times, most of all with the state sector of the economy. The first task of this government was to apply the stabilisation package agreed with the IMF in 1982. This was basically concerned with reducing inflation (over 100 per cent in 1982) and the deficit in the current account (the balance between imports and exports). The immediate measures applied to achieve these aims were a drastic cut in public investment, devaluation of the Mexican *peso* and a reduction of real wages by over 30 per cent.

In the following years, especially since 1985, the De la Madrid government and its successor Salinas de Gortari (1988–94) engaged in the most radical transformation of the Mexican economy since the 1930s. First, the protection offered to manufacture (and other sectors of the economy) was drastically curtailed. Output protected by import licences was reduced from 92 per cent in 1985 to 16.5 per cent in 1993, while the average tariff went down from 23.5 to 12.5 per cent in the same period (Tornell and Esquivel, 1995, Table 1). Second, the government engaged in a vigorous privatisation programme. Thus the number of parastate firms was reduced from 1,115 in 1982 to 218 in January 1999, and the process still continues.[3] An indication of the scale of these sales is that during the period 1988–97 the state sold 25 parastatals for a total of US$25.27bn (*The Economist*, 1997, p. 12). Third, a policy of export promotion was implemented. From the mid-1980s massive state resources were allocated to 'high exporting firms', a selected group of 100 firms (11 parastatal, 27 transnational and 62 private Mexican companies) providing them with up to 50 per cent of working capital available to the state. Further, the devaluation of the *peso* and decline in real wages increased the exporting capacity of the Mexican economy (Cypher, 1990, p. 184). Finally, FDI was stimulated by more favourable regulations, debt equity swaps and the privatisation thrust initiated in the mid-1980s. In this strategy the Mexican government was heavily supported by the Word Bank which lent Mexico US$5.7bn in 1986–88 or nearly 10 per cent of the total loans made by the Bank during that period.

As can be seen in Table 3.6, the results of these policies had been, to put it mildly, more than disappointing, especially if compared with the period 1940–80. GDP growth for the years 1985–95 had been 1.7 per cent p.a. and in per capita terms, negative, while manufacturing growth had been a moderate 2.7 per cent p.a., just above the population growth. In fact, as we will argue below, industrial growth would have been negative if the *maquila* programme had not been in operation.

MANUFACTURING GROWTH IN THE NORTHERN BORDER: THE *MAQUILAS*

In 1965 the Mexican government started a Border Industrialisation (or *maquila*) Programme initially designed to absorb the 'idle hands' left by the termination of the *bracero* (migrant labour) programme between the US and Mexican governments. Through the *maquila* programme US (and other foreign) firms were able to import into Northern Mexico raw materials, components, machinery, etc., provided that all their production was exported. Apart from the 'natural' advantages of the area such as unlimited supplies of cheap labour (mostly females) and its proximity to the USA, foreign companies found there a cooperative labour structure and a friendly government reception. The government for instance waived in the border its restrictions on foreign ownership allowing in most sectors a 100 per cent foreign ownership. Although initially limited to the 20 km lying south of the Mexican–US border, the scheme was extended in 1972 to Mexico as a whole, excluding only the three largest cities (Mexico, Guadalajara and Monterrey). Despite this, as late as 1993, the bulk of the labour force in the *maquilas* was still located in the border region (90 per cent), especially in Ciudad Juarez (24.4 per cent), Tijuana (14.2 per cent) and Matamoros (7 per cent) (Browne, 1994, p. 29, 49; Mercado, 1995, pp. 197–200).

As can be seen in Table 3.7, the number of firms, workers and value added generated in the *maquilas* has grown dramatically since the 1960s. Employment increased by a factor of 272 between 1967 and 1999 despite a minor decrease during the 1982 crisis. After that and due to the successive devaluations of the Mexican *peso* and a consequent decreasing wage bill for *maquila* owners, employment has grown vigorously until today.[4] It can be argued that in a country of 95 million people, 1 million jobs in the *maquiladoras* is little more than a drop in the ocean. At the same time they make up 20 per cent of total manufacturing employment. The *maquiladoras* are significant employers of women. In 1985 70 per cent and in 1999, significantly less (56 per cent) of the labour force were women (see Table 3.8). The pay and conditions for women workers, as well as the physical environment in the Mexican border towns in which over 6 million people live and work, are generally far inferior when compared to those in the USA (see Example 14).

The impact of the *maquilas* as a generator of foreign currency and therefore part of the solution to the successive Mexican balance of payment crises is clearer. In 1992 the *maquilas* single-handedly contributed 9.3 per cent of the total foreign exchange earned in Mexican exports (US$46bn). From the point of view of industrial policy, the areas in which the *maquilas* have shown the greatest weaknesses are in their contribution to a process of sustainable and value-adding industrialisation. This involves at least two aspects. First, the linkages of the *maquilas* to the rest of the Mexican economy and second, their capacity to act as agencies for technology transfer to the host country.

Linkages
Economic linkages are of two types. Backward linkages are the share of inputs (raw materials, components, services) bought in the Mexican economy thus stimulating its production. In this respect the impact of the *maquilas* has been minimal. In 1990–91 the total amount of inputs acquired by *maquilas* within Mexico (but outside the *maquila* sector) amounted to 1.8 per cent of the total, a small improvement on the 1.7 per cent registered in 1980. Moreover most of these inputs consist of services and raw materials and therefore its impact on Mexican industry is negligible. Forward linkages (*maquilas'* sales to intermediate goods industries) were initially not allowed by the regulation of the programme. However, in the 1980s they were allowed to sell to other *maquilas* and to sell in the Mexican market provided that they were buying inputs in the Mexican economy (Sklair, 1988, pp. 289, 294; Wilson, 1992, pp. 67, 120ff.). The creation of the North American Free Trade Agreement (NAFTA) seems to have created a greater stimulus for both forward and backward linkages. In relation to the former, from 1994 *maquilas* can sell 50 per cent of their output in Mexico, increasing that percentage by five points each year. On the other hand as of 2001 *maquilas* will not be able to import inputs duty free as is the case today, and that is said to have prompted *maquilas* to encourage their suppliers from abroad to move to Mexico and to 'buy Mexican'. The signs have not been encouraging.[5] Among reasons for the lack of interest of suppliers to 'buy Mexican', studies indicate lack of local supply, high costs, poor quality and delays in delivery (Mercado, 1995, pp. 194, 206–7).

Technology transfer
Technical processes in the *maquilas* have been improved since the early days of the *Maquila* Industry Decree in 1983. One indication of this progress is the value added per employee which has increased from US$5,870 in 1983 to US$7,794 in 1989. This has gone hand in hand with falling real wages, which are a large component of costs in the labour-intensive *maquilas*. Another indication of technological development in the *maquilas* is the diffusion in them of modern machinery and complex production processes (e.g. 'just in time production' and total production management), which are far less common in the rest of Mexico (Browne, 1994, pp. 31–2; Mercado,

1995, pp. 201–2; Shaiken, 1994; Carrillo, 1995). One realisation which was reached much earlier in studies of international outward processing in sectors such as garments, is that suppliers and TNCs have a material interest in the transfer technology, or at least ensuring that their contractors have the necessary level of technology to meet socially acceptable levels of quality in production. Typically this is associated with assembly-line and therefore, relatively standardised production.

CONCLUSIONS

The Mexican industry has changed dramatically in the last few decades. From a strategy emphasising protectionism and production for the home market, the Mexican government has moved to a clear export orientated model of industrialisation, which privileges FDI, production for foreign markets and lack of protection for the domestic industry (with a few exceptions such as the car industry). This change of gear was virtually forced on the government by the financial difficulties experienced by Mexico in the early 1980s although the export strategy was implicit much earlier in the development of the *maquilas* during the 1960s and 1970s. The latter have proved to mitigate unemployment and improve the trade balance but have so far contributed little to the process of sustainable industrialisation (and employment) or social development in the border region, due to the lack of linkages with the local economy and existing social reality.

EXAMPLE 14

'Maria Starves as Mexico Border Business Booms'

Dressed in one of the brightly flowered dresses beloved of Mexican women, Maria del Rosario Garcia lies listlessly on a sofa in the makeshift cardboard shack her friends have built around her. She has not eaten solid food for 19 days. Maria, a 42 year single mother, was sacked two days before she completed 20 years service entitling her to a payment of several million pesos. 'Going on hunger strike is the only way I can get the money to feed my children', she said, gesturing feebly to Maria, eight, and two year old Juan, playing by her feet. 'If I don't get compensation they will starve'. Maria's flimsy shack stands a few yards from the entrance of her former employers in the sprawling Mexican border town of Matamoros. The company, Kemet, a US electronics component manufacturer, paid her $60 dollars a week – a tenth of the wages paid to factory workers across the Rio Grande in Texas.

Encouraged by opponents of NAFTA, Maria has taken a stand against a *maquiladora*, one of 2,100 twin companies of US corporations with an economic stranglehold on the 1,250-mile US–Mexico border. In the past decade the number of *maquiladoras* has risen from 500 to 2,100 as household names such as GM and toy makers Fisher King have taken advantage of cheap Mexican labour and lax environmental controls. They employ half a million workers, mostly young women, and now provide Mexico's second biggest source of foreign exchange. But the people of Matamoros are paying a heavy price for jobs. Here, a mile across from the Texas city of Brownsville, raw human sewage runs into two man-made canals of thick industrial effluence known as the 'black rivers' that bisect the town. The heavy air that hangs over the shanty town or *colonias* which houses 250,000 people, tastes by turns acrid and sickly sweet. Water samples have found solvent levels 6,000 times higher than the US health standards.

Several *maquiladoras*, alarmed at bad publicity, have begun to establish water treatment plants. President Bill Clinton has pledged that public and private corporations will find $8 billion to clean up the border region and that this will be a key remit for NAFTA. (Source: Polly Ghazi, *Observer*, 14 November 1993.)

3.5

Prodromos Panayiotopoulos

China: Breaking the Iron Rice Bowl

OVERVIEW

China was one of the world's grandest ancient civilisations. Paper, gunpowder, items which were closely linked to Western industrialisation, were invented in China. In Imperial China the mandate of governance, passed from one ruler to another, was deemed to have arrived from Heaven. Increasingly a mandate with as much authority appeared in China in the form of European expansion. The last dynasty – the Ching (1644–1911) – came under intense pressure from European and Japanese expansion and was forced to open up the Chinese economy. Parts of China came under the control of European chartered companies. Resentment by the Chinese people against the humiliation of European rule led to the Boxer Rebellion in 1911. The Nationalist movement led by Sun Yat Sen came to power in 1912 and attempted to introduce liberal political and economic reforms in China and to re-establish relations with the foreign powers on a more equitable basis. The activities of pro-European warlords, the annexation by Japan of Manchuria (1937–45) and the protracted Civil War between the Nationalists and Communists (1927–49) led to a defeat for attempts to reform China during the inter-war period. The Communist Party of China came to power in 1949.

THE COMMUNIST PARTY OF CHINA AND INDUSTRIALISATION

The industrialisation and history of modern China is inextricably linked with the history of the Communist Party of China (CPC). The CPC was formed in Shanghai in 1921 and gained support amongst urban workers and intellectuals. In 1927 a workers' uprising in Shanghai was suppressed by the Nationalists and the CPC was decimated, losing its base amongst the emergent urban working class. In order to survive, the CPC under the new leadership of Mao Zedong established rural bases deep in the countryside. The Red Army harassed by the Nationalists was forced to undertake the Long March (1934–36) and was pushed even further into the interior. Over 50,000 died on the march which covered over 5,000 miles. This was a heroic period for the CPC and all future leaders of China traced their origins to this formative experience. The Long March allowed the Red Army (subsequently the People's Liberation Army) to regroup, to regain the initiative and to successfully mobilise the peasantry against the Nationalists and big landlords. The Communists came to power in 1949 and the Peoples' Republic of China was proclaimed.

China under Mao Zedong initially attempted to follow the Soviet model of industrialisation through the introduction of centralised planning and the concentration of resources in heavy industry. The First Five-Year Plan (1953–58) allocated 55 per cent of all investment to heavy industry. It proved difficult to imitate the Soviet model, however. Per capita income in China was four times less than that of Russia in 1928, when Russia itself initiated its first five-year plan (Harris, 1978). This meant that China had to extract an even greater surplus from agriculture (mainly in the form of cheap food) to pay for industrialisation. This would have called into question the willingness by the peasantry to continue to produce under such conditions and the CPC abandoned the policy. An alternative source could have been international borrowing. This avenue was closed, however, due to the embargo on capital investment in China imposed by the USA in 1949 and which lasted until the early 1970s.

The Great Leap Forward and Endogenous Industrialisation

The failure of the 1953–58 Plan to imitate the Soviet industrialisation model was coupled with an unwillingness by the Soviet Union to provide China with the latest technology and this laid the basis for Mao's growing rift with Moscow. This and the US boycott forced China into 'self-reliance'. Mao pre-empted the Second Five-Year Plan and launched in 1958–59 the Great Leap Forward. This policy aimed to mobilise China's vast human resources into a village-based industrialisation drive. Thousands of steel foundries were set up throughout the countryside and millions of peasants diverted from grain production. The strengthening of collective farms (People's Communes) was meant to increase labour productivity in agriculture and to release 'surplus' labour. The Great Leap Forward proved to be an unmitigated disaster. The Planners lied about meeting quotas and Mao set even more unreasonable targets. The following anecdote from Liu Binyan (leading Chinese dissident) was exemplary of the whole process.

One day, Bo Yibo was swimming with Mao. Mao asked him what the production of iron and steel would be for the next year. Instead of replying, Bo Yibo told Mao that he was going to do a turn in the water; Mao misunderstood him and thought he had said 'double'. A little later, at a Party meeting, Bo Yibo heard Mao announce that the national production of iron and steel would 'double' the next year.[1]

During the Great Leap Forward modern steel mills were deprived of iron ore and coal while the quality of the steel produced in the village furnaces was too poor to use. The rate of growth in Gross Domestic Product collapsed, from 20 per cent in 1956 to –30 per cent by 1960. The impact on agriculture was catastrophic. Rural labour was diverted into frenzied and fruitless efforts. Natural disasters compounded the problem and China faced famine. An estimated 30 to 50 million people died as a result of the biggest man-made famine in the twentieth century. Mao was forced to retreat and in 1959 stepped down as head of state.

The Great Proletarian Cultural Revolution

On 13 June 1966 exams were cancelled in China as the educational system became the battleground for a factional fight between Mao and the so-called revisionists for control of the CPC. The latter wanted to end China's isolation and to avoid a repetition of the Great Leap Forward experience. They gradually replaced collective farms with individual landholding and economic incentives like piece-work and greater managerial control in state enterprises. These changes were denounced by Mao as 'taking the road back to capitalism'. Mao counter-attacked to regain his position in the Party and mobilised masses of students into Red Guard units and used them to isolate, humiliate and break the influence of the revisionist group inside the Party. Mao called this campaign the Great Proletarian Cultural Revolution.

The Cultural Revolution consisted of mass meetings, show trials, street processions and street-fighting, as regular features of life. Homes were ransacked for proof of 'bourgeois' ideology. The experience resulted in severe economic dislocation as hundreds of thousands of young Red Guards were dispersed by Mao all over China to spread the Cultural Revolution. Having accomplished the task of bringing Mao back to power the Red Guards were then suppressed by Mao. The army took control of the universities, factories and villages. Many of the young people mobilised were killed and more were imprisoned in the *laogai* penal system. Millions remained exiled in villages far from their homes, for over a decade. Graphic descriptions of this experience can be found in Jung Chang's novel *Wild Swans*, and Chen Kaige's film *King of the Children*.

ECONOMIC REFORM AND PRODUCTION FOR EXPORT

China was shaken by the experiences of the Cultural Revolution and the Great Leap Forward. The major aims of policy in the early 1970s were for stability at home and in international relations and for increased levels of production. The CPC under Mao began to praise private landholding in the countryside. Many of the revisionists were reinstated. In 1971, President Richard Nixon visited China, breaking the US boycott of China which had lasted since 1949.

With Mao Zedong's death in 1976, Deng Xiaoping took power in 1978 following a two-year power struggle inside the CPC. Deng had suffered in the Cultural Revolution at the hands of the Red Guards and his eldest son was crippled by them, when in an attempt to escape a Red Guard beating he fell off a second-floor building and lay in the street for three days. No one had the courage to move him. The only official position held by Deng until his death in 1997 at the age of 92 was that of Honorary Chairman of the Chinese Bridge Association. Yet, Deng Xiaoping oversaw an unprecedented economic boom and was to have a profound influence on China's economic direction. Exports as a percentage of GDP increased from 7 per cent in 1982 to 21 per cent by 1995. Foreign Direct Investment which in 1982 was negligible had increased to $35bn by 1995. In 1988 *The Economist* named Deng Xiaoping as its 'Man of the Year'.

Deng represented elements of change and continuity in industrialisation policy in post-Mao China. The major change appeared in the move away from Maoist self-reliance and towards greater integration with the global economy through the promotion of rapid industrialisation in manufacturing sectors with high export capability. The key continuity appeared in the central role maintained by the CPC in all areas of economy and society. Deng Xiaoping himself was an unlikely figure to pick up the mantle of reform abandoned in China during the inter-war period. He was Mao's right-hand man in many Party purges and a leading member of the CPC from the Long March onwards. Deng was politically responsible for the Beijing Massacre (3–4 June 1989) during which the People's Liberation Army crushed the student pro-democracy occupation of Tiananmen Square. The Deng years saw increased internal debate in the CPC about the direction of industrialisation and wider economic policy. One key area of debate was how to overcome inequalities between different regions in China. A number of contradictory policies were applied in China since 1949 (see below).

Industrialisation and the regions: policy options

- The 'backward' areas are given preferential treatment to assist them to 'catch up' (regional balance).
- The most developed areas are encouraged to 'get rich first' (in the hope that growth in some areas will trickle sideways to other regions and downwards towards the poor).
- The adoption of an integrated system of production which encourages specialisation or 'strong points' of each region (the application of comparative advantage). (Gittings, 1997, p. 14)

During the 1950s and 1960s when China's economic policy consisted of self-reliance this tended to favour the 'backward' regions. In the 1980s and 1990s when policy encouraged integration into the global economy by making use of comparative advantage on a world scale, this tended to favour the 'advanced' mainly coastal regions of China. Material from the World Bank shows that the east and south coastal areas with a combined population of 282 million in 1992, enjoyed per capita income levels twice those of the 531 million people living in the southern and central hinterland. The World Bank indicates that regional inequalities have increased since 1985 (World Bank, 1997a). Other studies suggest that regional inequality was reduced after the economic reforms introduced by Deng in 1978, but has accelerated since the early 1990s (Jian et al., 1996). What is clear is that Deng Xiaoping adopted a more pragmatic approach both in dealing with regional disparities and in the preference of market mechanisms over centralised planning. This is illustrated by some of the 'sayings' of Deng, which were in effect compressed statements of policy.

Sayings by Deng

- 'It doesn't matter if a cat is black or white so long as it catches mice.'
- 'We should let some people get rich first, both in the countryside and in the urban areas. To get rich by hard work is glorious.'

Shenzhen Special Economic Zone: Guangdong Province

The Shenzhen Special Economic Zone (SEZ) exemplified the 'get rich first' approach which tended to favour the coastal regions of China. Shenzhen SEZ in Guangdong province adjoins Hong Kong and was established in 1980 as one of the earliest initiatives in production for export, often in the form of re-exports to Hong Kong. Some 30,000 enterprises have been established by Hong Kong industrialists in Guangdong employing an estimated 3 million workers (Gittings, 1997, p. 253). Many workers are recent rural to urban migrants. In Shenzhen, migrant labour accounted for at least 50 per cent of the city's total labour force in the mid-1990s.[2]

Guangdong province during the 1980s and early 1990s had the highest rate of foreign investment and per capita income in China and was the model applied by the government for China's integration into the world economy. By the early 1990s one-third of households in Guangdong owned a TV, a fridge and a washing machine (Gittings, 1997, p. 254). During 1997 the capital city of Guangzhou handled a sixth of China's imports and exports and per capita income stood at $2,333.[3] The purpose of Guangdong province and in particular Shenzhen SEZ was confirmed by Deng Xiaoping on a visit in 1992 as, 'to catch up with Asia's four little dragons [South Korea, Taiwan, Hong Kong, Singapore] in 20 years or even sooner' (Gittings, 1997, p. 232). Shanghai and other SEZs were urged to imitate Shenzhen's example. The visit by Deng (referred to as 'the Southern Expedition') was a very significant watershed in Chinese policy. From this point onwards the CPC came to accept, particularly in the light of the collapse of communism in Eastern European and the Soviet Union, that there was an inescapable general trend in the world economy in favour of the market mechanism and away from centralised planning.

The rapid growth of Shanghai (China's second largest city) was emblematic of the liberalisation which accelerated following the Southern Expedition in 1992. From 1992 to 1997 Shanghai's GDP grew by an annual rate of 14 per cent. Official estimates calculate that of Shanghai's 13 million people in 1997, 3 million were migrant workers.[4] The city accounts for 1 per cent of China's population, but 18 per cent of China's GDP and more than 20 per cent of total foreign investment. A vast building programme of roads, suspension bridges, high-rise retail and office blocks and housing is being undertaken. According to one estimate, the rush of construction projects brought one-fifth of the world's high-rise cranes to Shanghai.[5] Much of this was put on hold after the 1997 Asian crisis.

Conditions for workers in the cities and SEZs producing for export are at a very low level. Little value is attached to Health and Safety at work: in the city of Dongguan (in Guangdong province) for example, at least 60 workers were killed and 70 others injured when fire swept through a raincoat factory. The victims were trapped 'because exits were blocked by stockpiled goods'. This was the same reason given for the death of another 80 mainly women workers employed in a toy factory in Guangdong. These kinds of accidents have become common. In Shenzhen itself, industrial accidents resulting in death increased by over 170 per cent during the early 1990s (Gittings, 1997, pp. 256–7). Conditions in the *laogai* system are much worse (see Example 15).

'BREAKING THE IRON RICE BOWL'

The Chinese economy is now more open to world trade and its exports have to compete in global markets. The subjection of China's factories to global competition has made exporters far more sensitive to price. The wage bill of state-owned enterprises in particular has come under scrutiny and large-scale cost-cutting and redundancies have taken place and more are planned. China's initial comparative advantage in exports appeared in low wage, labour-intensive industries (which require lots of workers) and within which the wage bill is higher than more capital-intensive industries. The wage bill in China is even higher in the state-owned enterprises because they are obliged to provide workers and their families with a comprehensive welfare package of subsidised housing, education, health and pensions. Whilst the wage bill makes up 56 per cent of employee costs, the remaining 34 per cent consists of social costs with housing single-handedly accounting for 21 per cent of total costs (World Bank, 1995, pp. 28–9). This 'iron rice bowl' came under threat from the reforms introduced by Deng to make enterprises economically viable (self-financing) which envisaged the acceleration of job losses in the state sector and consequent losses of entitlement to benefits.

The Wuhan Iron and Steel company, for example, reduced the number of workers directly employed from 120,000 in 1992 to 70,000 by 1994. Many of the 50,000 'surplus' workers were relocated to other factories or were 'stood down' (*xia gang*) at reduced rates of pay and instructed not to report to work.[6] In 1994, Shanghai recorded 150,000 unemployed and 318,000 workers 'stood down'. The World Bank estimates that state enterprises had on their books about 15 million redundant workers in 1996 (World Bank, 1997a). Urban open unemployment in China during the mid-1990s was estimated at 15–17 per cent (Gittings, 1997, pp. 271–2).

State-owned enterprises have seen their contribution to industrial production fall dramatically since the introduction of economic reforms. Between 1978 and 1994 their contribution (in value terms) declined from 77.5 per cent to 34.0 per cent of total value added to the economy. The sharpest decline occurred after 1992. Enterprises owned by individuals doubled their contribution to industrial output since 1992 (to 11.5 per cent). 'Collective' enterprises mushroomed to represent by 1994 40.0 per cent of value added (see Table 3.9). Collective enterprises consist of Township and Village Enterprises (TVEs) owned by the community government representing the population. Day-to-day direction is given to managers through a 'management responsibility contract' but TVEs are typically supervised by local government officers who are frequently Party members. This has given immense scope for self-accumulation to Party entrepreneurs. Whilst TVEs have been offered as a way of transforming state-owned enterprises, there are question marks over their durability (see Byrd and Gelb, 1990).

FUTURE PROSPECTS

Future prospects in China are sensitively tied to the livelihoods made in the state-owned enterprises. The World Bank has called for sweeping privatisation and has argued that where small and medium enterprises predominate the government should completely withdraw as a matter of urgency (World Bank, 1997b). The Chinese government has responded by drawing up rules to facilitate mergers, bankruptcies and privatisation, as well as joint stock companies in which foreign investors can hold majority shares.[7] This trend was confirmed at the 15th Party Congress held in September 1997, which proposed to cut state losses in a timeframe of three years. The policies of economic reform were seen as 'irreversible' by the post-Deng Party leadership. The acceleration of redundancies and 'breaking the iron rice bowl' by allowing the state enterprises to go bankrupt could bring heavy social costs to China. This poses problems over legitimacy for the rulers of China. As John Gittings writes,

It was this 'iron rice bowl' which usually managed to secure at least the passive loyalty [of workers] if not their enthusiasm. It is this same bowl which the industrial reforms of the mid-1980s onwards have explicitly sought to crack. The result was the appearance in Tiananmen Square in May 1989 of the first organised independent workers movement. Many believe it was this phenomenon, so threatening to the Party leadership in the light of East European experience [such as the Solidarity trade union movement in Poland] which led to the armed suppression of the student democracy movement. (Gittings, 1997, pp. 271–2)

Future prospects in China have been influenced by the 1997 Asian crisis in one major way. The main conclusion drawn during the aftermath of the crisis was for the need to continue to exercise significant controls on the economy. Given the instability associated with collapsing exchange rates during the crisis, China has indicated that it will maintain fixed exchange rates and impose restrictions in the equity market (frequently in the guise of 'anti-corruption' drives). In this there is a significant irony. The eventual stabilisation of the Asian currencies brokered by the USA, the IMF and World Bank, rested on the understanding that China would not devalue its currency, since this could have led to another bout of exchange rate instability, further devaluations in the region and the resurgence of crisis.[8] In this respect, the US government and the global institutions owe a tremendous political debt to the Central Committee of the Chinese Communist Party.

Future prospects for China also include the negotiation of full membership of the World Trade Organisation (WTO). It is surprising, perhaps, that the world's most populous nation accounting for about 6.5 per cent of world merchandise trade (including Hong Kong) was not a member of the WTO until November 1999, even more surprising given that during 1996 China received 40 per cent of all Foreign Direct Investment in the developing countries (World Bank, 1997a), and is estimated by the year 2020 to be the world's second largest trading nation after the USA (World Bank, 1997c). China became the world's largest producer of crude steel in 1996.[9] China's application had been outstanding for 13 years as the USA put pressure on China to accept detailed agreements on the removal of tariffs, quotas, subsidies and other measures used to protect domestic (mainly state-owned) industries. This is an area in which the USA exercised strategic pressure, given that it is China's largest export market and accounts for most of China's large trade surplus ($38bn in 1995) due to China's Most Favoured Nation status. This has been a major factor in bringing China's foreign exchange reserves to an estimated $100bn by the end of 1996, placing it ahead of Germany.[10]

There are images which parallel the experiences of the Ching Dynasty in the dramatic manner by which – after 13 years of protracted negotiations – China joined the WTO. During negotiations in November 1999, talks were broken off by the US and negotiators had already packed their bags and were on their way to the airport when the talks were extended by an unscheduled fifth day, following the personal intervention of Chinese Premier Zhu Rongi.

On the fifth day the USA and China reached agreement paving the way to China's accession to the WTO. The agreement envisages a reduction in the average tariff level from 22.1 per cent to 17 per cent. On cars China has agreed to cut tariffs from 100 per cent to 25 per cent. On agriculture products tariffs were to be reduced to 14.5 per cent. In textiles it is envisaged that the USA will continue using bilateral quotas and anti-surge measures until the year 2009, and that monitoring against 'dumping' will continue for 15 years. The agreement also gives more freedom for foreign banks, the elimination of export subsidies, and has made special provision for US investment in Chinese Internet providers. In telecommunications China accepted 50 per cent foreign investment. This followed considerable debate inside the CCP, given the close links between telecommunications and China's defence capabilities. Major concessions were made by China in the oil and gas industry, which could increase the country's dependence on imported petroleum products.[11] This will also expose for the first time vanguard state-owned industries and the hundreds of thousands of workers employed by them, such as China National Petroleum Corporation (CNPC), China Petrochemical Corporation (Sinopec) and China National Offshore Oil Corporation (CNOOC), to competition with the Trans National Corporations.

CONCLUSIONS

Chinese state-directed industrialisation finds parallel experiences in the global experience, as do many of the problems encountered in its efforts: uneven development between and within regions, urban and rural households, state- and privately-owned enterprises, migrant workers and citizens, are structural characteristics of China's industrialisation and glob-alisation. A particular factor in the direction of industrialisation in modern China remains the critical influence of the Communist Party of China. During different historical periods the Party-state played a pivotal role in the making of policy and the direction of economic development in China. It is this continuity which presently guides China's attempts to complete two transitions at the same time – from a command to a market economy and from a rural to urban society. This has no other historical precedent.

EXAMPLE 15

Harry Wu: Working in the *Laogai* Penal System

Harry Wu was born in 1938 to a well-to-do family in Shanghai. This placed him under suspicion following the Communist victory in 1949. During the 'Let a Hundred Flowers Bloom' period, in which dissidents were encouraged to speak their minds, Harry then a 17-year-old student criticised the Russian invasion of Hungary – which was supported by the CPC. This resulted in him being branded as a 'counter-revolutionary rightist' and on 27 April 1960,

Public Security officers unexpectedly walked into Harry's classroom and announced that he was charged with a number of crimes, including stealing money. This was the beginning of 19 years of forced labour inside the *laogai* system (Wu, 1997, p. 54). Following his release and naturalisation in the USA, Harry Wu returned several times to China pretending to be a businessman, researching and film-making on prison labour conditions. During one such time Harry was arrested and released following the personal intervention of President Clinton. This took place while China was successfully renegotiating with the USA its Most Favoured Nation (MFN) status giving China preferential access to the lucrative US market.

The *laogai* system consists of forced prison labour in camps strategically situated all over China where millions of prisoners produce goods for Chinese industry and the export market. The *laogai* system consists of *laogai* itself (reform through labour), *laojiao* (re-education through labour) and *jiuye* (forced labour placement). It is difficult to estimate how much of China's economy is produced by prisoners. Beijing produced a special White Paper on labour camps in 1992, which said that 0.08 per cent of China's overall output came from prisons. According to Harry Wu it is more instructive to look at the numbers of people in the labour camps. The Chinese government has admitted that 10 million people have been sent to the camps since the Communist Party came to power in 1949 and that in 1995 there were 1.2 million workers in 685 camps. Harry Wu and other dissidents estimate that more than 50 million people have been sent to the *laogai* since 1949, and have current records on 1,155 camps and between 6 and 8 million prisoners, of whom perhaps 10 per cent are political prisoners (Wu, 1997, pp. 12–14).

Prison labour has been put to use in production for export. The difference under Deng Xiaoping was that while the prisoners continued with traditional areas of forced labour such as reclaiming wasteland, constructing roads, opening up mines, building dams, and undertaking agricultural projects (such as the growing of tea, cotton and grains), 'they also began to manufacture electronic, mechanical, and chemical products, for the export market' (Wu, 1997, pp. 81–2). Market reform was also introduced in the management of prison labour itself.

> Deng made every camp become an individual financial centre, just like a corporation or a factory. The operators had to pay for the uniforms, salary, benefits and education of their police and skilled workers. If, however, they covered their expenses, their workers received more benefits. The old-fashioned warden was now a production manager. (Wu, 1997, p. 140)

According to Harry Wu, China's rulers change the names of their prisons to make them sound like factories. The prison factories and prison farms have double addresses, double names, but Western businessmen who visit them never ask about the men and women in the blue shirts hunched over the assembly lines. Most of the buildings look normal, 'except for the watchtowers' (Wu, 1997, p. 117). Prisoners break rocks in the day and make artificial flowers for discount stores in America in the evening with 'trade marks in English, the prices in US dollars'. The following export products were amongst those identified by Wu as having been produced by prison labour: steel pipes, leather, garments, textiles, machinery, rubber accelerators, wine, rubber boots, perfume, hand tools, electric generators. 'China is selling kidneys and corneas to wealthy countries' (Wu, 1997, pp. 14–16).

Section 4

Commodity Studies

Introduction

Prodromos Panayiotopoulos

The purpose of this section is to illustrate dimensions of industrialisation and globalisation which can best be understood in commodity terms. Many of the poor developing countries show a high level of dependence on a limited range of primary commodity exports and as we noted previously in Sections 1 and 2 this often appears as a significant contributory factor to their poverty. In part, this represents a continuation of cash crop production set in motion by the impact of colonialism. It is also influenced by current country policies whether from government or the international agencies. The promotion of cash crops to increase export earnings is a key component of World Bank Structural Adjustment and IMF Stabilisation policies. Much of the experience of the Newly Independent Countries in the Third World consisted of attempts to diversify away from a primary commodity dependency and to industrialise. There are many commodities which influence the way national economies operate and the way people make a living in both historical and contemporary terms.

In this section we look closely at the role of copper and the way this cemented relationships of interdependence between Chilean miners and British smelters during the nineteenth century. We examine the role of tourism in the economic (and social) 'opening-up' of Spain, which itself in the 1950s was not that far removed from many of today's Third World lower-middle income economies. We also look at the global textile industry, both in respect of the strong protectionism which characterises the sector and in the significance of gender in structuring the pattern of employment within the industry. Whilst the choice of sectoral material is subjective, copper mining, tourism and the textile industry account for a significant chunk of non-agricultural employment. These industries employ millions of workers world-wide. Tourism also appears as a major source of foreign exchange earnings for a small number of Third World island states and coastal locations. Frequently tourism has been feverishly promoted for this purpose by many developing country governments.

The textile and garment industry accounts for the single largest source of manufacturing employment in many Third World countries and provides useful insights into how the 'global manufacturing system' operates. Concerns that 'sweatshops' and Third World production for export are linked, has informed the development in the USA of a mass student-based movement which is campaigning for labour rights and an end to sweatshops. The students have gathered wide community support. Many of the sweatshops produce garments for the High Street and this has opened them up to the possibility of consumer boycott. Sweatshops are by no means the property of the Third World: during the late nineteenth century they haunted the lives of immigrants in places like the East-End of London and the Bronx in New York and today similar experiences can be found in the major cities of Europe and the USA (see Section 2.4). These commodity case studies offer concrete sectoral manifestation of industries, which in various ways appear as the most prone to 'globalisation'.

4.1

Luis Valenzuela

Copper: Chilean Miners – British Smelters in the Mid-Nineteenth Century

OVERVIEW

Copper has played a central role in the globalisation of the Chilean economy from the early nineteenth century up until today. From 1844 (when reliable statistics for Chilean copper production began) to 1879 copper contributed 42.3 per cent of total Chilean exports, while in the last 30 years or so this proportion has increased to around 50 per cent. From the perspective of world trade, Chile has been among the major mine copper producers of the world. It was the largest producer during the late nineteenth century and again since 1990 (see Tables 4.1 and 4.2). Despite this leadership in mine copper production, Chile like other copper producers in the developing world such as Zambia and Peru, has two handicaps vis-a-vis the developed countries. First, there is a low level of processing, that is the transformation of copper ore or concentrates into refined copper ready for manufacturing (the production of wire, sheets, bolts, etc.). As can be seen in Table 4.1 Chile produces 22.2 per cent of the world's mine copper but refines only 11.1 per cent. This contrasts with Japan, with an insignificant production of mine copper (0.1 per cent) but a production of refined copper almost as large as Chile's. This situation is even worse in relation to consumption, that is the use of copper in the country to satisfy the needs of agriculture, industry or services. Here Chile's participation is minimal (0.6 per cent) and the indus-trialised countries' overwhelming (well over half the world's consumption). The case study looks at the emergence of the copper smelting industry in Chile in the mid-nineteenth century as an example of early specialisation and globalisation. One illustration of the evolving global division of labour was in the links established between Chile and South Wales. During the period analysed British smelters accounted for most of the world production of copper. The industry was centred in the South Wales Swansea Lower Valley which had access to both good dock facilities and abundant supplies of high grade anthracite coal. These smelters were the main purchasers of Chilean copper and, on the other hand, Chile provided the largest share of copper ore to be smelted in Britain.

EXPANSION OF THE CHILEAN COPPER INDUSTRY

Although copper was known, wrought and used by the indigenous
population of Chile some 2,000 years before the arrival of the Spaniards in
1541, copper did not acquire economic importance in Chile until the end of
the Colonial period (1541–1818). In the last decades of the eighteenth
century Chile started to produce copper in quantities above 1,000 tonnes
per annum. This was sufficient to satisfy the limited internal demand
(ornamental uses, domestic utensils, bells, etc.) and exports to Spain and
other Spanish colonies where it was used for purposes such as for sheeting
ships, the fabrication of cannons, pans for the processing of sugar, etc.
(CODELCO, 1975, pp. 5–17).

The process of independence from Spain (1810–18) and the ensuing
struggle among the different political factions was not conducive to economic
growth and copper production stagnated during the 1810s and 1820s.
However, from the late 1820s onwards several developments permitted a
tremendous increase in copper production: growing demand for copper in
the North Atlantic markets, especially in Great Britain; the introduction of
reverberatory furnaces which permitted the processing of copper sulphide
previously discarded as useless by Chilean miners; and legal deregulation
which allowed the export of copper ore (as opposed to copper bars whose
export was allowed).[1]

Growing Demand in the North Atlantic Market

In 1828 a change in the import duties in Britain permitted a dramatic growth
of imports of foreign copper ore into this country. Thus before 1828 imports
of copper ore into Britain never reached 1,000 tons per annum. By 1844
they reached 58,405 tons to decrease in the following ten years for reasons
which we will analyse below. Of the British imports for the period 1831–44,
31 per cent of the copper ore came from Chile and most of the rest (52 per
cent) from Cuba. This demand stimulated production in Chile. This increase
had at least one handicap: most of the increase in copper production was
exported as raw ore rather than smelted copper. This meant that the Chilean
economy did not reap the full benefits of these increases in production as the
price paid for the fine copper contained in the ore was significantly smaller
than that paid for the fine copper contained in copper bars.[2] Furthermore,
Chile was not affected by the beneficial multiplying effect of industrialisation
on the rest of the economy (i.e. increase in the demand of inputs such as coal,
firebricks, skilled labour, etc.). Conversely Britain was acquiring a raw
material necessary for its industrial development and increasing its smelting
capacity, generating hundreds or thousands of skilled jobs.[3] As we shall see
below this changed significantly during the late 1840s.

Introduction of Reverberatory Furnaces

In *c.* 1830 an Alsatian miner living in Chile, Charles Lambert, introduced the reverberatory furnace and modern techniques to process copper sulphide in Chile. Soon these techniques became known to other miners and were widely applied throughout the country. This increased production enormously as heaps of discarded regulus began to be processed and/or exported. On top of this miners started to dig further into their mines to reach the sulphide layer.[4]

Legal Deregulation

From 1828 onwards a number of British merchants and miners operating in Chile requested from the government licences to allow the export of copper ore or regulus. They were usually granted but only in 1834 was a law permitting the export of copper ore and regulus without prior licence decreed. In the following years special customs concessions were made to facilitate the export of copper ores from harbours close to the mines instead of the few ports so far authorised for export.

EXPORT CRISIS

The expansion of copper production that ensued in the 1830s and early 1840s had inherent problems which would become apparent during the 'export' crisis of 1844–45. First, reverberatory furnaces required much more fuel to smelt than the traditional blast furnaces. As a result firewood prices increased as the trees and bushes around the mines disappeared. Second, in 1842 new protectionist import duties were imposed on foreign ores in Britain. From 1828 to 1842 they were allowed duty free, provided that the copper produced with this ore was exported. In 1842, however, to protect the British copper mine owners, the government imposed duties ranging from £3 to £6 per ton on foreign ore. Chilean ore was affected by the higher rate as most of it was rich ore of 20 per cent copper content or over. Finally, in mid-1844 a comprehensive monopsony was formed among British smelters to depress the price of copper ore.[5] As a result of the new British duties and the formation of the smelters' monopsony, the price of copper ore went down by more than 10 per cent from the period 1837–43 to 1844–48. On top of this there was a small but significant rise in the freight rates between Chile and Britain. These factors created a crisis among the people engaged in the copper exporting business: Chilean miners and smelters, British merchants who handled the trade and British smelters who were deprived of a significant portion of high quality copper ore supply.

COPING WITH THE CRISIS

The 1844–45 crisis had positive effects for the Chilean copper industry (and for the country in general) but was negative for the British smelting industry. For the latter it meant the first step towards the loss of a profitable sector of industry. In Chile, the lack of a healthy market for their copper ore compelled miners to start or re-start smelting and new copper works were created and smelting capacity increased significantly. More importantly Charles Lambert started a second technological revolution in Chilean copper smelting by using Welsh coal instead of firewood and applying the Welsh smelting techniques. This permitted him to export from 1846 on, refined copper to South Wales equal 'in quality, shape and appearance' to Swansea's Best Selected copper. This initial technological breakthrough was followed by the British firm Mexican and South American Company which sent 20 British workers (mostly Welsh smelters) along with coal, tools and firebricks to erect a large copper works in the province of Coquimbo, and later by other Chilean firms.

In attempts at industrialisation, copper smelters operating in Chile had the full support of the government who excepted the export of copper from all taxes if smelted with Chilean fuel in the south of the country and freed the import of coal from all duties. It is paradoxical that as the result of the crisis and the ensuing miners' reaction and government support, there was a dramatic increase in the amount of copper smelted in Chile and a severe reduction in the amount of copper ore exported (see Table 4.2). This increase in smelted copper was permitted by the structure of the copper business world-wide. As copper smelting was concentrated in Britain and the main North Atlantic economies had not yet developed a significant smelting industry there was plenty of scope to export copper bars to countries other than Britain – where duties on copper bars were as prohibitive as those on copper ore. These included France, China and above all the United States.

Until 1850 the USA was the largest market for Chilean copper bars. This was due to the existence there of an important copper manufacturing industry not matched by a significant copper mining and smelting industry. This, however, started to change in the late 1840s when the USA began to develop both. The effect was felt by Chilean smelters in the mid-1850s when the import of Chilean bars in the US market started to decline significantly. By the late 1850s the USA was importing only one-third of the amount imported from Chile in the 1840s. The *coup de grâce* to the export of copper bars to the USA was given by the protective legislation of that country in 1862 which banned all imports of copper bars and in 1864 the imports of all sorts of copper.

By the early 1850s the British copper ore market became the major consumer of Chilean copper. The vast bulk, however, was imported in the shape of ore or regulus rather than bars, which were subject to stiff import duties. A significant factor in this period was the growth of the 'Manchester School' and the increasing dominance of 'free trade' in shaping British trade policy. Under these conditions Chilean miners saw the duty on imported ores reduced in 1848 to a nominal sum (one shilling per ton) and British merchants and smelters were allowed to pay better prices for Chilean ore. A dimension was that the comprehensive monopsony established in 1844 began to crumble with the creation of independent copper works (outside the cartel) in Britain thus stimulating competition. This resulted in the increase of the price of copper ore by between 30 to 40 per cent during the late 1840s and the 1850s, and a growing export of Chilean copper ore and regulus to South Wales.

CHILE–SOUTH WALES: A SYMBIOTIC RELATIONSHIP?

From the 1830s through to the 1860s Chile and South Wales had very close links which were solely driven by copper. During this period the town of Swansea in south-west Wales accounted for over 90 per cent of the copper smelted in the world. This was the beginning of a long relationship between Swansea's Lower Valley and the metallurgical industry: nearby Port Talbot became a major producer of steel during the nineteenth century and Llanelli of tin and aluminium in the twentieth century. Skilled workers and industrial processes from the Swansea area led the world and US industrialists such as Carnegie and corporations such as the Pittsburgh Steel Company were to adapt much of the technology developed in this area. The conditions facing foundry workers in Swansea's Lower Valley paralleled those of Chilean copper miners and both were equally dangerous (see Example 16). This is the subject of a permanent exhibition at Swansea's Industrial and Maritime Museum (also see Greenlaw, 1999).

Large quantities of Chilean copper and regulus arrived in the Swansea docks to be smelted and refined in the South Wales furnaces. On the other hand, Welsh coal and firebricks as well as other British produce were shipped from South Wales to Chilean ports close to the mines to pay for that copper and, incidentally, stimulating mining and smelting production. Newspapers in the Chilean mining towns closely monitored the movement of copper prices in Britain and the shipment of coal from South Wales, while the leading Welsh newspaper, *The Cambrian*, weekly reported on mining and smelting in Chile. More intriguingly, Chile-based miner Charles Lambert (see above) decided in 1851 to move his copper smelting operations from Coquimbo in Northern Chile to Swansea, retaining in Coquimbo the rich mine Brillador and a copper works which transformed ore into regulus to be sent to his works in Swansea. The plant in Port Tennant, Swansea, whilst not one of the largest, employed 350 workers. Lambert by importing semi-refined copper threatened the interests of other copper smelters, and 'the very existence of the Port Tennant works is said to have enraged the other copper magnates' (Gabb, 1992, p. 12).

The explanation of this relationship lies in the complementarity of the main economic activities of South Wales and Chile. The former was rich in coal suitable for copper smelting and over decades had developed the technical expertise which permitted it to concentrate 90 per cent of the British copper smelting capacity. On the other hand, the relative exhaustion of British copper mines during the nineteenth century forced smelters to look for sources of copper ore world-wide. The abundant and rich mines of Chile presented an obvious choice, especially as spare capacity for the return trips of British ships was available on the West Coast of South America.

As a result of this trade both partners benefited. Chile expanded its copper production to impressive levels and was able, with Welsh technical expertise and Welsh coal, to develop its primitive smelting industry to a level comparable to the largest copper works in South Wales. On the other hand, Chilean copper ore and regulus became extremely handy at a time when British copper mine production was failing (see Table 4.3). The relationship was, however, an unequal one. Before 1844 Chilean miners depended mostly on the British market, while Welsh smelters were able to buy ore from a variety of sources. The formation of the smelters' monopsony and the imposition of duties on imported copper by the British government in the 1840s exacerbated this weakness. After 1850 the trade became fairer as competition was restored and duties reduced. By the 1860s, however, Chile had developed its own smelting industry and was able to compete success-fully with the Welsh smelters in the world market. This provides an early example of industrialisation in Latin America.

The copper smelting industry also influenced the development of the town of Swansea as a metallurgical centre, as well as its political and social development. Copper magnates such as John Morris established the Landore Copper Works in 1790 and John Vivian set up the Hafod Works in 1810. The magnates and their families controlled the town of Swansea and entire areas of the town, such as Morriston and Hafod, are named after them. These magnates developed from an earlier group such as Morris, Lockwood and Co. who established the Forest Works in 1717, Joseph Percevall who set up in 1737 the White Rock Works in Landore, and the Penclawdd works which were set up relatively late in 1788 by Cheadle Brass Wire Co. Peter Fryer in a history of black people in Britain notes that the above industrialists benefited greatly from the slave trade: the Forest works produced rods and 'manillas' (manacles) used in the slave trade and that in the White Rock works 'one department was wholly engaged in the manufacture of copper rods and manillas'. In the Penclawdd works during the 1780s 'the entire output was used to buy slaves in Africa' (Fryer, 1984, pp. 418–19). A reminder of the symbiotic relationship established between Chilean miners and Welsh smelters in the Swansea Lower Valley has been the transforma-tion of the Vivians' octagonal Georgian House in Swansea, into 'Singleton Abbey', which today is the Registry of the University of Wales, Swansea (Gabb, 1992, p. 28).

CONCLUSIONS

This case study of early globalisation suggests an unequal interdependency between Chilean copper exporters and smelters in North America and Britain. Chile's role as an ore exporter made it prone to commodity substitution by the USA. In addition, Chilean exporters faced protectionist measures to benefit British monopsonistic interests. Paradoxically, this gave a push to the development of a Chilean copper smelting industry which continues to dominate the Chilean economy. The significance of this industry extends to all areas of life and is a concentrated manifestation of the political conditions of globalisation. For example, CODELCO the state-owned enterprise and one of the largest producers in the world has to hand over 20 per cent of its annual earnings to the military in order to pay salaries, and to purchase equipment mainly from the USA. The study suggests that whilst the development of copper in Chile and South Wales may reflect on natural endowment, the expansive global market is not governed by development in any single country or region. This early experience of globalisation shows how the livelihoods of Chilean miners and South Wales smelting and foundry workers, became linked in the world production, refining and manufacturing of this one commodity – copper.

EXAMPLE 16

An Accident in the Copper Mines of Chile, 1878

This is an edited version of the account of Chilean officials on the efforts carried out by a mining community to rescue a group of 17 miners buried in a copper mine in Northern Chile. It is worth noting that Antonio Alfonso, *Intendente* of the province of Coquimbo was, himself, a mining engineer who had worked several years in the Tamaya campsite. This probably explains his active participation in the rescue operation. These telegrams and letters can be found in the National Archive at Santiago, Chile, Fondo Ministerio del Interior, Vol. 824, pp. 230–46.

1. *Subdelegado* of the Tamaya mining camp to the Governor of Ovalle, Tamaya, 25 October 1878.

   Yesterday I was informed that in the campsite of Las Tortolas, 8 or 10 kms from this campsite, there has been a thrust [*derrumbe*] burying several mine workers. Immediately I went to the place of the accident [*siniestro*] from which I returned at 11p.m. with the knowledge [*certidumbre*] that there were 15 men buried alive including two foremen [*mayordomos*]. The mine owners Messrs Chadwick, told me they were buried 47 metres below the surface, and that the gallery in which they were working was blocked by 7 metres of rock as a result of the collapse of the ceiling of the gallery. At the moment active work is being carried out in order to rescue them. They have been buried for 52 hours and we do not know how long this situation will last.

2. Governor of Ovalle to the *Intendente* of Coquimbo, Ovalle, 26 October 1878.

[...] It is 2p.m. and the workers have been buried for 80 hours. The walls of the mine are very weak. As soon as we finish the excavation of a few metres, there is a new thrust which destroys the work that the carpenters had been able to support with wood. We are trying to send them milk mixed with brandy through a pump pipe. We can hear them, some of them have fainted but all 17 are alive...

3. *Intendente* of Coquimbo to the Minister of the Interior, Ovalle, 29 October 1878.

[I arrived in Ovalle last night.] At 5.30a.m. I started my journey to the mine and arrived at 7. In the mouth pit I met Mr Alejandro Chadwick who told me he was very disappointed as the gallery being cleared was totally choked [*ahogada*] and it was impossible to work in it. There is no map of the mine but Mr Chadwick who is a mining engineer drew a sketch of the mine and I went down to the gallery being cleared. Although there was a small fan in use [*ventilador*] the gallery was totally choked after the first 3 metres and lamps did not work [because of lack of oxygen].

At 6p.m. a ventilator Guibal, sent by the mine Pique, was installed. This worked very well and in no time the gallery affected by the thrust was cool and well ventilated and this permitted the workers to continue the rescue work. [An hour later] I left the gallery with the certainty that the workers would be saved. In the pit mouth there were very many people in a state of deep anxiety. I assured them that if there was not another thrust the buried workers would be out of the mine shortly.

At 7.15, I went back to Ovalle... The mines Pique, Chaleco, Rosario, San José and Dichosa put at the disposal of Messrs Chadwick all the people and resources needed. All mine workers carried out their jobs enthusiastically, although the excessive fervour of some of them became counterproductive...

[No other records exist from this point.]

Jose D. Garcia Perez

Tourism: The Spanish Tourist Industry

OVERVIEW

Tourism is a peculiar form of globalisation. It is for the purposes of national accounting classified as an export, despite the fact that it involves the import of large numbers of people. The tourist sector has been an important component in the industrialisation of Spain. It has been a significant provider of jobs in its backward link with construction and its forward link with catering services and manufacturing, as well as a vital foreign exchange earner. Foreign receipts from tourism contribute to the stabilisation of the Spanish balance of payments. These foreign exchange receipts, in strong currencies accepted in international markets, have been used to pay for imports for industrial and manufacturing development. The tourist industry continues to play a crucial part in the economy, although its growth has not been without social, economic and environmental costs and problems. To be able to assess the real contribution of tourism to development in Spain, it is therefore necessary that first we explore its evolution (the sequential growth in importance, the areas affected, and the international and national reasons and conditions for its development) in a historical perspective. Second, the examination of the main types of tourism, package holidays and second homes, reveal operational forms affecting its past, present and future economic, social and environmental functions.

HISTORIC CONSTRAINTS IN THE DEVELOPMENT OF TOURISM

Nineteenth-century Spain was not an attractive destination for northern European travellers. France, Switzerland, Germany, Italy, Egypt or Greece were far more popular than Spain, especially with early travellers – mainly from the English aristocracy and other European elite undertaking the 'Grand Tour' (Towner, 1985). Great deficiencies in transport and accommodation were two important constraints accounting for the small number of tourist visitors until the middle of the twentieth century. The areas visited before the 1950s were those mainly serviced by the railway system, which until 1855 was small and unconnected to France or Portugal. Large areas of the north-west, west and south-east of Spain did not have a rail system until 1936. It was not until 1968 that passengers could travel in the still small, but improved rail system connecting France with Madrid and other destinations in Spain. Travelling in Spain was perceived by early visitors as little more than an uncomfortable adventure in poor quality accommodation in a strange land. The seaside resort of San Sebastian was, however, visited by the Spanish Royal Family and became very popular with Spanish and French tourists in the nineteenth century. During the first half of the twentieth century a more affluent, but still small, middle class started to visit Spain in tours organised by companies like Thomas Cook. Governmental attempts to encourage the development of the tourist industry in 1936 involved plans for the improvement of accommodation (state-run accommodation in *paradores* and *albergues nacionales*) and transport by the newly formed national agency for tourism, the *Comision Nacional de Turismo*. This agency can be regarded as an example of a form of state planning for the sector which was well ahead of other European countries. However, the constraints of the First and Second World Wars, the Spanish Civil War (1936–39), which resulted in protracted military dictatorship and suspicion of foreigners, limited the possibilities of tourism development until the 1950s (Diaz Alvarez, 1990)

THE GROWTH OF MASS TOURISM AFTER THE 1950s

The development of the tourist sector since the 1950s was marked by a huge increase in the number of visitors. This was initially a reflection of full employment and rising incomes in Western Europe during the post-war boom. One dimension of this was the expansion of package holidays as a form of mass recreation for Western European workers to countries such as Spain, Greece and other southern European coastal resorts. In 1951, nearly 1.3 million people visited Spain; in the 1990s over 52 million foreign tourists and 13 million Spaniards (of these nearly 340,000 were Spaniards resident abroad) spent their holidays in Spain. The increase in arrivals by year is shown in Table 4.4.

The great increase in the number of tourists was a highly visible form of 'globalisation' in authoritarian Spain during the 1950s and 1960s. Tourism was crucial for industrialisation during these two decades. It increased demand for construction material of an industrial origin and also for manufactured goods and services consumed by tourists themselves. The value of tourist earnings as percentages of earnings from exports stood at 49 per cent in 1961 and a massive 111 per cent in 1965. By the 1990s the export of manufactured products became the leading foreign exchange earner and tourist earning had declined to 36 per cent of export earnings. The tourism industry remains a major employer and in the late 1980s and early 1990s, production and employment were greater in tourist accommodation and catering than in any of Spain's major industrial sectors, with the exception of metal products and machinery. In 1992 tourism still accounted for 9 per cent of the Spanish Gross National Product (GNP) (Barke et al., 1996).

The reasons for the large increase in the number of tourists were not only external but also internal. The internal reasons can be attributed to the proximity of Spain to Western Europe, and the natural, cultural, political and economic conditions of the country. The sunny weather, a coastal area with a wide selection of sandy beaches, as well as a rugged landscape, are natural attractive advantages. The Spanish Tourism Organisation and tour operators marketed the 'highly sociable' lifestyle of Spanish people, for example with its open-air popular *fiestas*, as attractive to visitors. Although at the early stages of mass tourism, in the early 1950s, the fascist government still regarded foreigners with suspicion, society was not 'uncomfortably' policed for visitors (apart from the occasional arrest for kissing in public or wearing shorts). The repressive character of the Spanish state against its own people was not visible, except to those politically well informed. The 'official' attitude towards foreigners changed as the development strategy of autarky was gradually abandoned and the possibility of making a profit from tourism became a reality. Due to this, the Spanish government removed the awkward prerequisite of entry visas and embarked on a strategy of promotion of mass tourism.

PACKAGE HOLIDAYS

The type of package holiday comprising 'sun and sand', sunbathing, swimming and night clubs in a setting of palm trees has been, according to Tamames and Rueda (1997), by far the most popular, and accounts for about 70 per cent of the total holidays taken in Spain. This type of holiday takes place mainly during the summer months in the areas between the Costa Brava in the north-east and the Costa del Sol in the south, as well as in the Balearic and Canary Islands. Majorca is a major destination for British tourists. The popularity of these summer package holidays has been complemented by the growth of extensive winter holidays targeting retired British persons, faced during the 1970s–1980s with high inflation and the rising cost of living eating into their savings and pensions. The inland areas in Madrid and Andalucia attract a particular kind of tourist more interested in cultural and historic aspects than in the sun and beach type of holiday. The northern Cantabric and Galician coasts attract a good number of Spanish visitors seeking a cooler climate and to get away from tourists.

The relationship between the concentrated marketing and retail operations of package tour operators in Northern Europe and the supply of holiday facilities by hoteliers in Spain, is an example of 'unequal exchange' in the global economy. The package holiday sector is controlled by the tour operators who provide the tourists in bulk and can determine the precise prices given to contract hoteliers (Gavira, 1974; Valenzuela, 1991). Most find it convenient not to own the hotels and apartments they control, as this avoids risks, running costs, depreciation and the headache of having to recruit and manage a large labour force. Although the expansion in the number of beds available has been considerable, demand in the summer months can be higher than capacity and situations of over-booking and/or extortionate prices have occurred. This prompted some (mostly German) tour operators in the 1950s and 1960s to invest in the construction of hotels and/or to provide financial facilities to Spanish hoteliers to expand. Although foreign hotel ownership remains small, it serves as a bargaining tool in the securing of rooms for tour operators. Most tour operators, particularly from Britain, rely on contractual arrangements of guaranteed quotas of rooms at low prices, rather than on direct investment in construction.

In this way tour operators are able to extract the best possible conditions from Spanish hoteliers. Their bargaining position is based on the large numbers of customers they can provide and the absence of a common umbrella under which Spanish hoteliers could negotiate. Tour operators are able to arrange very low prices for accommodation and food, and reserve rooms which are not paid for until they are actually used. They may not even have to inform the hotelier until a week before that these places will not be filled.

Another important source of revenue for tour operators is the organisation of extra activities during holidays, booked and paid for in the country of origin. Tour operators also invest in travel agencies in Spain, organising transportation, excursions and other services to visitors. They also make arrangements with charter airlines in Spain. Foreign airlines invest in Spanish charter firms ensuring the extra number of seats needed for their customers. It is in this form that a considerable part of the cost of holidays remains in the country of origin as tour operators' profit. 'It has been estimated that 58 per cent of the purchase price of package holidays in Spain never reaches Spain when foreign tourists travel in an airline of their country of origin' (Barke et al., 1996, p. 104). The growth of all-inclusive holidays and sea cruises leaves little distributional margin in the local economy. On cruises, for example, the stay in-country could be as little as a matter of a few hours (see Example 17).

APARTMENTS AND SECOND HOMES: TOURISM AS URBANISATION

Renting self-catering apartments or owning second holiday homes are the other main parts of the holiday industry. Many of these holidays are also organised by tour operators on similar lines as those above. There are, however, an important number of those operating at individual second home owner level. The way in which the construction of second homes, hotels and other installations took place, offers good insight into the political processes involved in the development of mass tourism and this allows us to place the economic, social and environmental effects of mass tourism in perspective. In the early stages of the development of tourism hundreds of hectares of land were urbanised for the construction of hotels and individual holiday villas. Between 1957 and 1967 the construction of villas changed from the building of individual properties to the promotion of villa estates and complexes by foreign and Spanish housing developers. It was at this stage when planning regulations under the Franco regime were at their minimum, and again during the building boom of 1977 and 1978, when the construction process accelerated very rapidly, that detrimental social, economic and environmental effects were at their most acute.

The operational stages of villa estate development are, first, that land is purchased, and second that the relevant building regulations for the legalisation of urbanisation, are structured around the purchase. This says something about the planning process. Third is the construction of the buildings, connection to services such as water, sewage, access, electricity, telephone, etc. and, finally, the sale. In the first stage the promoter buys the land from small landowners, or preferably a larger plot from a single owner, whose previous economy may well have been one of semi-subsistence. Selling land and finding employment as a waiter or chambermaid in the emerging tourism sector may have been perceived as more profitable than working the land. This was certainly the case for share-croppers and farm labourers who found much better paid employment in the building and catering industry. The seasonal nature of such employment, however, meant that winter consisted of hard months of unemployment. It was only during the late 1980s that a social programme was initiated by the Socialist administration in Andalucia, and for the first time in Spain, which introduced measures of support, including financial support for seasonal workers in agriculture and tourism.

Many land users in Spain who owned the land were reticent about abandoning agriculture for a job in catering or construction. In many cases it was not the prospect of becoming a waiter which motivated peasants, but rather the 'lure' of getting a good price for their land. Frequently people waited until land prices were at their highest, and this influenced decisions to sell. However, this required a good knowledge of land marketing and skills in speculation which most did not possess. The mechanisms for buying and selling land were in knowing the seller's weaknesses and bringing them together with a possible buyer. For this knowledge a commission might be earned by an intermediary. The collusion of interests between land speculators and Spanish *caciques* (i.e. people with credentials in the community because of their position of authority) were very high. Former large landowners, local councillors, mayors, bankers and senior church figures were key members of *caciques* and were in positions of influence and power which could be applied to entice small landowners to sell. Small landowners looking for advice from these sources were frequently advised to sell at prices which would double or treble only a few days later. In this manner many people in Spain were dispossessed.

The second operational stage of estate development, following land purchase, was the legalisation for urbanisation. This was typically marked by pressure exercised by building agents on local officials to change the classification of land from rural to urbanisable. The cases of corruption and constraints in the existing planning and building controls were responsible for a large amount of illegal construction. The prerequisites for the legalisation of urbanisation and building often have been flawed. The specific conditions of the approved building permissions were ignored and higher buildings (especially hotels) were built with impunity, sometimes only a matter of a few metres from the sea. In many cases bigger buildings than those specified by the land to building ratio were constructed, or/and constructed below the minimum distance from the level of high tide. These were regular practices. The urbanisation and building on land without permission at all, or only with partial permission, incurred a fine which was paid and included in the total cost, ultimately to be paid by the buyer.

This form of operation was not only the result of strong speculative practices but also due to the deficiencies of the existing regulations and controls in local authorities. Under Spanish planning law it was bureaucratically easier, and sometimes cheaper, to pay the fine than apply for permission. Since the local authority could not have pulled the existing building down, as planning legislation in Britain and the USA allows, paying the fine effectively legalised the status of the new building as a tourism installation. The control capabilities of local authorities were often dashed by the great increase in work resulting from the extremely rapid development in tourism. Jurdao (1990) provides an example of the degree of illegality as a result of reduced capabilities and corruption in the council of Marbella, the 'Jewel in the Crown' of Spanish tourism: the percentage of buildings finished without any documents in 1964 was 47 per cent, 30 per cent in 1966, 25 per cent in 1968, 22 per cent in 1971, and 19 per cent in 1972. The construction of high-rise buildings for tourism purposes has been marked by partial legality and this has been a key factor in producing the result of much higher density of tourists than either planned for or desired. It is in this context that the term 'concrete jungle' has been widely used to describe Spanish coastal resorts. The social mechanisms necessary for such large-scale informal land use require good political integration and high marketing skills by the promoter, such as good knowledge of prices and demand, as well as good links with possible buyers abroad. Specialised land developers and promoters' marketing entails 'inviting' possible buyers and their guests from Britain and Germany for weekend presentations in Spain at minimal cost (or no cost at all if they decided to buy), including accommodation, food, entertainment and always plenty to drink.

Many of the newcomers who purchased properties in Spain subsequently discovered problems. This is especially the case among those who bought a plot of land to build their own residence. The first step of fencing 'their' land may itself cause difficulties. It may be across public rights of way, divert streams which have traditionally been used by the local community or use all its water for the construction of a swimming pool, construct water wells lowering the normal water levels and diminishing the amount of water in natural springs, or construct cesspits which may contaminate the soil and natural water system, and so on. The construction of the building may also destroy a natural habitat. The collection of household refuse and the provision of medical and other services in these conditions of urban sprawl is expensive for local authorities. The environmental effects of waste disposal, especially sewers discharging into the sea, have been documented. One unforseen social consequence is reflected in the experience of many British pensioners, who having sold their homes in the UK to retire to Spain, now find themselves living in ghetto-like conditions of isolation from the host community. The feeling of loneliness can reach critical proportions with the death of a partner. Living one's last years with inferior health services to those available in the UK has been an additional discouraging factor in this kind of holiday retirement during the 1990s.

ENVIRONMENTAL AND SOCIAL EFFECTS

The ugly built environment of the 'concrete jungles' and concerns about the safety of the sea water have become major areas of policy in Spain and throughout the Mediterranean coastal regions. The contamination of Mediterranean waters has no readily available solution. The particular enclosed natural conditions, relatively small tides (less than a metre), small currents, and smaller waves than in the Atlantic, account for the low renewal of water in the Mediterranean sea. As a result, the spill of long outfalls on the coast remain near bathing areas. Any solution has to be found at the source rather than relying on the sea as a natural dispersant and treatment. Sewage bacteria, although not the most harmful if compared with viruses, are important as a perceived danger on the part of tourists. A recent example of the effect of a loss of confidence in the quality of sea water was the disastrous 70 per cent decline in bookings in the resort of Salou in 1989, 'following fears of a typhoid outbreak' (Barke et al., 1996, p. 120). Sewage in the water, increased by the large number of tourists, is the biggest problem facing the industry. Tourists become ill if they come in contact with sewage while swimming, or eat contaminated fish.

The tourist industry is sensitive to these problems and counteracts the effects of reports on contamination outbreaks with its own promotion. The most important coastal water test of the European Union (EU) (although basic, since it does not carry out tests for viruses) is for bacteria. The number of areas tested which comply with these European basic regulations have been increasing. According to information from the EU the vast bulk of points tested in Spain achieved the mandatory level (92.68 per cent) and 58 per cent achieved the higher guideline level in 1992. The Spanish tourist industry uses the Blue Flag symbol of the EU as an indication of the safety of its waters. The Blue Flag scheme assesses the quality of the water according to 27 criteria including beach management (adequate toilets and drinking water facilities), and provides up-to-date information on pollution incidents and water standards. These Blue Flag 'waving' promotional exercises by the tourist industry, portraying the 'Spanish coasts as among the cleanest in Europe', are meant to help to create a climate of confidence among tourists (Kirkby, in Barke et al., 1996, p. 102; Becker, 1995).

Improving the image of social life which may be encountered by the tourist has also been an important area of concern. Reports of rowdy behaviour by a minority of tourists ('lager louts') are a serious problem for the industry. The deteriorating social behaviour (the loutish conduct) of some of the British tourists during the 1990s – and some of their highlighted activities, such as exposing genitalia, urinating in public (often due to the lack of public conveniences) and so on – has infuriated the Spanish public. Much effort went into heavy policing in resorts such as Magaluf on the island of Majorca, and pressure has been applied by the Spanish government and local municipalities on tour operators to take more responsibility for their clients' behaviour. Advice given by the Spanish tourism organisation for hoteliers to move away from the mass market and towards 'quality' tourism is being given with even greater vigour. This offensive by the tourism industry has a considerable distance to travel. One optimistic sign, however, appears in the islands of Ibiza and Lanzarote, where 'famous boozing hell-holes' have been apparently transformed into attractive high quality resorts, largely due to the combined efforts of the Spanish tourist industry and local municipalities.[1]

CONCLUSIONS

The impact of the rapid development of tourism in Spain has radically changed the livelihoods of millions of people. People previously living from semi-subsistence agriculture now work in the building industry, in catering, as gardeners and as domestic servants. It can be said that the tourist industry created many jobs in the construction and hotel industries, but possibly destroyed as many amongst landless labourers and small peasants. The process of Spanish industrialisation was sensitively linked to tourism. The tourist sector acted as a leading economic sector gaining much needed hard currencies to pay for imports used in the engineering and car industries. At the same time, the interdependency between Western European tour operators and Spanish hoteliers is far from equal. Tour operators are very price sensitive and squeeze the local hotel industry. The 'success' of tourism has not been without social and environmental problems. The speculative form of growth resulted in the construction of high-rise buildings, the vast bulk of which were concentrated in the coastal areas, and characterised by unacceptably high levels of population density. This mass tourism resulted in significant reductions in the cost of holidays. The purpose-built concrete jungles of Can Picafort, Majorca and many others, stand as monuments to the days of unbridled land speculation and disregard for basic and transparent planning procedures. These edifices and the interests which benefited from them require a continuing spiral of further building and further increases in tourist numbers. This is more difficult to maintain today given the wider low-cost choices offered to European tourists in other parts of the world. In this sense European tourism has become more 'globalised'. One social and political legacy left by the development of tourism in Spain is the popular view that land speculators and the various *caciques* were the major beneficiaries of tourism development. An important factor was in the role played by the Franco dictatorship, which allowed even the most elemental norms of urban planning to be ignored, and sanctioned the imperfect, although in the short term lucrative, tourist industry. One condition which needs to be met if the balance of gains from tourism is to benefit Spain, is that contractor hoteliers need to obtain better prices from tour operators. Another is that policies have to be designed which redistribute the gains from tourism with far greater equity. Both have to be consistent with sustainable environmental management.

EXAMPLE 17

Working on a Cruise Liner

The *Island Breeze* is a cruise ship rather than a grand liner. At 38,000 tons, however, it is bigger than many of the ships used by Thompsons Holidays, the leading UK holiday operator. The *Island Breeze* is leased by Thompsons from the Greek-Cypriot owners, Louis Cruise Lines. Louis began its life during the 1950s in a dusty office in Ledras Street (Nicosia's old commercial centre) specialising in tours to the Holy Land. Today it owns 18 vessels and is amongst the top three cruise operators in the world.[2] The *Island Breeze* employs 612 workers and carries 1,383 passengers in 580 cabins. It sails from Palma, Majorca to Malta–Messina–Taormina–Naples–Menorca and back to Majorca. The high spot of the cruise is the visit to Pompeii. During the summer season it repeats this route 22 times. Time on shore was an average of six hours per landing. Most passengers take the offer of a 'two-centre' holiday and stay on an additional week in Puerto Polensa, which is a quieter resort on the island of Majorca. At a cost of £600 it was a relatively affordable holiday and part of a growing popular interest in cruising in the UK during the late 1990s. 'It's not a blue-rinse holiday' said the travel agent.

The ship employed workers from many nationalities. The skilled workers (plumbers, electricians, and nearly all ships-officers) were mainland Greeks. Many of the workers were frequently seen running about, trying to carry out emergency repairs. Once they were carrying out repairs in the adjoining cabin which suffered from high vibration and a water leak from the shower in an upstairs cabin. When I asked them [in Greek] what the problem was the engineer rolled his eyes and said 'problems... problems...'. The craft workers used to sit and drink during the evenings in an area of the ship permanently cordoned off and sign-posted with a 'wet-paint' notice. They invited me to join them during some of the evenings. Since I was a 'fellow' Greek and came originally from Cyprus they were particularly interested in my opinion of Louis. In fact my father used to work for Louis during the 1950s. I also gave them some Cypriot newspapers I brought with me which contained coverage of the latest Louis's takeover and its phenomenal rise on the Nicosia stock exchange. Many of these workers had experience with US cruise ships and Louis compared badly with them in terms of pay and conditions 'and passenger service' (as many emphasised). They said that they were the only workers who belonged to a trade union.

Most of the engine-room workers were from the West Indies. The *Island Breeze* used to in fact sail the Caribbean and this was the first time that it was used for a Mediterranean cruise. A number of these workers had stayed on, some in order to 'see Europe' for the first time. Many of the cleaning and room-service workers were from the Philippines, Burma and other Asian countries. The bar and waitering staff came from a wide range of nationalities: Italian, Portuguese, Bulgarian, Jamaican. Indeed it was the proud boast of the ship that it employed workers from 37 different nationalities. One of the highlights of the cruise was the spectacle of waiters, chefs, wine service staff, 'bus-boys' (trainee waiters who seemed to spray pepper and salt), as well as assorted craftworkers, assembled together by management on the second night of the cruise, for a rendition of *We Are The World*, as lights were dimmed and workers clutched their lit candles.

Mario is a waiter. He comes from Barbados in the West Indies and had worked on the *Island Breeze* for five years. He took the opportunity to visit the sights and to do shopping. He visited Pompeii, Menorca and Naples.

It's different when we used to work in the Caribbean. There used to be more black officers. Now it's just Greeks. No offence to you, but sometimes you can't understand what they are saying to you. There are only two black officers. When we were given the offer of 'redeployment' after they wound down the West Indian cruises hardly any of the black officers were 'redeployed'. They said they had a 'presentation problem'. Those of us who paid commission agents got offers to continue. You have to pay these agents for the ticket to work on a line. It cost me three months' pay, for others even more. To add insult to injury, you might have noticed these Eastern European bus-boys. We are supposed to be training them do our jobs! This will be the last season for me on the *Island Breeze*. 'We Are The World?' My ass!!

The passengers are also different compared to the West Indies. Then, most of the passengers were Americans and they tip much better than the British. For this reason you 'take care' of people. But the British don't tip and they always complain. Some of them – especially those who go on the two-week cruise – get really bad tempered. One guy gave me some racial abuse, which was rare on the West Indian cruise. Some people need to calm down before they go on holidays.

(Source: Mario Fernandez, Panayiotopoulos, P. Personal Communication, *Island Breeze*, 14 August 1997.)

4.3

Prodromos Panayiotopoulos

The Global Textile Industry: An Engendered Protectionism

OVERVIEW

The textile industry offers a commodity illustration of the 'global manufac-turing' system. The High Street fashion stores daily confront consumers in Europe and the USA with an expansive plethora of country of origin labels. Today more campaigners for labour rights, and consumers, are asking questions about what lies behind the country of origin and designer labels (see Klein, 2001). Concerns have surfaced about child labour and sweatshop conditions found in the production of clothing and footwear. In the USA the anti-sweatshop campaign turned during 1999 into the most powerful student movement since the anti-apartheid protests of the 1980s. Some 100 universities around the USA have groups affiliated to the United Students Against Sweatshops (USAS) and USAS was part of the mobilisation in Seattle. This case study allows us to investigate the relationship between gender and industrial work and the particular implications this sector has for working women world-wide. The industry also allows us an insight into inequalities in world trade as exemplified by the Multi-Fibre Arrangement (MFA). The MFA in different guises has 'regulated' world trade in the textile sector for over 40 years. It is scheduled for abolition in 2003. The MFA sets physical quotas on the amount of textile goods which can be exported by the developing countries to the markets of the developed industrial regions and national economies (USA, Europe, Japan).

THE TEXTILE INDUSTRY AND THE DEVELOPING COUNTRIES

The Newly Industrialised Countries (NICs) saw considerable state interven-tion to support the textile export sector. Nigel Harris (1990a) points to the selection of particular industries for export promotion which in the case of South Korea saw a graduation from labour-intensive industries such as garments and footwear, to more capital-intensive production such as ship-building and car production. Many developing countries promoted the textile industry as a means of addressing the 'employment question', that is, chronic unemployment and under-employment frequently manifested in high rural to urban migration (see Section 3.1). An important employment function of the sector was that it required less capital and generated more jobs, when compared to investment in other industrial sectors. This is typified by the continuing use of relatively simple and cheap technology in the form of the industrial sewing machine. The sector also became a crucial source of foreign exchange earnings, which are necessary for developing countries in order to pay for imports.

Despite the exceptionally high levels of protectionism found in this sector, textiles and footwear represented relative success in industrialisation policy by the developing countries during the 1970s. Many of the NICs, such as Taiwan and Hong Kong, initially depended heavily on the textile industry for their industrialisation[1] and the sector is a major employer in many of the poorest developing countries. During 1963 and 1980 the textile and garment sector accounted for 39.2 per cent and 34.9 per cent respectively of all employment in manufacturing industry in the Third World (Mark, 1985, pp. 11–15). During the 1990s the sector accounted for about a quarter to a third of manufacturing employment in the developing countries. In a number of the poorest countries the sector forms the largest sectoral contribution to Manufacturing Value Added (MVA) and the single most significant source of exports: Bangladesh, for example, saw 38 per cent of MVA and 78 per cent of merchandise exports accounted for by this sector (see Table 4.5). An equally important factor in the expansion of the sector has been high levels of relocation by Trans National Corporations (TNCs) to lower wage economies partly driven by a parallel reduction in transportation costs. Relocation has been particularly marked in the more labour-intensive garment sector within which labour costs are a more significant cost in production. During 1990 labour costs in the garment industry (per hour in US dollar terms) stood at 65 cents in India, 55 cents in China and 45 cents in Indonesia, compared to $10 in the UK and $12.50 in France.[2] Sensitivity to labour costs is a key factor in structuring the organisation of production and labour force composition in the garment industry.

Garment production consists of 'fragments' or component stages in production which require associated skills. Contractors and subcontractors in the industry are referred to as CMT units (Cut, Make and Trim). Cutting requires cutters and assistants, making requires sewing machinists and trimming requires pressers and workers to do the bagging (see Figure 2, previously cited). Most labour is required at the making stage which accounts for most of women's employment and which is associated with the lowest rates of pay. In reverse, cutting mainly employs men and is associated with the highest rates of pay. It is the sewing stage, i.e. the most labour-intensive stage of production, which has seen the most pronounced level of relocation to the developing countries. Production for export is structured in the form of outward processing which is also known as international sub-contracting. Whilst this appears in many diverse forms the major common purpose is to reduce labour costs and to bring together the different stages of production and distribution conducted on a global scale. A list of the main actors involved in outward processing and their specific contribution is attached to Figure 4.

THE TEXTILE INDUSTRY AND SWEATSHOPS

The conditions facing Third World workers have attracted growing attention. This is not the usual attention associated with Non Governmental Organisations (NGOs) which points to a grim enough picture of the human condition. Oxfam has run a Clothes Code Campaign and focused attention to the clothes trade in Bangladesh. Statements from women workers included, 'even when I was sick, I wasn't allowed any time off' and 'I am always afraid that if I make a mistake, they'll hit me'. Working conditions were appalling: few workers had contracts, if a worker was late for three days in a row, she lost a whole day's pay, some factories did not allow toilet breaks and young workers were likely to be beaten for making mistakes or for going to the toilet without permission.[3]

Attention has also been focused on sweatshops by a growing social and political student movement in the USA which is prepared to take direct action in order to force the TNCs into compliance on basic labour standards in their Third World factories. The target of the student anti-sweatshop movement became the $2.5bn collegiate licencing industry. Students have put university administrations under intense pressure to take responsibility for the conditions under which clothes bearing school logos are produced, and this demand led to sit-ins in the Universities of Arizona, North Carolina, Wisconsin-Madison and Michigan. The student groups involved in the sit-ins and 'name and shame' campaigns directed at particular companies came together and formed the United Students Against Sweatshops (USAS) during July 1998.[4]

There are very good reasons why students and young people are at the front of the anti-sweating movement in the USA. Many of the products – clothes and footwear – are aimed at them, with the 'sneaker' market alone valued at $6.8bn, of which about 40 per cent is controlled by Nike. This has made TNCs sensitive to the threat of boycott by young people and they have responded by offering concessions to the students. Reebok promised to improve conditions, which left the students unimpressed since there was little detail and no independent verification process. The students were particularly concerned that the Clinton-inspired Apparel Industry Partnership (AIP), bringing together representatives from the garment industry, unions, consumers, human rights groups and its monitoring organisation the Fair Labor Association (FLA), were incapable of monitoring and enforcement action against sweatshops. The FLA is a voluntary organisation which effectively allows the TNCs to monitor themselves. Yet, the FLA acted as sanctioning agency allowing manufacturers to sew 'No Sweats' labels into their clothes. This was seen by many students as official complicity in sweatshops and they began to look for unofficial channels in monitoring labour standards. One demand raised by the students was 'disclosure' by the TNCs of Third World production sites. Nike was forced to release the names of its 41 non-US factories making athletic wear for US universities. Until Nike released the names of the factories, the company, along with its competitors, argued that such information was a valuable corporate secret, which could be used by their competitors. Disclosure has allowed students not only to identify where production is located, but also to make links with workers employed in the factories. This has brought them into contact and alliances with unions and movements for workers' rights in the Third World and the USA. In the USA the student movement is working closely with The Union of Needle, Industrial and Textile Employees (UNITE), and it was partly due to pressure from students that UNITE withdrew from what was widely perceived as the 'sham' of the FLA.[5]

This new movement against sweatshops has taught many US students that behind Gap clothes, Reebok and Nike sportswear, or Disney's *Pocahontas* and *Lion King* T-shirts, are real-life human beings, workers who live and work in rat-infested conditions in poverty stricken countries like Haiti; that Honduran girls, some as young as 13, work 15 hours a day to make clothes for Wal-Mart by a company linked to leading US TV personality Kathie Lee Gifford; and that for each Liz Claiborne jacket which retails for $198 in the USA, a worker gets paid 74 cents in the *maquilas*.[6] Many US students have made connections between these issues and have challenged the sourcing policies of US universities and corporations. They also offered a direct challenge to the idea of 'partnership' between workers and owners of sweatshops and the proposition that the best way to deal with sweatshops is through market self-regulation. In doing so, they undermined the political legitimacy of the Fair Labor Association.[7]

TEXTILES AND PROTECTIONISM: THE MULTI-FIBRE ARRANGEMENT

The MFA sets quotas on the physical amount of textile goods which can be exported to the markets of the industrial economies. Since these markets are where the highest per capita incomes can be found, gaining market access is a critical issue for developing country exporters. The MFA illustrates a protracted history of protectionism (see below). It began its history in the USA during the late 1950s as a response by the US cotton textile industry towards Japanese competition. In 1961 the first Arrangement was effectively put in place, as an emergency measure of expected short duration. The quota system progressively extended its life for nearly four decades and increased the scope of protectionism, initially from cotton to cover all textile and garment exports from the developing countries. The MFA effectively devised special regulations for one group of products (textiles) and one group of countries (the developing countries). This represented a serious violation of the principle of 'non-discrimination' (that is, treating all trading partners as equals) which guided the work of the General Agreement on Tariffs and Trade (GATT), ostensibly set up in order to maintain 'free trade'. Textiles and garments became an exception to the general movement towards free trade in the post-war period.

Multi-Fibre Arrangement – RIP?

- The Short Term Arrangement Regarding International Trade in Cotton (STA): established in 1961 under US pressure to protect its domestic cotton industry from Japanese competition. Establishes a physical quota system.
- The Long Term Arrangement (LTA): established in 1962 and was renewed in 1967 and 1970 under the auspices of the General Agreement on Tariffs and Trade (GATT). The LTA extended the scope of quotas from cotton goods to all textiles and clothing.
- The First MFA: negotiated under European pressure in 1973 and identified the East Asian Newly Industrialising Countries rather than Japan, as the major threat to the European garment industry. The MFA extended the geographical spread of protectionism.
- The Second MFA: re-negotiated in 1977 with the EEC taking a leading role. The EEC threatened to act unilaterally and outside both MFA and GATT protocols. Protectionism fuelled by rising unemployment in Europe and the USA targeted the East Asian NICs with increased vigour.
- The Third MFA: re-negotiated during 1981 and tightened up some of the loopholes available to developing countries. The USA and the EU, for example, secured an 'anti-surge clause' which prohibited exporters from carrying-over unused quotas from the previous year.
- The Fourth MFA: re-negotiated in 1986, affirming all previous protocols.
- The re-negotiation of the MFA during 1989–90, was held up by the protracted trade disputes inside the GATT/World Trade Organisation, between the USA and the EU. A compromise was reached during 1992 between the EU, which favoured the eventual abolition of the MFA, and US textile groups which argued most fervently for its continuation. The accord proposed the phasing-out of all existing MFA quota restrictions by the year 2003.

Under the agreement reached between the USA and Europe it was projected that by the year 1994, 16 per cent of import quotas would be removed, followed by another 17 per cent in 1998, 18 per cent in 2002 and by January 2003, all the remaining quotas.[8] The abolition of the MFA would bring textiles under normal GATT/WTO rules for the first time. At the same time, however, in addition to the MFA restrictions there are also bilateral restrictions (that is, those imposed by one country on another). These take the form of 'voluntary' restraints, whereby the government of an industrial country would threaten to suspend imports from a developing country unless it accepted a 'voluntary' quota. This is usually sufficient to result in an 'agreement' (see Example 18A, 'China–USA: Trade in Silk'). During the early 1990s it was estimated that 80 per cent ($136bn) of world textile exports were regulated by MFA and bilateral quotas.[9]

The industrial countries use their strong bargaining power in the negotiation of quotas. In 1997 Vietnam – one of the world's poorest and newest producers – in order to get its quotas to the EU increased had to agree to give preferential treatment to European joint-owned companies rather than state-owned enterprises in the allocation of the use of quotas.[10] Bangladesh, which like Vietnam is an equally poor country, saw the USA, Europe and Canada applying export quotas and extending their product range during the late 1980s. Stocks of garments built up and many factories in Bangladesh closed down, laying off workers.[11] Despite the restrictions on exports Bangladesh experienced phenomenal rates of growth. This was a particular feature of the garment sector which single-handedly accounted for 51 per cent of total merchandise exports in 1992. The EU accounted for 55 per cent and the USA for 42 per cent of garment exports. Bangladesh became the USA's ninth largest supplier and its third largest for women's and girls' cotton non-knit shirts. It is the EU's third biggest supplier of T-shirts. In cotton shirt exports Bangladesh is second only to Hong Kong. Exports of garments to the USA were quota free in the mid-1980s but now face imposed quotas on 34 categories. During 1992/93 the quota utilisation rate was 100 per cent in all 34 categories with the exception of dressing gowns (where it was 91 per cent). This shows that Bangladesh could export far more if it were allowed to (Bhuiyan and Shaw, 1994, pp. 91–2).

Developing country exporters often resort to desperate measures when faced with the exhaustion of their quotas and the likelihood of factory closures. This can involve the use of fraudulent quota licences and export certificates. The MFA has contributed to the growth of international sub-contracting and one factor in TNC relocation has been to relocate to the developing countries not making full use of their quotas and which enjoy preferential market access to the EU or US market. One such example was illustrated in an attempt to capture 25 per cent of the world's cashmere market. This involved the collaboration of Japanese designer company (Hanae Mori), state-owned yarn producers in China and assembly-makers in Puerto Rico. Puerto Rico was chosen because it had under-utilised quotas in cashmere sweaters, and also had preferential access to the lucrative US market (Panayiotopoulos, 1996b, pp. 7–8). The implications of trade instability for livelihoods were illustrated in a study by the World Development Movement, which has campaigned against the MFA. The investigation of Bangladesh's textile industry found that not only was the MFA hurting the earning of foreign exchange, but also that it was hurting the poor and in particular the working poor, who constitute the single largest section of the poor in the Third World. The WDA found the MFA damaging not only to the employment prospects of the poorest countries, but also to the ability of the working poor to function in market economies, to meet basic needs, to gain access to services such as health and to educate their children (Jackson, 1992, p. 3).

TEXTILES AND WOMEN

The economic and social transformation explicit in Third World industrialisation has resulted in the growth of full-time women's employment in manufacturing industry. This is a particular feature of countries undergoing rapid industrialisation. High participation by women in the textile and garment industry appears as a characteristic feature of industrialisation and sectoral employment world-wide: in the Export Processing Zones (EPZs) of South Korea and Indonesia, the screwdriver (*maquiladoras*) plants on the US–Mexican border and the metropolitan cities of Los Angeles, London, New York, an element of convergence is the centrality of women workers in the sector's employment (see Yebra, 1996, pp. 1–18). One instrument which unites women world-wide is the industrial sewing machine (see Example 18B, 'The Sewing Machine').

The high participation by women in the textile and garment industry would give strength to the view that women, far from being marginal to industrialisation, are central to economic change and that Third World industrialisation would not be possible without the exploitation of women as cheap wage workers. This view informed what Ruth Pearson (1992) refers to as the 'new consensus' in conceptualising women's roles in much of the literature during the 1970s and 1980s. This view drew from socialist feminist analysis and research on the East Asian NICs and Export Orientated Industrialisation (EOI), which saw new potential for women's self-organisation as industrial workers. It was also a reaction to the 'old consensus' drawing from research on Latin American Import Substituting Industrialisation (ISI) and which was reflected in the work of Ester Boserup (1970). This view saw industrialisation, when compared to cottage industry, as a process which marginalised women in Latin American labour markets. Marginality theories were criticised for failing to explain the selective nature of women's incorporation in paid work, typified by sectors such as the garment sector (see Scott, 1986; Panayiotopoulos, 1996b).

Current analyses of women's economic activity point to the wide range of activities in which women engage in order to earn, or make, a living. These range from paid employment in assembly-line production in South East Asian Export Processing Zones, to precarious income generation in the 'informal sector'. The 'informal sector' consists of economic activities which are not registered for the purposes of GDP, or enforced by contractual relations and in which labour is not protected by any social legislation and is, therefore, cheaper. Women are highly represented in the 'informal sector' of the poorer economies (Atema and Panayiotopoulos, 1995). Current labour market trends have been described by the International Labour Organisation (1993) in terms of the 'global feminisation' of employment. By this the ILO meant that conditions of employment which were more systematically associated with women's work (unregistered, unprotected, short term, unskilled, low-paid) have now become general features of global labour markets. The conclusions drawn by the ILO were informed by a situation where, with the exception of the East Asian NICs (which faced periodic labour shortages), global labour markets have been characterised by high and persistent levels of unemployment during the 1980s and most of the 1990s: whether the above is a permanent or cyclical condition remains to be seen.

The ILO and other agencies involved in employment policy can be criticised for failing to adequately explain, (and in many cases perpetuate) assumptions that men and women are best suited for different kinds of work. A typical example is the way that many governmental and Non Governmental Organisations' (NGOs') vocational training programmes targeted at young people in the Third World invariably promote sewing skills amongst young girls and carpentry amongst young boys (Panayiotopoulos and Gerry, 1997). The way in which women learn skills, acquire training and employment in sectors such as garments, footwear and electronic component assembly, is neither 'natural' nor a simple matter of individual decision making. Women's participation in garment sector employment is driven by the increased economic pressure on working-class women to be providers, which is indicated in the growing number of households headed by women: in Kenya 32 per cent and in the Third World an estimated 35 per cent of households are headed by women (Atema and Panayiotopoulos, 1995, p. 2). This has put great pressure on women's time to meet productive and reproductive roles. At the same time, women's employment is also structured by prevalent ideas in society about what constitutes 'women's work' and frequently there are conflicts between the economic needs of working-class women and dominant ideas in society about the role of women. Women world-wide have won a paradoxical victory in the global garment industry, or at least the ability of millions of them to work in this sector. Explanations for women's over-representation in the garment industry include:

Explanations for women's participation in the garment industry

- Biological reductionism: a range of assumptions and practices applied by production management which point to a range of 'natural' and 'feminine' aptitudes of women as a group, such as 'nimble fingers', 'quick eyes', greater 'docility' and 'dexterity' than men as a group. The conclusions which follow from this approach are that women are biologically designed and have a comparative advantage for more detailed work such as assembly-line production.

- Social construction: the way young girls and young boys are socialised (learn according to prevailing norms) to become men and women and the way this is reflected in the learning of skills. This influences the formal education, vocational training programmes and apprenticeships. It is also reflected in the learning of skills in the domestic economy (such as sewing), frequently from older women family members. Because these skills are learned in the domestic economy, they are attached with low value and are frequently classed as 'unskilled'.

- Production and reproduction: wage work carried out by women cannot be understood without reference to the 'double burden' faced by women both as workers and as mothers, wives and daughters, with major responsibility for a range of 'reproductive' activities. These include childbearing, childcaring and daily household maintenance (cooking, cleaning, and so on). Homeworking is a prevalent way of organising work in the garment industry because it combines domestic work with paid labour and it addresses these two dimensions of women's lives (Pearson, 1992; Panayiotopoulos, 1992b; Yebra, 1996).

Biological reductionism finds a parallel expression in attempts at explaining the concentration of women workers in the 'caring' professions, such as nursing, teaching and voluntary work. A crude deduction is that women as carers for children can also 'naturally' become the carers of society as a whole. This view has steered World Bank and NGO funded programmes in the Third World towards the conclusion that women are 'naturally' competent community managers. Prevailing norms whilst culturally diverse are often reflected in views such as that men should earn a 'family wage' or that women work for 'pin-money' (additional extras to household income). These conclusions can justify low pay for women and legitimise discriminatory practices such as the Delhi Agreement regulating labour relations in India: this saw women workers laid-off first during periods of economic recession. The view that young women are transient workers to whom motherhood and childcare responsibilities are ascribed as disadvantages, often means that personnel managers do not readily invest resources in training women.

The relationship between women's productive and reproductive activities influences the hours that women work, as well as the choice of sector and the kind of work carried out by them. Work patterns in the garment industry are often designed to accommodate women with school children. Many women look to self-employment and work in the 'informal sector' as a way of having more flexible hours of work which can allow them to negotiate multiplex activities (Atema and Panayiotopoulos, 1995). In the garment industry, the major reason for homeworking is that women have children of pre-school age with no one to help in looking after them. Another factor in homeworking is that it can address economic necessity (earning an income) in ways which conform to prevailing ideas about women's seclusion. There are important tensions in many cultures between beliefs about women and the practical lives of working women world-wide (see Example 18C).

CONCLUSIONS

The textile and garment industry acts as a microcosm of the contradictions in globalisation. Many US students and Western consumers of garments and sportswear produced in the Third World by US and European companies, have drawn the conclusion that globalisation far from leading to development goes hand in hand with sweatshops. Given the centrality of women's employment in this sector, this amounts to sweating women on a global scale. The industry also allows us to investigate the contradiction between the rhetoric of 'free trade' and the practice of protectionism characterised by the MFA. Protectionism can be seen as damaging both to the developing countries and to neo-liberal thinking which proposes that since developing countries are characterised by an abundance of labour and a scarcity of capital, then any 'comparative advantage' to be had in manufacturing industry involved the promotion of labour-intensive industries such as textiles. The MFA is particularly damaging to the developing countries, therefore, as it undermines this comparative advantage in world markets. Ironically the MFA also hurts the industrial countries too since a particular dimension of globalisation in the textile industry consists of high levels of intra-industrial trade (that is, trade within the same sector). This means that a large part of so-called garment exports from the developing countries can in fact be previous imports from the industrial countries themselves (in the form of machinery, synthetic fibres, zips, buttons). Limiting developing country imports to the industrial countries would, therefore, lead to a necessary reduction in industrial country exports, too. The MFA can be seen as damaging in gender sensitive ways given the high levels of women's employment in the sector. In this sense we can talk of an 'engendered' protectionism, though this is rarely seen in such terms by the World Trade Organisation, the World Bank and other policy makers.

    In trying to understand the relationship between women and the textile and garment sector, one paradox is that whilst the sector is a central employer for women world-wide, it is characterised by a scarcity of current research on the lives of working women and the way in which women negotiate multiplex roles under difficult circumstances. Often, assumptions about women as 'docile' workers or/and 'little women' tend to ignore capacities by women for creative self-organisation in the workplace.[12] Commodity analyses of 'women's work' allow us the ability to investigate tensions between prevailing ideas and beliefs in society about women, and the actual lives of working women themselves.

EXAMPLE 18A

China–USA: Trade in Silk

Whilst the MFA is scheduled for abolition by the year 2003, the four-stage reduction envisaged in the quotas left responsibility for compliance and time-tabling to the importing countries themselves. The USA made the decision to leave quota restrictions in place for the maximum period allowed. An added irony was that in the first three months following the signing of the GATT/WTO deal in December 1994, the USA negotiated new bilateral agreements and imposed at least a dozen new quotas. An example of this was the imposition of quotas on Chinese silk imports to the USA. The quotas on silk were applied for the first time. What made this particularly important was that silk is not even covered by the MFA. Neither could the USA raise the argument that the quotas were imposed to protect the domestic textile industry. In the case of silk there is no US industry to protect. The new quotas were an important pointer to the post-MFA environment, as one in which the USA intends to continue vigorously with bilateral restrictions.

The main argument by the importers was that the growth of Chinese silk exports was damaging the market in two ways: first, it 'disrupted' the traditional silk market. Leading retailers and fashion houses in Western Europe argued that Chinese silk clothing (blouses and shirts) were displacing European production and 'devaluing silk's up-market image'. Second, Chinese silk products became 'more affordable' as Chinese exports grew in volume terms, so they began to compete head-on with cotton and synthetics (*Textile Outlook International*, 1994, pp. 3–6).

Other than the gusto shown by the USA in protecting its citizens from cheap (and good quality) silk wear, for many commentators on the textile and garment industry the response of the Chinese government was surprising. Normally Chinese negotiators are seen as tough, yet in this instance they very quickly agreed to all US demands for bilateral quotas on silk. One major reason for China's agreement was that China was trying to secure the renewal of its Most Favoured Nation (MFN) status with the USA. This allows China preferential access to the US market or the same treatment afforded to WTO members despite China's non-membership of the WTO. The MFN was renewed.

EXAMPLE 18B

The Sewing Machine

Helen Chenut asks, 'How often have women been told that machines have revolutionised their lives?' and suggests that it would upset many modern myths to rewrite – from a feminist perspective – the history of the mechanisation of women's work both at home and in the workplace. Chenut (1983, pp. 68–9) points to the sewing machine as providing a good case of gender characterised technology. Designed and manufactured with women in mind, 'the Singer' as it came to be known the world over, revolutionised humble sewing tasks: during the 1850s a skilled tailor sewing by hand could average up to 35 stitches per minute. In 1880 the new, powered Singer machine could work at the rate of 2,000 stitches per minute. In 1900 Singer introduced a new machine capable of sewing over 4,000 stitches per minute (Godley, 1996, pp. 11–12). This, as we shall see, in no way liberated women's work in the garment industry.

It is worthy of note, that shortly after Singer obtained a pattern for his machine and began production in his Glasgow factory, an advertisement appeared in the *Illustrated News* of 25 June 1853 stating:

> The sewing machine has within the last two years acquired a wide celebrity and established its character as one of the most efficient labour saving instruments ever introduced to public notice... We must not forget to call attention to the fact that this instrument is peculiarly calculated for female operative [*sic*]. They should never allow its use to be monopolised by men. (Cited by Chenut, 1983, p. 68)

Drawing on skills women already possessed, the sewing machine increased the speed for producing finished clothes. This did not, however, alter the low wages or the low status attributed to women in the garment industry. As part of the overall process of mechanisation throughout the nineteenth century, the Singer strengthened the piece-work system linking wages more tightly to production especially for women, and divided the labour process into separate operations. In the men's wear factories or sweatshops women sewed just sleeves or button-holes and rarely handled the more noble operations connected either with the cutting or final product.

The sewing machine is a hybrid instrument: both a home utensil and a factory machine, it bridges the gap between a domestic and an industrial economy. By the 1890s, a lighter and cheaper model, practical for home use, entered many working-class homes as married women saw the advantage of supplementing family incomes by taking in sewing. Between 1880 and 1905 over 3 million Singers were sold in the UK alone (Godley, 1996, p. 13). It was only a short step from here to the sweatshops denounced at the turn of the century. Even more insidious were the 'pay as you earn' schemes inducing women to buy a home sewing machine which included a contract with a local garment manufacturer. To pay for the machine, mothers, aided by their children, worked 15 hours a day.

Chenut writes that 'the sewing machine was also attacked on the grounds that the way it was operated had an immoral affect on women's bodies' (Chenut, 1983, p. 69). The early machines manufactured by Singer were worked by a foot treadle until being replaced by an electric motor. The peculiar motion necessary to operate the foot treadle was said to have vicious effects described and denounced at the Socialist Workers' Congress in Marseille by Citoyan Dauthier:

> Several women workers in my *atelier* [small factory] are sick, all due to the same cause: the continuous leg movements, the shaking, the rocking of one's whole body, exhaust them and gives them pains in their backs and stomachs. A large number of them frequently experiencing genital excitement so strongly that they need to stop work...and resort to a cold water wash. (Cited in Chenut, 1983, p. 69)

With the introduction of the electric motor, these specific physical effects disappeared, but the economic and cultural association – even identification – of women with the sewing machine remains an important continuity. (Source: Chenut, 1983, pp. 68–9; Godley, 1996, pp. 8–25.)

EXAMPLE 18C

Women and Trade Unions in the Indian Garment Export Industry

A study of women workers in the Delhi garment export industry by Sujata Gothoskar (1992), carried out under the auspices of the Indian Association of Women's Studies, investigated the relationship between women and trade unions. Delhi accounts for 60 per cent of garment export earnings and employs about 100,000 registered workers and a larger number of homeworkers. Most of the factory women interviewed worked as machinists, passers, cotton cleaners. Many were interviewed at home because employers refused permission to do so at the factory. The study found very low levels of unionisation. Only five out of 30 firms surveyed were unionised and three of them had a union for men only.

The study pointed to a number of factors which influence the ability of women to organise in unions: the fragmented nature of production and the mobility of the industry which sees many firms closing down and re-opening in a different place with a different name; the non-application of labour legislation; high levels of segregation of workers in different departments of the same plant. This was reinforced by a ban on talking while working in many factories. A general 'climate of repression' existed inside the plants. Many women expressed a fear of 'social stigma' attached to women's participation in public actions, such as strikes and demonstrations which challenge prevailing social norms about women's conduct. A more frequent response by many women was that they 'did not have time' to join a union, mainly due to the burden of housework (Gothoskar, 1992, p. 107). Most of them were young women, many of whom were new entrants to employment and as such were more vulnerable. In a number of factories young women were employed on condition that they did not marry, and since most were working out of economic necessity (often due to the death of an earning member of the family) 'were left with the only option – of not marrying' (Gothoskar, 1992, p. 99). Younger women came under intense pressure to comply with lower pay and the worst conditions. One key factor was the fear of sexual harassment and this partly explained why women worked in lower paying but more 'safe' (often smaller) firms with little union presence.

While the study found powerful reasons why the women were not members of trade unions, a sizable proportion of the sample (37 per cent) felt that they needed a union. Permanent jobs and Provident Funds (weekly savings by union members used for personal emergencies) were mentioned positively. A number of women had taken part in previous attempts to organise in unions. Most of these attempts failed. In one case a woman entre- preneur recounted a strike which had taken place in her factory two years before. The same strike was recounted by a woman worker:

'The woman entrepreneur was still bitter about the experience and vowed never to employ women again because "they are worse than the men when it comes to action and militancy". The ostensible reason for her to recruit such a large number of women was that she "always wanted to do something for the poor women" but regretted having thought that women were "timid and peace loving". She narrated incidents of how two women agitators shouted filthy abuse at her and how the women were the major participants on the *gherao* carried out against her'. (Woman entrepreneur, cited by Gothoskar, 1992, p. 110)

The woman worker (Godavari) 'recalled that many months passed but nothing happened when they approached a union for help in recovering three months wages owed to them by the owner. Another union was approached and "this union really fought our case". After protracted negotiations the women came out on strike. What brought the dispute to rapid conclusion [the strike lasted for eight hours] was that "one day we the women decided to *gherao* the owner. Despite feeling afraid we decided not to let the car [with the owner in it] move out of the factory. We encircled it. There was a scuffle in which a woman's leg was fractured but we refused to move. The police was called but we shouted and screamed until the owner agreed to give us our wages". The women won the three months wages they were owed, but only received money for two months ("the union must have kept the other"). For Godavari it was a bitter victory. Her husband who supported the strike throughout the four month dispute, as well as her son, asked her to give up the job, which she did. "Everyone had started talking about me. Sometimes I used to come home late at night. And people started talking bad things about us. It affected my son"'. (Woman worker, cited by Gothoskar, 1992, pp. 111–12)

(The *gherao* is form of direct action used by workers in labour disputes and consists of workers surrounding managers and bosses and refusing to let them out of their offices, or in this case their car.)

Conclusions

Prodromos Panayiotopoulos and Gavin Capps

Development and its Discontents

THE GLOBAL ECONOMY, THE NATION STATE AND DEVELOPMENT

The development of capitalism on a world scale was a protracted affair with roots which can be traced to the emergence of the European medieval cities and the growth of trade in specialised industries. The expansion of competing European powers and the long transition from mercantilism to industrial capitalism formed much of the context for the development of the global economy until the middle of the eighteenth century. From the late eighteenth century onwards, the Industrial Revolution radically transformed the economy and society of initially Britain and subsequently the other western European countries. During the mid-nineteenth century Britain made a potent connection between industrialisation, the state and imperial expansion. In the twentieth century the USA pioneered fordist mass-production techniques and this, more than any other factor, allowed the USA to challenge Britain's supremacy in manufacturing and in the world economy. Whilst industrialisation began in Europe, the book argues that by this it is not meant that industrialisation is the property of Europe. The book offers illustrative material which points to the 'export' of industrialisation both by colonial expansion and imitative policies by the ex-colonies. This means that industrialisation has spread, albeit unevenly, to all parts of the globe, incorporating as in the cases of the Asian and Latin American NICs, Japan and North America, particular characteristics in the functioning of markets and corporate organisation.

Two universal assumptions in imitative industrialisation were the expectations that this would result in the strengthening of the nation state: another stated objective in all industrial policy in the Third World was that industrialisation would raise per capita incomes and improve the human condition. Invariably industrialisation became interlocked with notions of development and national progress. It is this notion, more than any other, which is being challenged by globalisation.

Studies of countries, regions and commodities offer concrete illustration of the emergence and changes to an interdependent world economy. This interdependency is neither a lineal nor stationary condition, let alone one characterised by equality between the world's nation states. The nature of this interdependency, whether it represents a new phenomenon called 'globalisation' or represents important continuities in world development, is debatable, as are some of the political conclusions on the 'irresistibility' of globalisation. What is clearer, is that the more industrialised a commodity, sector, country or region is, so the more it is integrated and subject to changes in the global economy. Each swing in the price of a commodity or currency, each austerity programme and 'rescue' package launched by government and the international agencies, impacts in often unpredicted ways on developing countries and the livelihoods of millions of people throughout the Third World. There is more than a sense of irony, therefore, to the proposition that industrialisation was intended to strengthen the nation state in its international relations.

GLOBALISATION, INDUSTRIALISATION AND THE STATE

In attempting to provide explanations for the transformation of national economies it has been argued that in many situations the role of the state was critical to the initiation of industrialisation. The state as agency in Third World industrialisation has longer roots than contemporary neo-liberal arguments about globalisation suggest. This saw the consolidation of Import Substitution Industrialisation (ISI) in inter-war Latin America, from a 'forced' response to external shock to a recognisable national industrial policy. This was mirrored in global experiences during the inter-war depression, which ranged from Stalinist 'forced' industrialisation in Russia, to extensive state intervention during the 1930s in virtually all the advanced industrial economies, whether in the form of New Deal public work schemes in the USA, or the militarisation of entire national economies in war-time Europe. It was under these conditions that the analysis of the 'Leviathan State' presented by Nikolai Bukharin (1982, pp. xxxi–lviii) – an analysis which proved useful in explaining the evolution of the Stalinist regime in the Soviet Union itself – pointed towards an omnipotent unity of state and national capital. In diverse political formations and at different historical periods – South Korea, Brazil, China, Argentina, India, Turkey, Russia, Japan, the state protected and subsidised infant state-owned industries acting as a critical agency for accumulation and industrialisation.

The state played a significant role in the global dispersion of industrialisation characterised by the NICs. This experience challenges the various theories which point to the structural constraints facing Third World countries in the world economy. A number of broad and inter-exchangeable structural-constraint theories have been identified. These include classical dependency theories such as 'unequal exchange', more current globalisation analyses associated with the 'new international division of labour' and the 'global manufacturing system'. All point towards externality as the key determinant in economic and political development and offer powerful evidence of structural constraint (see Frobel et al., 1980; Harris, 1990a; Hirst and Thompson, 1996). Globalisation theories suggest that the world system acts in a positive, negative, (but rarely neutral) way on national economies (Panayiotopoulos, 1995).

The wider application of state direction to promote industrialisation has been described as 'state capitalism' (see Harris, 1990a; Harman, 1996). State capitalism acted in many situations and particularly so in the Third World, as a necessary precondition for globalisation, or the internationalisation of national economies. This condition intensified with state-directed industrialisation, paradoxically driven by policies initially framed to promote national economic development and self-reliance, in order to combat underdevelopment and to lessen dependency on the world economy and fluctuations in commodity prices. In practice the more industrialised an economy became so the less self-reliant it was. As Nigel Harris notes,

> If 'dependency' indicated the economic relationship between a country and the world, the more developed the country, the more dependent it was – that is, the more domestic activity was determined by external relationships. (Harris, 1990a, p. 123)

In this sense, globalisation represents the crisis of state capitalism on a world scale.

CONTRADICTIONS WITHIN GLOBALISATION

One important proposition in the Millennium is that the crucial question to ask is not 'how far' a state can control key economic variables but (more significantly) what happens *after* the state as 'historical animator' is confronted by the very forces it has helped to promote (such as the *Chaebol*), outgrowing the confines of a given nation state. Given the weight attached to economic liberalisation, globalisation and production for export in developing country industrial policy – exemplified by attempts to imitate the Export Orientated Industrialisation (EOI) market-friendly strategies of the East Asian NICs – then these sorts of questions have become increasingly poignant. The active promotion of export-led industries means that national economies which industrialise under the current conditions of globalisation, now find themselves more vulnerable to external shocks and less prone, therefore, to state planning.

Regional and country studies point to three major contradictions within globalisation. First, on the one hand they offer powerful evidence that capitalism is expanding the boundaries of human contact, in ways which were unimaginable in previous historical periods. Nowhere is this more apparent than in the expansive global manufacturing production system and the activities of Trans National Corporations in sectors such as garments, footwear and electronic component assembly. TNCs unite workers with differing social characteristics, such as 'race', religion, gender and nationality, in most countries of the world. At the same time, however, capitalist states and regional trade blocs apply restrictions in the movement of goods and services and impose selective immigration controls on workers and asylum seekers from the Third World which make use of the very same social characteristics.

The second major contradiction within globalisation appears in the tendency for economics and politics to be moving in opposite directions. One general observation is that whilst the world we live in is far more economically interdependent and 'globalised' than at any previous point in human history, nationalism remains the dominant political ideology on a world scale. This creates problems of analysis for those who see in globalisation a source for optimism. Nigel Harris writes (1990a, p. 202) that 'one of the sources of optimism is in the weakening of the drive to war [in that] as capital and states become slightly dissociated, so the pressures to war are slightly weakened'. Harris further notes, that under these conditions 'there promises to be some decrease in the belief that killing foreigners is a good thing'. Critics of this benign view of globalisation point to wars and military interventions in the Falklands, Somalia, the Gulf and the Balkans, as representing neither a weakening of pressure to war, nor a lessening in the belief (amongst rulers, at least) that killing foreigners is a price worth paying to defend strategic interests (see Callinicos, 1991, 1994; see also, Harman, 1991, 1992; German, 1999). They point to a more complex world, but nevertheless one characterised by the 'return' of a bloody imperialism, a condition which both globalisation and post-modernist/post-colonial theories tend to ignore or to underestimate. Military intervention by the developed countries and their use of technological superiority to impose political solutions typically (but not exclusively) in the Third World, provide contextual explanation for the durability of nationalist ideologies. The development of globalisation does not result in the 'withering away of the state', least of all those of the imperialist countries. One continuity appears in the high incidence of military conflict waged by the national or supranational states. Chris Harman (1996, p. 30) argues that the world system remains 'unstable and dangerous precisely because capitals retain ties to states with the possibility of resort to force'.

One of the complexities of military intervention at the end of the twentieth century appeared in the imposition of 'humanitarian aid'. This saw the selective application by the USA of UN Security Council Resolutions (the so-called 'Clinton doctrine'). This underpinned US intervention in Somalia, Bosnia, Kosovo and gave NATO the confidence to act unilaterally in Yugoslavia. The above when coupled with the collapse of communism has contributed to the neo-liberal argument, popularised by amongst others Francis Fukuyama, that the market with the USA as its epicentre is the custodian of both history and the core values of civil society (see Fukuyama, 1995). The Gulf and Yugoslavian Wars suggested, however, that the ability of the USA to act was in part conditioned by the level of political support which it could mobilise in Europe, the Arab countries and so on. This is neither fixed nor predetermined and suggests something less than 'world domination', despite the collapse of communism.

One sobering reflection on the persistence of nationalism is that the twentieth ended as with the nineteenth century, in a war in the Balkans. Over 20 Newly Independent Countries, most of them in the heartland of Europe, have emerged as the result of the collapse of communism. This second great wave of decolonisation which parallels the experiences of Africa and Asia in the post-war period, has led to an unprecedented expansion in the number of nations. Many of the Newly Independent Countries of Eastern Europe, Central Asia and the Caucasus, have broken out of the 'prison house of nations' which characterised both Tsarist and Stalinist Russia and as with the Third World, they too made use of the discourse of 'national liberation' (Harris, 1990b). This is an illustration of how the world is a more complex place within which nationalism represents an important continuity. The international agencies driven by free market globalisation theories, find it difficult to understand the phenomenon of nationalism or be clear about the role of the nation state in development. The World Bank in its most current *World Development Report*, for example, identifies the intersection between international and sub-national levels of the global economy as the optimum area for development intervention. This says little, if anything, about the role of development at the national level (see World Bank, 2000).

A third major contradiction within globalisation is the tendency for development and industrialisation to be highly selective and uneven in its distribution. This can appear in differences in the levels of foreign direct investment and the distribution of industry between regions and countries, as well as within countries and in the role of particular industries in national economies. Uneven development is neither a new nor ephemeral phenomenon. It lies at the heart of the world system, which becomes a world system of extremities in both the level of economic development and in the state of the human condition. The poverty-stricken North-East region of Brazil, the island of Haiti which sees the lowest per capita incomes in the Western Hemisphere, the South Wales Swansea Valley which faces worse levels of unemployment than most places in Britain, were all at one time or other, the 'most' developed parts of the world. The impact of boom and slump cycles, as well as industrial policy, are some of the factors which explain changes in the composition of the world economy's growth centres. As old areas, industries, skills and trades are abandoned, so new areas, industries and skills become more integrated into the world system and in quite unpredictable ways. The Newly Industrialised Countries became the most significant new growth centres in the world economy at the end of the twentieth century. As such the NICs came to represent the most concentrated form of uneven development inside the world economy. The dynamic nature of uneven development is also illustrated in the experiences of particular industries, such as the global textile industry, the copper mining and refining industry, and in the global restructuring of the tourism sector. The crisis which faced the Asian NICs and the question marks raised over their future direction, are neither new nor particularly Asian. Rather, they are substantially the result of changes in the world economy which made possible industrialisation in the NICs in the first place. The dynamic nature of uneven and combined development means that neither industrialisation nor development can be seen as representing a terminal condition.

A number of contradictions within globalisation were revealed during the 1997 Asian crisis. One appeared in a tendency for industry and finance to be moving in opposing directions. This was typified by the sliding of the South Korean *Chaebol* into financial bankruptcy, whilst at the same time retaining some of the most up to date and competitive industrial capacity in the world. This was illustrated in the fortunes of Daewoo, which simultaneously became the largest corporate bankrupt in history and the most productive car maker in the world. Another contradiction emerged in the poverty of neo-liberal theory in offering explanations for the Asian crisis and for the persistence of poverty in the Third World, despite very high rates of growth in the NICs. For neo-liberals the mono-causal explanation for crisis has been the application of the idea of 'crony capitalism': this condition points to deficiencies in the political institutions of capitalism, rather than any structural faultlines in capitalism itself. It is a convenient way of explaining the crisis. Crony capitalism has been discovered in formal democracies and dictatorships in South East Asia, in Eastern European and sub-Saharan African countries undergoing transition, in Latin America's resurgent relationship with populist politics, and in fact just about everywhere in the world. The idea that poverty is the result of deficiencies in the developing countries themselves, and in particular their ('corrupt') governments, has been a standard neo-liberal residual explanation for lack of growth in most of the poor countries of the world. It is this simplistic stereotype which has been applied by the World Bank and the IMF today to explain the market crisis in Asia. This detracts attention from the role of markets, and in particular financial markets in the development of the Asian crisis. The crony capitalism thesis presents a highly ideological and unsatisfactory explanation for crisis. There remains the need to more clearly identify precise mechanisms in the relationship between nation state, globalisation and development.

DEVELOPMENT

It is relevant in the conclusion to remind ourselves about the scale and nature of the problem facing the human condition in the twenty-first century. For many people in the world the development problem is an employment problem. Many cannot find work, or sufficient work, and this is a particular problem facing young people internationally but even more so in the Third World where young people constitute a larger section of the population (Panayiotopoulos and Gerry, 1997). One encouraging development appears in the role of endogenous growth and employment generation by the 'informal sector(s)' of the Third World. Growth has been sufficiently pronounced in this area for the ILO to include in its 1997 World Labour Report a section on 'Industrial Relations in the Informal Sector' (see ILO, 1997, pp. 175–214). At the same time, the 'informal sector' is strongly associated with poverty and represents for most of the urban poor in the Third World, bare subsistence (see Atema and Panayiotopoulos, 1995). For many workers in the developed countries the 1990s were 'lean times' which showed the limits of nationally based trade union action (Moody, 1997). Viviane Forrester (1999) writes eloquently about the 'economic horror' facing millions of workers who lose their jobs or are afraid of losing their jobs, whose peace of mind is shattered by both economic hardship and the loss of self-esteem which in market economies is strongly linked with paid employment.

For many people in the Third World the development problem is the struggle to exist. The United Nations Children's Fund (UNICEF) in its current report on the *State of the World's Children* points to how little has been achieved since the targets established at the World Summit for Children in 1990. The report states that 'the world has more children living in poverty now than it did ten years ago [and] is more unstable and violent than it was in 1990'. It argues that 'as globalisation proceeds along its inherently asymmetrical course' children remain main victims of poverty (UNICEF, 2000, pp. 21, 27). The global number of people living in poverty has increased to 1.2 billion (one in five) of whom 600 million are children. In the UK and USA a fifth to a quarter of children live in poverty. In the decade since the adoption of the Convention of the Rights of Children in 1989, more than 2 million children have been killed, more than 6 million injured in armed conflicts and 15 million have become refugees. More than 500 million children – nearly one in four – live in dangerous and unstable conditions. The report condemned the failure of governments and international agencies to tackle the Aids epidemic. Each day Aids was estimated to infect 8,550 children and young people. In Africa 2 million people have died from Aids in 1998 and the pattern is likely to repeat itself in south Asia (UNICEF, 2000).

There are intense debates about the direction of development. For neoliberals the standard argument is that free trade and the market are the only forces capable of delivering sustainable growth and development. This is clearly re-stated by US Treasury Secretary Lawrence Summers, who writes in defence of the World Trade Organisation, that 'more than 50 years of global trade agreements have confirmed what economics have always taught: that increasing trade between nations promotes prosperity, and by promoting prosperity, trade promotes peace'.[1] The assumptions of a benign and universal body of economics inexorably moving the world towards global integration, did not prove very convincing to the large numbers of 'anti-capitalist' protesters who gathered outside the WTO Seattle Conference.

The protest saw one of the largest mobilisations in the USA since the demonstrations against the Vietnam War in the 1960s, and brought together a variety of people and causes: longshoremen, who had closed down the port of Seattle, auto workers, the Teamsters Union, worried about their jobs; students campaigning against sweatshops, people opposed to environmental degradation, Third World debt, poverty, GM food companies and corporate greed. One black worker was quoted as saying, 'I work at the Boeing factory in Seattle. It's a huge plant with 80,000 workers. I do not trust the people who treat us badly in the plant to run the world.'[2] The protesters were united in a common opposition to a vision of the world in which the price mechanism alone structures world trade and much of everyday life. Seattle pointed to a growing resistance against a neo-liberal vision of globalisation. It also saw for the first time a curfew used in a US city since the Second World War – when it acted as a prelude to the internment of Japanese-Americans. Over 600 people were arrested at Seattle.

The Conference collapsed and failed to agree on a common programme on free trade. One contributory factor was the atmosphere of tension created by the demonstration and the police response, which included at one stage the gassing of some of the delegates. The blockade by the protesters also meant that some of the delegates failed to gain entrance into the hall (including UN General Secretary, Kofi Annan) on the opening day. Another contributory factor was the arrogance of the US delegation. The insistence by Ms Barshefsky, US Trade Representative, to both lead the US delegation and chair the meeting was tactically unwise. US trade negotiators are more at home in bilateral negotiations in which the USA is in a stronger position, and as such, Ms Barshefsky was badly equipped to show the necessary level of dialogue in complex negotiations, and this angered many of the delegations from the Third World. As some of the spirit of the surrounding streets began to permeate into the conference hall itself, the proceedings grew more chaotic, and it was reported that 'developing country delegates pounded their desks, booed and catcalled in protest at the brusque chairmanship [sic] of Charlene Barshefsky, US trade representative. Some threatened to walk out of the talks early'.[3]

Development is an area of struggle over meaning which has been shaped by changes to the world economy, the activities of TNCs and by the economic development policies pursued by the international agencies and Third World states. It is also shaped by competing claims to development which influence the redistributory functions of the local state. Analyses (such as 'crony capitalism') which attach primacy to the role of the state in economic development, frequently fail to explain in a satisfactory manner the relationship between different classes in society and the state, how this may influence the form of any given state and the implications this has for the distribution of the benefits of development. Holloway (1994, p. 29) writes that states are 'a form of social relations' which themselves are a reflection of the changing relationship between classes in any given society. As the relationships between classes in society change, so does the particular form in which states appear. In this sense, all states and their institutional arrangements are contingent rather than fixed and subjected to processes of deconstruction and reconstruction. The nature of the relations between state and capitalist development needs to be understood in the specific circumstances and epochal location within which competing claims to development are articulated.

Alternatively, globalisation analyses which attach primacy to the role of externality in shaping the pattern of economic development and see the role of the state and development assistance as a counter-balance to structural constraints faced in global markets, similarly say little about the politics of the state itself, or those of the development agencies themselves (see Hirst and Thompson, 1996, pp. 170–94; also see Hancock, 1991), or see the need to investigate the relationship between politics and economics per se. This absence of politics is rather surprising since both in the Latin American and wider experience, 'development purposes have been politically-driven' (Leftwich, 1994, p. 380), expressed in the wish to 'catch up' and which frequently (and necessarily so) applied the discourse of nationalism and state direction. Globalisation analyses which point to external constraints as causal explanation similarly fail to explain in a satisfactory manner the role of complex local factors (and actors) in globalisation, and the nature of the relationships which shape state and development. As such, globalisation theories fail to identify competing claims to development, how this may define the local state, or how this may change over time.

The institutional arrangements of the state, which underpinned the economic miracles in Brazil and South Korea and which made it possible over a prolonged period, were not only internal variables, but necessarily so. In Latin America, ISI was sensitively linked to populist and nationalist political mobilisations. The institutional arrangements linking state and *Chaebol* in South Korea were shaped by the role of the military and the politics of anti-communism. In many developing countries and in particular those undergoing industrialisation, the key institutional arrangement which shaped relations between state and economic development was in attempts at the subordination of working-class interest to that of the 'national' interest. These arrangements, sometimes involving co-option and frequently physical coercion, are neither automatic nor externally driven, but rather, they presuppose ideas, politics, traditions and legitimisation processes embedded inside a given society: these are the sort of factors which become manifest in specific analysis of particular situations, and by and large, are factors to which globalisation theories do not speak. The relationship between state and development and industrialisation and globalisation, may be seen as a reflection of the wider idea of policy as profoundly a political process and one characterised by competing claims to the distribution of the benefits of development and industrialisation in the global economy. Who controls the state and by implication who controls society, has critical implications for shaping the pattern of 'winners and losers' in development. The lives of workers offer graphic detail and insight into the processes behind globalisation, industrialisation and the cruelty we call 'development'. In this lies a voice for optimism. There are very few countries in the world where the rulers do not have to worry about workers, trade unions and periodic industrial action. At Seattle, US labour unions were a key part of the broad anti-capitalist coalition. In many African and Eastern European countries workers were instrumental in the development of pro-democracy movements. George Orwell's Winston Smith drew the conclusion that 'if there is a future, it lies with the proles'. A more optimistic conclusion might be to look to the spirit of resistance to global capital illustrated by Seattle.

Appendix 1

Of Noble Savages and Lazy Natives

'THE OTHER'

Societies and groups of peoples in different historical periods employed many ways by which they could be distinguished from each other. Frequently this appeared in customs involving the denial of certain kinds of food, the wearing of certain kinds of clothing, or the following of particular occupations. The ancient Greeks and Romans distinguished themselves from the 'barbarians' in the north (such as the Ancient Britons) in terms of perceived cultural deficiencies: that they (the barbarians) did not speak Greek or Latin languages; that they did not worship the Olympic and minor gods, appreciate Graeco-Roman science, philosophy, literature, music and so on. Similarly during the conflict between Islam and Christendom during the Middle Ages, the 'divide' was constructed in terms of 'believer' or 'infidel' of a given religion. Implied in the above was the possibility of transgressing identities based on cultural norms: one could for example, learn a language or convert to another religion.

Many examples suggest that historically, the construction of identities was conceptualised in cultural terms – which are themselves subject to change – rather than in the unchanging terms implied in the use of a fixed biological attribute such as skin pigmentation (colour) as a way of constructing the 'other'. It is of note that both in the Ancient and Arab worlds the Greeks, Romans and Arabs, whilst practising slavery, did not attach to this any colour specificity.

The use of colour as a way of conferring inferior identity to Africa, its people, communities and their environment, points to departures in the way Europe understood Africa and its people. Martin Bernal (1987, 1991) for example shows that the 'Ancient Model' pointed towards (black) Egypt as the centre of civilisation – a proposition accepted by the Greeks and Romans themselves. This was, as Bernal (1987, p. 189) argues, displaced by the 'Aryan Model' of (white) Greece as the cradle of civilisation during the beginning of the nineteenth century, as a result of four main factors: Christian reaction; the increasing association between Europe and Christendom; the rise of the concept of progress and its association with an industrialising Europe; the growth of racism; and as also due to a romantic Hellenism – a movement amongst English intellectuals, such as Lord Byron – which campaigned for the independence of Greece from the Ottoman Empire.

Ignacy Sachs (1976) points to European perceptions of blackness during the Middle Ages in two contrasting images: the devil was often presented in popular folklore as black (usually in the guise of a black Ethiopian). At the same time, however, there were a number of North African saints who also were black, such as St Maurice, St Zeno and St Cassius. There were paintings of a black Madonna, and during the fourteenth century one of the Magi was depicted as being black. Quite clearly, at this period of little knowledge by Europe of Africa, blackness was articulated in an ambiguity whereby the colour black could be equally perceived by Europeans in terms of devil or saint.

The ambiguity over the colour black was illustrated in a theological debate in sixteenth-century Venice, one of the strongest sea-powers amongst the Italian city-states. Venetian society at the time was characterised by the expansion in the numbers of black slaves servicing its expanding galleon ships. Implied in this was that blackness denoted an inferior status. That black slavery at the time was not as prevalent as it was to become, was partly reflected in the threat by the Pope to excommunicate the Venetians for being slave-owners. The subject of the theological debate was, 'can a black person be canonised?' By implication the question was: *can a black slave be canonised?* This latter implication posed problems for slave-owners, since the act of canonisation explicitly places a saint above all other mortals, including slave-owners. It was, as Ignacy Sachs argues, about this time that many of the paintings in the nativity play begin to depict all three Magi as white.

THE AMBIGUITY OF THE 'NOBLE SAVAGE'

The concept of the noble savage was the most characteristic expression of European ambiguity towards black Africa during the period of early exploration and limited contact between the two continents. The concept proposed that Africans were closer to and in communion with nature, and in this there was a begrudging admiration for the world of freedom the noble (but simple) savage may enjoy, untainted as he/she was by the corrupting influence of commerce and cities. A general romanticisation of nature found expression in late eighteenth-century France, in the educational ideas of Rousseau, as well as the economic ideas of the Physiocrats (the founders of political economy) who argued in the *Tableau Economique*, that agriculture was the only productive sector.

The application of the concept of the noble savage needs to be understood in the context of a Europe facing rapid changes and challenges, such as: the 'discovery' of peoples outside the framework of Biblical reference; the growth of the ideas of the Enlightenment; and a sense of loss of nature and community arising out of incipient industrialisation, growing urbanisation and land enclosure; the above were to inform European perceptions of black, African and nature. At the same time the Africans and other races were presented as savage, ignorant, unchristian, thieving and in need of civilising. The concept might have said more (therefore) about an expanding Europe itself, rather than the Africa it sought to describe.

Henry Rider Haggard, Edgar Rice Burroughs (the creator of Tarzan), Captain W.E. Johns (the creator of Biggles) and Rudyard Kipling were some of the many authors who, in varying ways and with varying emphases on noble or savage, acted as popular translators of cultural representation and misrepresentation of other cultures and the 'Dark Continent' in particular. John Newsinger (1986) suggests that Burroughs' work *Tarzan of the Apes* is the story par excellence of the white man's conquest of African savagery. As Newsinger writes:

> When Professor Archimedes Porter, his daughter Jane, and the rest of a sorry band of castaways stumbled across an apparently abandoned cabin on the savage African coast, they were confronted by a notice: 'This is the House of Tarzan, the killer of Beasts and Many Black Men. Do Not Harm the Things Which Are Tarzan's. Tarzan Watches'. In this way were white men and women first made aware of the Apeman's existence. (Newsinger, 1986, p. 59)

The conquest by Tarzan of African savagery is a triumph of white, European heredity and superior breeding, a fact of which Lord Greystoke becomes aware in this incident: one of the blacks kills Kala (the gorilla who nurtured Tarzan) while out hunting and Tarzan pursues him through the jungle. He eventually kills the man, banging him by the neck and stabbing him in the heart, and is about to eat part of the corpse when something stops him:

> a qualm of nausea overwhelmed him... All he knew was that he could not eat the flesh of this black man, and thus hereditary instinct, ages old, usurped the function of his untaught mind and saved him from transgressing a worldwide law of whose very existence he was ignorant. (Burroughs, 1980, p. 103)

Biggles, as with Tarzan, assisted in informing the children of the generation brought up during the period of the end of Empire and the 'winds of change' (growth of independence) in Africa. According to a survey carried out by UNESCO during 1964, Biggles was rated the most popular juvenile hero in the world and was placed 29th on the list of the world's most translated books. Brian Street (1975) notes that the savage is presented in W.E. Johns' work as inevitably hostile. In describing one adventure by Biggles and his friends, Ginger and Bertie, before even a foot is set on land the estimation by Biggles is that of, 'crocodile-infested rivers, swamps, virgin jungle and warlike tribes of head-hunting cannibals... In short it's just about one of the worst pieces of territory in the world' (Johns, 1955, p. 65). When the inhabitants of the territory are met, the encounter is described in this fashion:

> The blacks, seeing them stopped dead, huddling, crouching, staring. Their great mops of hair and bodies daubed with white clay, their mouths stained with betel-nut, and with boars tasks thrust through their nostrils, they presented a picture of bestial savagery not easily forgotten. (Johns, 1955, p. 84)

Biggles is presented as inevitably involved in physical confrontations with savage natives and blacks, with Biggles and friends invariably 'winning the day' with volleys of strategically placed buckshot:

> Half a dozen shots were sufficient to alter the entire situation. The attackers leapt high into the air as the leaden hail smacked into their bare skins... They may have thought these wounds were fatal. At any rate they were soon hopping and jumping back towards the forest from which they had emerged. (Johns, 1955, p. 85)

SLAVERY: THE AMBIGUITY DISSOLVED

Factors behind the dissolution of the ambiguity implied in the noble savage and the growth of explicit ideas of racial superiority need to be related to the changing nature of the encounter between Europe and Africa: from the initial period of early European exploration, to the triangular trade, to the scramble for Africa and extended territorial acquisition. Each of these periods implied changes to the economic arrangements which made use of land, labour and capital.

The making of a new and more interdependent world order by an expanding and industrialising Europe was expressed in more spatially expansive and increasingly complex patterns of trade. The triangular trade involved: UK manufacturing workers and exporters; slavers and the elites of African society; plantation owners of the New World; African slave labour upon which the plantation economy depended (see Williams, 1966; James, 1980). The commodities produced by the plantation economy – such as sugar, cotton, tobacco – marked key departures in the world economy. The previous era of mercantilist 'windfall' profits rested on trade in a limited range of luxury goods (such as spices, silk) or precious metals, or in the case of England the looting of Spanish ships. The plantation economy by contrast, produced mass goods, the consumption of which characterised an industrialising Europe.

Explicit in colour-specific slavery was a process whereby Africans were denied humanity. Eric Williams (1966, p. 46) points to the following: during 1783 the captain of the slave ship *Zong* facing an acute shortage of water threw overboard 132 slaves, who drowned. The owners brought an action for insurance alleging that the loss of slaves fell within the clause of the policy which insured against 'perils of the sea'. Chief Justice Manfield made the judgement that 'the case of the slaves was the same as if horses had been thrown overboard' and damages of 30 pounds were awarded for each slave. Williams comments that the idea that the captain and crew should be prosecuted for mass homicide never entered into the head of any humanitarian.

THE 'LAZY NATIVE'

The slave trade decisively dissolved the initial romantic ambiguities contained in the noble savage presented during the exploratory period of the colonial encounter. Rapid economic expansion by an industrialised Europe was characterised by increasingly more complex demands made on indigenous labour supply. Often this was expressed in a distinction between non-settler and settler colonies; indeed, it was amongst the settler colonies of South-East Africa characterised by an increasing demand for African *wage* labour that the concept of the 'lazy native' was to implant in popular white culture and colonial development policy a new key term of reference.

Attempts to intensify the level of work carried out by African labour for European employers in mines, factories and plantations, and concerns expressed amongst them over worker diligence, implied new ways of mobilising labour. This, as Henry Bernstein notes (1988, p. 42), also implied a novel irony:

It is ironic too – and would hardly have escaped the attention of the 'natives' – that the virtues of intensive manual labour were advocated (and enforced) by groups of Europeans notable for their aversion to it, whether colonial officials, missionary 'princes' of the church, traders, land-owners or the managers of mines and plantations.

Appendix 2

The Third World: An Activity

The purpose is to use a readily available source of information about the Third World in order to look at the nature of media coverage and the images and perceptions presented by such coverage. This can be critically evaluated in its own right and in the light of the examples and case study material. Much of this exercise will be conducted independently of the classroom situation. The findings, however, and explanation for the findings, may act as the basis for classroom discussion.

1 INTRODUCTION

The project requires you to formulate a critical argument about the treatment of Third World issues by the media in the form of a report for a concerned group. You should choose a topic in which you are personally interested, and investigate its coverage in the media, relating topical social, economic and political development to material in the course.

2 THE ISSUES

How do various media sources select Third World events and issues as news stories, and what approaches do they use in their coverage (for example, in their use of 'fact', opinion, language and visual effects)?

To what extent, and in what ways, are particular images and ideas encouraged or reinforced by the selection and treatment of information about the Third World by the media sources used? How do these views relate to relevant analyses in the course materials?

You may be concerned with a particular topic (for example, the social impact of the 'Asian Crisis') which you think receives insufficient and/or biased media treatment, and you may want to make out a case for certain changes to be made. So you should think about the *objectives* behind your choice: what are you trying to investigate and why? What is the hypothesis under examination?

3 GETTING STARTED

You have to decide:

a. on a topic from one of the four categories listed below under 'Practical Advice';
b. to whom you are making a report and what sort of report;
c. which media sources you are going to use for your investigation;
d. the time-span your investigation is going to cover;
e. what methods of data analysis you are going to use, appropriate to your topic and report.

4 INITIAL PROJECT PROPOSAL

You need to have thought carefully about these five points (which are discussed in 'Practical Advice' below), and be able to outline what you plan to do in relation to each. Although you will not be able to collect all the information you need at this stage, you should make a preliminary survey of the media sources you wish to use to make sure that your project is feasible. You should also indicate the topic you have chosen.

5 PRACTICAL ADVICE

Choosing a Topic

Your topic should fall into one of the following categories:

a. A recent *event*: examples during the 1990s included wars, in the Gulf, Balkans, the United Nations intervention in Somalia, the crisis in Rwanda;
b. An *issue*: examples might be the role of aid, disasters, the impact of 'structural adjustment', the pro-democracy movements, the role of Non Governmental Organisations, role of trade unions;
c. A particular *country or region*, such as Southern Africa, East Asia, or the treatment of Third World immigrants, in the USA or UK, over a period of time (say six weeks) comparing its coverage in different media sources;
d. *Sub-Saharan Africa*: its coverage in general in a selection of sources over a limited period of time (say two weeks).

Be practical in your choice. Only choose an event that isn't recent if you have reasonable access to back copies of media material, through cuttings, libraries or other sources. Try and relate your topic to the material you have studied in the book. An appreciation of the case studies and examples as well as the application of concepts and ideas elaborated in the book, should act as an aid and inform a critical evaluation of the treatment of Third World issues by the media.

Choosing a Target Group

Your choice of topic may be influenced by the *target group* of your report. In selecting a target group, you should consider what sort of case you plan to make in your report: for example, is it to change an editorial line? is it to influence the way journalists write? is to argue for more balanced coverage of Africa on television? Make sure the argument is directed at a specific group (for example, heads of journalism training centres, community education organisers in US and UK cities).

Choosing Sources

First, you need to decide which material sources you are going to use for your project, and the extent of coverage required to obtain the back-up material you need: newspapers, magazines and journals, radio, television, or some combination of these. Your choice may be affected by the likelihood of your topic being covered. This needs to be given some thought. The initial proposal containing a preliminary survey of sources should address this point. In addition you need to be sensitive to circulation and viewing figures when assessing media scope.

Second, you need to decide over what time period you are going to monitor your sources. If you are going to use radio or television, you may want to make a sample of particular kinds of broadcasts such as the news. Do remember, however, that radio and television are more difficult to draw as evidence to your report (and more difficult for your teacher to check) than written sources. Remember also time constraints involved in deciding on sources. It can take a long time to scan many newspapers. In addition, many newspapers can cost a lot of money.

So select your sources carefully and make a preliminary investigation of what they may reveal. A first survey will save you time later and help you to set limits on your material by discarding sources which may not be useful for the purpose of your project. Alternatively you may purposely include a study of a mass circulation paper with little (if any) coverage of Africa, so as to draw some qualitative insight.

Collecting and Analysing Your Data

How you analyse your data depends partly on the objectives of your report and what you want to find out to substantiate your case.

First, there are *quantitative* measures. These are particularly important for establishing the extent of coverage within and between sources and for comparing coverage of your topic with other topics, or of the Third World with other general content. Common quantitative methods are measuring column inches for comparison with columns given to other subjects both within and between sources. For broadcasting, calculating time allocated to your topic compared with other coverage (for example, on the news) would give you a quantitative measure. Indicators for assessing treatment of Third World issues can include: the amount of space given, the incidence of coverage, the number of issues covered, and so on. Work out a systematic way of categorising data.

Second, there is *qualitative* investigation. This includes analysing depth and level of coverage, forms of bias in presentation, use of language, use of 'omission', and distortion of facts. This calls for evidence of attempts to check 'facts' by making comparisons between media sources, links made to the course material, analysis of opinions, a critique of the ways information and opinions are presented, the extent to which sensitivity is shown to the diversities in Third World societies, and so on.

6 WRITING YOUR REPORT

First, don't forget that you are making out an argument to a group of people in your report, so it should be persuasive.

Second, you might like to use the following format to plan your report:

1 Introduction

- to whom is your report addressed?
- what is your report about (argument/hypothesis)?
- what are the stages of it?

2 Stages

- of source identification
- of preliminary survey/feasibility study
- of undertaking project

3 Findings

- the presentation of evidence/data
- what conclusions are drawn from the findings?
- do you make any recommendations?

4 Appendices

- Tables, pictures
- List of sources, references

Tables

Table 1.1 **Percentage Share of Agriculture and Industry in the Economies of Selected Developed and Developing Countries and their Average Incomes**

Country	Share of Agriculture (%)	Share of of Industry (%)	Average Income(a) per person (US$) 1985	1997
UK			8460	20710
1801	32	23		
1901	6	40		
France			9540	26050
1835	50	25		
1962	9	52		
Germany(b)			10940	28260
1860	32	24		
1959	7	52		
USA			16690	28740
1869	20	33		
1963	4	43		
Japan			11300	37850
1878	63	16		
1962	26	49		
Russia(c)			4550	2740
1928	49	28	(for 1980)	
1958	22	58		
Bangladesh			150	270
1960	61	8		
1985	57	14		
Kenya			290	330
1960	38	18		
1985	41	20		

continued

Table 1.1 **continued**

Country	Share of Agriculture (%)	Share of of Industry (%)	Average Income(a) per person (US$) 1985	1997
Thailand			800	2800
1960	40	19		
1985	27	30		
Bolivia			470	950
1960	26	25		
1985	17	30		
Turkey			1080	3130
1960	41	21		
1985	27	35		

(Source: Kitching, 1989, p. 7; Allen and Thomas, 2000 p. 512.) (a) Per capita GNP. (b) Figures are for the Federal Republic of Germany, 1993. (c) 1928 and 1958 figures are for USSR.

Table 1.2 **Pattern of British Overseas Investment, 1860–1929 (%)**

Area of World	1860–70	1881–90	1911–13	1927–29
British Empire				
(Total)	36	47	46	59
Canada	25	13	13	17
Australia and New				
Zealand	9.5	16	17	20
India	1.2	15	10.5	14
Other	0.3	3	5.5	8
Argentina, Chile,				
Mexico and Brazil	10.5	20	22	22
USA	27	22	19	5.5
Europe	25	8	6	8
Other	1.5	3	7	5.5

(Source: Barratt-Brown, 1974, pp. 190–1)

Table 1.3 **World Output of Principal Tropical Primary Commodities, 1880–1910 (in 000s tons)**

Primary Commodity	1880	1900	1910
Bananas	30	300	1800
Cocoa	60	102	227
Coffee	550	970	1090
Rubber	11	53	87
Cotton Fibre	950	1200	1770
Jute	600	1220	1560
Oil seeds	–	–	2700
Raw sugar cane	1850	3340	6320
Tea	175	290	360

(Source: Hobsbawm, 1996c, p. 348)

Table 1.4 **Pattern of World Trade, 1876–1983**

Year(s)	Industrial countries with other industrial countries (%)	Industrial countries with non-industrial countries (%)	Industrial countries total share of world trade (%)	Non-indust. countries with other non-indust. countries (%)	Non-indust. countries with industrial countries (%)	Non-indust. countries total share of world trade (%)
1876–80	50	23	73	4	23	27
1913	49	23	72	5	23	28
1928	46	23	69	8	23	31
1935	26	32	57	12	30	43
1953–55	40	25	65	10	25	35
1966	62	18	80	4	16	20
1973	61	18	79	6	15	9
1979	56	19	74	7	19	26
1983	47	20	67	9	23	32

(Source: Gordon, 1988, p. 47)

Table 1.5 **Britain's Rivals: Protectionism, Industrialisation and Militarisation**

Country & Average Level of Tariff in 1914 (%)	Steam Power 1847–50 (in Horse Power 000)	Steam Power 1876–80 (in Horse Power 000)	Armies 1879 (000s) (Peacetime)	Armies 1913 (000s) (Mobilised)	Navies 1900 (in no. of battleships)	Navies 1914 (in no. of battleships)
Germany (13)	–	5120	419	3800	14	40
France (20)	370	3070	503	3500	23	28
Russia (38)	70	1740	766	4400	16	23
Austria with Hungary (18)	100	1560	267	3000	6	16
USA (57 in 1897)	1680	9110	–	–	–	–
Britain (0)	1290	7600	136	700	49	64

(Source: Hobsbawm, 1996b, p. 309; 1996c, pp. 39, 351)

Table 1.6 **Global Share of Manufacturing Production, 1870–1984**

Year(s)	The Developed Countries (excluding Japan) (%)	The Centrally Planned Economies & Japan (%)	The Developing Countries (%)
1870	93	4	3
1896–1900	91	6	3
1913	91	5	4
1926–29	89	7	3
1938	76.7	12.9	10.4
1948	76	10	14
1966	65.8	22	12.2
1973	58.7	27.3	14
1979	54.5	30.9	14.6
1984	52.8	33.6	13.9

(Source: Gordon, 1988, p. 33)

Table 1.7 **Percentage of Business for TNCs in Home Country, 1992–93**

Country	Manufacturing Sales (%)	Service Sales (%)	Manufacturing Assets (%)	Service Assets (%)
USA	64	75	70	74
Japan	75	77	97	92
Germany	48	65	na	na
France	45	69	55	50
UK	36	71	39	61

(Source: Adapted from Hirst and Thompson, 1996, pp. 91–6)

Table 1.8 **FDI Flows to Developing Countries, 1973–93 (US$ billion annual averages)**

Region	1973–76	1977–82	1983–89	1990–93
Africa	1.1	0.8	1.1	1.4
Asia	1.3	2.7	5.2	19.8
Middle East and developing Europe	−1.0	2.5	2.6	1.6
Latin America	2.2	5.3	4.4	11.0
Total	3.6	11.3	13.3	33.8

(Source: Hirst and Thompson, 1996, p. 67)

Table 1.9 **The World's Labour Force* by Country Income Group and Region**

Income Group/Region	Millions of Workers			Percentage of Total		
	1965	1995	2025	1965	1995	2025
World	1329	2476	3656	100	100	100
Income Group						
High income	272	382	395	21	15	11
Middle income	363	658	1020	27	27	28
Low income	694	1436	2241	52	58	61

continued

Table 1.9 **continued**

Income Group/Region	Millions of Workers			Percentage of Total		
	1965	1995	2025	1965	1995	2025
Region						
Sub-Saharan Africa	102	214	537	8	9	15
East Asia and Pacific	448	964	1201	34	39	33
South Asia	228	440	779	17	18	21
Europe and Central Asia	180	239	281	14	10	8
Middle East and N. Africa	29	80	204	2	3	6
Lat. America and Caribbean	73	166	270	5	6	7
High Income OECD	269	373	384	20	15	10

* Ages 15 to 64
(Source: World Bank, 1995, p. 11)

Table 2.1 **Brazil: Foundation Dates for Largest Economic Groups and American Subsidiaries**

	Pre-First World War	1914– 29	1930– 45	Post-Second World War	Total	
Largest locally owned economic groups	64%	28%	8%	0%	100%	(25)
Largest foreign owned economic groups	20%	37%	16%	27%	100%	(30)
Subsidiaries of American industrial firms	0%	11%	21%	68%	100%	(131)

(Source: Evans, 1979, p. 105).

Table 2.2 **Asian Debt By Maturity, 1997 ($USbn)**

Borrower Two Years	Up to Two Years		From Two Years		Unallocated	
	$USbn	%	$USbn	%	$USbn	%
Indonesia	38.2	20.3	17.0	27.4	3.5	14.6
Malaysia	16.9	9.0	8.2	13.2	3.7	15.3
Philippines	8.6	4.6	4.0	6.5	1.5	6.2
Thailand	50.2	26.6	16.5	26.6	2.7	11.2
South Korea	74.3	39.5	16.4	26.4	12.7	52.7
Total	188.2	(100%)	62.1	(100%)	24.1	(100%)

(Source: Bank for International Settlements, *Financial Times*, 'Surge in bank lending to Asia', 5 January 1998)

Table 2.3 **Africa: Single Commodity Dependence (as % of total export earnings)**

Algeria	petroleum	37.6	Liberia	iron ore	63.5
Angola	petroleum	95.8	Malawi	tobacco	55.0
Benin	cotton	20.7	Mali	animals	58.6
Burkina Faso	cotton	48.0	Mauritania	iron ore	45.0
Burundi	coffee	87.0	Mauritius	sugar	59.7
Central African			Morocco	phosphates	28.5
Republic	coffee	28.7	Namibia	diamonds	40.0
Chad	animals	58.7	Nigeria	petroleum	90.5
Congo P.R.	petroleum	93.1	Rwanda	coffee	73.0
Cote d'Ivoire	cocoa	24.2	Sudan	cotton	42.0
Egypt	petroleum	55.8	Swaziland	sugar	35.2
Equatorial Guinea	cocoa	71.5	Tanzania	coffee	40.0
Ethiopia	coffee	66.0	Togo	phosphates	47.0
Gabon	petroleum	69.0	Tunisia	petroleum	47.1
Gambia	groundnuts	45.0	Uganda	coffee	95.0
Ghana	cocoa	59.0	Zaire	copper	58.0
Guinea	bauxite	52.2	Zambia	copper	98.0
Guinea-Bissau	groundnuts	29.0	Zimbabwe	tobacco	20.0
Kenya	coffee	30.0			

(Source: North–South Institute, 1988, p. 3, figures are for 1986; Coote and LeQuesne, 1996, p. 6, figures are the average for 1982–86)

Table 2.4 **Annual Gains from Trade Liberalisation by 2002 as Result of GATT 1992 Renegotiation (in US$bn)**

Low income Asia	1.8	Other Latin America	4.4
China	37.0	Brazil	3.4
India	4.6	Mexico	0.3
Sub total	43.4	Subtotal	8.1
Upper income Asia	20.6	USA	18.8
Indonesia	−1.9	Canada	2.5
Subtotal	18.7	Australia/New Zealand	1.1
		Japan	25.8
Other Africa	−0.6	EC	80.7
Nigeria	−1.0	EFTA	12.8
South Africa	−0.6	Subtotal	141.7
Maghreb	−0.6		
Subtotal	−2.8	Eastern Europe	1.4
		Former Soviet Union	0.8
Mediterranean	−1.6	Subtotal	2.1
Gulf region	3.1		
Subtotal	1.5	Total	218.3

(Source: *Financial Times*, Samuel Britan, 'Where is Gatt's $200bn really coming from?', 4 October 1993)

Table 2.5 **A Garment Factory in Tottenham, North London: Labour Force Characteristics**

Factory			
1 entrepreneur	male		Greek Cypriot (brother)
1 master cutter	male		Greek Cypriot
1 assistant cutter	male		Greek Cypriot
1 sample machinist	female		Greek Cypriot (sister)
2 special machinists	female		Greek Cypriot (aunt)
7 machinists	female	4	Afri-Caribbean
		3	Greek Cypriot
1 driver	male		Greek Cypriot (brother)
3 passers	female	2	Greek Cypriot
		1	Irish
2 pressers	male	2	Afri-Caribbean
Subtotal 19			

continued

Table 2.5 **continued**

Homeworkers			
4 machinists	female	4	Afri-Caribbean
6 machinists	female	6	Greek Cypriot
10 machinists	female	10	Indian
1 driver	male	1	Indian
Subtotal 21			
Total (40)	33 female	18	Greek Cypriot
(of whom 30	7 male	11	Indian
are machinists)		10	Afri-Caribbean

(Source: Panayiotopoulos, 1993, p. 151)

Table 3.1 **Clothing Exports* from Cyprus to Libya: Selected Indicators, 1979–86**

Year	As % of all clothing exports	As % of all manufactured exports	As % of all exports
1979	18.5	6.0	3.2
1980	32.0	10.0	6.0
1981	40.0	13.0	8.2
1982	4.5	1.5	0.8
1983	24.0	8.5	5.1
1984	54.0	24.0	14.3
1985	38.2	15.2	9.5
1986	7.0	2.8	1.6

* of industrial origin
(Source: Panayiotopoulos, 1996a, p. 9)

Table 3.2 Indices of Manufacturing Production: South Korea, 1987 (1980=100)

Food, beverages, tobacco	162.4
Textiles, clothing, leather	162.5
Wood, wood products (incl. furniture)	153.6
Paper, printing, publishing	183.5
Processed raw materials (chemicals, petrol, rubber, coal)	179.6
Non-metallic mineral products (china, glass, etc.)	191.9
Iron, steel and other basic metals	246.1
Fabricated metal products, machinery, equipment	421.7
Other	211.6
Weighted average for manufacturing	233.9

(Source: Bank of Korea (1988) *Monthly Bulletin of Statistics*, Vol. 42, pp. 108–9)

Table 3.3 Labour Disputes 1975–89: South Korea

No. of Disputes								
1975	1976	1977	1978	1979	1980	1981	1982	1983
133	110	96	102	105	407	186	88	98
1984	1985	1986	1987	1988	1989			
113	265	276	3749	1833	1532			

(Source: Bello and Rosenfeld, 1990, p. 43)

Table 3.4 Foreign Direct Investment in Mexico, 1940–98 (US$ billion)

Year	Total	Manufacturing	Manufacturing as a % of total
1940	358	10	2.8
1950	415	133	32.0
1957	739	335	45.0
1967	1143	890	66.3
1978	3712	2752	74.1
1990	30300	18877	62.3
1991	41876	na	na
1994–98*	57000	na	na

* New net FDI that should be added to accumulated FDI.
(Source: For 1940–78, Gereffi and Evans (1981, pp. 36–7); for 1990, Székely (1994, p. 155) and Barry (1992, p. 305); for 1991, Concheiro Bórquez (1996, p. 130); for 1994–98, *El Economista*, 9 March 1999).

Table 3.5 **Mexican Foreign Debt: 1970–96 (in U$bn)**

Year	Public	Total	Year	Public	Total
1960	0.8	na	1985	na	99.4
1965	1.7	na	1990	na	101.9
1970	3.2	7.0	1994	na	135.5
1975	11.5	20.2	1996	na	174.2
1981	42.6	75.0	1999	90.0	160.0

(Source: For 1970–85 total debt, Lustig and Ros (1987, p. 65); for public debt 1960–81, see ECLAC (1990, pp. 502–3). For total debt 1990–94, see ECLAC (1995), for 1996, EIU (1997, p. 5) and for 1999, *La Crónica*, 1 July 1999)

Table 3.6 **Mexican Gross Domestic Product, Industrial Production and Demographic Growth, 1940–95 (average annual rates of % growth)**

Year	GDP	Manufacturing	Population
1940–50	6.7	8.1	2.8
1950–60	5.8	7.3	3.1
1960–68	6.4	8.2	3.3
1970–80*	7.1	6.6	2.6
1980–85*	1.1	1.2	2.2
1985–90*	1.7	4.2	2.0
1990–95*	1.5	1.2	1.8
1985–95*	1.6	2.7	1.9
1996	5.1	na	na
1997	7.0	na	na
1998	2.0 (e)	na	na

* At constant prices. (e) estimate.
(Source: for 1940–68, Hansen (1971, p. 42); for 1970–95, calculated from ECLAC (1990, pp. 338–9; 1995, pp. 188–9 and 194–5; and 1996, pp. 192–3,198–9 and 175); for 1996–98, United Nations (1998, p. 128))

Table 3.7 *Maquila* **Industry by Plants, Employees, Value Added and Labour Cost, 1967–98**

Year	Number of plants	Number of workers	Value added (U$m)	Average hourly labour cost in *Maquilas* (in US$)
1967	72	4000	77	na
1970	160	20327	86	na
1975	454	67214	321	na
1980	620	119546	771	2.41
1981	605	30973	974	2.57
1982	585	127048	812	1.78
1983	600	150867	825	1.28
1984	672	199684	1161	1.43
1985	760	211968	1266	1.39
1986	890	249833	1295	1.02
1987	1125	305523	1635	1.04
1988	1396	369489	2339	1.17
1989	1655	429725	3057	1.30
1990	1930	460293	3362	1.35
1991	1954	489000	4100	1.60
1992	2129	511000	4300	1.64
1993	2149	535410	na	na
1997	2634	898786	8834	na
1998	2905	981302	na	na
1999	na	1088668	na	na

(Source: for 1967–92, Browne (1994, p. 33); for 1993, Mercado (1995, p. 198); for 1997–98, *Financial Times*, 7 October 1998; and for 1999, *La Crónica*, 1 June 1999).

Table 3.8 **Women's Employment in the *Maquilas***

Year	No. of women	%
1976	50628	90.0
1983	79074	76.6
1984	106904	71.0
1985	115970	70.0
1999	609650	56.0

(Source: for 1975, see Bustamante (1983, p. 252); for 1983–5, Castilla and Torres (1991, p. 580); and for 1999, *El Economista*, 30 July 1999)

Table 3.9 **Chinese Industrial Gross Output: Value by Ownership Type (% of enterprises owned by)**

Year	State	Collectively	Individually	Other
1978	77.63	22.37	0.00	0.00
1981	74.76	26.62	0.04	0.58
1984	69.09	29.71	0.19	1.01
1987	59.73	34.62	3.64	2.02
1990	54.60	35.62	5.39	4.38
1991	52.94	35.70	5.70	5.66
1992	48.09	38.04	6.76	7.11
1993	43.13	38.36	8.35	10.16
1994	34.07	40.87	11.51	13.55

(Source: Prof. Xiang Bing, CEIBS Working Paper No. 002, CEIBS, Shanghai)

Table 4.1 **Main Producers and Consumers of Copper, 1993 (%)**

	Mine Copper Production	Copper Refining	Copper Consumption
Chile	22.2	11.1	0.6
USA	19.3	19.7	21.2
USSR	9.1	9.8	7.8
Canada	7.8	4.9	1.8
China	3.5	6.1	8.3
Zambia	4.5	–	–
Japan	0.1	10.4	12.2
Germany	–	5.5	7.9
Belgium	–	3.0	2.8
Italy	–	0.6	4.4
France	–	0.6	4.2
UK	–	0.4	2.9
Taiwan	–	–	4.2
7 largest economies	27.2	42.0	54.5

(Source: Vera, 1996, p. 231)

Table 4.2 **Chilean Copper Production, 1700–1970 (in tonnes)**

Year	Chilean production (tonnes)	As % of world production	Year	Chilean production (tonnes)	As % of world production
1741–60	0.7	22.6	1891–1900	23.2	6.2
1761–1800	2.0	37.7	1901–10	33.0	4.8
1801–10	1.5	10.0	1911–20	69.3	6.2
1811–20	1.5	9.5	1921–30	112.8	8.6
1821–30	2.1	8.5	1931–40	294.1	18.1
1831–40	4.9	14.4	1941–50	438.5	18.8
1841–50	8.7	19.0	1951–61	447.5	13.2
1851–60	21.0	31.5	1961–70	640.9	12.1
1861–70	40.0	40.8			
1871–80	45.7	33.6			
1881–90	35.3	15.7			

(Source: CODELCO, 1975, p. 485; Schmitz, 1979, pp. 60–78)

Table 4.3 **British, Chilean and World production of Mine and Smelted Copper, 1831–70 (yearly averages in 000s tonnes)**

Years	Mine Copper			Smelted Copper		
	UK	Chile	World	UK	Chile	World
1831–40	14.6	4.8	34.0	16.1	3.2	66.7
1841–45	11.2	9.4	43.0	24.0	3.8	40.8
1846–50	12.3	10.9	48.5	24.3	7.2	66.4
1851–60	15.7	20.6	63.5	26.7	8.1	39.3
1861–70	11.8	38.8	96.0	31.9	20.4	52.6

(Source: Schmitz, 1979, pp. 64–5, 209; Valenzuela, 1990, p. 658)

Table 4.4 **Tourist Arrivals to Spain over time (thousands)**

	1951	1955	1960	1965	1970	1975	1980	1985	1990
Spanish residents abroad	73	130	686	1180	1448	1721	1510	1991	3299
Foreign visitors	1190	2392	5427	13071	22657	28401	36517	41244	48745
Total	1263	2522	6113	14251	24105	30122	38027	43235	52044

(Source: compiled from Towner, 1985; Tamames and Rueda, 1997)

Table 4.5 **Textiles and Garments as Percentage of Manufacturing Value Added and as Percentage of Merchandise Exports (Selected Countries 1970–93)**

Country/ Income Group	As % of Manufacturing Value Added (MVA)		As % of Merchandise Exports	
	1970	1992	1970	1993
Low Income				
Bangladesh	47	38	na	78
India	21	15	27	30
Pakistan	38	19*	75	78
China	13*	13	29**	31
Sri Lanka	19	29	3	52
Egypt	35	23	65	20
Lower Middle Income				
Indonesia	14	16	–	17
Morocco	16*	18	5	25
Paraguay	16	16	7	23
Thailand	14	16	8	15
Turkey	15	14	35	40
Upper Middle Income				
Uruguay	21	18	34	28
Greece	17	13	14	28
South Korea	12	11	41	19
Portugal	19	23	26	30
High Income				
Hong Kong	41	35	44	52**
Italy	13	14	14	12

* Figure for Pakistan is for 1989. Figure for China and Morocco, is for 1986.
** Figure for China and Hong Kong is for 1965.
(Source: UNDP, *World Development Report 1995*, Tables 6 and 15; *World Development Report 1992*, Tables 6 and 15)

Figures

Economic Policy: Import Substitution	Economic Policy: Export Orientation
Import controls and high tariffs Exchange controls/fixed rate Price controls/state subsidies State investment/ownership Restrictions on Transnationals	No import controls/low tariffs No exchange controls/market rate Market prices/no subsidies Private capital/ownership Freedom for Transnationals
Industrial Policy: Import Substitution Industrialisation (ISI)	**Industrial Policy: Export Orientated Industrialisation (EOI)**
A developing country uses foreign exchange earned in commodity exports to import investment goods (for example, sewing machines) to make garments in order to substitute for currently imported goods.	A developing country uses labour-intensive technologies and comparative advantage consistent with factor endowment, to produce competitive exports (such as garments).
The same developing country uses its foreign exchange to import capital goods instead (such as the machinery used to make sewing machines).	Labour-intensive industrialisation creates higher direct sectoral employment, when compared to the promotion of capital-intensive industrialisation.
Foreign exchange is used to import capital goods which can be used to *make* capital goods: that is, to develop the ability to make machines which make sewing machines, as well as machinery used in other sectors.	The creation of greater employment opportunities in labour-intensive industrialisation, makes a significant contribution towards the development of a more equitable size distribution of income.
The country develops an important technological capability. The capital goods sector can be applied to produce any other imported manufactured product across a range of sectors.	EOI leads to a more efficient allocation of scarce resources, resulting from the stimulus of international competition, with beneficial effects on growth and development.

Figure 1 **Import Substitution and Export Orientated Industrialisation: Economic and Industrial Policy**

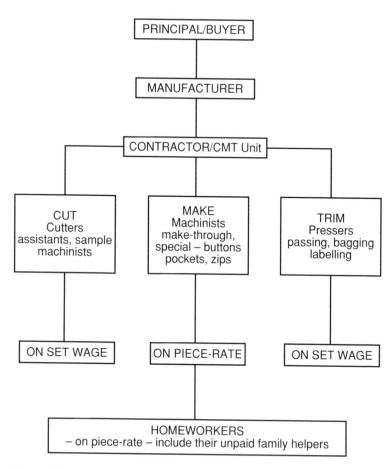

(Source: Panayiotopoulos, 1996a)

Figure 2 **Organisation of Production and System of Payment in the London Garment Industry**

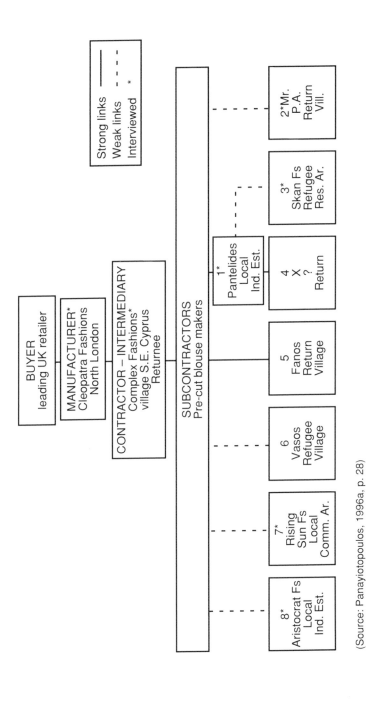

Figure 3 **Complex Fashions: Subcontracting Network**

(Source: Panayiotopoulos, 1996a, p. 28)

245

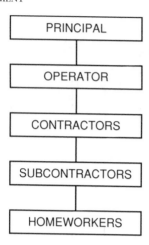

Figure 4 **International Subcontracting in the Global Garment Industry**

Explanatory Note

- **Principal**: the person or company located abroad who places the order and provides the design and cloth for the operator. Typically this consists of the large departmental chain stores (e.g. Marks & Spencer) who have huge retailing capacities. Production at this point is characterised by high levels of concentration in ownership.
- **Operator**: also referred to as a manufacturer, is the person or company in the developing country who may work the cloth to finished or semi-finished stage according to the specifications (design) provided by the principal. The goods are then shipped back to the principal. Labour is frequently the only contribution made by the operator to the production process.
- **Contractors and Subcontractors**: the persons or companies who are supplied work orders by the operator and who are responsible for all or most of production. Contractors may themselves use subcontractors if they cannot meet the order. Homeworking, usually by women, is a major form of labour recruitment. Production at this point is characterised by high levels of proliferation in small CMT units (Cut, Make and Trim).

Notes

SECTION 2.1

1. The *Grande Carajas Programme* was financed by the international donors during the late 1980s as 'the' answer to Brazil's debt crisis. Beef, mining and large-scale rice production for the Japanese market were some of the areas of investment. Antony Hall, 1989, refers to the 'Prussian model' (of large *Junker* estates) to describe this scale of development. Single handedly, this programme plans by the year 2000 to bring into production 16 per cent of the entire Brazilian Amazonian land mass.

SECTION 2.2

1. The IMF insisted in 1998 that 'the Fund did see the trouble coming'. But that 'it could not persuade the affected countries to act early enough because they were in denial about the problems' (of 'overvalued' currencies and inflated share prices). See Michel Camdessus, Managing Director of the IMF, interview with the *Financial Times*, 'Defending the Fund', 9 February 1998. Michel Camdessus took early retirement in November 1999.
2. See for example, Nigel Harris, 1995a, 'Can the West Survive?' *Competition and Change*, Vol. 1, pp. 111–22.
3. *Far Eastern Economic Review*, 'Can Asia be Revived?', 18 June 1998, pp. 10–15.
4. Jeffrey Sachs is a consultant with some experience working for the IMF. Amongst his 'successes' are Bolivia and Russia. See *Financial Times*, 'Personal View. Jeffrey Sachs', 11 December 1997. It is examples such as these, which reinforce the view that the poverty reduction efforts of both the IMF and the World Bank neither facilitate dialogue nor consensus building. See Toye, J. and Jackson, C. (1996) 'Public expenditure policy and poverty reduction: Has the World Bank got it right?' Institute of Development Studies, Sussex, Bulletin, No. 1, pp. 56–68. Under the circumstances of crisis, building consensus proves even more politically difficult; also see Chris Harman (1997) 'Do the Tigers face extinction?', *Socialist Review*, No. 214, pp. 9–12; and special edition of the *New Internationalist* (1999) 'Indonesia. Power of Protest', No. 318.
5. See *Financial Times*, 'World Bank sounds alarm over risky emergency loans', 25 September 1998.
6. See *Financial Times* coverage, 'South Korean manufacturers stage sharp export growth', 25 August 1995; 'Samsung drives on to globalisation', 25 October 1994; 'Chung Hwa confirms £260m plant', 15 November 1995; 'UK catches cold', 15 August 1998; 'Hyundai halts plant construction', 27 June 1998.
7. Fermont, C. et al. (1998) 'Indonesia in Revolution', *International Socialism Journal*, No. 80, pp. 3–71; *Financial Times*, 'ILO warns of social unrest in Asia', 16 April 1998.
8. *Financial Times*, 'Poverty coming back to Asia', 28 September 1999.

9. John Sweeny, *Observer*, 'Migrants poisoned and deported', 26 April 1998. Another source of violence against immigrants has been that directed against the pawns of Indonesia's transmigration policy in areas such as East Timor and Papua New Guinea, see Kilvert, A. (1996) 'Golden promises', *New Internationalist*, No. 305, pp. 16–18.
10. *Guardian*, 'Crisis culls list of Asia's super rich', 23 June 1998.
11. Michel Camdessus, *Financial Times*, 'Defending'.
12. Martin Wolf, *Financial Times*, 'Indonesia's legacy', 26 May 1998. One legacy of Indonesia's rescue package was the political power this gave to the IMF. This is not a view shared by the IMF, which typically sees itself as a neutral organisation providing technical assistance. It denies any link between aid and politics. Yet in September 1999 the IMF and the World Bank made it known to the Indonesian government that future aid would be linked to progress on East Timor. This saw protests from Japan, that the cutting of aid could destabilise Indonesia's economy and affect Asia's fragile economic recovery (see, *Financial Times*, 'IMF and World Bank played role in climbdown', 13 September 1999).
13. *Financial Times*, 'Tokyo launches £77bn crisis package', 25 April 1998.
14. *Financial Times*, 'Indonesia the focus of transparency', 28 July 1999.
15. See *New Internationalist* (1999) 'Tree that grows money', No. 318, pp. 12–13, and *Financial Times*, 'Indonesia incorporated', 16 January 1998.

SECTION 2.3

1. *Financial Times*, 'Commodity prices and development in the 1980s', 9 September 1991.
2. *Financial Times*, 'Africa's share of world exports declines further', 19 June 1990.
3. *Financial Times*, 'Drive to give third world farmers fair deal', 16 September 1992.
4. *Financial Times*, 'Drive'; see also, the example of bananas, in the *New Internationalist* (1999) special edition 'The big banana split', No. 317.

SECTION 2.4

1. *Financial Times*, 'Customs VAT raids lead to 44 arrests', 1 March 1990.
2. In a previous work, however, Waldinger and Lapp, 1993, p. 23, described this kind of thinking 'as a pseudo-problem of social control'. Gans, 1992, p. 173, writes that 'a significant number of the children of poor immigrants, especially dark-skinned ones, might not obtain jobs in the mainstream economy' and that 'US cities cannot stand a cohort of immigrants' children who will join very poor blacks, Hispanics, and Anglos on the corner or in lines of the welfare agencies' (p. 189). Thanks Roger Waldinger for helpful comments on an earlier version of the chapter.
3. *Financial Times*, 'EU moves against black economy', 8 April 1998.
4. Peter Booth, National Secretary, Transport and General Workers Union, quoted from *Observer*, 'Final Cut', 13 September 1998.
5. *Parikiaki Haravghi*, 'Endymatoviomihania: apo to kako sto hirotero', 15 October 1998.
6. Neither does the methodology allow for an estimation on returns based on gender, race or between documented and undocumented workers. Borjas and Tienda, 1993, for example, in reviewing evidence from an amnesty programme which gave the opportunity to undocumented workers in the USA to adjust their status (and which included information on previous employment), show that undocumented immigrants who form a significant proportion of labour in the enclave economy, earn less than legal immigrants; further, given that most are manual workers, it is not surprising that this wage disadvantage increased with age.
7. Against the uncritical acceptance of entrepreneurship as a prescriptive remedy and 'a kind of policy Prozac for those disadvantaged by racism' (Barret et al., 1996, p. 803).

SECTION 3.1

1. For a detailed assessment of the factors leading to Partition and its economic consequences see P. Panayiotopoulos, 1999, 'The Emergent Post-Colonial State in Cyprus', *Commonwealth & Comparative Politics*, Vol. 37, No. 1, pp. 31–55.
2. The information here draws from a comparative study of Cypriot entrepreneurs in the London and Cyprus clothing industries undertaken for the purposes of a PhD. The research included the interviewing of 46 entrepreneurs in southern Cyprus. The enterprises employed a total of 1,726 workers or approximately 10 per cent of the sectoral total, see Panayiotopoulos, 1993, pp. 15–16.
3. For a detailed assessment of one such network of subcontracting and problems raised by this mobility for local authority planning in north London, see Panayiotopoulos, 1992a, pp. 57–72.
4. See 'Survey of the West Midlands Textile Industry', *Financial Times*, 3 October 1996; Personal Communication, George M. Georgiou, Central Bank of Cyprus, Nicosia, 10 October 1996.
5. Andreas Pavlikas, Head of Research for PEO trade union federation, quoted from *The Cyprus Weekly*, 'Women pay price of Customs Union', 15 December 1998.

SECTION 3.2

1. *Financial Times*, 'European Car Industry', 1 November 1995.
2. *Financial Times*, 'Survey of Spain', 30 July 1995.
3. Regional unemployment in Andalucia stood in the mid-1990s at 30 per cent. Only East Germany saw similar rates of mass unemployment (see, *Financial Times*, 'Spain').

SECTION 3.3

1. See Sung Hwaan Jo, 1982, 'The changing position of the agricultural sector in the South Korean economy, 1955–1977', in C. Hou and T. Yu, *Agricultural Development in China, Japan and Korea*, Taiwan, p. 232; Bank of Korea, 1988, *Monthly Bulletin of Statistics*, Vol. 42, February, p. 123.
2. *Financial Times*, 'South Korean–US cinema dispute heads for happy ending', 18 August 1989.
3. *Financial Times*, 'South Korean cinema. Actors oppose US on quotas', 3 December 1998.
4. See coverage in the financial press, *Financial Times*, 'S. Korean growth rate hit by sharp drop in exports', 28 March 1990; 'Motor industry misfires along the road to success', 28 March 1990; 'Red ink stains South Korea's pride in its trade', 19 February 1991; 'Seoul suffers record deficit', 13 October 1991.
5. *Financial Times*, 'Export setback gives Seoul record deficit', 17 February 1997.
6. See Kyong Dong Kim (1985) 'Social change and societal development in Korea since 1944', *Korea and World Affairs*, Vol. 9, No. 4, p. 769; Bank of Korea (1988) *Monthly Bulletin of Statistics*, Vol. 42, pp. 122–3.
7. See *Financial Times*, 'Hyundai in row about attacks on trade unionists', 12 January 1989. It was reported that Hyundai Construction 'organised the kidnapping of a white collar union leader', and that senior management of Hyundai Engineering 'may have organised a group of men who attacked [the] unionists with clubs and pipes'.
8. *Financial Times*, 'Textile labour costs. High wages to plague South Korea', 1 December 1989.
9. Amongst the list of books which are illegal to read in South Korea, are publications by Professor Alex Callinicos, Tony Cliff, and *Why We Hate Mondays*, a translation of articles from *Socialist Worker* written by John Molyneux: this was on the grounds that

'it contained many rebellious arguments'. See *Socialist Worker*, 'Trial begins for the "crime" of reading', 4 July 1998. One significant political development in South Korea during 1999 has been an initiative by a number of KCTU officials and left-wing intellectuals to form a Democratic Labour Party (DLP). See Callinicos, A., 1999, 'Reformism western style?', *Socialist Review*, November 1999, p. 24.

10. For coverage on the *Chaebol*, see *Financial Times*, 'Chaebol select their core sectors', 14 January 1994; 'South Korean groups target core business', 19 January 1994; 'Boost for S. Korean deregulation', 5 December 1994.

11. See International Monetary Fund (1997) *World Economic Outlook*.

12. *Far Eastern Economic Review*, 'On the brink', 15 December 1998, pp. 118–20; also see *Financial Times*, 'Asian ratings downgraded to junk bond status', 23 December 1997, and 'Asian equity markets', 20 February 1998.

13. *Financial Times*, 'Surge in bank lending in Asia', 5 January 1998.

14. *Financial Times*, '$2bn prop for ailing Seoul banks', 10 December 1997.

15. The UK contributed $1.5bn and China $600m. See *Financial Times*, 'S. Korea gets $55bn package', 4 December 1997.

16. Jeffrey Sachs writes that 'the IMF insisted that all presidential candidates immediately "endorse" the agreement' (an agreement) 'they had no part in drafting or negotiating – and no time to understand', see *Financial Times*, 'Personal View. Jeffrey Sachs', 11 December 1997.

17. *Financial Times*, 'South Korea announces IMF bail-out conditions', 7 December 1997; *Far Eastern Economic Review*, 'Opening Korea', 26 March 1998.

18. *Financial Times*, 'Seoul under pressure on "shameful" IMF deal', 24 November 1997.

19. Daewoo accounts for 5 per cent of South Korean GDP and employed directly an estimated 150,000 workers (and even more via contractors) worldwide. It is equivalent to the GDP of the Philippines and its debt alone equalled the GDP of the Czech Republic. See *Financial Times*, 'Daewoo discovers it is not too big to be allowed to fail', 17 August 1999.

20. See *Financial Times*, 'Daewoo debt estimated at $73bn', 5 November 1999, and 'Size of Daewoo debt angers creditors', 7 November 1999. Also see Economist Intelligence Unit, 1999, *Motor Business International*, Fourth Quarter, EIP, London, pp. 25–6.

21. For the first six months of 1999 the South Korean National Statistical Office reported that industrial output increased by an annualised rate of 33.1 per cent. During the third quarter of 1999, South Korean GDP grew by 12.3 per cent, the fastest growth since 1988, and for the whole of 1999 GDP grew by 7 per cent. See *Financial Times*, 'Seoul's industrial output jumps', 30 August 1999, and 'S. Korea appears to turn corner', 23 November 1999. This sharp economic rebound was the result of strong exports, particularly of electronic products such as semiconductors.

SECTION 3.4

1. We have applied here the criteria used by Sutcliffe, 1971, pp. 16–23. These consist of the following conditions: (a) industry must contribute at least 25 per cent to the country's GDP, (b) manufacture must constitute at least 60 per cent of industry (which also includes mining and construction) and (c) at least 10 per cent of the whole population must be employed in industry. Only two other Latin American countries fulfil these requisites: Brazil and Argentina, although Colombia, Chile and Uruguay only narrowly fail to achieve these conditions.

2. Here we define industry as manufacturing production on a large scale involving the use of complex techniques and an advanced division of labour within the productive units, and using mostly non-human sources of energy. See Hewitt et al., 1992, pp. 3–6.

3. At the moment there are 48 parastate companies in the process of privatisation, including the electricity industry. However, the attempts to privatise the petroleum

industry (the parastatal Pemex) has so far failed. See *La Cronica*, 1 March 1999 and *The Economist*, 1 May 1999.

4. The same trend, but with lower rates of growth, operated in the number of firms and the amount of value added.

5. *Financial Times*, 'Buying Mexican fails to inspire', 7 October 1998.

SECTION 3.5

1. Liu Binyan, quoted from Ahmed Shaikh (1997) 'China: from Mao to Deng', *International Socialist Review*, No. 1, p. 14.

2. *Beijing Review*, 18–24 July 1994.

3. *Financial Times*, 'Chinese city driven by Pearl River vision', 4 February 1997.

4. *Financial Times*, 'Shanghai sees rise in invisible unemployed', 6 February 1996.

5. *Financial Times*, 'Shanghai fighting to regain title', 2 July 1997.

6. *New York Times*, 'Workers stood down', 6 May 1994.

7. *Financial Times*, 'State sector rationalisation', 25 April 1996. A key aspect of industrial management in the state-owned enterprises was the decentralisation of management functions to plant level.

8. China made tremendous sacrifices by not devaluing the *renminbi*. One result was that its trade surplus was reduced drastically (by 64.5 per cent during the first six months of 1999) as Chinese exports lost some of their competitiveness when compared to a resurgent South Korea and other South East Asian countries. See *Financial Times*, 'China's trade surplus declines', 14 November 1999.

9. *Financial Times*, 'China tops world steel league', 26 August 1996.

10. *Financial Times*, 'New Dawn in the East', 26 August 1996.

11. *Financial Times*, 'China, US and the WTO', 15 November 1999.

SECTION 4.1

* Unless otherwise stated all the information in this section comes from Valenzuela 1990 and 1992.

1. During the nineteenth century copper was traded in the world market in four main shapes: (a) copper ore of different qualities usually of 10 to 30 per cent copper content, (b) regulus or matte, the product of a first firing of around 30 to 60 per cent copper content, (c) Copper bars of smelted copper of 90 to 96 per cent fine copper, the product of usually two firings and (d) refined copper of over 99 per cent fine copper for which several roastings and firings were necessary. Nowadays Chile exports mainly refined copper of over 99.5 per cent obtained either by electrolysis (the purest type) or fire-refining.

2. For the period 1841–77 average prices for copper in Chile were as follows: 17.95 pesos per *quintal* of copper bar and 11.28 per *quintal* of fine copper contained in the ore. As in that period Chile exported 24.8 million *quintales* of fine copper (over 1 million tonnes), the country would have received an 'income' of 444.8 million *pesos* (£88.9m) if it had sold all its copper in the shape of copper bars but only 279.5 million *pesos* (£55.9m) if it had sold it in the shape of raw ores.

3. On the development of the copper smelting industry in Britain, see R.O. Roberts, 1980.

4. Normally Chilean mines have a superficial deposit of oxidised copper, beyond that a zone of sulphide copper is found. See Pederson, 1966, pp. 28–9.

5. This followed a three-year period of fierce competition among British smelters which substantially increased the price of copper ore. Monopsony is a combination of purchasers of a given commodity to depress its price (a cartel, or monopoly).

SECTION 4.2

1. See *Financial Times*, 'Famous boozing hell-holes', 19 August 1995. One contributory factor has been the displacement of Magaluf as the centre of non-stop partying by Ayia Napa in south-east Cyprus. Much of the tourism installations in Ayia Napa and elsewhere in Cyprus were built on land owned by the Orthodox Church which has extensive interests in the tourism industry.
2. See *The Cyprus Weekly*, 'Louis Cruise Line shares edge towards £10', 5 November 1997.

SECTION 4.3

1. A distinction can be made between textiles and garments. Textiles have seen much greater application of capital and this has seen most productivity gains made by the TNCs and industrial countries. Garments require far more labour and less capital and has been the area of greatest gain by the developing countries.
2. *Financial Times*, 'Labour cost comparisons', 3 October 1991.
3. Oxfam Clothes Code Campaign (see, 'The clothes trade in Bangladesh', 3 October 1999, www.oxfam.org.uk/campaign/clothes/ciobanio.htm, pp. 1–4; also see Sweatshop Watch, 'The Garment Industry', www.sweatshopwatch.org/swatch/industry). The purpose of the Oxfam campaign is to appeal to the leading UK chain stores to accept minimum standards. Their response, exemplified by M&S in a recent court case (involving allegations by Granada TV over the use of child labour in Morocco) has been that they are neither legally nor morally responsible for the actions of their contractors and subcontractors. The Judge agreed with M&S.
4. See Jennifer Roesch, 1999, pp. 7–14.
5. *Financial Times*, 'US students to campaign on sweatshops', 19 October 1999; also see UNITE's website, 'Stop Sweatshop News', www.uniteunion.org/sweatshops/newsthisweek/s7–21–99.html
6. On Disney products sourced in Haiti, see Murray MacAdam 1998, 'Working for the rat', *New Internationalist*, No. 308, pp. 15–17, and Andrew Ross, 1997, p. 97. On Liz Claiborne jackets, see National Labour Committee, www.nlcnet.org/behindclosed/nicaragua.htm. On the production of jeans, see the *New Internationalist* special edition (1998) 'The big jeans stitch-up', No. 302.
7. This was not difficult to achieve given that Kathy Lee Gifford, Liz Claiborne and Nike, who were identified by the students as employing sweatshop labour, also all sat on the Board of the FLA.
8. *Financial Times*, 'Many textiles quota curbs may linger on', 21 February 1991; also, 'US textile curbs come under fire', 9 March 1995.
9. *Financial Times*, 'MFA extended', 10 November 1993.
10. *Financial Times*, 'Vietnam in EU pact on textiles', 30 October 1997.
11. World Bank, 1990, p. 123.
12. One such example in pre-Suharto Indonesia was described by a visiting Indonesian woman trade union activist as the 'screaming strike'. This consisted of 'women having "visions" about "dead babies" and engaging in what has been described as mass hysteria involving uncontrolled screaming. This shuts down the line. On occasion the whole factory can close down. In one factory I was involved in, there were two "screaming strikes". One happened when the overtime was cut to time and a quarter (from time and a half) and the other when workers were told they had to work compulsory overtime' (Personal Communication, London, 26 November 1997). For more overt attempts at union organisation by women, see Smyth and Grijns, 1997; Asia Monitor Resource Centre (AMRC), 1998; and Ungpakorn, 1999, pp. 68–78 ('Strong women in an underwear factory'), and pp. 78–86 ('Organising').

See also interview with Dita Sari, Indonesian trade union organiser, following her release from prison, in *New Internationalist* (1999) 'Good Citizen Sari', No. 318, pp. 11–12. See also attempts by women workers to resist redundancies in the *Maquiladoras*, Miriam Louie (1998) 'Life on the line. Jean sweatshops', *New Internationalist*, No. 302, pp. 20–3; see also their organisation's (Fuerza Unida) website at www.igc.org.fuerzaunida

CONCLUSIONS

1. Quoted from *Financial Times*, 'A trade round that works for people', 29 November 1999.
2. Rocky Caldwell, quoted from *Socialist Worker*, 'Taking on the rule of money', 18 December 1999.
3. See *Financial Times*, 'A goal beyond reach', 6 December 1999.

References

Akyaz, Y., Chang, H.-J. and Kozul-Wright, R. (1998) 'New Perspectives on East Asian Development', *Journal of Development Studies*, Vol. 34, No. 6, pp. 4–37.

Allen, T. and Thomas, A. (1992) *Poverty and Development in the 1990s* (Oxford: Oxford University Press).

Allen, T. and Thomas, A. (2000) *Poverty and Development into the 21st Century* (Oxford: Oxford University Press).

Amsden, A.(1989) *Asia's Next Giant: South Korea and Late Industrialisation* (London: Oxford University Press).

Anderson, H. and Flatley, J. (1997) *Contrasting London's Incomes: A Social and Spatial Analysis* (London: London Research Centre).

Anson, R. (1997) 'EU Clothing Production May Have a Future, Editorial', *Textile Outlook International*, November, pp. 3–5.

Asia Monitor Resource Centre (AMRC) (1998) *We in the Zone. Women Workers in Asia's Export Processing Zones* (Hong Kong: AMRC).

Atema, J. and Panayiotopoulos P. (1995) *Promoting Urban Informal Enterprises: a Case Study of the ActionAid-Kenya Kariobangi Savings and Credit Programme*, Papers in International Development No. 15 (Swansea: Centre for Development Studies).

Auty, R. (1994) *Economic Development and Industrial Policy: Korea, Brazil, Mexico and China* (London: Mansell).

Auty, R. (1995) 'Industrial Policy Capture in Taiwan and South Korea', *Development Policy Review*, Vol. 13, pp. 195–217.

Bank of Korea (1988) *Monthly Bulletin of Statistics*, Dec. Vol. 42 (Seoul: Bank of Korea).

Barke, M., Towner, J. and Newton, M.T. (eds) (1996) *Tourism in Spain. Critical Issues* (Wallingford: CAB International).

Barnes, P. (1994) 'Profile of Marks and Spencer: A Growing International Presence', *Textile Outlook International*, September, pp. 128–44.

Barratt-Brown, M. (1974) *The Economics of Imperialism* (London: Penguin).

Barret A.G., Jones, T. and McEvoy, D. (1996) 'Ethnic Minority Business: Theoretical Discourse in Britain and North America', *Urban Studies*, Vol. 33, Nos. 4–5, pp. 783–809.

Barry, T. (1992) (ed.) *Mexico. A Country Guide* (Albuquerque: Inter-Hemispheric Resource Centre).

Becker, C. (1995) 'Tourism and the Environment', in A. Montanari and A. M. Williams (eds) *European tourism: Regions, spaces and restructuring*, pp. 25–53 (Aldershot: J. Wiley and Sons).

Bello, W. and Rosenfeld, S. (1990) *Dragons in Distress: Asia's Economic Miracle in Crisis* (London: Pelican).

Bernal, M. (1987) *Black Athena: the Afroasiatic Roots of Classical Civilisation. Vol. 1 Fabrication of Ancient Greece 1785–1985* (London: Free Associated Press).

Bernal, M. (1991) *Black Athena: the Afro-Asian Roots of Classical Civilisation. Vol. 2 The Archaeological and Documentary Evidence* (London: Free Associated Press).

Bernstein, H. (1988) 'Labour Regimes and Social Change Under Colonialism', in B. Crow and M. Thorpe (eds) *Survival and Change in the Third World*, pp. 31–58 (Cambridge: Polity Press).

Bernstein, H. et al. (1992) 'Capitalism and the Expansion of Europe', in T. Allen and A. Thomas (eds) *Poverty and Development*, pp. 168–84 (Oxford: Oxford University Press).

Bernstein, H. and Crow, B. (1988) 'The Expansion of Europe', in B. Crow and M. Thorpe (eds) *Survival and Change in the Third World*, pp. 9–30 (Cambridge: Polity Press).

Bhuiyan, M. and Shaw, H. (1994) 'Profile of the Textile and Clothing Industry in Bangladesh', *Textile Outlook International*, May, pp. 91–2.

Bohning, W.R. (1972) *The Migration of Workers in the United Kingdom and the European Community* (Oxford: Oxford University Press).

Bonacich, E. (1972) 'A Theory of Ethnic Antagonism: the Split Labour Market', *American Sociological Review*, No. 37, pp. 34–51.

Bonacich, E. (1973) 'A Theory of Middleman Minorities', *American Sociological Review*, No. 38, pp. 583–94.

Bonacich, E. (1993) 'Asian and Latino Immigrants in the Los Angeles Garment Industry: an Exploration of the Relationship between Capitalism and Racial Oppression', in I. Light and P. Bhachu (eds) *Immigration and Entrepreneurship: Culture, Capital and Ethnic Networks*, pp. 51–74 (New Brunswick: Transaction Publishers).

Bonacich, E. (1994) 'Asians in the Los Angeles Garment Industry', in P. Ong, E. Bonacich and L. Cheng (eds) *The New Asian Immigration in Los Angeles and Global Restructuring*, pp. 137–63 (Philadelphia: Temple University Press).

Borjas, G. and Tienda, M. (1993) 'The Employment and Wages of Legalised Immigrants', *International Migration Review*, Vol. 27, No. 4, pp. 712–47.

Boserup, E. (1970) *Woman's Role in Economic Development* (London: Earthscan).

Brett, E.A. (1973) *Colonialism and Underdevelopment in Africa* (London: Heinemann).

Browne, H. (1994) *For Richer, for Poorer. Shaping US–Mexican Integration* (London: Latin American Bureau).

Buffie, E. (1988) 'Mexico 1958–86: From Stabilizing Development to the Debt Crisis', in J. Sachs (ed.) *Developing Country Debt and the World Economy*, pp. 141–68 (Chicago: Chicago University Press).

Bukharin, N. (1982) *Selected Writings on the State and the Transition to Socialism*. R.B. Day (ed.) (Nottingham: Spokesman).

Burroughs, E.R. (1980) *Tarzan of the Apes* (New York: Ballantine, first published 1912).

Bustamante, J.A. (1983) 'Maquiladoras: a New Face of International Capitalism on Mexico's Northern Frontier', in J. Nash and P. Fernandez-Kelly (eds) *Women, Men, and the International Division of Labor*, pp. 224–56 (Albany: State University of New York Press).

Byrd, W. and Gelb, A. (1990) 'Why Industrialise? The Incentives for Rural Community Governments', in A. Byrd and L. Qinsong (eds) *China's Rural Industry*, pp. 51–75 (New York: Oxford University Press).

Callinicos, A. (1987) 'Note on Racism in Ancient Greece', *International Socialism*, No. 37, pp. 133–7.

Callinicos, A. (1991) 'The End of Nationalism? A Review of Nigel Harris, *National Liberation*', *International Socialism*, No. 51, pp. 57–70.

Callinicos, A. (1994) 'Marxism and Imperialism Today', in A. Callinicos, et al. (eds) *Marxism and the New Imperialism* (London: Bookmarks).

Cárdenas, E. (1984) 'The Great Depression and Industrialisation. The Case of Mexico', in R. Thorp (ed.) *Latin America in the 1930s. The Role of the Periphery in World Crisis*, pp. 222–41 (London: Macmillan).

Carlin, N. (1987) 'Was there Racism in Ancient Society?', *International Socialism*, No. 36, pp. 93–119.

Carrillo, J. (1995) 'Flexible Production in the Auto Sector: Industrial Reorganization at Ford Mexico', *World Development*, Vol. 23, No. 1, pp. 87–101.

Castilla, B. and Torres, B. (1991) 'Las maquiladoras en Yucatan', in R. Pozas and M. Luna (eds) *Las Empresas y los empresarios en el Mexico contemporáneo*, pp. 559–88 (Mexico: Grijalbo).

Castles, S. and Kosack, G. (1973) *Immigrant Workers and Class Structure in Western Europe* (Oxford: Oxford University Press).

Chenut, H. (1983) 'The Sewing Machine', in W. Chapkis and D. Enloe (eds) *Of Common Cloth. Women in the Global Textile Industry*, pp. 68–9 (Amsterdam: Transnational Institute).

Chossudovsky, M. (1996) *The Globalisation of Poverty: Impacts of the IMF and World Bank Reforms* (London: Zed Books).

CODELCO (Corporacion del Cobre, Chile) (1975) *El Cobre Chileno* (Santiago: Codelco).

Collier, P. and Gunning, J. (1999) 'The IMF's Role in Structural Adjustment', *The Economic Journal*, November.

Concheiro Bórquez, E. (1996) *El gran acuerdo* (Mexico: Ediciones Era).

Coote, B. and LeQuesne, C. (1996) *The Trade Trap: Poverty and the Global Commodity Markets* (Oxford: Oxfam Publications).

Coquery-Vidrovich, C. (1988) *Africa, Endurance and Change South of the Sahara* (Berkeley: University of California Press).

Cypher, J.M. (1990) *State and Capital in Mexico. Development Policy since 1940* (Boulder: Westview Press).

Das, S. K. and Panayiotopoulos, P. (1996) 'Flexible Specialisation. New Paradigm for Industrialisation for Developing Countries?', *Economic and Political Weekly*, December 28, pp. 57–61.

Diaz Alvarez, J. (1990) *Geografia del turismo* (Madrid: Editorial Sintesis).

Dobb, M. (1971) *Studies in the Development of Capitalism* (London: Routledge).

Doogan, Alison (ed.), Capps, G., Panayiotopoulos, P., Hintjens, H. and Gerry, C. (1996) *Winners and Losers: African Society and Development South of the Sahara* (Swansea: Centre for Development Studies/Oxfam).

Economist, The (1991) 'Where Tigers Breed: A Survey of Asia's Emerging Economies', London, 16 November.

Economist, The (1997) 'A Survey of Business in Latin America', 6 December.

Economist Intelligence Unit (1997) *Country Report: Mexico*, 3rd quarter (London: EIU).

Evans, P. (1979) *Dependent Development: the Alliance of Multinational, State and Local Capital in Brazil* (New Jersey: Princeton University Press).

Evans, P., Rueschmeyer, D. and Skocpol, T. (eds) (1985) *Bringing the State Back In* (Oxford: Oxford University Press).

Fernandez-Kelly, P. and Garcia, A. (1989) 'Informalisation at the Core: Hispanic Women, Homework, and the Advanced Capitalist State', in A. Portes, M. Castells and L. Benton (eds) *The Informal Economy: Studies in Advanced and Less Developed Countries*, pp. 247–64 (London: Johns Hopkins Press).

Financial Times (1998) 'Mexico: Manufacturing. A Marked Improvement in Sales', 7 October.

FitzGerald, E.V.K. (1984) 'Restructuring through the Depression: the State and Capital Accumulation in Mexico, 1825–1840', in R. Thorp (ed.) *Latin America in the 1930s. The Role of the Periphery in World Crisis*, pp. 242–78 (London: Macmillan).

Foo, L. (1994) 'The Vulnerable and Exploitable Immigrant Workforce and the Need for Strengthening Worker Protective Legislation', *The Yale Law Journal*, Vol. 103, No. 8, pp. 2213–37.

Forrester, V. (1999) *The Economic Horror* (Cambridge: Polity Press).

Frobel, F., Heinrichs, J. and Kreye, O. (1980) *The New International Division of Labour. Structural Unemployment in Industrial Countries and Industrialisation in Developing Countries* (Cambridge: Cambridge University Press).

Fryer, P. (1984) *Staying Power: the History of Black People in Britain* (London: Pluto Press).

Fukuyama, Francis (1995) *Trust: The Social Virtues and the Creation of Prosperity* (New York: Hamish Hamilton).

Furtado, Celso (1976) *Economic Development of Latin America: Historical Background and Contemporary Problems* (Cambridge: Cambridge University Press).

Gabb, G. (1992) *Lower Swansea Valley: Later Copper Works* (Swansea: Maritime and Industrial Museum Services).

Gallego, F. (1979) *Los comienzos de la industrializacion en España* (Madrid: Ediciones de la Torre).

Gans, H.J. (1992) 'Second-generation Decline: Scenarios for the Economic and Ethnic Futures of the Post-1965 American Immigrants', *Ethnic and Racial Studies*, Vol. 15, No. 2, pp. 173–92.

Gavira, M. (1974) *España a go-go. Turismo charter y neocolonialismo del espacio* (Madrid: Ediciones Turner).

Gereffi, G. and Evans, P. (1981) 'Transnational Corporations, Dependent Development, and State Policy in the Semiperiphery: a Comparison of Brazil and Mexico', *Latin American Research Review*, Vol. 16, No. 3, pp. 31–63.

German, L. (1998) 'Tiger, Tiger Burning Bright: Indonesia Erupts', *Socialist Review*, June, No. 220, pp. 10–13.

German, L. (1999) (ed.) *The Balkans, Nationalism and Imperialism* (London: Bookmarks).

Gittings, John (1997) *China. From Cannibalism to Karaoke* (London: Pocket Books).

Godley, A. (1996) 'The Emergence of Mass Production in the UK Clothing Industry', in I. Taplin and J. Winterton (eds) *Restructuring Within a Labour Intensive Industry*, pp. 8–25 (Aldershot: Avebury).

Goodwin, M. (1996) 'Governing the Spaces of Difference: Regulation and Globalisation in London', *Urban Studies*, Vol. 33, No. 8, pp. 1395–406.

Gordon, D. (1988) 'The Global Economy: New Edifice or Crumbling Foundations?', *New Left Review*, No. 187, pp. 24–64.

Gothoskar, S. (1992) (ed.) *Struggles of Women at Work* (New Delhi: Vikas Publishing House).

Greenlaw, J. (1999) *The Swansea Copper Barques and Cape Horners* (Swansea: Bryn Press).

Griesgraber, J.M. and Gunter, B.G. (1996) (eds) *The World Bank: Lending on a Global Scale* (London: Pluto Press).

Griesgraber, J.M. and Gunter, B.G. (1997) (eds) *World Trade: Towards Fair and Free Trade in the Twenty-first Century* (London: Pluto Press).

Gutiérrez del Valle, R.M. (1990) *Las actividades industriales* (Madrid: Editorial Sintesis).

Gyoung-hee, Shin (1998) 'The Crisis and the Worker's Movement in South Korea', *International Socialism*, No. 78, pp. 39–54.

Haber, S. (1989) *Industry and Underdevelopment. The Industrialization of Mexico, 1890–1940* (Stanford: Stanford University Press).

Hall, A. (1989) *Developing Amazonia: Deforestation and Social Conflict in Brazil's Carajas Programme* (Manchester: Manchester University Press).

Hammond, J.L. and Hammond, B. (1948) *The Village Labourer: Volume I* (London: Guild Books).

Hammond, J.L. and Hammond, B. (1948) *The Village Labourer: Volume II* (London: Guild Books).

Hamnett, C. (1996) 'Social Polarisation, Economic Restructuring and Welfare State Regimes', *Urban Studies*, Vol. 33, No. 8, pp. 1407–30.

Hancock, G. (1991) *The Lords of Poverty: the Freewheeling Lifestyles, Power, Prestige and Corruption of the Multibillion Dollar Aid Industry* (London: Macmillan).

Hansen, R.D. (1971) *The Politics of Mexican Development* (Baltimore: Johns Hopkins University Press).

Harman, C. (1991) 'The State and Capitalism Today', *International Socialism*, No. 51, pp. 57–71.

Harman, C. (1992) 'The Return of the National Question', *International Socialism*, No. 56, pp. 3–63.

Harman, C. (1996) 'Globalisation: a Critique of the New Orthodoxy', *International Socialism*, No. 73, pp. 3–35.

Harris, N. (1978) *The Mandate of Heaven* (Londonn: Quartet).

Harris, N. (1990a) *The End of the Third World: Newly Industrialising Countries and the Decline of an Ideology* (London: Penguin).

Harris, N. (1990b) *National Liberation* (Reno: University of Nevada Press).

Harris, N. (1995a) 'Can the West Survive?' *Competition and Change*, Vol. 1, pp. 111–22.

Harris, N. (1995b) *The New Untouchables: Immigration and the New World Worker* (London: Penguin).

Harrison, J. (1978) *An Economic History of Modern Spain* (Manchester: Manchester University Press).

Hatori, T. (1989) 'Formation of the Korean Business Elite During the Era of Rapid Economic Growth', *The Developing Economies*, Vol. XXV, No. 4, pp. 346–62.

Hellenier, G.K. (1998) 'The East Asian and Other Financial Crisis – Causes, Responses and Prevention', in K.S. Jomo (ed.) *Tigers in Trouble*, pp. 232–8 (London: Zed Books).

Hewitt, T. (1992) 'Developing Countries: 1945 to 1990', in T. Allen and A. Thomas (eds) *Poverty and Development in the 1990s*, pp. 221–37 (Oxford: Oxford University Press).

Hewitt, T., Johnson, H. and Wield, D. (1992) *Industrialization and Development* (Oxford: Oxford University Press).

Hill, C. (1969) *Reformation to Industrial Revolution* (London: Penguin).

Hirst, P. and Thompson, G. (1996) *Globalization in Question: the International Economy and the Possibilities of Governance* (London: Polity Press).

Hobsbawm, E. (1996a) *The Age of Revolution 1789–1848* (London: Weidenfeld and Nicolson).

Hobsbawm, E. (1996b) *The Age of Capital 1848–1875* (London: Weidenfeld and Nicolson).

Hobsbawm, E. (1996c) *The Age of Empire 1875–1914* (London: Weidenfeld and Nicolson).

Holloway, J. (1994) 'Global Capital and the National State', *Capital and Class*, No. 52, pp. 23–49.

Hoogvelt, A. (1997) *Globalisation and the Post-colonial World: the New Political Economy of Development* (London: Macmillan).

Humphries, J. (1988) 'Industrialisation in Brazil. The Miracle and its Aftermath', in B. Crow and M. Thorpe (eds) *Survival and Change in the Third World*, pp. 216–42 (London: Polity Press).

Institute of the Democratic Trade Union Movement (IDTUM) (1998) *The Great Economic Crisis and the IMF's Trusteeship* (Seoul: IDTUM).

Institute for Migration and Ethnic Studies (IMES) (1998) *Immigrant Businesses in Manufacturing: the Case of Turkish Businesses in the Amsterdam Garment Industry* (Amsterdam, University of Amsterdam: IMES).

International Labour Organisation (ILO) (1993) *Annual World Labour Report* (Geneva: ILO).

International Labour Organisation (ILO) (1997) *Industrial Relations, Democracy and Social Stability*. Annual World Labour Report (Geneva: ILO).

International Monetary Fund (IMF) (1997) *World Economic Outlook*. Annual Report (Washington, DC: IMF).

International Monetary Fund (IMF) (1998) *World Economic Outlook*. Annual Report (Washington, DC: IMF).

Jackson, B. (1992) *Threadbare: How the Rich Stitch up the World's Rag Trade* (London: World Development Movement).

James, C.L.R. (1980) *Toussaint Louverture and the San Domingo Revolution* (London: Alison and Busby).

Jenkins, R. (1992) 'Industrialization and the Global Economy', 'Theoretical Perspectives' and 'Re-interpreting Brazil and South Korea', in T. Hewitt et al. (eds) *Industrialisation and Development*, pp. 13–40, pp. 128–66 and pp. 167–201 (Oxford: Oxford University Press).

Jian, T., Sachs, D. and Warner, A. (1996) *Trends in Regional Inequality in China*. National Bureau of Economic Research, Working Paper 5412 (Washington, DC: World Bank).

Johns, W.E. (1955) *The Boy Biggles* (London: Dean and John).

Johnson, C. (1982) *MITI and the Japanese Miracle: the Growth of Industrial Policy, 1925–1975* (Stanford: Stanford University Press).

Jomo, K.S. (ed.) (1998) *Tigers in Trouble: Financial Governance, Liberalisation and Crisis in East Asia* (London: Zed Books).

Jones, T. (1993) *Britain's Ethnic Minorities* (London: Policy Studies Institute).

Jurdao, F. (1990) *España en venta* (Madrid: Endymion).

Kabeer, N. (1994) 'The Structure of "Revealed" Preference: Race, Community and Female Labour Supply in the London Clothing Industry', *Development and Change*, Vol. 25, No. 2, pp. 307–31.

Kidron, M. (1968) *Western Capitalism since the War* (London: Pelican).

Kidron, M. (1974) *Capitalism and Theory* (London: Pluto Press).

Kiely, R. (1995) *Sociology and Development: the Impasse and Beyond* (London: University College of London Press).

Kindleberger, C. (1967) *Europe's Post-War Growth. The Role of Labour Supply* (New York: Harvard University Press).

Kitching, G. (1982) *Class and Economic Change in Kenya* (London: Yale University Press).

Kitching, G. (1989) *Development and Underdevelopment in Historical Perspective: Populism, Nationalism and Industrialization* (London: Routledge).

Klein, N. (2001) *No Logo* (London: Flamingo).

Kwong, P. (1997) 'Manufacturing Ethnicity', *Critique of Anthropology*, Vol. 17, No. 4, pp. 365–87.

Lagendijk, A. (1994) 'The Impact of Internationalisation and Rationalisation of Production on the Spanish Automobile Industry', *Environment and Planning*, Vol. 26, pp. 321–43.

Lagendijk, A. (1995a) 'The Foreign Take-over of the Spanish Automobile Industry: a Growth Analysis of internationalisation', *Regional Studies*, Vol. 29, No. 4, pp. 381–93.

Lagendijk, A. (1995b) 'Spatial Effects of Internationalisation of the Spanish Automobile Industry', *Tijdschrift voor Economische en Sociale Geografie*, Vol. 86, No. 5, pp. 426–52.

Lal, D. (1983) *The Poverty of 'Development Economics'* (London: Institute of Economic Affairs, Hobart Paperback No. 16).

Lee, D. (1992) 'Commodification of Ethnicity. The Sociospatial Reproduction of Immigrant Entrepreneurs', *Urban Affairs Quarterly*, Vol. 28, No. 2, pp. 258–75.

Lee, E. (1996) 'Globalization and employment: Is Anxiety Justified?', *International Labour Review*, Vol. 135, pp. 485–99.

Lee, E. (1997) 'Globalization and Labour Standards: a Review of Issues', *International Labour Review*, Vol. 136, pp. 173–91.

Leftwich, A. (1994) 'Governance, the State and the Politics of Development', *Development and Change*, Vol. 25, pp. 363–86.

Light I., Bernard R. and Kim, R. (1999) 'Immigrant Incorporation in the Garment Industry of Los Angeles', *International Migration Review*, Vol. XXXIII, No. 1, pp. 5–25.

Love, J.L. (1980) 'Raul Prebisch and the Origins of the Doctrine of Unequal Exchange', *Latin American Research Review*, Vol. XV, No. 3, pp. 47–72.

Luedde-Neurath, R. (1988) 'State Intervention and Export-orientated Development in South Korea', in G. White (ed.) *Developmental States in East Asia* (Basingstoke: Macmillan).

Lustig, N. and Ros, J. (1987) *Country Study 7: Mexico* (Helsinki: World Institute for Development Economics Research of the United Nations University).

McGrew, A. (1992) 'The Third World in the New Global Order', in T. Allen and A. Thomas (eds) *Poverty and Development in the 1990s*, pp. 255–72 (Oxford: Oxford University Press).

Mark, J. (1985) *The MultiFibre Arrangement: Unravelling the Costs* (Ottawa: North South Institute).

Marx, K. (1970) *Capital: Volume I* (London: Lawrence and Wishart).

Marx, K. and Engels, F. (1971) *The Communist Manifesto* (Moscow: Progress Publishers).

Mavros, E. (1989) 'A Critical Review of Economic Development in Cyprus', *The Cyprus Review*, Vol. 1, No. 1, pp. 11–66.

Mercado, A. (1995) 'Implicaciones del desarrollo de la industria maquiladora en la modernización tecnológica de México', in P. Pozo (ed.) *Aspectos tecnológicos de la modernización industrial de México*, pp. 85–112 (Mexico: Fondo de Cultura Económica).

Messerlin, P. (2000) *Measuring the Costs of Economic Protection in Europe* (Washington: Institute for International Economics).

Metcalf, H., Modood, T. and Virdee S. (1996) *Asian Self- Employment* (London: Policy Studies Institute).

Meyer, M.C. and Sherman, W.L. (1991) *The Course of Mexican History* (New York: Oxford University Press).

Mitter, S. (1986) 'Industrial Restructuring and Manufacturing Homework: Immigrant Women in the UK Clothing Industry', *Capital and Class*, No. 27, pp. 37–80.

Moody, K. (1997) *Workers in a Lean World: Unions in the International Economy* (New York: Verso).

Moser, C., Herbert, A. and Makonnen, R. (1993) *Urban Poverty in the Context of Structural Adjustment. Recent Evidence and Policy Responses*. The World Bank Urban Development Division, Discussion Paper No. 4. (Washington: World Bank).

Myrdal, G. (1968) *Asian Drama* (New York: Pantheon Press).

New Internationalist (1990) 'The Poor Step Up Trade Wars', February, No. 204, Special Edition on Trade.

Newsinger, J. (1986) 'Lord Greystoke and Darkest Africa: the Politics of the Tarzan Stories', *Race and Class*, Vol. 28, No. 2, pp. 59–73.

North–South Institute (1988) *Commodity Trade: the Harsh Realities* (Ottawa: North South Institute).

Odinga, O. (1985) *Not yet Uhuru* (London: Hill and Wang).

Ogle, G.E. (1990) *South Korea: Dissent Within the Economic Miracle* (London: Zed).

Ong, P. and Valenzuela, A. (1997) 'The Labour Market: Immigrant Effects and Racial Discrimination', in R. Waldinger and M. Bozorgmehr (eds) *Ethnic Los Angeles*, pp. 165–91 (New York: Russell Sage Foundation).

Owen, D. (1997) 'Labour Force Participation Rates, Self-employment and Unemployment', in V. Karn, (ed.) *Ethnicity in the 1991 Census*, pp. 29–66 (London: HMSO).

Panayiotopoulos, P. (1990) 'Cypriot Entrepreneurs in the North London Clothing Industry: A Colonial Legacy', in *The Proceedings of the First International Symposium on Cypriot Migration: a Historical and Sociological Perspective*, pp. 285–331 (Nicosia: Science Research Centre).

Panayiotopoulos, P. (1992a) *Local Government Economic Initiatives. Planning, Choice and Politics: the London Experience*, Papers in International Development, No. 7 (Swansea: Centre for Development Studies).

Panayiotopoulos, P. (1992b) 'The Cypriot Clothing Industry' *The Cyprus Review*, Vol. 4, No. 1, pp. 77–123.

Panayiotopoulos, P. (1993) 'Cypriot Entrepreneurs in the Clothing Industry. North London and Cyprus: a Comparative Analysis'. PhD Thesis (Swansea: University of Wales).

Panayiotopoulos, P. (1995) 'The Developmental State in Crisis: the Case of Cyprus', *Capital and Class*, No. 57, pp. 13–53.

Panayiotopoulos, P. (1996a) 'Challenging Orthodoxies: Cypriot Entrepreneurs in the London Garment Industry', *New Community*, Vol. 22, No. 3, pp. 437–60.

Panayiotopoulos, P. (1996b) 'The State and Enterprise in the Cypriot Clothing Industry under Conditions of Globalisation', *Cyprus Journal of Economics*, Vol. 9, No. 1, pp. 5–29.

Panayiotopoulos, P. (1999) 'The Emergent Post-Colonial State in Cyprus', *Commonwealth & Comparative Politics*, Vol. 37, No. 1, pp. 31–55.

Panayiotopoulos, P. (2000) 'The labour regime under conditions of globalisation in the Cypriot garment industy', *Journal of Southern Europe and the Balkans*, Vol. 2, No. 1, pp. 75–88.

Panayiotopoulos, P. and Gerry, C. (1997) 'Learning from State-sponsored Youth Enterprise Promotion in the Commonwealth Developing Countries', *Third World Planning Review*, Vol. 19, No. 2, pp. 209–27.

Panpillón Olmedo, R. (1991) *El deficit tecnologico español* (Madrid: Instituto de Estudios Económicos).

Pearson, R. (1992) 'Gender Issues in Industrialisation', in T. Hewitt, H. Johnson and D. Wield (eds) *Industrialisation and Development*, pp. 222–47 (Oxford: Oxford University Press).

Pederson, L.R.(1966) *The Mining Industry of the Norte Chico, Chile* (Evanston, IL: Dept of Geography, North Western University).

Penninx, R., Schoorl, J. and van Praag, C. (1993) *The Impact of International Migration on Receiving Countries: the Case of the Netherlands* (Amsterdam: Swets and Zeitlinger).

Pereira, L.B. (1984) *Development and Crisis in Brazil* (London: Westview).

Petras, E. (1992) 'The Shirt on Your Back: Immigrant Workers and the Reorganisation of the Garment Industry', *Social Justice*, Vol. 19, No. 1, pp. 76–114.

Pilger, J. (1995) 'Natural Born Partners', *New Statesman and Society*, 10 March.

Portes, A. (1994) 'The Informal Economy and its Paradoxes', in N. Smelser and R. Swedbergh (eds) *The Handbook of Economic Sociology*, pp. 426–49 (New York: Princeton University Press).

Portes, A., Castells, M. and Benton, L.A. (eds) (1989) *The Informal Economy: Studies in Advanced and Less Developed Countries* (London: Johns Hopkins Press).

Portes, A. and Jensen, L. (1989) 'The Enclave and the Entrants: Patterns of Ethnic Enterprise in Miami Before and After Mariel', *American Sociological Review*, No. 54, pp. 929–49.

Portes, A. and Zhou, M. (1996) 'Self-Employment and the Earnings of Immigrants', *American Sociological Review*, No. 61, pp. 219–30.

Prebisch, Raúl (1959) 'Commercial Policies in the Underdeveloped Countries', *American Economic Review*, May, pp. 251–74.

Prebisch, Raúl (1984a) 'Five Stages in My Thinking on Development', in G. Meier and D. Seers (eds) *Pioneers in Development*. A World Bank publication (Oxford: Oxford University Press).

Prebisch, Raúl (1984b) *Power Relations and Market Laws*, Working Paper No. 35 (University of Notre Dame: Kellogg Institute for International Studies).

Quirós, J.M. (1973) 'Memoria de estatuto', in E. Florescano and I. Gil (eds) *Descripciones economicas de la Nueva Espana, 1784–1817*, pp. 231–64 (Mexico City: D.F.J. Mortiz).

Raghavan, C. (1997) 'A New Trade Order in a World of Disorder?', in J.M. Griesgraber and G. Gunter (eds) *World Trade: Towards Fair and Free Trade in the Twenty-first Century*, pp. 1–33 (London: Pluto Press).

Ram, M. and Jones, T. (1998) *Ethnic Minorities in Business* (Milton Keynes: Open University Business School).

Rath, J. (2000) 'Introduction' in J. Rath (ed.) *Immigrant Businesses. The Economic, Political and Social Environment*, pp. 1–19 (Houndmills: Macmillan).

Republic of Cyprus (1980) *Economic Report* (Nicosia: Government Printers).

Republic of Cyprus (1981) *Cyprus Economic Development 1960–1980* (Nicosia: Public Information Office).

Republic of Cyprus (1994) *Ministry of Labour and Social Insurance Annual Report* (Nicosia: Government Printers).

Roberts, R.O. (1980) 'The Smelting of Non-Ferrous Metals since 1750', in G. Williams (ed.) *Glamorgan County History*, Vol. V, pp. 47–96, Cardiff.

Roesch, J. (1999) 'The New Movement against Sweatshops', *International Socialist Review*, No. 9, pp. 7–14.

Ross, A. (ed.) (1997) *No Sweat, Fashion, Free Trade and the Rights of Garment Workers* (New York: Verso).

Rostow, W.W. (1960) *The Stages of Economic Growth: a Non-Communist Manifesto* (Cambridge: Cambridge University Press).

Rubin, I.I. (1989) *A History of Economic Thought* (London: Pluto).

Sachs, I. (1976) *The Discovery of the Third World* (Cambridge, MA: MIT Press).

Samuelson, A. (1948) 'International Trade and the Equalisation of Factor Prices', *Economic Journal*, No. 59, pp. 181–97.

Sanders, J. and Nee, V. (1987a) 'Limits of Ethnic Solidarity in the Enclave Economy', *American Sociological Review*, No. 52, pp. 745–73.

Sanders, J. and Nee, V. (1987b) 'On Testing the Enclave Economy Hypothesis', *American Sociological Review*, No. 52, pp. 771–3.

Sanders, J. and Nee, V. (1992) 'Problems in Resolving the Enclave Economy Debate', *American Sociological Review*, No. 57, pp. 415–18.

Sassen, S. (1988) *The Mobility of Labour and Capital: a Study of International Investment and Labour Flow* (New York: Cambridge University Press).

Sassen, S. (1989) 'New York City's Informal Economy', in A. Portes, M. Castells and L. Benton (eds) *The Informal Economy: Studies in Advanced and Less Developed Countries*, pp. 60–77 (London: Johns Hopkins Press).

Sassen, S. (1991) *The Global City: New York, London, Tokyo* (New Jersey: Princeton).

Sassen, S. (1995) 'Immigration and Local Labour Markets', in A. Portes (ed.) *The Economic Sociology of Immigration: Essays on Networks, Ethnicity and Entrepreneurship*, pp. 87–127 (New York: Russell Sage Foundation).

Sassen, S. (1996) 'New Employment Regimes in the Cities: the Impact of Immigrant Workers', *New Community*, Vol. 22, No. 4, pp. 579–94.

Saul, J. (1983) 'The State in Post-colonial societies: Tanzania', in H. Goulbourne (ed.) *Politics and State in the Third World*, pp. 70–92 (London: Macmillan).

Schmitz, C.J. (1979) *World Non-Ferrous Metal Production and Prices, 1700–1976* (London: Sage).

Scott, A. (1986) 'Women and Industrialisation: Examining the "Female Marginalisation" Thesis', *Journal of Development Studies*, No. 4, pp. 649–80.

Shaiken, H. (1994) 'Advanced Manufacturing and Mexico. A New International Division of Labor?', *Latin American Research Review*, Vol. 29, No. 2, pp. 39–71.

Sharp, R. (1994) *Senegal: a State of Change* (Oxford: Oxfam Publications).

Shivji, I.G. (1976) *Class Struggle in Tanzania* (London: Heinemann).

Simmons, P. (1995) *Words into Action: Basic Rights and the Campaign Against World Poverty* (Oxford: Oxfam Publications).

Sklair, L. (1988) 'Mexico's Maquiladora Programme: a Critical Evaluation', in G. Philip (ed.) *The Mexican Economy*, pp. 286–27 (London: Routledge).

Smyth, I. and Grijns, M. (1997) 'Unjuk Rasa or Conscious Protest? Resistance Strategies of Indonesian Women Workers', *Bulletin of Concerned Asian Scholars*, Vol. 29, No. 4, pp. 13–22.

South Commisssion (1990) *Report of the South Commisssion: the Challenge to the South* (Oxford: Oxford University Press).

Sparks, C. (1998) 'In the Eye of the Storm', *International Socialism*, No. 81, pp. 3–54.

Steadman Jones, G. (1976) *Outcast London: a Study in the Relationship between Classes in Victorian Society* (London: Peregrine).

Stopford, J. and Strange, S. (1993) *Rival States, Rival Firms: Competition for World Market Shares* (Cambridge: Cambridge University Press).

Storkey, M. (1993) *Identifying the Cypriot Community from the 1991 Census* (London: London Research Centre).

Storkey, M. (1994) *Ethnic Minorities in London: One City, Many Communities* (London: London Research Centre).

Storkey, M. and Lewis, R. (1997) 'London: a True Metropolis', in P. Ratcliffe (ed.) *Ethnicity in the 1991 Census*, pp. 210–25 (London: HMSO).

Street, B.V. (1975) *The Savage in Literature* (London: Routledge).

Sutcliffe, R.B. (1971) *Industry and Underdevelopment* (London: Addison-Wesley).

Székely, G. (1994) 'The Consequences of NAFTA for European and Japanese Trade and Investment in Mexico', in V. Bulmer-Thomas and N. Craske (eds) *Mexico and the North American Free Trade Agreement. Who Will Benefit?*, pp. 149–62 (Basingstoke: Macmillan).

Tamames, R. and Rueda, A. (1997) *Estructura economica de España* (Madrid: Alianza Universidad Textos).

Textile Outlook International (1994) Editorial, 'USA Puts MFA on Life Support', March, pp. 3–6.

Thorp, R. (ed.) (1984) *Latin America in the 1930s. The Role of the Periphery in World Crisis* (London: Macmillan).

Todaro, M. (1997) (sixth edn) *Economic Development in the Third World* (London: Longman).

Tornell, A. and Esquivel, G. (1995) 'The Political Economy of Mexico's Entry to NFTA', *National Bureau of Economic Research* Working Paper No. 5322, Mexico City.

Towner, J. (1985) 'The Grand Tour: a Key Phase in the History of Tourism', *Annals of Tourism Research*, Vol. 12, No. 3, pp. 297–333.

Toye, J. (1989) *Dilemmas of Development: Reflections on the Counter-Revolution in Development Theory and Policy* (Oxford: Basil Blackwell).

Tussie, D. (1987) *The Less Developed Countries and the World Trading System: a Challenge to the Gatt* (London: Frances Pinter).

Ungpakorn, J.G. (1997) *The Struggle for Democracy and Social Justice in Thailand* (Bangkok: Workers Democracy Book Club).

Ungpakorn, J.G. (1999) *Thailand: Class Struggle in an Era of Economic Crisis* (Bangkok: Workers Democracy Book Club).

United Kingdom Department of Employment (1976) *Immigrants in the Labour Market*. Unit of Manpower Studies Project Report (London: HMSO).

United Kingdom National Statistics (1998) *Labour Market Trends*, June (London: HMSO).

United Kingdom Office of Population (1961) *Census of Population for 1961* (London: HMSO).

United Kingdom Office of Population (1991) *Census of Population for 1991* (London: HMSO).

United Nations (1998) *World Economic Survey 1998* (New York: United Nations).

United Nations Conference on Trade and Development (UNCTAD) (1990) *Africa's Commodity Problems: Towards a Solution*. UNCTAD Secretariat, Task Force on UN-PAARD (Geneva: UNCTAD).

United Nations Conference on Trade and Development (UNCTAD) (1994) *Liberalising International Transactions in Services: a Handbook* (Geneva: UNCTAD/World Bank).

United Nations Development Programme (UNDP) (1961) *Cyprus – Suggestions for a Development Programme of Technical Assistance* (Geneva: UNDP).

United Nations Development Programme (UNDP) (various issues) *Human Development Report*. Annual Report (New York: Oxford University Press).

United Nations Economic Commission for Latin America and the Caribbean (ECLAC) (1990, 1995, 1996) *Statistical Yearbook for Latin America and the Caribbean* for these years (Santiago: ECLAC).

United Nations International Children's Emergency Fund (UNICEF) (2000) *State of the World's Children* (New York: Oxford University Press).

Valenzuela, L. (1990) 'Challenges to the Copper Smelting Industry in the World Market, 1840–1860', *Journal of European Economic History*, Vol. 19, pp. 57–86.

Valenzuela, L. (1992) 'The Chilean Copper Smelting Industry in the Mid-Nineteenth Century: Phases of Expansion and Stagnation, 1834–1858', *Journal of Latin American Studies*, No. 24, pp. 507–50.

Valenzuela, M. (1991) 'Spain: the Phenomenon of Mass Tourism', in A. Williams and G. Shaw *Tourism and Economic Development. Western European Experiences*, pp. 34–51 (London: Belhaven Press).

Van Der Wee, H. (1987) *Prosperity and Upheaval: the World Economy 1945–1980* (London: Penguin).

Van Geuns, R. (1992) 'An Aspect of Informalisation of Women's Work in a High-Tech Age: Turkish Sweatshops in the Netherlands', in S. Mitter (ed.) *Computer-aided Manufacturing and Women's Employment: The Clothing Industry in Four EC Countries*, pp. 125–37 (London: Springer-Verlag Press).

Vázquez Barquero, A. (1988) 'Small-scale Industry in Rural Areas: the Spanish Experience Since the Beginning of this Century', in K. Arrow (ed.) *The Balance between Industry and Agriculture in Economic Development*, pp. 25–52 (London: Macmillan).

Vera, M. (1996) *El cobre en el centro de la política* (Santiago: Mariel).

Wade, R. (1990) *Governing the Market: Economic Theory and the Role of Government in East Asian Industrialisation* (New Jersey: Princeton University Press).

Wade, R. (1996) 'Japan, the World Bank, and the Art of Paradigm Maintenance: the East Asian Miracle in Political Perspective', *New Left Review*, No. 217, pp. 3–36.

Wade, R. and Venereso, F. (1998) 'The Asian Crisis: the High-Debt Model versus the Wall Street-Treasury-IMF Complex', *New Left Review*, No. 228, pp. 3–23.

Waldinger, R. (1996a) *Still the Promised City? African-Americans and New Immigrants in Postindustrial New York* (Cambridge, MA: Harvard University Press).

Waldinger, R. (1996b) 'From Ellis Island to LAX: Immigrant Prospects in the American City', *International Migration Review*, Vol. 30, No. 4, pp. 1078–86.

Waldinger, R. (1997) 'Ethnicity and Opportunity in the Plural City', in R. Waldinger and M. Bozorgmehr (eds) *Ethnic Los Angeles*, pp. 445–70 (New York: Russell Sage Foundation).

Waldinger, R. and Lapp, M. (1993) 'Back to the Sweatshop or Ahead to the Informal Sector', *International Journal of Urban and Regional Research*, Vol. 17, No. 1, pp. 6–29.

Watkins, K. (1995) *The Oxfam Poverty Report* (Oxford: Oxfam Publications).

Watkins, K. (1997) *Globalisation and Liberalisation: Implications for Poverty, Distribution and Inequality* (Oxford: Oxfam Publications).

White, G. (ed.) (1988) *Developmental States in East Asia* (Basingstoke: Macmillan).

White, G. and Wade, R. (1988) 'Developmental States and Markets in East Asia: an Introduction', in G. White (ed.) *Developmental States in East Asia*, pp. 1–17 (Basingstoke: Macmillan).

Wield, D. and Rhodes, E. (1988) 'Divisions of Labour or Labour Divided?', in B. Crow and M. Thorpe (eds) *Survival and Change in the Third World*, pp. 288–309 (London: Polity Press).

Wilkie, J.W. (1970) *The Mexican Revolution. Federal Expenditure and Social Change since 1910* (Berkeley: University of California Press).

Williams, E. (1966) *Capitalism and Slavery* (London: Capricorn).

Wilson, P.A. (1992) *Exports and Local Development. Mexico's New Maquiladoras* (Austin: University of Texas Press).

Wolf, E.R. (1990) *Europe and the People Without History* (London: University of California Press).

World Bank (1987) *Cyprus: a Long-Term Development Perspective*, A World Bank Country Study (Washington, DC: World Bank).

World Bank (1989) *Sub-Saharan Africa. From Crisis to Sustainable Growth*. A Long-Term Perspective Study (Washington, DC: World Bank).

World Bank (1990) *Poverty*. Annual World Development Report (Washington, DC: Oxford University Press).

World Bank (1993) *The East Asian Miracle. Economic Growth and Public Policy*. Policy Research Report (New York: Oxford University Press).

World Bank (1994) *Adjustment in Africa. Reforms, Results and the Road Ahead*. A World Bank Policy Research Report (Oxford: Oxford University Press).

World Bank (1995a) *Workers in an Integrating World*. Annual World Development Report (Washington, DC: Oxford University Press).

World Bank (1995b) *China: Macroeconomic Stability in a Decentralised Economy*. A World Bank Country Study (Washington, DC: World Bank).

World Bank (1996) *From Plan to Market*. Annual World Development Report (Washington, DC: Oxford University Press).

World Bank (1997a) *China 2020: Development Challenges in the New Century* (Washington, DC: World Bank).

World Bank (1997b) *China's Management of Enterprise Assets: the State as a Shareholder* (Washington, DC: World Bank).

World Bank (1997c) *China Engaged: Integration with the Global Economy* (Washington, DC: World Bank).

World Bank (1999) *Global Economic Prospects and the Developing Economies* (Washington, DC: World Bank).

World Bank (2000) *Entering the 21st Century*. Annual World Development Report (Washington, DC: Oxford University Press).

Wu, Harry (1995) *Laogai. The Chinese Gulag* (London: Vintage).

Wu, Harry (1997) *Harry Wu. Troublemaker* (London: Vintage).

Wynia, G. (1984) *The Politics of Latin American Development* (Cambridge: Cambridge University Press).

Yebra, D.M. (1996) *Homework on the Mexican Border*. Discussion Papers in Sociology, No. S96/5 (Leicester: Department of Sociology, University of Leicester).

Zwanenberg, R.M.A. and King, A. (1975) *An Economic History of Kenya and Uganda 1800–1970* (London: Macmillan).

Further Reading

Below is a collection of material which may be useful in finding out more about particular issues. It is by no means exhaustive, but does indicate ways in which further reading can be undertaken. Some thought has gone into providing material which is relatively accessible to the reader. The reading ranges from academic books and articles in scholarly journals, to books on development and globalisation produced for a wider readership. Some literary texts are also included. Further on there is a section on magazines and newspapers, which are either about the study of the Third World or which include extensive coverage of Third World issues. An asterisk denotes introductory reading. A list of websites relevant to some of the concerns raised by the book is included at the end. The quality and availability of sites can vary, and they are not a substitute for reading and engaging in debate. The websites listed belong to institutions or organisations, such as the World Bank and the International Labour Organisation. Many of them belong to trade unions. This can be a useful source for updating knowledge and can act as a channel for international communication. Some thought has also gone into ensuring breadth and balance in further reading, as well as the availability of sources. This allows for diverse interpretation and makes for some interesting comparisons.

BOOKS AND ARTICLES

Note: * represents introductory reading

*Allen, T. and Thomas, A. (2000) (eds) *Poverty and Development into the 21st Century* (Oxford: Oxford University Press).

Amsden, A. (1989) *Asia's Next Giant: South Korea and Late Industrialisation* (London: Oxford University Press).

Bello, W. and Rosenfeld, S. (1990) *Dragons in Distress: Asia's Economic Miracle in Crisis* (London: Pelican).

Bonacich, E. (1993) 'Asian and Latino Immigrants in the Los Angeles Garment Industry: an Exploration of the Relationship between Capitalism and Racial Oppression', in I. Light and P. Bhachu (eds) *Immigration and Entrepreneurship: Culture, Capital and Ethnic Networks*, pp. 51–74 (New Brunswick: Transaction Publishers).

Boserup, E. (1970) *Woman's Role in Economic Development* (London: Earthscan).

Browne, H. (1994) *For Richer, for Poorer. Shaping US–Mexican Integration* (London: Latin American Bureau).

Bustamante, J.A. (1983) '*Maquiladoras*: a New Face of International Capitalism on Mexico's Northern Frontier', in J. Nash and P. Fernandez-Kelly (eds) *Women, Men, and the International Division of Labor*, pp. 224–56 (Albany: State University of New York Press).

*Callinicos, A. (1994) 'Marxism and Imperialism Today', in A. Callinicos et al. (eds) *Marxism and the New Imperialism* (London: Bookmarks).

Callinicos, A. (1999) *Social Theory: a Historical Introduction* (Cambridge: Polity Press).

*Chossudovsky, M. (1996) *The Globalisation of Poverty: Impacts of the IMF and World Bank Reforms* (London: Zed Books).

Coote, B. and LeQuesne, C. (1996) *The Trade Trap: Poverty and the Global Commodity Markets* (Oxford: Oxfam Publications).

Coquery-Vidrovich, C. (1988) *Africa, Endurance and Change South of the Sahara* (Berkeley: University of California Press).

*Danaher, K. and Burbach, R. (2000) *Globalise This!* (Maine: Common Courage).

*Doogan, Alison (ed.), Capps, G., Panayiotopoulos, P., Hintjens, H. and Gerry, C. (1996) *Winners and Losers: African Society and Development South of the Sahara* (Swansea: Centre for Development Studies/Oxfam).

Fernandez-Kelly, P. and Garcia, A. (1989) 'Informalisation at the Core: Hispanic Women, Homework, and the Advanced Capitalist State', in A. Portes, M. Castells and L. Benton (eds) *The Informal Economy: Studies in Advanced and Less Developed Countries*, pp. 247–64 (London: Johns Hopkins Press).

Foo, L. (1994) 'The Vulnerable and Exploitable Immigrant Workforce and the Need for Strengthening Worker Protective Legislation', *The Yale Law Journal*, Vol. 103, No. 8, pp. 2213–37.

*Forester, V. (1999) *The Economic Horror* (Cambridge: Polity Press).

Frobel, F., Heinrichs. J. and Kreye, O. (1980) *The New International Division of Labour. Structural Unemployment in Industrial Countries and Industrialisation in Developing Countries* (Cambridge: Cambridge University Press).

*Fryer, P. (1984) *Staying Power: the History of Black People in Britain* (London: Pluto).

Fukuyama, Francis (1995) *Trust: the Social Virtues and the Creation of Prosperity* (New York: Hamish Hamilton).

*German, L. (ed.) (1999) *The Balkans, Nationalism and Imperialism* (London: Bookmarks).

Geuns, Van, R. (1992) 'An Aspect of Informalisation of Women's Work in a High-Tech Age: Turkish Sweatshops in the Netherlands', in S. Mitter (ed.) *Computer-aided Manufacturing and Women's Employment: the Clothing Industry in Four EC Countries*, pp. 125–37 (London: Springer-Verlag Press).

*Gittings, John (1997) *China, From Cannibalism to Karaoke* (London: Pocket Books).

Gothoskar, S. (ed.) (1992) *Struggles of Women at Work* (New Delhi: Vikas Publishing House).

*Griesgraber, J.M. and Gunter, B.G. (eds) (1996) *The World Bank: Lending on a Global Scale* (London: Pluto Press).

*Griesgraber, J.M. and Gunter, G. (eds) (1997) *World Trade: Towards Fair and Free Trade in the Twenty-first Century* (London: Pluto Press).

Hall, A. (1989) *Developing Amazonia: Deforestation and Social Conflict in Brazil's Carajas Programme* (Manchester: Manchester University Press).

*Hancock, G. (1991) *The Lords of Poverty: the Freewheeling Lifestyles, Power, Prestige and Corruption of the Multibillion Dollar Aid Industry* (London: Macmillan).

*Harman, C. (1999) *A People's History of the World* (London: Bookmarx).

*Harris, N. (1990a) *The End of the Third World: Newly Industrialising Countries and the Decline of an Ideology* (London: Penguin).

—— (1990b) *National Liberation* (Reno: University of Nevada Press).

*—— (1995) *The New Untouchables: Immigration and the New World Worker* (London: Penguin).

*Hewitt, T., Johnson, H. and Wield, D. (1992) *Industrialization and Development* (Oxford: Oxford University Press).

*Hirst, P. and Thompson, G. (1996) *Globalization in Question: the International Economy and the Possibilities of Governance* (London: Polity Press).

*Hobsbawm, E. (1996a) *The Age of Revolution 1789–1848* (London: Weidenfeld and Nicolson).

—— (1996b) *The Age of Capital 1848–1875* (London: Weidenfeld and Nicolson).

—— (1996c) *The Age of Empire 1875–1914* (London: Weidenfeld and Nicolson).

*Hoogvelt, A. (1997) *Globalisation and the Post-colonial World: the New Political Economy of Development* (London: Macmillan).

International Labour Organisation (ILO) (1997) *Industrial Relations, Democracy and Social Stability*. Annual World Labour Report (Geneva: ILO).

International Monetary Fund (IMF) (1998) *World Economic Outlook*. Annual Report (Washington, DC: IMF).

*Jackson, B. (1992) *Threadbare: How the Rich Stitch up the World's Rag Trade* (London: World Development Movement).

*James, C.L.R. (1980) *Toussaint Louverture and the San Domingo Revolution* (London: Alison and Busby).

Jomo, K.S (ed.) (1998) *Tigers in Trouble: Financial Governance, Liberalisation and Crisis in East Asia* (London: Zed Books).

Kidron, M. (1974) *Capitalism and Theory* (London: Pluto Press).

Kiely, R. (1995) *Sociology and Development: the Impasse and Beyond* (London: University College of London Press).

Klein, N. (2001) *No Logo* (London: Flamingo).

Lagendijk, A. (1994) 'The Impact of Internationalisation and Rationalisation of Production on the Spanish Automobile Industry', *Environment and Planning*, Vol. 26, pp. 321–43.

Lal, D. (1983) *The Poverty of 'Development Economics'* (London: Institute of Economic Affairs, Hobart Paperback No. 16).

Love, J.L. (1980) 'Raul Prebisch and the Origins of the Doctrine of Unequal Exchange', *Latin American Research Review*, Vol. XV, No. 3, pp. 47–72.

Montanari, A. and Williams, A.M. (eds) (1995) *European Tourism: Regions, Spaces and Restructuring* (Aldershot: J. Wiley and Sons).

*Moody, K. (1997) *Workers in a Lean World: Unions in the International Economy* (New York: Verso).

Myrdal, G. (1968) *Asian Drama* (New York: Pantheon Press).

Odinga, O. (1985) *Not yet Uhuru* (London: Hill and Wang).

Ogle, G.E. (1990) *South Korea: Dissent Within the Economic Miracle* (London: Zed).

*Ousmane, S. (1986) *God's Bits of Wood* (Nairobi: Heinemann).

Panayiotopoulos, P. (1995) 'The Developmental State in Crisis: the Case of Cyprus' *Capital and Class*, No. 57, pp. 13–53.

*—— (1996a) 'Challenging Orthodoxies: Cypriot Entrepreneurs in the London Garment Industry', *New Community*, Vol. 22, No. 3, pp. 437–60.

*—— (1999) 'The Emergent Post-Colonial State in Cyprus', *Commonwealth & Comparative Politics*, Vol. 37, No. 1, pp. 31–55.

—— (2000) 'The labour regime under conditions of globalisation in the Cypriot garment industy', *Journal of Southern Europe and the Balkans*, Vol. 2, No. 1, pp. 75–88.

Panayiotopoulos, P. and Gerry, C. (1997) 'Learning from State-sponsored Youth Enterprise Promotion in the Commonwealth Developing Countries', *Third World Planning Review*, Vol. 19, No. 2, pp. 209–27.

Pearson, R. (1992) 'Gender Issues in Industrialisation', in T. Hewitt, H. Johnson and D. Wield (1992) (eds) *Industrialisation and Development*, pp. 222–47 (Oxford: Oxford University Press).

Pereira, L.B. (1984) *Development and Crisis in Brazil* (London: Westview).

Portes, A. (1994) 'The Informal Economy and its Paradoxes', in N. Smelser and R. Swedbergh (eds) *The Handbook of Economic Sociology*, pp. 426–49 (New York: Princeton University Press).

Portes, A., Castells, M. and Benton, L.A. (eds) (1989) *The Informal Economy: Studies in Advanced and Less Developed Countries* (London: Johns Hopkins Press).

Portes, A. and Zhou, M. (1996) 'Self-Employment and the Earnings of Immigrants', *American Sociological Review*, No. 61, pp. 219–30.

Prebisch, Raúl (1959) 'Commercial Policies in the Underdeveloped Countries', *American Economic Review*, May, pp. 251–74.

Ram, M. and Jones, T. (1998) *Ethnic Minorities in Business* (Milton Keynes: Open University Business School).

Roberts, R.O. (1980) 'The Smelting of Non-Ferrous Metals since 1750', in G. Williams (ed.) *Glamorgan County History*, Vol. V, pp. 47–96, Cardiff.

Roesch, J. (1999) 'The new Movement against Sweatshops', *International Socialist Review*, No. 9, pp. 7–14, Chicago.

*Ross, A. (ed.) (1997) *No Sweat: Fashion, Free Trade and the Rights of Garment Workers* (New York: Verso).

Rubin, I.I. (1989) *A History of Economic Thought* (London: Pluto).

Sanders, J. and Nee, V. (1987) 'Limits of Ethnic Solidarity in the Enclave Economy', *American Sociological Review*, No. 52, pp. 745–73.

*Saskia, S. (1991) *The Global City: New York, London, Tokyo* (New Jersey: Princeton).

Shaiken, H. (1994) 'Advanced Manufacturing and Mexico. A New International Division of Labor?', *Latin American Research Review*, Vol. 29, No. 2, pp. 39–71.

Sharp, R. (1994) *Senegal: a State of Change* (Oxford: Oxfam Publications).

Simmons, P. (1995) *Words into Action: Basic Rights and the Campaign Against World Poverty* (Oxford: Oxfam Publications).

Sklair, L. (1988) 'Mexico's Maquiladora Programme: a Critical Evaluation', in G. Philip (ed.) *The Mexican Economy*, pp. 286- 327 (London: Routledge).

Smyth, I. and Grijns, M. (1997) 'Unjuk Rasa or Conscious Protest? Resistance Strategies of Indonesian Women Workers', *Bulletin of Concerned Asian Scholars*, Vol. 29, No. 4, pp. 13–22.

South Commisssion (1990) *Report of the South Commisssion: the Challenge to the South* (Oxford: Oxford University Press).

Sparks, C. (1998) 'In the Eye of the Storm', *International Socialism*, No. 81, pp. 3–54.

Steadman Jones, G. (1976) *Outcast London: a Study in the Relationship between Classes in Victorian Society* (London: Peregrine).

Stopford, J. and Strange, S. (1993) *Rival States, Rival Firms: Competition for World Market Shares* (Cambridge: Cambridge University Press).

Todaro, M. (1997) (sixth edn) *Economic Development in the Third World* (London: Longman).

Toye, J. (1989) *Dilemmas of Development: Reflections on the Counter-Revolution in Development Theory and Policy* (Oxford: Basil Blackwell).

*Traven, B. (1997) *The Rebellion of the Hanged* (London: Alison and Busby).

*Ungpakorn, J.G. (1997) *The Struggle for Democracy and Social Justice in Thailand* (Bangkok: Workers Democracy Book Club).

—— (1999) *Thailand: Class Struggle in an Era of Economic Crisis* (Bangkok: Workers Democracy Book Club).

*United Nations Development Programme (UNDP)(various issues) *Human Development Report*. Annual Report (New York: Oxford University Press).

United Nations International Children's Emergency Fund (UNICEF) (2000) *State of the World's Children* (New York: Oxford University Press).

Valenzuela, L. (1990) 'Challenges to the Copper Smelting industry in the World Market, 1840–1860', *Journal of European Economic History*, Vol. 19, pp. 57–86.

—— (1992) 'The Chilean Copper Smelting Industry in the Mid-Nineteenth Century: Phases of Expansion and Stagnation, 1834–1858', *Journal of Latin American Studies*, No. 24, pp. 507–50.

Wade, R. (1990) *Governing the Market: Economic Theory and the Role of Government in East Asian Industrialisation* (New Jersey: Princeton University Press).

—— (1996) 'Japan, the World Bank, and the Art of Paradigm Maintenance: the East Asian Miracle in Political Perspective', *New Left Review*, No. 217, pp. 3–36.

Wade, R. and Venereso, F. (1998) 'The Asian Crisis: the High-Debt Model Versus the Wall Street-Treasury-IMF Complex', *New Left Review*, No. 228.

Waldinger, R. (1996) *Still the Promised City? African-Americans and New Immigrants in Postindustrial New York* (Cambridge, MA: Harvard University Press).

Waldinger, R. and Bozorgmehr, M. (eds) (1997) *Ethnic Los Angeles* (New York: Russell Sage Foundation).

*Watkins, K. (1995) *The Oxfam Poverty Report* (Oxford: Oxfam Publications).

*Went, R. (200) *Neoliberal Challenge, Radical Responses* (London: Pluto).

White, G. (ed) (1988) *Developmental States in East Asia* (Basingstoke: Macmillan).

Wilson, P.A. (1992) *Exports and Local Development. Mexico's New Maquiladoras* (Austin: University of Texas Press).

World Bank (1990) *Poverty*. Annual World Development Report (Washington, DC: Oxford University Press).

—— (1993) *The East Asian Miracle. Economic Growth and Public Policy*. Policy Research Report (New York: Oxford University Press).

*—— (1995) *Workers in an Integrating World*. Annual World Development Report (Washington, DC: Oxford University Press).

—— (2000) *Entering the 21st Century*. Annual World Development Report (Washington, DC: Oxford University Press).

Wu, Harry (1995) *Laogai. The Chinese Gulag* (London: Vintage).

*—— (1997) *Harry Wu. Troublemaker* (London: Vintage).

Wynia, G. (1984) *The Politics of Latin American Development* (Cambridge: Cambridge University Press).

JOURNALS, MAGAZINES, NEWSPAPERS

Capital and Class
Development in Practice (an Oxfam publication)
Economic and Political Weekly (Bombay)
The Economist (London)
Far Eastern Economic Review
Financial Times (London)
Institute of Development (Sussex, UK) Discussion Papers
International Labour Review (an ILO publication)
International Socialism Journal
Journal of Development Studies
Journal of Ethnic and Migration Studies
Latin America Research Review
The New Internationalist
New Left Review
Race and Class
Review of African Political Economy
Small Enterprise Development (Intermediate Technology)
Socialist Worker
Third World Quarterly
Urban Studies
World Development Journal

WEBSITES

Centre of Indian Trade Unions (CITU)
http://www.citu.org.in/
Confederation of South African Trade Unions (COSATU)
http://www.cosatu.org.sa/
Fuerza Unida
www.igc.org/fuerzaunida
Global Labournet (Directory of directories on Labour Movement)

http://www.solinet.org/lee/labour49.htm
International Labour Organisation: Employment and Social Policy
http://www.ilo.org/public/english/20gb/docs/gb273/sep-4.htm
International Labour Organisation and Small Enterprises
http://www.ilo.org/public/english/65entrep/papers/sed.2/htm
Korean Confederation of Trade Unions (KCTU)
http://www.kctu.org/
Latin American Auto Workers
http://www.mesharpe.com/65601990.htm
National Labour Committee – USA
www.nlcnet.org/behindclosed/nicaragua.htm.
OXFAM Clothes Code Campaign
www.oxfam.org.uk/campaign/clothes/ciobanio.htm; also see 'Sweatshop Watch' at
www.sweatshopwatch.org/swatch/industry
Peoples Democratic Party (PRP) Indonesia
www.peg.apc.org/-asiet/
Trade Unions and Human Rights
http://www.gov.sk.ca/shrc/ixunions.htm
Trade Unions and NGOs
http://www.igc.org/dgap/beleong.htm
UNITE – and Anti-Sweatshop Campaign
www.uniteunion.org/sweatshops/newsthisweek/s7–21–99.html
World Bank and Small Enterprises
http://www.worldbank.org/htm/fpd/privatesector/sme.htm

Glossary

Absolute poverty – A situation where individuals, communities, or sections within communities are able to meet only bare subsistence and essentials of food, clothing and shelter, at a minimum level of living.

Aggregate demand – A measure of the real purchasing power of a country's economy which includes total expenditure in consumption, investment and net exports.

Alternative Trade Organisations (ATOs) – Specialised NGOs involved in 'fair trade', with the expressed non-profit making purpose of empowering local communities and introducing socially acceptable labour standards. Some ATOs are driven by ethical investment policies and others by a sense of political solidarity with the Third World. Partly because ATOs are a relatively new structure for NGOs their impact is difficult to estimate.

Autarky – A closed economy that attempts to be completely self-reliant.

Balance of payments deficit – The balance of payments consists of flows of goods, services and money. A country is in deficit when its income from exports and cash inflows is less than its payment for imports, cash outflows and debt repayments.

Bretton Woods institutions – The institutions founded under US leadership at the conference of Bretton Woods, New Hampshire, USA in 1944, that is, the World Bank, the International Monetary Fund, and subsequently the General Agreement on Tariffs and Trade – forerunner of the World Trade Organisation.

Capital-intensive production – Production technologies which require a higher proportion of capital relative to other factors of production, i.e. labour and land.

Chaebol – Large South Korean companies which originated and in many cases still remain as family-owned enterprises and which account for most of the employment and exports by South Korea. The *Chaebol* pursued a TNC strategy in the 1990s both in response to protectionism by the EEC and USA, and rising domestic labour costs. This saw the relocation of productive capacity to Europe, the USA and other South East Asian countries. The 1997 Asian crisis weakened the *Chaebol* and this has made them vulnerable to predation by US and European rivals.

Common Agricultural Policy (CAP) – A system of agricultural subsidies used by the European Community. These consist of buying and hoarding food at prices above those it would command under normal market conditions and subsidies for 'set aside' purposes, i.e. to grow nothing. The impact of CAP policies is to artificially increase prices for consumers in Europe. The hoarding of surpluses which accounts for about half of the total value of the product also depresses agricultural prices for producers in the Third World. Since subsidies are given on the basis of unit of production, the major beneficiaries of the CAP have been the large agricultural TNCs.

Comparative advantage – A country can be said to have a comparative advantage over another country if it can produce a commodity at a lower cost, relative to other commodities produced. There are two variations of comparative advantage. The first is associated with natural endowment, such as the role of climate and soil in the production of tropical commodities. The second is associated with country policy attempts to create a comparative advantage, such as in manufacturing industry, which may not be consistent with its natural endowment. The development of dynamic comparative advantage was an important factor in industrialisation by the NICs.

Debt crisis – Extreme difficulties faced by Third World countries in repaying their loans since 1982, caused mainly by rising rates of interest, declining commodity prices and the growth of short-term lending by progressively de-regulated financial markets.

Deflation – A sustained fall in the general price level.

Devaluation – A decrease in the value of a currency.

Economic Commission for Latin America and the Caribbean (ECLAC) – A regional branch of the United Nations which became a considerable intellectual force through the publication of technical and statistical analyses of economic trends in Latin America. *The ECLA School* as it became known, shaped wider structuralist thinking about the development of under-development in the Third World.

Economic Planning Board (EPB), South Korea – The EPB was the centre of South Korean industrialisation for a period of over 20 years. It controlled industrial and financial policy, and drafted plans to which the *Chaebol* had to conform. It regulated the internal price regime, the transfer of technology, imposed severe restrictions on foreign competition and used export subsidies to steer production towards export.

Economies of scale – The expansion in the scale of productive capacity by a company or industry leading to increases in output and decreases in the cost of production per unit of output.

European Economic Community (EEC) – The Common Market was established under the Treaty of Rome in 1957 as a European free trade zone, which has progressively enlarged its membership to most European countries, including Eastern European countries most of which have pending membership. Agricultural subsidies in the form of the CAP brought the EEC into conflict with the USA in the recent renegotiation of the GATT/WTO world trade agreement. The EEC has supported the MFA in textiles and uses extensive immigration controls on the free movement of labour.

European Union (EU) – The EU represents the development of the EEC from a common trading zone to an economic and political union with common monetary, political and military institutions. Country members of the EEC are at different stages of harmonisation and compliance with full EU membership. This has been influenced by popular movements in many European countries against policies such as reduction in government expenditure as a precondition for monetary union. In some member states such as the Scandinavian countries and Denmark, EU policy on labour rights and the environment represents a deterioration in existing national standards.

Exchange rate – The rate at which central banks will exchange one country's currency for another.

Export Credit Guarantee Scheme (ECGS) – An insurance scheme for exporters used in many countries. This guarantees payment for a proportion of the value of goods exported if payment has not been received by a specified period of time. The major beneficiaries of the scheme are the TNCs.

Export Orientated Industrialisation (EOI) – A policy which gives primacy to production for export as a means of generating foreign exchange earnings and improving the balance of payments.

Export Processing Zones (EPZs) – Sometimes also referred to as Free Trade Zones (FTZs). EPZs and FTZs are fenced-off industrial estates designed specifically for the purpose of production for export. In order to attract inward investment Third World countries offer incentives to TNCs such as tax holidays, freedom from foreign exchange restrictions, rights to profit repatriation, freedom to import tax-free raw materials and machinery destined for export production, and so on. The first FTZ was established in Taiwan in 1965. Now they exist in all countries of the globe.

Factors of production – The inputs required to produce goods and services. The basic factors of production are land, labour and capital.

Fair Labor Association (FLA) – Established by the Clinton administration as a pioneering example of social partnership. Its purpose was to meet rising concerns in the USA about Third World sweatshop conditions in factories used or owned by US corporations producing goods for the US market. The FLA was widely discredited for including on its Board companies identified by the USAS as using sweatshop labour. Trade unions and NGOs withdrew from the FLA.

First World – The advanced, capitalist economies of Western Europe, North America, Oceania and Japan.

Foreign Direct Investment (FDI) – Represents private sector investment by TNCs and Western banks, as well as development assistance by the international agencies and governments. FDI distribution in the developing countries is highly selective.

Free market – An economic system in which all the resources necessary for the production and trade of goods and services are privately owned and allocated exclusively by a price system.

Free trade – Trade in which goods and services can be imported and exported without any kind of restriction.

General Agreement on Tariffs and Trade (GATT) – An Agreement signed by 23 countries in 1947, in Geneva, under US leadership. Most of the Third World countries were colonies at the time and were not represented. It set out rules of conduct in world trade and aimed to eliminate tariffs and barriers to free trade, whilst at the same time sanctioning protectionism by the developed countries in agriculture and textiles. Forerunner of the World Trade Organisation (WTO).

Gross Domestic Product (GDP) – The value of goods and services produced in the country within a given period.

Gross National Product (GNP) – The value of goods and services produced by nationals within and outside the country such as remittances by migrant workers.

Gross National Product per capita (GNP per capita) – A measure of the average income of a country's residents which ignores the actual distribution of income in society.

Human Development Index (HDI) – Devised by the UNDP in 1990 as a composite indicator of economic and social welfare which gives equal weight to purchasing power, life expectancy and literacy.

Import coefficient – the change in the value of imports generated by a given change in Gross National Product (GNP).

Import Substituting Industrialisation (ISI) – A policy used by many of the large Third World countries to industrialise, which aims at the replacement of imports by domestic production through the use of high import duties or/and quotas, or prohibition.

International Bank for Reconstruction and Development (IBRD) – Commonly referred to as the World Bank, founded in 1944 at Bretton Woods. A commercial lending and technical institution whose stated aims are to promote long-term development, but whose policies of Structural Adjustment have contributed to the growth of impoverishment in the Third World. Produces an annual *World Development Report*.

International Development Association (IDA) – The 'soft lending' section of the World Bank, which lends to the poorest of the developing countries at concessionary rates of interest.

International Federation for Alternative Trade (IFAT) – Brings together specialised NGOs involved in alternative trade such as ATOs, for the purposes of facilitating marketing networks and advocacy for fair trade.

International Labour Organisation (ILO) – Established at the end of the First World War by the Treaty of Versailles in 1919 and which subsequently became a specialised agency of the United Nations in 1945. The ILO has transformed from an organisation originally concerned with manpower supply, training and global labour standards to the leading advocate for small enterprises and the 'informal sector' in the Third World.

International Monetary Fund (IMF) – One of the Bretton Woods institutions which became a specialised agency of the United Nations in 1947. The IMF monitors the world's currencies and regulates the international monetary exchange system, in order to maintain an orderly system of payments between all countries. It attempts to control fluctuations in the world's exchange rates. To this end it lends on a short-term basis to countries facing serious balance of payments deficits. The IMF attaches harsh conditions ('conditionality') to lending which have contributed to the growth of poverty in the Third World.

Invisible hand – The term originates from Adam Smith's influential book *Wealth of Nations* published in 1776, to describe a condition where the unbridled pursuit of individual self-interest in free markets results in the maximisation of social welfare.

Labour-intensive production – Production technologies which require a higher proportion of labour relative to other factors of production, i.e. capital and land.

Labour productivity – The level of output per unit of labour input, usually measured as output per man-hour or man-years. This measurement derives from the proposition that relative commodity prices depend on relative amounts of labour used to produce them. Marxist economics are based on this labour theory of value.

Least Less Developed Countries (LLDCs) – Made of approximately 30 of the poorest and least industrialised of the Third World countries. An LLDC is characterised by very low GNP per capita incomes, levels of adult education and contribution by manufacturing industry to the country's economy.

Manufacturing Value Added (MVA) – The percentage of GDP deriving from manufacturing. This total 'value added' is a market measure of the proportion of the output of the economy that comes from manufacturing and is an indicator of the proxy level of industrialisation in a country.

***Maquiladora* Programme** – A programme created by the Mexican government in 1966 with the purpose of increasing employment in the border region by encouraging US TNCs to make use of low-cost Mexican labour. Gave special exemption to investors from normally strict controls on foreign investment.

Market failure – An economic term describing the variation between how markets behave and how they should according to abstract notions of markets. A condition which results from market imperfections such as monopoly and lack of knowledge, rather than any structural defects in market mechanisms of allocation. Market failure frequently legitimised state intervention in the working of markets in the Third World.

Most Favoured Nation (MFN) – Third World countries which gained for political and economic reasons, preferential access to the US economy. In the 1970s–80s this was associated with South Korea and in the 1990s with China.

Multi-Fibre Arrangement (MFA) – An instrument of protectionism used in the global textile industry. The MFA originated in the USA during the early 1960s as a response to Japanese cotton imports and evolved into a general instrument used against all developing countries. The MFA sets physical limits in developing country textile exports to the markets of the developed countries. The application of import quotas for one group of countries (the developing countries) and in one sector (textiles) is a clear breach of WTO principles of non-discrimination in international trade.

Neo-liberal – A theoretical position which looks to free markets, free trade, comparative advantage and the prowess of the 'invisible hand' for answers to Third World poverty. Neo-liberalism is a term which can be used to describe the policies pursued by the IMF, World Bank and the WTO. EOI represents the application of neo-liberal thinking to industrial policy.

Newly Industrialising Countries (NICs) – The countries which industrialised later than was the experience in North West Europe and the USA and which consist of three geographical blocs of countries: the Southern European, Latin American and South East Asian NICs.

Non Governmental Organisations (NGOs) – Private sector organisations which began as voluntary responses to the various crises and emergencies manifest in the Third World, but which in the case of international NGOs have come to depend partly or wholly on funds from Western governments and the international donors. Third World NGOs do not have the resources of the large international NGOs and operate very differently from them: they are nearer to communities, more accountable to them and more responsive to their needs and retribution. These grassroots NGOs are also referred to as People's Organisations.

North American Free Trade Association (NAFTA) – A trilateral free trade zone established in 1992 under US leadership, bringing together the USA, Mexico and Canada. It aims to remove barriers to internal trade and investment and to harmonise rules on labour, health and environmental standards. NAFTA was a response by the USA to European Community enlargement. NAFTA sees the *Maquiladora* border region as a model for the Americas and NAFTA itself.

Organisation for Economic Cooperation and Development (OECD) – Established at the end of the Second World War to coordinate the delivery of US aid to Europe in 1948. Today the OECD brings together the world's industrial countries and its major objective is to assist the economic growth of its member nations. Mexico and South Korea are also members.

Organisation of Petroleum Exporting Countries (OPEC) – An organisation, sometimes referred to as a cartel, made up of 13 major oil exporting Third World countries. Eight of the members are North African and Middle East countries.

Physical Quality of Life Index (PQLI) – An internationally recognised composite indicator of social welfare, which gives equal weight to life expectancy, infant mortality and literacy.

Price elasticity of demand – The relationship between the quantity of goods and services demanded and changes to the prices of given goods and services. Typically this translates to low elasticity of demand in agricultural products and low prices for Third World commodity exports.

Purchasing Power Parity (PPP) – Determined by calculating the income necessary to satisfy basic needs in any country in US dollars.

Second World – The advanced, communist/state capitalist economies of Eastern Europe and Russia which made extensive use of centralised planning. Since the collapse of communism in Eastern Europe many countries have faced a transition trap, where for political reasons they can neither fully dismantle the state-owned enterprises, nor fully embrace private capitalism. The World Bank has been referring to these countries as 'economies in transition' since 1989.

Sources of income – The different ways people make a living, which illustrate their economic positioning in society, i.e. profit-capitalist, wages-worker, rent-landlord, interest-savings.

Structural Adjustment Programmes (SAPs) – A standard set of policies which condition World Bank lending and which include the privatisation of state-owned enterprises, cut-backs in public sector expenditure and removal of restrictions on the activities of TNCs. SAPs are meant to address the long-term, macroeconomic problems facing developing countries, and 'adjust' them towards economic liberalisation, free trade and production for export. As with IMF conditions, SAPs have been a major contributor to the growth of poverty in the Third World.

Terms of trade – The movement between export and import prices. Declining terms of trade represent a condition where developing countries have to export even more in volume terms in order to pay for the same quantity of imports. Given that most Third World countries export primary commodities and import manufactured goods, this typically means they have to produce even more commodities, which reduces export prices even further.

Textile and garment industry – The textile industry is a general term which signifies everything from the production of natural and synthetic fibres to their transformation into apparel fibre, household goods and industrial products. The garment industry, also called the 'clothing' or 'wearing apparel' industry, produces outergarments, undergarments and clothing accessories.

Third World – The present 150 or so developing countries of Asia including Central Asia, Africa, the Middle East and Latin America. Characterised by common problems such as the experience of colonialism, the persistence of poverty, dependence on agriculture and commodity exports and technology imports. The differentiation of the Third World between the NICs and the LLDCs has accelerated during the last 25 years.

Trans National Corporations (TNCs) – Large enterprises which have a home base in one of the industrial economies but operate, typically through subsidiaries, in many other countries. TNCs use their economic power to monopolise the entire economies of the poorest Third World countries and commodities such as fuel, minerals, tropical fruits. Third World countries such as South Korea and India have seen the growth of indigenous TNCs, with the South Korean *Chaebol* as the most prominent example during the 1990s.

United Nations Conference on Trade and Development (UNCTAD) – Established in 1964 by the United Nations as a forum for developing country interests in international trade. The first General Secretary of UNCTAD was Raúl Prebisch who argued that world trade was characterised by 'unequal exchange'. Whilst a considerable intellectual force in the development of structuralist ideas during the 1960s and 1970s, UNCTAD has been progressively marginalised inside the UN structures substantially as the result of US financial pressure.

United Nations Development Programme (UNDP) – Established in 1966 as an agency for delivering and coordinating Technical Assistance to development projects in the Third World. Since 1990 the UNDP has published annually a *Human Development Report* which uses methods such as the HDI to provide useful information on the human condition in the Third World.

United Students Against Sweatshops (USAS) – A movement amongst US students which has targeted the collegiate wear market and has demanded that university administrations and TNCs accept responsibility for labour conditions in factories contracted to produce garments and footwear for US universities.

World Trade Organisation (WTO) – The successor of GATT. Provides rules governing world trade which are based in free trade thinking. The dismantling of import duties and tariff barriers to trade, the ending of protection for domestic infant industries and extensive privatisation of the country's economy are conditions of entry. The WTO argues that issues such as labour rights, environmental degradation, health and safety of consumers and producers, cannot be allowed to interfere with the rights of TNCs to conduct 'free trade'. The WTO has become the unacceptable face of globalisation and its Seattle Conference during December 1999 became the battleground of some of the largest protests seen in the USA since the Vietnam War.

Notes on Authors

Gavin Capps Gavin Capps is a PhD Candidate in the Development Studies Institute at the London School of Economics and a Visiting Lecturer at the University of the North West, South Africa. He has previously tutored in Development Studies at the Open University, School of Oriental and African Studies, Swansea University, University of Central Lancashire and London School of Economics. He has carried out research on the promotion of rural enterprises by Non Governmental Organisations in Botswana and is currently conducting research on land reform and traditional authority in South Africa. He has a long-standing interest in adult and development education and was the lead author of *African Society and Development: Winner and Losers South of the Sahara* (1996) – a development education publication co-produced by the Centre for Development Studies, Swansea, and Oxfam, Wales.

Dr Jose D. Garcia Perez is a Lecturer in Development and Environmental Management at the University of Central Lancashire, Preston. He teaches courses on Development and Environment, Tourism with special interests in Eco-tourism and Social Forestry, drawing from Southern European and Latin American material. He has contributed to the teaching of programmes aimed at non-conventional students and has interests in adult and trade union education. He is currently working on a research project which is investigating the impact of the promotion of small enterprises by the European Community in the northern Iberian Peninsula.

Dr Prodromos Ioannou Panayiotopoulos is a Lecturer in Development Studies at the School of Social Sciences and International Development, the University of Wales, Swansea and the Open University in the UK. He teaches Development Studies and researches on Third World employment, small enterprises and the garment industry. He has taught courses on Poverty and Development and Globalisation and Development, Labour, Employment and the Urban Economy in the Third World, and a Small Enterprise course for post-graduate mainly overseas students. He is also an Associate Lecturer for the Open University course on World Development and has provided assistance in the development of the AS Level in World Development for the UK school curriculum. Some of his publications include 'The Emergent Post-Colonial State in Cyprus', *Commonwealth & Comparative Politics*, Vol. 37, No. 1 (1999), pp. 31–55; 'The

280

Developmental State in Crisis: the Case of Cyprus', *Capital and Class*, No. 57 (1995), pp. 13–53; 'Challenging Orthodoxies: Cypriot Entrepreneurs in the London Garment Industry', *new Community*, Vol. 22, No. 3 (1996a), pp. 437–460; 'The State and Enterprise in the Cypriot Clothing Industry under Conditions of Globalisation', *Cyprus Journal of Economics*, Vol. 9, No. 1 (1996b), pp. 5–29; 'The Labour Regime under Conditions of Globalisation in the Cypriot Garment Industy', *Journal of Southern Europe and the Balkans*, Vol. 2, No. 1 (2000), pp. 75–88. Has collaborated with Chris Gerry in the writing of 'Learning from State-sponsored Youth Enterprise Promotion in the Commonwealth Developing Countries', *Third World Planning Review*, Vol. 19, No. 2 (1997), pp. 209–27; with Subesh K. Das in 'Flexible Specialisation. New Paradigm for Industrialisation for Developing Countries?', *Economic and Political Weekly*, 28 December (Bombay, 1996), pp. 57–61; and Yusef Abu ElJedian in 'Small Enterprises in the Gaza Strip, the Case of the Plastic and Rubber Industry', *Third World Planning Review*, Vol. 16, No. 4 (1996), pp. 455–75.

Dr Luis Valenzuela is a Lecturer in Development Studies at the School of Social Sciences and International Development at the University of Wales, Swansea. He has taught first year students on development in historical perspective and teaches second and third year students on the Sociology of Development – Latin American perspectives, Race, Ethnicity and Class, and football. He has researched extensively on industrialisation in Latin America with a special interest in the Chilean copper industry. Publications include, 'Challenges to the Copper Smelting Industry in the World Market, 1840–1860', *Journal of European Economic History*, Vol. 19 (1990), pp. 57–86 and 'The Chilean Copper Smelting Industry in the Mid-Nineteenth Century: Phases of Expansion and Stagnation, 1834–1858', *Journal of Latin American Studies*, No. 24 (1992), pp. 507–50.

Index

U.W.E.L. LEARNING RESOURCES